PENGUIN LITERARY BIOGRAPHIES
SECRETS OF A WOMAN'S HEART
The Later Life of Ivy Compton-Burnett
1920–1969

Hilary Spurling was educated at Somerville College, Oxford, and worked as a waitress before becoming theatre critic of the *Spectator* and its literary editor in the 1960s. Her books include the first half of this biography, *Ivy When Young*, and a *Handbook to Anthony Powell's Music of Time*. She reviews books for the *Observer*, is married to the playwright John Spurling, and has three children.

Hilary Spurling was awarded the Duff Cooper Memorial Prize for *Ivy When Young* and *Secrets of a Woman's Heart*.

HILARY SPURLING

SECRETS OF A
WOMAN'S HEART

The Later Life of Ivy Compton-Burnett
1920–1969

Penguin Books

Penguin Books Ltd, Harmondsworth, Middlesex, England
Viking Penguin Inc., 40 West 23rd Street, New York, New York 10010, U.S.A.
Penguin Books Australia Ltd, Ringwood, Victoria, Australia
Penguin Books Canada Ltd, 2801 John Street, Markham, Ontario, Canada L3R 1B4
Penguin Books (N.Z.) Ltd, 182–190 Wairau Road, Auckland 10, New Zealand

First published by Hodder and Stoughton 1984
Published in Penguin Books 1985

Copyright © Hilary Spurling, 1984
All rights reserved

Made and printed in Great Britain by
Richard Clay (The Chaucer Press) Ltd,
Bungay, Suffolk
Typeset in Bembo

FOR MAUREEN

'I don't see why spinsters have any less success,' said Isabel.

'Well, they have no proof that they have been sought,' said Miss Mitford.

'Have you ever been sought?' said Venice . . .

'You must not probe the secrets of a woman's heart,' said Miss Mitford . . .

Parents and Children, p. 86

CONTENTS

LIST OF ILLUSTRATIONS

Front-cover photograph

Ivy Compton-Burnett in the summer of her first success with *Brothers and Sisters*, published in 1929 (*photo. by Claude Harris*)

Photographic inset

FOREWORD

TEN YEARS AGO when I wrote the first half of this biography of Ivy Compton-Burnett, it seemed to me that her life was, as she herself implied, virtually over by the end of the First World War. Now I think it might as easily be argued that the opposite was true. *Ivy When Young* ended with her struggling for survival, emotionally stripped and physically shattered by the War, and by a tragic family history in the years immediately before it. This book is the story of the writer who responded triumphantly to the defeats and suffering of the past. It begins with her planting her first postwar book like a small unexploded bomb, and shows her gradually building up, layer by layer, the extraordinary protective armour that made her in the last part of her life one of the literary legends of her day.

Her public image was so intimidating that, when I started talking to her friends a year or so after her death, I found it hard at first to credit the gentle, considerate, amusing and affectionate private person many of them described. The discrepancy was one of several surrounding Ivy Compton-Burnett. She looked and dressed all her life like a Victorian maiden lady yet she thought in ways so unconventional that even now in 1984 – the centenary of her birth – the full implications of her writing have hardly yet sunk in. 'Compton-Burnett is a radical thinker, one of the rare modern heretics,' wrote Mary McCarthy (who said that Ivy in her long black skirts, Edwardian hairnet and buckled shoes, lunching at the Ritz in the early 1960s, reminded her of her redoubtable Irish Catholic grandmother). 'It is the eccentricity that has diverted attention from the fact that these small uniform volumes are subversive packets.'[1]

Ivy was frightening and she knew it, for she wrote about what still seem some of the most threatening issues of our time. For more than forty years she used the domestic novel, ostensibly distanced by her Victorian style and setting, to explore atrocity, violence, the corruption of language and the totalitarian abuse of power. She was not interested in conventional politics and she had no patience with radical or any other sort of chic. She visited none of the world's trouble spots, indeed she travelled at all only under protest. What interested her was people (apart from writing – and a celebrated weakness for expensive chocolates, soft fruit and garden flowers – she had practically no other interests). Above all she was concerned with the lengths to which the strong are prepared to go to exploit and crush the weak. No enormity was hidden from her, which perhaps explains why her popularity increased dramatically in the Second War when uncertainty and fear played so large a part in everyday reality. Nervous readers, before and since, have echoed the protesters in her books:

> 'Oh, must we be quite so honest with ourselves, my dear?'
> 'We do not know how to avoid it,' said Terence. 'That is why there is horror in every heart, and a resolve never to be honest with anybody else.'[2]

Remarks like this one aim to tease, especially to tease biographers, as Ivy herself was well aware. 'I have had such an uneventful life that there is little to say,' she wrote,[3] and turned down her publisher's suggestion for an autobiography on the grounds that she had done nothing and been nowhere. Clearly the solution to the central puzzle of her life and work – the deceptively old-world appearance and the subversive content – could only lie in some attempt to see what Ivy saw in her own heart. She left no explanations, no journal and comparatively few letters: even to her dearest friends she was generally terse, rarely intimate and always punctiliously obedient to her generation's rule against gossiping by post. Gossip – 'simple candid probing of our friends' business'[4] – was her delight, but she understood inquisitiveness too well – 'Our curiosity is neither morbid nor ordinary. It is the kind known as devouring'[5] – not to take precautions. Her private papers when she died amounted to little more than a shoebox half full of appointment diaries, and a small, apparently random selection of fanmail.

I could not have reconstructed Ivy's early years without the help of her sisters, Vera and Juliet Compton-Burnett; but the only comparable witness for the second half of her life – her companion, Margaret Jourdain – was dead; and whatever Ivy's feelings may have been, about Margaret or anything else, she confided them to no one. Among her friends – nearly all much younger in the last years of her life – even the fondest and most pressing never came anywhere near eliciting more from Ivy than she wanted known. My first clue came from an enemy, the distinguished antiquarian

Dame Joan Evans, who at first refused to see me because, as she wrote, 'I am afraid I dislike Miss Compton-Burnett too much to do anything to contribute any help towards any of her numerous biographies.' A year later, after the publication of *Ivy When Young*, I was sent for by Dame Joan: 'I must tell you why I detested Miss Compton-Burnett' were her first words in an interview that made it plain that Ivy was no stranger in fact to the jealousy, love of power and unscrupulous manipulative skills she wrote about in fiction.

But, if she found her tyrants in herself, Ivy also found the gaiety, courage and endurance of their victims, as well as the sympathetic understanding of the observers who stand, appalled and helpless, on the edges of the action in her books. 'I am so glad you think I am a compassionate writer, as I always feel myself so very pitiful,' she wrote to a fellow novelist soon after the Second World War.[6] Though her own books seemed to wartime readers both exhilarating and consoling, Ivy could never bring herself to read historical or fictional accounts of either of the two great Wars. The Victorian disguise she eventually adopted in both fact and fiction seems to have served as some sort of barricade: an essential device for distancing herself from horrors she saw, whether in herself or in the world at large, too clearly for comfort. But when this book begins, at the start of the 1920s, she had no such defences. Her family life was in ruins, her last link with the only world she knew had been snapped by the death of her brother Noel on the Somme in 1916, she herself had nearly died in the great influenza epidemic of 1918; and it was in the aftermath of this illness, at a time of overwhelming lethargy, loneliness and despair, that she took in Margaret Jourdain as a lodger.

People who knew them both in those days remember Margaret as from the first the dominant partner. Something of the strength and support Ivy got from their relationship is reflected in the special enthusiasm with which she wrote afterwards about single women ('You would not have liked to be married?' 'No, I never wanted a full, normal life'[7]), celebrating their humour, affection and stability, coming down always firmly in favour of their way of life when set beside the preposterous minefield of the family. Ivy and Margaret became inseparable: though they were not in any obvious or accredited sense a lesbian couple, Margaret's liberating influence was evidently crucial.

Margaret was a feminist pioneer in practice if not in theory, firmly established by the 1920s at the top of a profession staffed otherwise throughout her working life almost exclusively by men. She struck her contemporaries as phenomenally independent, unsentimental, free from obligation to anyone or anything. No one asked her about her past (even old family friends knew comparatively little about the Jourdains' immediate history, which proved to be as painful and explosive as anything the Compton-Burnetts had known); neither her friends nor Ivy's were apparently inclined to speculate about the private feelings or motives behind what seemed at the time an unremarkable, thoroughly practical arrangement between landlady and lodger. Margaret lived vigorously in the present, and even Ivy gave a contemporary setting together with an unmistakable flavour of the 1920s to the novel, *Pastors and Masters*, which she started writing a few years after meeting Margaret.

This was where I chose to begin – with a book that produced in its relatively few readers a bewildered double-take, and a relationship that seemed if anything more baffling still. All I could be sure of was that the two were inextricably entangled, for Ivy was one of those writers whose life and work are one. It would have been impossible to write her biography without writing also about her books: it was in any case the books that first awoke in me a curiosity Ivy might not have liked but which she would undoubtedly have understood.

One unexpected pleasure of writing this book has been the way in which, after a worse start than most, Ivy's life got steadily better in middle and old age. Another has been that, in the course of countless conversations about Ivy, many of her friends became mine too. Among these I owe most to Madge Garland and Robert Liddell, the late Herman Schrijver and Sonia Orwell whom I should particularly have liked to thank before she died for her incomparably generous encouragement, advice and insight. My debt to Vera and the late Juliet Compton-Burnett remains immense; next to them, my thanks go to Anthony Compton-Burnett for permission to quote from Ivy's published and unpublished works, and the late Hester Marsden-Smedley (together with her daughter, Henrietta Williamson) for her unpublished memoir, her constant practical help and the long loan of both Ivy's and Margaret's papers (chief among these were the minute appointment diaries in which both intermittently recorded visits and visitors, parties given and attended, professional contacts, trips and holidays; Ivy's press cuttings, practically complete from 1925 to Margaret's death in 1951 after which the collection lapsed; Margaret's Account Book, 1902–1924, address books and a few odd scraps of correspondence).

My next great debt is to the novelist Elizabeth Taylor, who gave me permission before she died to quote from the remarkable letters she wrote to Robert Liddell about Ivy, and to all the others who took notes at the time, in particular Barbara and the late Walter Robinson, Rosamond Lehmann, Lady Anne Hill, and James Lees-Milne whose published diaries and private conversation have been invaluable. I have already thanked those who helped me with *Ivy When Young* but there are many others to whom I owe special gratitude (some for the second time) for kindness, patience and stamina in answering my enquiries: James Brandreth, Rex Britcher, Professor Charles Burkhart (whose pioneering books remain indispensable to anyone interested in Ivy), Lettice Cooper, Kay Dick, Marjorie and the late Ralph Edwards, Kathleen Farrell, Dr. George Furlong, the late Cicely Greig, Livia Gollancz, Heywood Hill, the late Soame Jenyns, Francis King, the late Olivia Manning, Elka Schrijver, the late Elizabeth Sprigge and Vere Watson-Gandy.

My best thanks go also to Margaret Hawkins, Gertrude McCracken, K. E. Currey and the other inhabitants, past and present, of Sutton Veney, who told me about the Noyes sisters – Liza Banks, Joan McWilliam, Anne Northcroft and Caroline Walker; to Peter Thornton and his staff at the Furniture and Woodwork Department of the Victoria and Albert Musuem for information, advice and access to Margaret's furniture notes (specially interesting to me because they were jotted down on the backs of discarded letters, receipts, income tax returns, royalty statements, etc., including odd pages of typescript from Ivy's novels and even her torn-up contracts with Heinemann); and to Dr. John Rollett, the connoisseur and collector of Jourdainiana, but for whom much in Margaret's early life might have remained a blank.

I am also grateful to the following for help, information and permission to reproduce or quote from material in their possession: Jennifer Adamson, Sybille Bedford, the late Katharine Blackie, Margaret Branch, Livia Breglia, Gerald Brenan, Anna Browne, John and Sheila Bush, Glen Cavaliero, Sarah Coffin, Professor Christopher Cornford, John Cornforth, Anne Doe, Valerie Eliot, Renée Fedden, Yvonne Ffrench, Roy Fuller, the late David Garnett,

Victoria Glendinning, Cecil Gould, Rupert Hart-Davis, Violet Henriques, Iseult Hickie of Kensington Central Library, Kathy Huff (for an unpublished bibliography), Lucille Iremonger, Arthur J. Jourdain, Joy Jourdain, Richard Kennedy, Dorothy Kerr, A. J. B. Kiddell of Sotheby's, Moll Lampard, Edith Lamont, J. A. Laurence, Lady Macalister, Mary Maguire, Lady Mander, Douglas Matthews and the staff of the London Library, Mary McCarthy, Robin McDouall, Lady Medawar, Peter Mellors, Esther Millar, the late Raymond Mortimer, Hugh Noyes, Dr. Stephen Pasmore, Dulcie Pendred, the Phoenix Trust, Michael Pinney, Sir John Pope-Hennessy, the late Mario Praz, Marion Rawson, Maria Rejt, Graham Reynolds, Joanna Routledge, Carol Rygate, Natasha Sokolov, Humphrey and Sir Stephen Spender, Dame Freya Stark, Jane Stockwood, Jenny Stratford, Dorothy Stroud, Christopher Sykes, Michael Tayler, Mr and Mrs Richard Thesiger, Feliks Topolski, Clissold Tuely, Dame Janet Vaughan, Alison Waley, Sir Angus Wilson, Sir Peter Wilson and Norman Wright.

Lastly, I should like to thank Maureen Forrest who first introduced me to Ivy's books, and John Spurling without whom I should probably not have begun and certainly never have finished writing her life.

HILARY SPURLING

CHAPTER ONE

'Not one of those modern people'

i

WHEN IVY COMPTON-BURNETT published *Pastors and Masters* at the beginning of 1925, her friends reacted with varying degrees of shock, disbelief and dismay. Margaret Jourdain, who lived with her, said that the first she knew of the book's existence was one morning when Ivy, laid up with a chill, fished out a copy from under the bedclothes.[1] 'Margaret was horrified,' said Joan Evans, 'really horrified when that first novel was produced.' Joan herself was indignant. Other people, like Margaret's professional colleague Ralph Edwards and her old ally in the country Hester Pinney, were frankly incredulous. Hester Pinney's daughter, known as Little Hester, accepted the copy Ivy gave her without even bothering to open it: 'My mother, when I told her about the gift, said that as usual I'd got it all wrong. I ought to know by this time that Margaret was the one who wrote.'[2]

In Ivy's circle this was the general view. A friend who met both ladies some time in 1926 was astonished to find, when someone referred to one of the pair as 'the writer', that it wasn't Margaret he meant.[3] Ivy's lapse into authorship was something Margaret's friends found it best to ignore. People who visited their various flats in the 1920s and 1930s remember Ivy as drab, inconspicuous, inscrutable, generally mute: 'She was a rather stout, middle-class woman who poured out cups of tea for all the young men who came to see Margaret,' said Herman Schrijver (who was one of Margaret's young men himself in 1927). 'Ivy had no conversation of any sort or kind in those days . . .'[4] Herman, whose first move on meeting Ivy had been to go out and buy *Pastors and Masters*, maintained that for years he was her only reader, or at any rate the only one she knew.

Ivy's friends in the early 1920s had nearly all met her through Margaret, who was beginning by this time to be widely feared and respected as an authority on English furniture and interiors. She moved in a thoroughly conservative and quite unbookish, in some

cases near-philistine world of collectors and country-house journalists, museum officials, dealers, decorators and their clients. From
the start Margaret herself set the tone for furniture friends who
boasted over the next forty years and more that they could make
neither head nor tail of the writings of I. Compton-Burnett. 'Of
course I never read Ivy's trash,' Margaret is said to have told Roger
Hinks[5]; and the saying, by no means strictly truthful, well illustrates her characteristically brusque version of the Pinneys'
offhandedness (the younger of the two Hesters did eventually get
through her copy of *Pastors and Masters* but, though she remained a
friend to the day Ivy died, this was the first and last time she read one
of her books).

It was a state of affairs Ivy did nothing at all to discourage. The
novelist David Garnett said that she looked like a schoolmistress
and scarcely spoke when he first met her, at a lunch given for
Margaret in 1923.[6] To the critic Raymond Mortimer, Ivy's earliest
and most effective champion in the literary world, she seemed
'always more like the governess than the governess's employer'.[7]
This was a common impression, and one she took pains to produce.
Her highly stylized looks, the air of strange formal distinction she
acquired in later life, grew from what had been in these years a form
of the nondescript colouring adopted by the better type of governess in her books: meek, plaintive, underrated creatures, often
queerly dressed in styles long since discarded by everyone else,
always effectively sustained against pity or contempt by a rather
startling degree of self-knowledge and an even more worrying
understanding of other people.

Margaret and Ivy made an odd couple in their long skirts that
neither rose nor fell with the switchback lunges of hemline in the
1920s, and hairstyles unchanged since their girlhood. But where
Margaret (who was ugly and forceful and eight years older than
Ivy[8]) wore lace jabots, dashing plumed and flowered hats, gold
chains, feather boas, finery of all sorts with a watch in her belt and a
dangling Regency spyglass, Ivy dressed like Miss Ridley, the
governess in *The Present and the Past*, 'to make a whole that
conformed to nothing and offended no one. She made no mistakes
in her dress, merely carried out her intentions.'[9] Friends of Margaret visiting the flat for the first time barely noticed her ('*No one
ever went to see Ivy, or would ever have been asked by her,*' said
Raisley Moorsom, who had known them both almost from the start

of their assocation); and the few like Herman who tried to draw her out found it uphill work.

Like her own governesses, Ivy must have had much to put up with in these years by way of condescension from people who, in so far as they were aware of her at all, suspected that her social origins were a great deal humbler than Margaret's. But, like Miss Mitford, the governess in *Parents and Children*, she gave no quarter and expected none. Miss Mitford with her immediate successor, Miss Lacy in *Elders and Betters*, is among the most nearly contented characters in Ivy's books: a colourless exterior and constrained social manner mask, in each case, a curiosity too concentrated to operate without some sort of camouflage, since each shares with Ivy 'a knowledge of books which was held to be natural in her life, and a knowledge of people which would have been held to be impossible, and was really inevitable'.[10]

This was a side of Ivy not often glimpsed, unless perhaps by the brides or fiancées of Margaret's young men, several of whom found Ivy's silent scrutiny quite as unsettling as Margaret's tart comments. Juliet Compton-Burnett remembered from before the First World War her sister's habit of looking people over—their faces, their expressions, their hands as they took tea—'one might say to a degree that was hardly respectable'. Marjorie Edwards, Ralph's wife, produced for inspection soon after their marriage in the 1920s, found Ivy 'most alarming' at this first encounter. So did Viva Booth, whose engagement in 1926 to another gifted youth, Willie King of the British Museum, earned her Margaret's undisguised disapproval:

> She was an ugly, bosomy spinster with fluffy blonde hair and she used a spy-glass, the better to stare with. She was very clever . . .
> At that time [Ivy] was also plump and bosomy, with streaky grey-brown hair the shape of a mob-cap, kept in place with a string round her head—which colour and shape never varied during the forty years I was to know her. She had written a book, *Dolores*, with no success and had attempted to call in the copies.

Dolores, published in 1911, had never been heard of in a circle still barely aware in 1926 of *Pastors and Masters*, but the general impression of novel-writing as a dim and faintly discreditable activity is accurate enough. 'Margaret's spy-glass and Ivy's hard stares, and the company of these intellectual women, were only for the strong.'[11]

But in those days it was only young women who found Ivy formidable. To Margaret's young men—for Margaret required, and saw that she got, a steady stream of young men to sit at her feet, pick her brains, join her for lunch, escort her round the sale rooms or on country-house visits—Ivy rated less attention than the chair she sat on. The celebrity was Margaret, who had few rivals as an expert in a field cultivated until recently on a more or less haphazard basis by amateur antiquarians. Caustic and categorical, vehement, argumentative and often cuttingly funny, Margaret was capital company, centre of an energetic social life and a prime source of professional contacts not otherwise easily come by. Moreover, when they first set up house together in 1919, she had far better literary credentials than Ivy, who had published a single, forgotten and remaindered novel at her own expense before the war, and showed no sign of producing another.

Margaret was a published poet and prose poet, editor and essayist, translator and disciple of Baudelaire and the symbolists, as well as a regular reviewer for the literary weeklies on subjects ranging from Voltaire and the Greeks to Trollope, Samuel Butler and Henry James. Her reputation for painstaking scholarship had taken years to build up and, at the beginning of the 1920s, before Ivy's own routine of working at home was established, the two would spend mornings working together in the reading room at the British Museum. On the rare occasions when she could be brought to relax with people she knew well, Miss Jourdain's 'young friend'[12] seemed in those days the lightminded one of the two, gigglier and giddier than Margaret: 'Ivy was slightly silly. She was very young and sort of fluffy, and bubbling over with humour,' said her brother's old Cambridge friend, Raisley Moorsom. 'Everything that happened to her, and everything she said, was a great joke.' She herself always drew a sharp distinction between scholarship, or 'serious books', and her own kind of writing—the sort everyone reckons to be able to do because, as another novelist says sharply in *Daughters and Sons*, 'people think it needs brains and no training'.[13]

What one might call the running gag in Ivy's books about the superiority of scholars (as opposed to the intrinsic frivolity of novelists) has the wry, affectionate note of a private joke; and there is no shortage of evidence that, for all her disclaimers, Margaret did in fact read Ivy's books with understanding and pleasure. Like the learned Miss Marcon in *Daughters and Sons*, who also travelled regularly to the British Museum to research her next book in the reading room, Margaret in some moods took a genuine pride in her friend's success ('that wonderful child! To write like that, sitting at home, and not have to go by train to get it! I do look up to her!'[14]). Her asperity seems to have been, in part at least, a game played according to Ivy's rule of secrecy and discretion. 'I think people work at different levels of consciousness,' Ivy said long afterwards. 'I think I must work rather low down.'[15] Certainly there had never been any question, even in the days when she wrote *Dolores* sitting side by side with her brother Noel in the schoolroom at home, of anyone seeing a word she had written before the manuscript was completed.

Negotiations with publishers over that first book had been as darkly concealed as, by Margaret's account, they were for the second. Ivy placed *Pastors and Masters* in the autumn of 1924 with a small firm of 'vanity' publishers called Heath Cranton in Fleet Lane, paying for publication herself as she had paid for *Dolores*, and receiving in return the published price of 3s 6d per copy, less Cranton's commission of twenty per cent, or eightpence a volume.[16] Margaret's copy must have been produced from under the bedclothes early the following February; and, if it is clearly impossible for the two women to have lived at close quarters for more than five years without one suspecting that the other was writing a book (Margaret had published at least three in the time), the answer probably lies in a pact between them which Margaret described to Joan Evans: 'Ivy has written a book and I expect it's very bad. We have decided that I shan't read it, and then there'll be no trouble about it.'[17]

Part of the anticipated trouble was undoubtedly social. Margaret's upper-class friends seem to have felt that everything they deplored about Ivy—her drabness, isolation, lack of small talk, the fact that she came, socially speaking, from the wrong drawer—was compounded by her having written a novel ('It seems such a light sort of thing,' as Sir Michael Egerton says in *A God and his Gifts*. 'But of course people do earn by it, even more than by serious books they say'[18]). Even Ivy's maid felt (like the Egertons' butler) so ashamed when the butcher remarked on 'her lady' having written a novel that she drew herself up and said witheringly: 'My lady has no need.' ★

Few people Ivy knew were likely to take the *New Statesman* which saluted *Pastors and Masters* that summer as 'a work of genius'.[19] *Vogue* was more in their line, and perhaps somebody spotted the young Raymond Mortimer recommending Ivy's novel ('The wit of it often, the acidity and quiet cynicism always, are a delight . . .') as a New Book for the Morning Room Table in April. But Margaret and most of her friends read or wrote for *Country Life*, where Ralph Edwards (who had begun his career on the staff just after the war, and ended it running the Victoria and Albert Museum's department of Furniture and Woodwork) reviewed Ivy's early work with no great enthusiasm strictly as a favour to Margaret.[20] His cautious reception of books that struck him as unhealthy, unsettling and too smart by half reflects widespread agreement in furniture circles that Ivy had much better stick to her place as Margaret's companion and housekeeper. 'I was more and more dazzled by Margaret's erudition. Ivy was always in the background,' wrote young Hester Pinney, whose first attempts to launch herself in London owed much to Margaret: 'The delightful company I met were Margaret's friends. The fine books on furniture and *Country Life* articles were Margaret's work. It was Margaret who told me Ivy was scribbling in little notebooks.'[21] By the end of the 1920s, and throughout the 1930s, when Ivy's growing reputation in the literary world could no longer be entirely discounted at home, Margaret's friends retaliated by referring to Ivy as 'Margaret Jourdain's Boswell', a nickname invented by Basil Marsden-Smedley (who had married young Hester in 1927) and widely circulated among people who took much the same view of the novelist's trade—'scratching and scribbling and shuffling papers!'[22] —as friends and relations generally do in Ivy's books.

Admittedly, there was a special stigma attached to the sort of books Ivy wrote. 'Mayfair murders I call them,' † said Margaret, who would declare, when Herman asked after Ivy, that she was 'writing

★ This was Herman Schrijver's story (Burkhart 2, p. 81), but Ivy told Nathalie Sarraute that it was the grocer who said to the maid how shocked he was to see a lady like Miss Compton-Burnett with her name in the newspapers. ' "But what could I do?" said she with a sigh. "I had to earn my living" ' (letter to H.S., 30 March 1973).
† Though they contain quite a few actual or attempted murders, none of Ivy's novels could be described as remotely connected with Mayfair (then a favourite

one of her silly little books'.[23] Silliness in this context had a particular connotation for people of Margaret's background and generation. It went with lightness, brightness, irreverence, sophistication, and was a word often on the lips of indignant elders deploring the baffling, morbid, neurotic, unpleasant and unnatural tendencies of hardboiled modern youth. All these terms were applied to one or other of Ivy's four early novels by critics who found her tone indefinably suspect. Reviewers of the old school could never feel entirely happy with dapper, self-confident, irrepressibly flippant young men like Julian Wake in *Brothers and Sisters*, or Felix Bacon ('one thing about me is that limpness gives the effect of grace'[24]) in *More Women Than Men*: decadents (to use the contemporary term) who lay themselves out to tease with their sleek and frivolous wit, their passion for clothes and parties and gossip ('simple, candid probing of our friends' business'[25]), their profoundly sceptical view of their own and other people's motives. Even the most oppressed and downtrodden youths in the later novels of I. Compton-Burnett never quite lost the enthusiasm with which their predecessors, in the 1920s and early 1930s, repudiated duty, self-respect, usefulness, manliness and every other virtue the old and orthodox might be supposed to hold dear:

> 'Well, a man is a man,' said Mr. Bigwell.
>
> 'That is rather sweeping,' said Oliver. 'I am not.'
>
> 'Neither am I,' said Mr. Spode. 'And I should not think Cassidy is.'
>
> 'Of course not,' said Oliver, 'when he keeps a boys' school. And my meaning is simple, not sinister.'[26]

This sort of thing was naturally hard to take for people whose standards of style, daring and wit had been set by Barrie, Wells and A. A. Milne. Equally naturally, it went down well with modern youth. 'It seemed absolutely wonderful, something quite, quite new,' said Rosamond Lehmann, who was in her mid-twenties (and

---

setting with fashionable novelists like Evelyn Waugh, Aldous Huxley, Michael Arlen, Nancy Mitford, etc.). *Murder in Mayfair* by Ivor Novello opened at the Globe Theatre in 1934, but Margaret seems to have borrowed the phrase from a legal friend who claimed that undetected murder among the middle class was by no means uncommon: 'He used to call them "Mayfair murders" ' (Burkhart 1, p. 26).

already a best-selling author herself) when Raymond Mortimer
introduced her to Ivy's writing: 'I was so dazzled by it, she became
my favourite novelist immediately.' Word got round on the fringes
of Bloomsbury, passed by people like Eddie Sackville-West, Henry
Lamb and Margaret's friend Francis Birrell at the bookshop he ran
with David Garnett: a good many lifelong readers of I. Compton-
Burnett (Ivy always insisted on disclosing her initial only, never her
full name, on her title pages) were originally recruited by Garnett's
review of *More Women Than Men* in the *New Statesman*, published in
1933 round about the time Raymond Mortimer took over as
literary editor.

It was the Compton-Burnetts' old family friend Arthur Waley
who had first mentioned *Pastors and Masters* to Mortimer, then still
in his twenties, a columnist on *Vogue* in its brief palmy period as an
avant-garde organ, and already beginning to make a name for
himself as a critic in stern pursuit of new and original talent. 'Was it
possible that there could be a *bâteau*, however *ivre*, moderner than
himself?'[27] asked Harold Nicolson, whose own tastes, in literature
at least, were decidedly more conventional (though both Harold
and his wife, Vita Sackville-West, were shortly afterwards roped in
to spread word of Mortimer's latest discovery). If Mortimer was
one of the first to notice I. Compton-Burnett in 1925, ten years later
he was also the first to point out that her strange, concentrated,
almost abstract way of writing produced the same effect—an
initial, often disturbing sense of unfamiliarity, followed by successive shocks of recognition—as the Post Impressionists had done on
a public accustomed to Victorian naturalism in painting.

But when Ivy finished writing *Brothers and Sisters* at the end of
1928, she knew none of these people except Frankie Birrell, who
had known her brother Noel at King's and turned up again afterwards as one of Margaret's liveliest, seediest and most amusing
young men. Perhaps it was Birrell who persuaded her, directly or
indirectly, to send the manuscript to the Hogarth Press where
Leonard Woolf turned it down, together with J. B. Yeats' *Sligo*
(' "She can't even write," he said . . . "At least this man, Yeats,
knows how to write" '[28]). Ivy went back to Cranton who, having a
good many copies of her last book still on hand, held out no great
hope for the next which he took on the same terms as before.[29]
Brothers and Sisters was published in April and, according to Hugh
Walpole, 'would have been read by scarcely more than a dozen

persons had not a group of professional critics connected with a literary journal made loud and violent outcry about it'.[30]

Mortimer was at the back of this outcry which culminated—to Cranton's astonishment and Woolf's consternation—in *Brothers and Sisters* becoming one of the year's minor publishing sensations. Walpole's 'professional critics' were part of the reviewing stable built up by Woolf himself as literary editor of the *Nation*, which had carried a review by Mortimer,[31] combining his accolade for Miss Compton-Burnett with a shrewd attack on the vulgar commercialism of Walpole's own newly founded Book Society. The Society, a controversial body already under attack from the book trade, capitulated handsomely by making *Brothers and Sisters* runner-up to its very next Book of the Month in May: a choice confirmed at the end of the month by a perceptive and characteristically generous puff in the London *Evening Standard* from Arnold Bennett.* Bennett had long since enthusiastically accepted the role assigned him by Virginia Woolf of philistine, materialist and literary reactionary number one; but, though he might grumble ('The novel has incurred the laudation of select highbrows—which of course put me against it'), it did him no harm with the trade or the reading public, who knew that Bennett meant business. *Brothers and Sisters* promptly went into a second edition which brought a fresh crop of reviews in the middlebrow weeklies in June, all agreeing they had never read anything like it.

Ivy was taken up, talked about, asked to parties, pursued by photographers and gossip columnists (she posed for her picture but drew the line at reporters, being, as she told *Ideal Home* in October,

---

* According to Richard Kennedy's charming account in *A Boy at the Hogarth Press*, Bennett hailed *Brothers and Sisters* as A WORK OF GENIUS. What he actually said was rather more guarded, and seems to have been tacked on as an afterthought at the foot of a piece about making money from first editions:

> I am not sure but I think it quite possible that a work lying at the moment here . . . will one day be the cause of research, envy, covetousness and other vices: . . . *Brothers and Sisters* by I. Compton-Burnett . . . though by no means easy to read, it seems to me an original work, strong and incontestably true to life. I. Compton-Burnett may be a new star, low on the eastern horizon. (*Evening Standard*, 30 May 1929)

The idea of the Book Society had been originally put forward by Bennett, who proposed holding Walpole's post of chairman himself; and no doubt he watched its initial flounderings with a certain quiet satisfaction.

'a writer who will not have publicity at any price'). Frankie Birrell asked her to lunch on 9 April to meet Vita Sackville-West who took her the same afternoon to call on Virginia Woolf (describing Ivy in a letter next day to Harold Nicolson as a 'little spinster of at least 50, very shy, very nervous, very overwhelmed by the admiration we heaped on her, and at being carried off to see Virginia who wants the refusal of her next book'[32]). Birrell brought Raymond Mortimer to tea at Ivy's flat a week later, while Vita (who gave *Brothers and Sisters* one of its sharpest and most enthusiastic reviews on the B.B.C. on 2 May) dined alone with Ivy on the fourteenth and returned to a rather grander luncheon two days later. She and Mortimer were both entertained at parties composed otherwise entirely of Margaret's more presentable furniture friends like the Kings, together with a choice selection of her young men—Roger Hinks from the British Museum, Leigh Ashton (eventually head of the V&A), the architect Basil Ionides and the society painter Willie Ranken: a guest list calculated to leave envoys from Bloomsbury feeling almost as flummoxed as Ivy's own skilled impersonation of a governess of the old school.

But Ivy had become overnight a catch for literary hostesses as diverse as Mrs Robert Lynd (who regularly entertained high livers and plain thinkers, like the Victor Gollanczes and the J. B. Priestleys, to games, charades and singsongs at her Hampstead Friday nights), and the elderly but still furiously competitive Violet Hunt. Rose Macaulay, who sent a card for her party in July and dined at the flat the night after, became a close friend, and so did Mrs Hunt. For the first time in her life Ivy was courted by agents and publishers: she accepted the advances of Rose's and Vita's energetic young agent, David Higham of Curtis Brown, and had the gratification of turning down not only the Woolfs' Hogarth Press but also Sylvia Lynd with messages from Methuen in favour of a contract for her next three novels from Heinemann, topped off by hopeful overtures from Donald Brace of the American firm Harcourt, Brace (who brought out *Brothers and Sisters* that autumn in the U.S.).[33]

ii

Ivy was forty-five. She had never been fêted like this before, never attracted attention, scarcely even had friends of her own, let alone parties: 'in a sense she had no youth,' as William Herrick says of his sister Emily in *Pastors and Masters*, 'just as in a way she will have no old age.'[34] At the end of the First World War, Ivy had drawn a line beneath everything that had happened in her first thirty-five years. She never again discussed her early life, indeed knew hardly anyone with whom she might have discussed it. Escape from the past, always a theme in I. Compton-Burnett, is nowhere more explicit than in *Brothers and Sisters* which, for all its melodramatic apparatus of missing documents and long-lost parents, contains at its core a faithful account of events in the Compton-Burnett household at Hove in the early years of the century. Like the young Staces running away to London at the end of that novel, Ivy had seen her youth wasted in Hove, her life several times blasted in it, her parents cut off in their prime.

Her own subsequent attempts to take cover in London in 1915 could hardly have been worse timed. When people asked afterwards about the gap between *Dolores*, published in 1911, and *Pastors and Masters* fourteen years later, Ivy put it down to 'family troubles and responsibilities and the loss of a brother in the war'.[35] The war itself, her brother Noel's death on the Somme, his wife's attempted suicide, the actual suicides of Ivy's two youngest sisters on Christmas Day, 1917, followed by her own nearly mortal illness: all these culminated in a period of prolonged mental and physical prostration, what Ivy herself described as a kind of death in life,[36] from which she only gradually recovered after Margaret moved into her flat in 1919.

It is the dislocation caused by this series of catastrophic upheavals that presumably explains why, though she was born in 1884 within a year or two of such giants of the Modern Movement as James Joyce, D. H. Lawrence and for that matter Virginia Woolf, I. Compton-Burnett can hardly be said to belong in their company. Membership of the Movement was not in any case a claim she would have cared to make, or see made on her behalf: her own view came closer to Felix Bacon's boast, in *More Women Than Men*, 'I am not one of those modern people; I try always to seem a survival from the old world.'[37] But in this characteristically misleading scheme she was only partly successful. Settings in the 1890s, plots which reminded her earliest reviewers of high Victorian tearjerkers like *East Lynne* and *The Wide, Wide World* or the still more bizarre excesses of *Irene Iddesleigh*, none of these eccentric trappings could entirely conceal the boldness that struck her contemporaries as very far from old world.

Dolores, published in the same year as Lawrence's *The White Peacock*, respectively three and four years before Joyce's and Virginia Woolf's first books, had been a thoroughly misconceived homage to George Eliot (its original title, *Unhistoric Acts*, came from the last sentence of *Middlemarch* and its plot from *Scenes of Clerical Life*). Its very turgidity shows how fiercely Ivy had struggled, like the great moderns, with a dead form. 1911 was also the year in which Ivy's mother died, the year she found herself facing what must have seemed like life imprisonment inside the family, the year when (according to her sister Vera) 'the iron entered into her soul'.[38] Her writing career, in some sense her life itself, came to a standstill. For the next decade and more Ivy went underground. But the tide of destruction which, in her own phrase, 'quite smashed my life up'[39] also dismantled much that she relinquished without regret. By the time she took to scribbling again in the penny notebooks in which she had written *Dolores*, the assumptions and outlook underlying that false start had been drastically realigned. In the sense that Ivy's imagination was shaped and profoundly modified by the experiences of 1914 to 1918, she belongs essentially to the postwar generation of writers; and it is scarcely surprising that, when she eventually made her debut alongside the much younger novelists who surfaced towards the end of the 1920s, she had in some ways more in common with the young Evelyn Waugh or Anthony Powell than with her own contemporaries.

Ivy emerged from years of despair and stagnation with something of the survivor's elation, the gallows gaiety that overtakes Robin Stace in *Brothers and Sisters* when his family's fortunes touch rock bottom (' "You are not letting anything get the better of you, I know." "Things have done that, without any slackness of ours," said Robin'[40]). A heady sense of release and liberation runs through her early work, in the ebullient elderly novelists or would-be novelists of *Pastors and Masters* (' "Real books coming out of our own heads!" said Bumpus. "And not just printed unkindness to other people's" '[41]) as in the ceaseless party-giving and -going of *Brothers and Sisters*. No writer agreed more readily than Ivy with 'readers who demand of a novel that it should be light, malicious and high-spirited' in Peter Quennell's definition (the phrase comes from his *New Statesman* review of Powell's *Agents and Patients* but might as well have been applied to any one of Ivy's four early novels); and there is no mistaking the relief with which an earlier *New Statesman* reviewer switched, in June 1925, from a polite if faintly derisive account of Lawrence's *St. Mawr* to something decidedly less strenuous: 'As for *Pastors and Masters*, it is astonishing, alarming. It is like nothing else in the world. It is a work of genius. How to describe it—since there is nothing of which to take hold?'[42]

Much the same mixture of delight and bewilderment greeted Waugh's *Decline and Fall* three years later, together with the same charges of insubstantiality, brittleness and oddity. Indeed there is a marked affinity between Dr Fagan's famously shady establishment in *Decline and Fall* and the equally run-down prep school in *Pastors and Masters*★ with its watery marmalade, its alternately tearful and tittering small boys, its overworked and hopelessly underqualified staff, its indolent headmaster trading on the dubious services of a partner called Merry whose gift for ingratiating himself with parents amply compensates for his lack of any more palpable educational advantage (' "Isn't it generous of him to spend his life giving to others what he has not had himself?" "Why not hand over prayers to him, and retire, Herrick?" said Bumpus. "If he can read" '[43]).

The satirical exuberance of I. Compton-Burnett's first postwar novel never entirely left her though she never again let it play quite so freely as it does on dilapidated characters like Merry, or those quintessential poor relations, the Batemans (' "I wish it was us who had a party," said Tilly, who was an almost startling example of failure to rise above a lack of advantages'[44]) in *Brothers and Sisters*. It runs strongly to the last in the butlers whose aggressive feats of oneupmanship are recorded in an almost Wodehousian spirit of detached appreciation—one thinks of Bullivant, in *Manservant and Maidservant*, magnanimously clearing the dead jackdaw from a smoking chimney with the unction he might have reserved, in a better class of household, for dislodging champagne corks; or

★ Both no doubt derive ultimately from Dickens' Dotheboys Hall, a debt freely acknowledged in Emily Herrick's account of the thirty-nine boarders filing out of their basement dining room in *Pastors and Masters* (p. 48): 'There are those hundreds of helpless children, coming up from that cellar that we have never seen. I wish Dickens was alive to expose schools. Mr. Merry has stopped to look back at Mrs. Merry, as if she were a dumb pet that understood.'

Buttermere in *Men and Wives*, first and perhaps most infuriating of all his tribe, showing the family solicitor where to wash his hands for luncheon: ' "The water is hot, sir," said Buttermere, standing by the open door and producing the impression that for many people he would have turned the tap.'[45] Anti-romanticism, always unremitting in I. Compton-Burnett, is implicit in the gaiety, malice and high surface polish of her literary, rather than her literal generation. It is the frame of mind responsible for a whole race of cynics like Theresa Fletcher in *Pastors and Masters* (' "It is unworthy of you to expect people to be prompt," said Bumpus. "Such a cold, self-esteeming thing to be." "I am cold and self-esteeming," said Theresa'[46]) as well as the urbane young men whose obstreperous wit was so highly prized in the 1920s. 'Given favourable conditions,' wrote the American critic O.J., reviewing *Brothers and Sisters* in the *New Republic*, 'a work such as this might conceivably, like a new *Euphues*, mould social talk for a decade.'[47]

Brothers and Sisters went down especially well in the U.S. where its author was several times contrasted with 'that other great master of conversation, Ernest Hemingway', and the 'coolness and candour' of her sexual deviants greatly preferred to the self-indulgence of a dozen other novels on 'problems of sexual abnormality' crossing the Atlantic in 1929 in the wake of Radclyffe Hall's *Well of Loneliness* trial the year before. Basil Davenport, voting incest theme of the year in the *Saturday Review*, compared Ivy's casual approach favourably with William Faulkner's Jacobean intensity in *The Sound and the Fury*—not, as Davenport explained, that he meant any disrespect to the latter, 'only to point out that Mr. Faulkner writes of a decaying, old-world family with a heritage of insanity and Miss Compton-Burnett of some healthy moderns'.[48] The distinction is salutary, and perhaps it seemed so to Ivy at the time; at any rate, Davenport went on to discern in *Brothers and Sisters* the programme she was to follow for the rest of her career:

It is the only book where one can find implicit what every twentieth century reader of the *Oedipus Tyrannus* must have felt, that a prohibited marriage ignorantly contracted may be a calamity but is after all nothing to blind oneself about . . . One suddenly sees that she [Sophia Stace, prototype of Ivy's mother, who dominates the book] is all that is worst in the nineteenth century, and the young people with their forthrightness and independence, all that is best of the twentieth. Their modernity gives them almost the qualities of the children in *The Innocent Voyage*,★ the ability to go through the fire and escape the burning. All other books on this theme are stories of the present defeated by the past; *Brothers and Sisters* is a story of the present hurt by the past, but not defeated.

Like so much else in the fiction of I. Compton-Burnett, *Brothers and Sisters* works by extracting its larger application from things that had happened in fact. In a sense, Ivy could never escape from the world that had ended with the First World War: in 1941, Margaret warned Francis Wyndham (who had posted a fan letter from school, and received in reply an invitation to visit) that 'Ivy lives in the past, and nothing after 1914 has any reality for her'.[49] To Anthony Powell, meeting her for the first time a few years later, she seemed 'a quite unmodified pre-1914 personality'.[50] New acquaintances often felt like this about Ivy, and the reaction goes back to the crucial years before 1919 when her violent slamming of doors on the past had entailed an equally harsh rejection of the present. *Pastors and Masters* marked a recovery consolidated four years later in *Brothers and Sisters*, where the incestuous complications provide a fictional gloss or counterpart to material supplied by Ivy's own unhappy family: here for the first time she turned back to her father's death and its disastrous effect on her despairing, despotic, hysterically unstable mother, the cat-and-mouse régime that followed, the children's helplessness in the ten years of steadily increasing strain that bound Ivy so intimately to her own two brothers. But, as Elizabeth Bowen pointed out, I. Compton-Burnett was 'not merely copying but actually continuing the Victorian novel',[51] and it was something that could only be done from a firm stance in the present, in the light of that hard, frank, pertinent stare her contemporaries found so essentially modern. Ivy lived the rest of her life, in fact, on the principle that even a family history as calamitous as the Oedipuses' was nothing to blind oneself about. Perhaps she remembered Davenport's review when, twenty years later, she made Bridget Chase confront precisely this situation in fiction:

★ The American title of Richard Hughes' *High Wind in Jamaica*, also first published in 1929 along with Hemingway's *A Farewell to Arms*, Henry Green's *Living*, J. B. Priestley's *The Good Companions* and Michael Arlen's *Lily Christine*.

'People are so noble in trouble,' said Bridget. 'We forget how well they come out under a test. And we have been brave enough ourselves not to put out our eyes. Perhaps people are braver than they used to be.'

'Perhaps we are fortunate,' said Selina, drily. 'Or perhaps fashions have changed. It does not seem that Oedipus was thought to have acted oddly under the circumstances.'[52]

iii

People driven to extremities of one sort or another were to be Ivy's permanent preoccupation. But in the 1920s and 1930s she was still sufficiently a child of her time to extract much entertainment from the contemporary scene. *Pastors and Masters* takes place at the time it was written, *Brothers and Sisters* has begun to move rather shakily —and the next two books more firmly—back before the First World War. But drinks before dinner together with the speed, ease and frequency of divorce in *Men and Wives* (1931) make the period setting a fairly hit-and-miss affair, as it still is in *More Women Than Men* (1933) with its horse-drawn carriages and almost regal widows' weeds ranged uneasily alongside talk of trades unions, equal pay for women and telephone trunk calls. The high spirits —what disgruntled reviewers took for cynicism—of Ivy's characters at this stage reflect an emancipation widespread after the First World War. In all four early novels the pomposity and sentimental rhetoric of overbearing elders are systematically undercut by 'frank modern children'[53] like Ruth Giffard, defending her engagement in *More Women Than Men*, or Griselda Haslam breaking hers off in *Men and Wives*:

'It is Griselda, wild and sorrowing and burdened, whom I love, as I shall never love another woman.'

'If you think of me in that way, you do already love another woman.'[54]

Decor and dress sense, class and sex distinctions loom larger than ever again in these early books whose fictional world seems as often as not contiguous with Ivy's own circle at the time. Even Margaret's professional interests tend to spill over, most noticeably in the village of Moreton Edge in *Brothers and Sisters* with its commuters travelling up and down between London and their handsome, half-timbered or Queen Anne houses in the country, and its marked attention to furnishings—the Drydens' enforced economy at the rectory contrasting with the Staces' family portraits, or the Wakes' pursuit of expensive simplicity in a tumbledown cottage on the main street. At the beginning of the 1920s Margaret wrote a regular column for *Eve* on 'Furniture for the Country Cottage', urging the simple virtues of solid oak, recommending humble Georgian or Queen Anne pieces for the parlour with Toby jugs on the chimneypiece, generally promoting the fashionable taste for romantic rusticity embodied in the Wakes' cottage and its 'carefully cottage-like furnishings', its sitting room renamed the parlour, even its modest jug of columbines (' "I grew them, and cut them, and put them in that pot," said Julian. "Every little womanly touch in this cottage is mine" '[55]).

Julian himself is precisely the sort of escort regularly featured in gossip column or social calendar by illustrated papers like *Eve*. His ability to relieve his feelings by having a real tidy-up or a good cry, his gallantry towards older women, preference for his own sister's company, successive proposals to the sisters of two of his best friends on grounds that only marriage can excuse fading charm ('though of course I agree that nothing ought to excuse it'[56]): all unmistakably reflect the limp-wristed vogue endorsed by so many outrageously witty and talented men-about-town in the 1920s. Margaret's and Ivy's great friend Ernest Thesiger was one of them. Gossipy, acerbic, inquisitive and entertaining, Ernest was in his prime between the two world wars (and, to borrow Robin Stace's phrase from *Brothers and Sisters*, 'I can hardly tell you how utterly he was in it'[57]). In a decade of parties, he had figured on notable occasions from the Women's Ball at the Albert Hall in 1919—Lady Diana Manners and other Greek beauties led by Ernest as Pan, in a goatskin designed by Lady Lavery—to Norman Hartnell's circus party ten years later when Ernest, at fifty, came as a lion tamer in red tights and close-fitting black trunks. Like Julian, Ernest had married his best friend's sister (the friend, Willie Ranken—who had been a contemporary at the Slade and used to walk about town with Ernest, both wearing bouquets in their buttonholes—shaved off his hair at the news[58]). He collected rings and pink lustre, and, when his house in Montpelier Terrace was featured in *House and Garden*, made a point of demonstrating how he had marbled the bathroom himself, worked his own *gros point* carpets, painted his own Chinese wallpaper, appliquéd the curtains and frescoed a sky on his wife's bedroom ceiling.

Ernest's taste, according to *Eve*,[59] was the last word in wallpaper and white waistcoats. His face, as he said himself, was too queer to be caricaturable but, as a founder member of the Men's Dress Reform Society, he liked to show off his legs in pale moleskin shorts or a still more striking cerulean velvet pair, worn with matching silk blouse and muffler, in which he outshone even Shaw at the Malvern Festival in 1932. He designed his own clothes, painted in oils, learnt lace-making to run up a christening veil for a niece. It was Ernest who made the Aubusson carpet and dining-room fire screens for Queen Mary's dolls' house (his aunt had been her mother's lady-in-waiting, and Queen Mary herself supplied the model for Ernest's own increasingly regal bearing in later life); Willie did the still life over the sideboard; they were both expert needlemen, apt to take out their embroidery and sit stitching on trains to the consternation or mirth of other incredulous passengers.

Ernest had been wounded in both hands as a private on the Western Front in 1915, and came home to make his name on the stage that autumn in *A Little Bit of Fluff*, playing the sort of stage dolt—'a lank, weedy, cadaverous, plaintive-eyed ninny with a nose as sharp as a pen—a kind of modern Slender'[60]—which afterwards became his speciality. His Bertram Tully was a wild success with the troops ('Mr. Ernest Thesiger is a scream'[61]), and was followed after the war by the boatman in Barrie's *Mary Rose*, a haunting Captain Hook and triumphant Dauphin in Shaw's *St. Joan*: perhaps his greatest hit in a long line of what the *Queen* called 'unhealthy parts'[62] like Bagoas the Eunuch in Bennett's *Judith* ('exquisite as a lady's lampshade with his swinging skirts and fringes, evil as the flash of a poisoned scimitar in an Eastern alley', wrote an apprecia- tive Rebecca West[63]) or the catamite Piers Gaveston in Marlowe's *Edward II*. He left the cast of *St. Joan* in 1925 to do a Noël Coward number in drag with Douglas Byng for C. B. Cochrane's revue. He was Henry in *Gentlemen Prefer Blondes* at Blackpool and Miles Malpractice in Waugh's *Vile Bodies* at the Arts. Ernest once com- plained that Somerset Maugham never sent him anything: 'B-but, I am always writing p-parts for you, Ernest,' said Maugham. 'The trouble is that somebody called Gladys Cooper *will* insist on p-playing them.'[64]

Ernest represented, in short, everything that was silliest and most provoking in the social life of the time. He said, when he published his autobiography in 1927, that he charged people £50 for a mention and £75 to be left out.[65] A master of double, triple, even (according to Beverley Nichols) quadruple meaning, he had brought subversion to a fine and frivolous art. People thought him heartless, self-centred, cynical, but nobody questioned his nerve. For Ernest, who was a grandson of the first Lord Chelmsford and cousin to the Viceroy of India, to have become a professional painter and ended up on the stage was something unheard of. It was an extremist's version of his father's reaction to the tailor who suggested that a gentleman in his position ought not to carry his trousers about in a parcel: ' "A gentleman in my position can do *anything*," said my father indignantly. "That is the only point of being a gentleman in my position." '[66]

It enabled Ernest all his life to combine refusal or failure to conform with a front of unimpeachable moral and social rectitude. He delighted the children of Margaret's friend, Nelly Levy, by showing them his green-painted toenails,[67] and there are many stories (decidedly risqué in those days) of his unbuttoning at conventional dinner parties to fish out the pearls he wore under his shirt. Loyalty, independence, sensitivity, pluck were the qualities he liked best in himself, and he freely confessed himself a snob ('I have always maintained that the only way to make an impression on a celebrity is to insult them at sight'[68]), with a particular bias towards royalty and what he called 'gilded bounders'.

But Ernest was also irresistibly drawn to the obdurate, unfashionable and odd. He went out of his way to be attentive to social misfits like Mrs Arnold Bennett, the despised or neglected 'lesser halves of the great'* (a category for which Ivy certainly qualified among Margaret's friends when Ernest first knew her). He had long been a connoisseur of lady novelists, having built up quite a

---

* See his story of meeting Mrs Bennett at a party:

Everyone was at that party—even I—and naturally everyone was in their gladdest of rags. Except one person. Seated in a conspicuous position was a somewhat grim-looking woman, strangely dressed, and wearing a large crimson jockey cap, adorned with a marabou! . . . 'I wore it,' she explained, 'so that everyone in the room should say, "Who on earth is that woman in the hat?" and then they would be told, "That is Mrs. Arnold Bennett." You see,' she added, 'no one seems to know that there *is* a Mrs. Arnold Bennett.' (*Practically True*, p. 129)

collection as a young man in the first decade of the century—Miss
Mary Cholmondeley, Miss Florence Montgomery, Mrs Fuller-
Maitland and Mrs Evan Nepean had all been courted by Ernest
—and holding that all the best novels since the war had been written
by women. He knew Ivy's friend Violet Hunt, and the redoubtable
May Sinclair whom Ivy met at parties given by Hester's uncle,
Alban Head, and who was one of the very few people capable of
flustering Ernest:

> Even now that I know her well, I am careful what I say, when I
> am confronted with someone who looks more like a nursery-
> governess than a brilliant writer, and whose knowledge of the
> world and keen sense of humour are locked away behind a prim,
> pinched smile; and every time I read one of her books I wonder
> how anyone so reserved and conventional can know all the
> dreadful things she does. But appearances in writers, and espe-
> cially women writers, are terribly deceptive![69]

Ernest's addiction to writers would have done him no good among
Margaret's friends, many of whom in any case dismissed him as a
snob and a rattle and worse, to be tolerated chiefly for his wife's
sake: 'He was a sort of butterfly,' said one[70], 'or more like a
mosquito.' But Ivy liked him, more than Margaret did, precisely
because of his rattling, his garrulity, irony, gregariousness, because
nothing ever nonplussed him, and no doubt partly also because of
the genuine sympathy that made him seek out Marguerite Bennett
and get past the guard of May Sinclair. Ernest laid claim to
clairvoyance, or at least to a knowledge of people that matched
Ivy's own and was based on the same strict professional habit of
detailed observation:

> I have sometimes been asked whether it is not very awkward to
> know so much about people, but I have never found it so. '*Tout
> comprendre c'est tout pardonner*' is one of my favourite mottoes . . .
> to know *everything* about a person, as I do when I know anything
> at all, puts one almost in the position of a benignant deity to
> whom everything can be confided without fear of blame or
> misunderstanding . . .[71]

He and Ivy would sit over their needlework together ('Nothing is more terrifying to me than to see Ernest Thesiger sitting under the lamplight doing this embroidery,' wrote the young Beverley Nichols[72]), sewing and talking in a spirit that was, by Ernest's own account, not unlike the Scropes' in *The Present and the Past*:

> 'I never feel disapproval,' said Elton. 'It is a feeling foreign to my nature. I hardly need to know all to forgive all. Considering the pleasure of knowing, that is only fair. I can hardly bear to know it, I forgive so much. I think people do such understandable things.'
>
> 'Yes,' said Ursula. 'I am often ashamed of understanding them.'[73]

Of all Margaret's friends Ernest was probably Ivy's ultimate favourite, together with the Dutchman Herman Schrijver who had been her first fan. Herman, another prime gossip and wit who, like Ivy, believed the worst of human beings, was making his way between the wars with fair success as an interior decorator. His clients among the wealthy and great eventually numbered Guinnesses and Keplers, financiers and socialites, Ernest Simpson and 'more than one of Ernest's wives',[74] and at the beginning of the 1930s he even had a hand in doing up Fort Belvedere for the future king. But his father, who managed a diamond-cutting and -polishing works, had lost all his money in England after the war and returned to Amsterdam, leaving Herman to start his career in 1925, at the age of twenty-one, as a shop clerk at Peter Jones in Sloane Square on £5 a week.[75] A Jew and a foreigner, without money or connections, must have been open to innumerable slights in the world Herman was setting out to conquer. Even Margaret, who acknowledged no conventional prejudices against friends or clients ('She didn't mind if they were Jews or dagoes, provided they were rich enough'[76]), referred to Herman with her customary air of scorn as 'Ivy's Jewish friend'.

Although she had made the introduction herself, Margaret was not always best pleased to find Herman intrigued and attracted by something in Ivy to which other friends remained largely impervious; and perhaps Ivy for her part responded to Herman in the first place because she was, in some sense, a fellow outsider. She loved his flightiness, cheerfulness, unfailing pessimism, his wild overstatements and darting, allusive, fantastically embroidered accounts of his own and other people's professional and sexual manoeuvrings for power. More than that, she came eventually to depend on him for the unconditional, unspoken, mutual acceptance and understanding that had always been her essential emotional demand of other people. Not that their intimacy grew straight away. Ivy had been as constrained with him to start with as she was with everyone else. 'I found it very difficult to talk to her,' said Herman, who required all his considerable powers of persuasion as well as heroic persistence to reach the stage at which he not only read her books but, by his own account, contributed to them as well. 'Ivy was really interested in people as material for her novels, in people's money, in their sex lives, particularly incest and servants'[77]: all subjects on which Herman spoke with authority and with an ingrained scepticism deeply congenial to Ivy.

It was Herman who reversed the tag, 'Kindness in another's trouble,/Courage in one's own.' 'Oh no, darling,' he said once to a friend[78] in distress, 'I've always thought it ought to be, "Courage in another's trouble,/Kindness in one's own."' No one delighted more fondly than he did in his friends' cleverness, beauty or wit; and no one could beat him at speaking evil behind people's backs, a talent Ivy admired as much as Hope Cranmer in *Parents and Children*: 'I like my friends when they are doing it. It makes them so zestful and observant. Original too, almost creative. You see, I am speaking good behind their backs . . .'[79] Herman believed, with Hope and most of the practical observers in Ivy's books, 'that every human being loves himself or herself best, and that for this very reason they prefer their own sex to the other'.[80] But, where characters like Hope (Rachel Hardistie in *Men and Wives* and Felix Bacon in *More Women Than Men* are parallel cases) combine this belief with notably successful marriages, Herman went further and held that all men were essentially homosexual. One of the games[81] he described playing with Ivy consisted in her attempting to name any heterosexual man they both knew while he refuted her claims so that (except for an early hit with Basil Marsden-Smedley) Ivy scored nil.

Exaggeration was a fixed principle, almost a mania with Herman ('Why make any statement unless you exaggerate?' he once blithely asked . . . 'What's wrong with too much?'[82]); and the game, if it took place at all, must have done so after the Second World War, almost certainly after Margaret's death, since Margaret would never have permitted such licence. 'She wasn't intolerant but she wouldn't have thought it *bon ton*,' said their friend Soame Jenyns of the British Museum, who maintained that Margaret was well aware of disreputable proclivities among some of her friends whereas Ivy took in nothing at all. But Ivy had always kept an eye on what she called 'homos' at a time when this, or any similar term, was unmentionable in polite society, let alone literature.*

It is not easy to reconstruct the taboos which prevented people from talking freely or writing about, sometimes even from recognizing, things we now accept as casually as Ivy did from the start in her books. The war had released what the literary elder statesmen of the day—people like Edmund Gosse and E. F. Benson, both of whom had ruthlessly suppressed unorthodox sexual leanings in their own lives—thought of as a 'flood of erotic fiction', in which for the first time 'sexual perversion' had become a legitimate, if still loathsome topic: 'Though all normal folk naturally regarded it [homosexuality] with disgust, it had to be recognised as a pathological deformity of the mind rather than a mark of unspeakable moral obliquity.'† In this heated atmosphere, it is no wonder if Ivy's attitude seemed at the time almost preposterously unemphatic.

Homosexuality, taken for granted among the dons in *Pastors and Masters*, crops up intermittently in her books thereafter with couples like the cook and parlourmaid in *Elders and Betters* ('If it was hinted that their devotion bordered on excess, Ethel would reply with quiet finality that they were first cousins'[83]). But it is most pervasive in *More Women Than Men* which came out in 1933 at the height of the vogue for deviant literature, and which dwells with quite uncharacteristic firmness on the mechanics of seduction

---

* According to Anthony Powell, excisions demanded by the apprehensive publishers (Chapman and Hall) of Waugh's *Decline and Fall* in 1928 included the remark that Captain Grimes did not like women, together with the phrase 'nothing happened' applied to his marriage ('boiler room' was also substituted for 'lavatory' where the boys smoked, and the Welsh station master was made to pimp for his sister-in-law, not his sister), *Messengers of Day* (Heinemann, 1978), p. 105.
† *As We Are Now* by E. F. Benson (Longmans, 1932), p. 262. But high-mindedness did not prevent Benson inserting a good many steamy scenes in bathroom or swimming pool into his own popular prep-school novel, *David Blaize* (Hodder and Stoughton, 1916): 'He was completely dishevelled and yet a very jolly object, and was quite altogether wet, his knickerbockers clinging like tights to his thighs, which showed pink through them . . .' (p. 141).

among both homo- and heterosexuals, not forgetting shades in between (' "I cannot imagine any useful and self-respecting person of either sex wanting to belong to the other," said Josephine. "Neither can I, a person of that kind," said Felix[84]). Faint but insistent signs of lesbian activity in the senior common room of the girls' school in which the book is set are complemented by the longstanding affair between the drawing master, Felix Bacon, and the headmistress's brother, the Rev. Jonathan Swift: a ménage disrupted after twenty years by Felix's engagement to one of the mistresses, whereupon Jonathan proposes setting up house with his son, brought up from infancy by his sister, on grounds that kinship is the natural tie ('Of course it is. But you wanted an unnatural one,' says Felix[85]).

Ivy's matter-of-factness is as different from the absurd high jinks of squibs like Compton Mackenzie's *Extraordinary Women* (1929) as from the no less extravagant, confessional earnestness of Radclyffe Hall and her followers. 'A most gentlemanly book' was Rose Macaulay's phrase for *The Well of Loneliness*[86]; and the point of Ivy's riposte is the thoroughly ungentlemanly spirit in which she deals with the way people actually behave, as opposed to the ways in which social and literary convention decreed that they ought. Ralph Edwards, who knew Ivy by this time well enough to feel rightly uneasy about *More Women Than Men*, warned *Country Life* readers that most of them would be well advised to steer clear of 'a study in morbid psychology,* the more extraordinary because the author is clearly unaware that her characters are beyond the pale of normal experience'.[87] Ralph Straus in the *Sunday Times* was not so much affronted as aggrieved, almost plaintive: 'Do men exist like . . . Jonathan, or the lady-like Felix, or Jonathan's son Gabriel—dim creatures who hardly seem to be male at all?'[88]

It was another thirty years and more before characters like Jonathan and Felix became commonplace in English fiction. In 1933 even David Garnett, who had also met Ivy and might have known better, was too puzzled by the flavour of 'this queer writer'[89] to register how accurately she reproduced the manners and mores described only long afterwards in his own and other people's memoirs of the period. Ivy's Victorian schoolmasters and mis-

* 'Morbid' was the conventional codeword for homosexual: Felix describes Jonathan's feelings for himself as 'a morbid attachment'.

tresses reminded him at the time of lavender and old silk, Meredith, Wilde and the Marx brothers. But anyone who has read recent accounts of what went on among the London intelligentsia in Bloomsbury and elsewhere between the wars will find something distinctly familiar about Ivy's portrait of a small, self-conscious and inward-looking society of intellectuals, waspish, hard-up and far from smart, almost all single and sexually on the make, fascinated by and madly curious about each other's ages, clothes, looks, incomes, sexual inclinations and changes of partner.

Ivy herself reacted with amusement and some complacency to charges of innocence or immodesty. Museum friends like Ralph Edwards and Soame Jenyns, who tended to doubt whether Margaret's unworldly, inexperienced companion understood quite what she was saying, might have taken a tip from the novelist Robert Liddell, who raised the question openly the first time he met Ivy and Margaret:

> Margaret picked up my suggestion that some of the good characters were not sexually irreproachable.
> 'The doubtful Felix?' she said. 'Our landlady when we were staying in Cambridge said to me: "Miss Burnett must be a little naive. That young man sitting on an old man's knee: some people would think it improper." '
> 'I thought it was meant to be improper,' I said.
> 'Oh, it was meant to be improper,' said Ivy, in a full, satisfied tone. She went on to say, 'One cut out a scene because one didn't want trouble.'[90]

Avoiding censorship trouble—the sort of thing frowned on by Jonathan's sister in 'some modern books I could mention'[91]—was not the least advantage of Ivy's old-world style. Far from inhibiting conversation or behaviour (the divorce and illegitimacy rates, not to mention general crime, being consistently high in Compton-Burnett novels), it permitted a freedom by no means always inherent in 'the loose and easy realism of most novelists'. The point was taken at the time by another novelist, Alice Herbert (author of the bestselling *Heaven and Charing Cross* in 1922), who noted in her review of *More Women Than Men* that I. Compton-Burnett's Victorianism was barely skin deep:

Her people 'converse' a little like Jane Austen's . . . Here non-modernity stops: for her sense of our own time is acute and very penetrating. The 'young' man Felix could never have been drawn in a novel of fifty years ago, nor the ethereally delicate hints given here and there of tendencies—not modern indeed, but un-acknowledged in the old days.[92]

It is young men like Felix and Julian Wake who represent all that most appealed to Ivy in the contemporary scene. Their talk is what E. M. Forster called 'easy and modern',[93] as far removed from the shock and pioneering sexual excitement of Lawrence as from the Victorians' blanket inhibitions. But their homosexuality is inciden-tal, or important only in so far as it enables them to remain detached from the scenes of family violence which, after *More Women Than Men*, occupied the foreground of Ivy's novels. Cool, clever, self-contained jokers like Felix remain steadfastly kind, if helpless, in the face of greed, lust, rage, jealousy, the explosive passions I. Comp-ton-Burnett set herself to confront, in book after book, with the hard, dry, unblinking realism that puts her so utterly apart from her great romantic contemporaries like Lawrence and Virginia Woolf.

Virginia Woolf herself readily agreed with Vita's cousin, Eddie Sackville-West, that the Hogarth Press ought to have published *Brothers and Sisters* in 1929, but it was a blunder she could not bring herself to regret—'There is something bleached about Miss Comp-ton-Burnett: like hair that has never had any colour in it.'[94] As a shy, nervous 'little spinster', Ivy inevitably invited condescension from patricians like Vita and Virginia (the patronizing tone of Vita's description was not lost on Ivy, who startled the French novelist Nathalie Sarraute—coming to pay homage nearly forty years later to the two chief radical innovators in the English novel—by saying that Virginia Woolf was a terrible snob[95]). As a writer, she was too different and at the same time too formidable ever to make much headway with Virginia. Though there were only two years be-tween them in age, Virginia was already in her professional prime at their first meeting, and Ivy seems to have seen her as belonging in some sense to an older generation—or at least to have regarded her with that special ambivalence artists tend to feel for their immediate predecessors. To the end of her life Ivy retained strong reservations about Virginia Woolf's novels, combined with rather uncharacter-istically high expectations of her as a person: 'She was a bit malicious, you know—she'd say the most dreadful things about people,' Ivy reported long afterwards to her friend Barbara Robinson. 'Of course, one does oneself. But one doesn't expect it of Virginia Woolf.'[96]

For a few months in the summer of 1929 it looked as though Ivy herself was well on the way to becoming a literary celebrity in her own right. A steady stream of admirers called at the flat for the first time to see Ivy, not Margaret, coming away often more mystified than when they arrived. Lytton Strachey was said to admire her, and so did 'that living index of printed books', J. F. Cox of the London Library, who recommended all his customers to read her.[97] I. Compton-Burnett was a name to conjure with by the early 1930s, especially with the second wave of Bloomsbury intellectuals; so much so that she seemed positively tainted to Anthony Powell, then in his twenties, starting his career by working for Duckworths (Waugh's former publishers who had lost Decline and Fall by over-assiduous censorship) and vehemently rejecting all shades of received opinion: 'my own generation regarding Bloomsbury as no less elderly, stuffy, anxious to put the stopper on rising talent, than the staunchly anti-avant-garde Duckworths.'[98] Ivy's growing fame continued to keep Virginia Woolf awake at nights ('Dead and disappointing . . . No life in it,' she wrote in her diary, contrasting her own reviews for The Years in March, 1937, unfavourably with Ivy's for Daughters and Sons: 'Much inferior to the bitter truth and intense originality of Miss Compton-Burnett. Now this pain woke me at 4 a.m. and I suffered acutely'[99]).

But, after the success of Brothers and Sisters, Ivy politely but firmly turned down further overtures from the literary world. The layers of protective camouflage so carefully built up in ten years as Margaret's companion proved too convenient to be dismantled. Though she preserved her press cuttings, kept an intermittent eye on publicity and always remembered the gratitude due to her early reviewers, Ivy never again made—or permitted Margaret to make—the slightest move to mark, let alone celebrate, publication of one of her books. Intrigued or bewildered readers who wanted to know more about her had to make do with rumours circulating by word of mouth. Ivy herself sank comfortably back into her old role of spectator at Margaret's parties, ignored or dismissed by people who made a point of not reading her books: a choice perhaps best understood by analogy with the contented lives of her own governesses who also prefer to make their own terms among people who treat them at best with a certain indifferent respect. The image of the alarming Miss Mitford settling herself to her own satisfaction with her book and her box of sweets in *Parents and Children* is not unlike the picture passed on to Elizabeth Wiskemann when, as a young woman at the beginning of the 1930s, she first heard of I. Compton-Burnett from Bunny Garnett and other Bloomsbury friends: 'They said there was someone—a woman who lay all day on a sofa writing with a pencil in a notebook—and that she was the one to watch.'[100]

FOR THE NEXT twenty . . . . more Ivy seems to have accepted her role in much the same spirit as Dudley Gaveston, in *A Family and a Fortune*, who indignantly rejected other people's assumption that he couldn't go on playing second fiddle all his life: ' "Yes I can," said Dudley . . . "It is a great art and I have mastered it." '[1] The centre of the stage suited Margaret as much as an onlooker's part suited Ivy, and middle age suited them both. They had arrived together, and for the first time in each case, at an orderly and highly agreeable existence designed to please nobody but themselves; and both agreed with Miss Mitford who said, when asked if she would have liked to be married, 'No. I never wanted a full normal life.'[2]

Few writers have celebrated the single state more cordially than Ivy, who did it with especial vigour in her early books. There is clearly something of her relationship with Margaret in the placid companionable intimacy of those two sceptical veterans, Emily Herrick and Theresa Fletcher in *Pastors and Masters*; the pleasures of spinsterhood, and even honorary spinsterhood, provide a theme nicely contrasted with the sombre tensions of family life in her next novel but one, *Men and Wives*; while the 'mature and settled spinsters'[3] of *More Women Than Men* have reached a state of such superlative satisfaction with themselves and their ways that even the intrepid Felix admits himself taken aback. All four early books are full of characters teetering on the brink of marriage, finding excuses for it, turning it down, or cheerfully making the best of it like Rachel Hardistie who freely admits that her single years were the happiest time of her life:

'Of course I see how civilised it is to be a spinster,' said Rachel. 'I shouldn't think savage countries have spinsters. I never know why marriage goes on in civilised countries, goes on openly. Think what would happen if it were really looked at, or regarded as impossible to look at. In the marriage service, where both are done, it does happen.'[4]

Civilized living for Ivy and Margaret meant reading, writing, paying visits, travelling and the cultivation of friends. 'The life those two led between the wars was very intelligently planned, and very very pleasant,' said Hester Marsden-Smedley.[5] It approximated (in so far as life in a series of comparatively cramped London flats ever could do) to the sober eighteenth-century pattern Margaret recommended to readers of *Eve*, in an article describing an unfashionably small, plain Georgian house called Wandle Bank in Surrey:

> It dates from a period of prosperity and comfort among middle class families, unspoiled by a passion for dimension and display. Here are rooms to live in, to write in, to dine in. Here is no suggestion of torture chambers in which crowds of semi-detached strangers trample on each other's gowns and reputations . . .[6]

Neither Margaret nor Ivy could ever abide a crowd but they regularly entertained four or five friends at a time, often more, at the tea parties they gave in the late afternoons for anyone who cared to drop in ('Good many' is Ivy's complacent comment in her diary when one of these occasions had been a success). Margaret liked to lunch out with one or other of her young men, Ivy generally lunched at home alone or with a friend. But there were people for tea most days, others came to dine or stay at the flat, and 'Play at night' is a frequent entry, sometimes as often as once or twice a week in the winter, in Ivy's diaries. Husbands were invited if need be without their wives, children only if kept well in hand. Young couples might find themselves put into cold storage for five or ten years at a time ('After that, in their view, the marriage ought to be breaking up anyway,' said Elliott Felkin's daughter, Penelope Douglas, to whom this had happened), or tolerated on the sort of footing Hemingway described in his account of how he and his first wife made friends with Gertrude Stein and Alice B. Toklas in Paris in the early 1920s: 'They . . . treated us as though we were very good, well-mannered and promising children and I felt that they forgave us for being in love and being married—time would fix that . . .'[7]

Margaret and Ivy could put rather a strain on a young or inexperienced hostess who did not know them well or feared that her standards might fall short of theirs: they both had hearty appetites, 'fell to', then expected to be entertained by guests whose conversation might not always come up to scratch. But however scathing Margaret might be, she was always amusing; and she and Ivy made excellent hosts on their own ground, or on any of the countless excursions organized by Margaret, who had access to collections up and down the country at a time when few of the great country houses were yet open to the public. She was often on the move, sprinting about with Ivy, or Herman or Ralph or Basil Ionides, hiring a car to drive down to Hatfield or Knole for the day, staying at pubs near Chatsworth or Beaulieu, haring up by train to the Buccleuchs' and the Duke of Argyll's in Scotland for Chippendale.

Ivy, who never cared a button for furniture, china or the decorative arts, enjoyed these outings less for the homes than the gardens. Flowers were her delight, especially wild ones, and, if soft fruit were in season, she would make straight for the raspberry canes or strawberry beds, spending sometimes so much time under the nets on country-house weekends that Margaret declared she had been obliged to stop taking her altogether because of gardeners' complaints. Every year they went on a round of visits to Margaret's friends—the Marcons at Highclere in Berkshire, the Noyes sisters in Wiltshire, Lady Waechter at Ramsnest in Surrey and, later, Lord Bearsted's daughter, the Hon. Mrs Ionides, at Buxted Park in Sussex. Ivy would arrive punctually in the hall after breakfast, 'fully gloved and booted for her hour in the garden'[8] like the governess, Miss Ridley in The Present and the Past, ready to be taken for a walk or a drive or once, when they came over from East Meon to call on Raisley Moorsom at Ramsden End in Hampshire, for a bathe in the sea. Raisley drove them to West Wittering or Headingham where both ladies, highly delighted ('Ivy was terrifically excited, like a child'), put on old-fashioned, high-necked, long-sleeved bloomers and paddled about in the waves.

Summer meant a month in the country, generally by the seaside —they took rooms at Orford, Dunwich and Dymchurch on the east coast in successive years in the 1920s, as well as paying visits to

Devon and Cornwall, and they were among the early guests in 1927 at Portmeirion in North Wales. This was Ivy's idea of a holiday, and was invariably followed by two or three weeks travelling on the Continent which was Margaret's: comfortable, leisurely journeys planned to take in museums and art galleries with flowers and patisseries for Ivy (one of her grudges against abroad was its dearth of tea shops) and, for Margaret, a visit to the Elliott Felkins in Geneva (Elliott, who had been a disciple of Lowes Dickinson at King's with Raisley and Noel Compton-Burnett, worked in the 1920s and 1930s for Dickinson's beloved League of Nations).

When Margaret stayed at the Felkins' small flat, Ivy went to an hotel up the road or sometimes stopped at home altogether, for she felt that a single annual trip abroad was as much as anyone could properly be asked to put up with. 'It was always nature Ivy spoke of,' said Vera Compton-Burnett, describing her sister's account of these travels, 'never castles or museums or Margaret's antiquarian things. But if there were wild narcissi on the mountain, she'd send a postcard about that.' Ivy in those days had not yet come to dislike 'abroad' as she was to do later, after Margaret's death, when she not only stopped going herself but kept a blacklist of people who lived there. But it is always a sinister spot in her books: abroad is where people go to forget the past, saddle themselves with unwanted bastards or attend to business affairs that generally end in false reports of their death (in some cases they might have been better dead since something fishy nearly always happens behind the backs of anyone rash enough—like Charlotte Lamb in *Manservant and Maidservant*, Fulbert Sullivan in *Parents and Children*, Ellen Mowbray in *A Father and his Fate*—to set foot abroad). It was not for nothing that Margaret wrote Ivy's name in her notes under a contemporary account of Lord Holland by someone who clearly shared Ivy's view of people going too far too often: 'He has already been long enough on the Continent for any reasonable end, either of curiosity or instruction, and his availing himself so immediately of this opportunity to go to a foreign country again looks a little too much like distaste for his own.'[9]

At home the housekeeping was Ivy's province, as it had been since she took over the household in Hove when her mother died in 1911. She ordered supplies, dealt with tradesmen, saw to the china and linen cupboards, carved at table (always the woman's part in

Victorian families) and supervised the maid Jessie. 'My maid is a very pleasant creature and I trust will remain contented,' Ivy wrote after Jessie first arrived in November 1919. 'I am on the alert for any sign of dissatisfaction so that at any cost to myself it may be soothed. She calls me 'm, not miss. I suppose she thinks I have reached that time of life when it is suitable.'[10] Jessie who was tiny, not much taller than a circus dwarf, moved flats three times with 'her ladies', stopping in the end for nearly twenty years (the next maid stayed another ten which suggests that Ivy's soothing power must have been equal to her disreputable habit of getting her name in the newspapers). Like the knowledgeable and inquisitive Miranda Hume in *Mother and Son*, Ivy was keenly interested in every domestic process from plumbing to coffee-making or the price and quality of butchers' cuts—'Ivy used to say that she thought she would have been rather good below stairs herself'[11]—while Jessie had a gift for the sort of traditional English cooking Ivy liked: roast meat or fowls, great joints of boiled ham and bacon, steamed salmon with lavish helpings of parsley butter, followed by nursery puddings like junket, meringues and stone cream. 'Everything good and plentiful and in season,'[12] as the housekeeper says in *Mother and Son* of a meal specifically designed to impress Mrs Hume (Ivy's friends in the 1950s liked to speculate as to the exact nature of the dish singled out for praise at this luncheon: Roger Hinks wanted it to be Apple Charlotte, Robert Liddell backed the rum-flavoured blancmange which was one of Ivy's own favourites at the time[13]).

Ivy could never bring herself to taste caviare any more than she would drink champagne ('D'you heat it?' she asked plaintively when someone[14] brought her a bottle). Margaret, who had more sophisticated tastes in food though she scarcely set foot in the kitchen, chose the wine and collected what were in those days exotic, even faintly daring French recipes for lobster, sauces, meat cooked with herbs and wine. It was also Margaret who kept meticulous lists of their friends' preferences: 'Ernest Thesiger *likes* Indian tea. Dislikes eggs. Dislikes ices. Jane Thesiger likes vegetable soup. Ices. China tea without milk. Schrijver likes salt beef and dumplings; black coffee; Irish stews, plum pudding, ginger and celery stuffed with cheese.'[15] Food at Ivy's table was ample and excellent, by no means always the rule among the English intelligentsia then or now: 'Plain living and high thinking are best,' as somebody says in *Daughters and Sons*, 'but our standard of thinking is not high enough to warrant the living's being too plain.'[16]

The living was in fact so rich, both ladies so large and growing larger, that at the end of 1926 Margaret consulted 'an oddity among beauty doctors',[17] Laurence Lazarus Heyman ('*Viennese* . . . very foreign, gay . . . Probably a gambler . . . I put it on record that I think him quite trustworthy, and very intelligent, though I have not much illusions about beauty doctors generally; and the fee charged seems very high'). Dr Heyman's banting (or slimming) cure lasted five years, involving regular weighings, the consumption of vast quantities of mauve pills and cachets, and, from 1928 to 1933, weekly, bi-weekly, sometimes even daily trips to his consulting rooms in New Cavendish Street at a cost of £1,500 apiece, a staggering sum for people normally as prudent as Margaret and Ivy. It worked (these were the years in which both Margaret and Ivy acquired a trick of pulling out the loose folds of their bodices and looking complacently down to check that their dresses were indeed becoming several sizes too large). Dr Heyman's key point, worth any amount of trouble and expense in Margaret's view, was that patients might eat as much as they liked without fear of getting fat ever afterwards: both friends took full advantage of this dispensation for the rest of their lives, and Ivy at least never grew stout again.

Apart from holidays (and the banting régime) Ivy's own daily routine barely changed throughout the 1920s and 1930s: writing (which she did in an armchair in the sitting room,[18] keeping her current notebook stuffed under the cushions) was seldom permitted to encroach on more than one or two mornings a week, and there were long fallow periods between books. Shopping took up much time and attention. So did fittings for hats, shoes, corsets, coats-and-skirts (Ivy got her beautifully cut, severely simple black suits, like her furs, from Bradleys in Chepstow Place, Bayswater; Margaret's suits—also of the finest quality, and equally indifferent to fashion—were in grey gaberdine). Ivy's companion on these expeditions was usually one or other of the very few friends she had salvaged from the past. Her sister-in-law, Noel's widow, Tertia Burnett (who had married Horace Mann as her second husband in 1920), would come up generally at least once or twice a month from Potter's Bar, meeting Ivy at Smith's or Barkers or Boots, and going on for lunch to Tertia's club or the Case Café in Wimpole Street.

Tertia was then, perhaps in a sense always would be, still in mourning for Noel: their courtship had been so intense, the marriage so brief (it lasted thirteen months, all but two of which Noel spent in the trenches), his death such a crushing blow that nothing afterwards could ever quite match up to the past. Certainly not Horace Mann, who was another of her brother Jack Beresford's friends and thirteen years older than Tertia. Never a particularly forceful character, Horace worked for the Board of Education, read Chinese in his spare time, painted a little and rapidly resigned himself, like Emily Herrick's putative husband in *Pastors and Masters*, to having his predecessor installed 'as a sort of upper husband'[19] in a marriage that could never hope to be more than second best. Tertia remained childless and indefinably blighted, or at least nipped in the bud: always retiring, she became in later life something of a recluse and, though Ivy could be very funny at her sister-in-law's expense, she clearly always felt a protective duty towards her.

But Tertia had been eclipsed all her life by her elder sister Dorothy who had shared Ivy's top flat at 59, Leinster Square until she left to marry Alan Kidd in 1917. Dorothy, proprietary by nature, had a habit of annexing and renaming people or places she fancied: Asquith (who had paid marked attention to Dorothy as a young girl) was christened 'the Oracle', Ivy became 'Miss I' and Ivy's flat 'the perfect rooftree' so that, after Margaret moved in, the couple were known ever after as 'the Rooftreeites'.[20] Both Beresford sisters were beautiful, dreamy, unworldly and intensely competitive. But where Tertia's nervous energy turned inwards and tended to falter under the burden of early unhappiness, Dorothy was disposed to accept or exact tribute from a wider circle. The Beresfords, like the Burnetts, were a booky family and Dorothy, who had grown up transcribing her blind father's songs, sonnets and sermons for publication, had inherited his passionate devotion to literature, along with the family pride and the no less notorious family temper.

The novelist J. D. Beresford was her second cousin, and she herself came between brothers who had both published poems: the elder, Dick, had been shipped off to the colonies as a black sheep before the First World War, leaving Jack (who had always planned to write, like his best friend Noel Compton-Burnett) with more than his share of impecunious relatives to support, which he did by going into the Treasury. But, while Jack built up a substantial literary reputation on the side between the wars (as the editor and essayist J. B. Beresford), Dorothy held out against 'the urge to write'[21] with a determination for which she took credit, 'feeling all round me the fearful tyranny of the over-full inkpot and the unwanted word'. Quick, sensitive, acutely observant, widely read but otherwise uneducated save for what she had picked up from her father, Dorothy was one of those people—all too familiar in the novels of I. Compton-Burnett—who have brains but no training and cannot for the life of them see why writers make such a fuss about writing ('I always feel I could write a novel if I tried. But I am a bad person for trying and that is the truth,' as another of them says in *A God and his Gifts*[22]).

She had known Ivy since they were both dutiful daughters before the First World War, marooned at home in their mid-twenties, watching their younger brothers flourish at Cambridge and later in the larger literary world of London. Dorothy, who had the advantage in looks and was Ivy's equal in wit (she told T. S. Eliot that the three tall, pale, long-fingered Sitwells put her in mind of 'a stained glass window, hands joined in admiration of one another'), had never been prepared to let Ivy 'come the bluestocking' over her. But, when Jack and Noel both married within a few months of one another in 1915, Dorothy and Ivy were united by a disapproval exacerbated in each case by a family break-up that left the two elder sisters high and dry. If mutual displeasure at Noel's marriage to Tertia first drew Ivy and Dorothy together, the war further strengthened an alliance based perhaps as much on respect for each other's intensity of feeling as on their shared love of nature and still greater love of Jane Austen:

My mother and Ivy spoke together intimately [wrote Dorothy's son, Roger Kidd, who was born in 1923 and had grown up listening to these conversations from infancy]. My mother had a direct, unpremeditated approach to things which Ivy responded to: they were able to relax in each other's company. They appreciated each other's value for truth and spontaneity. Ivy was amused by my mother's remarks, and my mother laid store by Ivy's observations—one was never quite sure whether they were talking about relations, friends or characters from a novel.[23]

Dorothy was always ambivalent about Ivy's novels. 'You may impress others but you don't impress me,' she said, and remained perpetually on the alert to forestall any attempt at exploitation on Ivy's part ('Whatever you do, Ivy must never get to hear of this or it'll all come out in a novel,' she said once of a particularly juicy family scandal). She liked Keats, Wordsworth and the Romantics, Sir Thomas Browne, Thomas Traherne and J. D. Beresford's protégée Dorothy Richardson, what she called 'the Immensities' in life or literature; and she seems to have felt, like so many critics of Ivy's novels, that it was rash, if not wrong, to probe the seamier side of human endeavour: 'Too much analysis of our darker moments brings little help unless it leads to a stronger realisation that Beauty is Truth, Truth Beauty . . .'[24]

Ivy herself had learnt from the repeated shocks of her early life to welcome passivity as thankfully as the young Staces—'spotless dullness is what Andrew and I are so gifted at'[25]—looking forward to an uneventful middle age in *Brothers and Sisters*. But spotless dullness was emphatically not among Dorothy's gifts: 'You could describe Dorothy as wicked, as all sorts of things, but you could never describe her as dull,' said one of her nieces.[26] High-handed, strong-minded, by turns ecstatic and cutting but always 'utterly alive', as she herself said of a friend, Dorothy found an appreciative audience in Ivy whose grudge against 'people in life'[27]—as distinct from people in books—was precisely their lack of this sort of vitality and high definition.

However much it might rankle, Dorothy was inclined on the whole to accept Ivy's literary success as an asset: 'She was a very rare creature, one of the rarest of her generation,' said Dorothy who never got out of the habit of seeing Ivy regularly, even in the years when she was most taken up with running her own much larger household in Kensington, together with a nursery and husband ('I don't know how he bore Miss I always,' she said thoughtfully long afterwards). When Margaret spent a fortnight in Paris in the autumn of 1931 with a new friend, Lady Assheton-Smith, Dorothy, Tertia and Jack's wife Janet took it in turns to see Ivy nearly every day for lunch or tea; and, five years later, when Margaret was again away staying with the Felkins at Geneva, it was Dorothy who moved into the flat to keep Ivy company.

Alan Kidd had been another of the husbands Jack Beresford was always said to have brought home for his sisters. He was tall, dark and handsome, a successful civil servant with substantial private means and an equable nature that ideally complemented his wife's freaks of temperament. But he lost a good deal of money in the slump, and died suddenly of septicaemia after a family fishing holiday in Scotland in 1933 leaving Dorothy, with the ten-year-old Roger, his nurse (known as the 'Ancient Retainer') and a greatly reduced income, to join her sister in the ranks of affliction and grief. She was inconsolable; and though, unlike Tertia, Dorothy refused to succumb to straitened circumstances thereafter, she too turned for support to Ivy and Margaret. Outings with Roger and the Rooftreeites provided frequent distraction, and sometimes all four spent holidays together in the country, reading and walking and talking: 'We made constant visits to places, museums, galleries, these were always a delight to my mother and me,' wrote Roger. 'I remember no difficulties, only a sense of ease and pleasure. These expeditions were always planned by Margaret quietly and efficiently to give amusement to us all.'[28]

ii

In so far as Ivy took any further part in family life after her own home had disintegrated, it was supplied by the Beresfords far more effectively than by her two sisters whom she scarcely saw from one year to the next, and then only on a strictly business footing. Under the terms of their mother's will Ivy had been appointed head of the family, a duty she punctually discharged to the end of her life since Vera and Juliet—for fifty years her sole surviving charges—were neither of them interested in managing money. Ivy's fellow trustees in the various trust funds set up by their parents had been Noel and the family solicitor, Martyn Mowll, both of whom died in 1916. From then on she presided alone at the quarterly meetings held in Mowll's London office for which Martyn's nephew, Rutley Mowll, travelled up from Dover with his head clerk to submit the books and go through the accounts. 'She kept a tight eagle eye on her finances,' said the accountant who, like his father before him, had made a fourth at these meetings, and at the luncheons held afterwards in a nearby hotel. 'She scrutinised everything and demanded cogent reasons. There was never any question of her sisters being consulted.'[29]

Dr Compton-Burnett's estate had been made up of almost a

hundred properties, mostly round Clacton and Hove, any one of which might involve separate negotiations with tenants, rental agreements, mortgages, insurance policies, permission to erect a telegraph pole or a shed in the garden.[30] By the end of the First World War, Ivy and her sisters had sold the family home—Number 20, The Drive, Hove—which all three recalled with acute dislike. But they still possessed a string of houses up and down the country, marking the various stages of their father's rise to prosperity: his old home and consulting rooms at 17, Hamilton Square, Birkenhead; the larger house with its own stabling and gardens that he bought in Lee High Road, just beyond fashionable Blackheath, when he set about establishing a London practice in Wimpole Street; the highly desirable red brick villa in the country at Pinner where his first wife died and where his second wife came as a bride, nine months before Ivy was born in June 1884; and the first seaside home to which he moved his young family when Ivy was seven years old at 30, First Avenue, Hove.

But the bulk of their property consisted in shops and terraced houses on the outskirts of Hove, together with a number of more substantial establishments designed for the affluent middle classes, all put up on building plots bought by Dr Burnett as the town expanded westwards over fields by the sea towards Aldrington where he had once taken his Sunday walks, and where he now lay buried in St Leonard's graveyard with his second wife beneath a cross commemorating also their sons Guy and Noel, and their two youngest daughters Katharine and Primrose, who had died together of an overdose of veronal in 1917, aged twenty-two and eighteen. His growing estate had been a source of pride and pleasure to Dr Burnett, and after his death it remained dear to the heart of his wife who expressly stipulated in her will that no part of it should be sold. But filial piety was not proof against market forces, and by the early 1920s Ivy and Rutley Mowll were systematically getting rid of the family holdings, selling off whole streetsful at a time and investing the money instead: a state of affairs which, as Noel had once said to Ivy when property values slumped in 1916, was 'enough to make our parents curse God to his face'.[31]

Rutley Mowll (who would in due course be succeeded as Ivy's solicitor by his son Wilfred) was himself the son of Worsfold Mowll who had loomed over Ivy's childhood, paying regular visits to Hove to advise her father and, when Dr Burnett died, to regulate and control her mother's affairs. These Mowlls were a masterful race: sober, godly, righteous, physically commanding, each one overtopped—at any rate in the memory of people who knew them—only by his predecessor. Worsfold's father had been active, like Ivy's maternal grandfather, in the fierce public welfare battles that rocked Dover in the 1850s and 1860s. Worsfold himself, who had seemed to the little Compton-Burnetts a sombre embodiment of authority and repression, supplied the model for more than one of the tyrants in Ivy's books; Martyn was remembered by her sisters as 'only less Worsfold than Worsfold'; and Rutley came out of the same mould. 'He was a massive and awe-inspiring figure,' wrote the novelist Roy Fuller, who as a young solicitor in the late 1930s had several times appeared before Rutley Mowll in his capacity as coroner for East Kent. 'Can he still have worn a frock-coat? He certainly habitually wore one of those hats that start as a top-hat and finish as a bowler. I was terrified of him, but though severe he was always courteous and just.'[32]

Ivy herself, however circumspect she may have seemed to social acquaintances, left her professional advisers in no doubt that she was 'an exceedingly forceful woman'.[33] To her sisters, now that her power over them rested on consent not coercion, she remained inscrutable. The bitter struggles of the past were never mentioned between them, indeed they seldom talked about anything beyond what was for tea, or the sort of news that might as well go on a holiday postcard. 'Her manner was touch-me-not. So far and no further,' said Juliet. She and Vera had by this time found their own release from oppression and grief in theosophy, becoming disciples of Rudolf Steiner and turning the house they shared with Myra Hess in St John's Wood into an 'art house', filled with music, painting, modelling, eurhythmics, all activities that Ivy flatly deplored. She herself had once proposed moving into 8, Carlton Hill with her sisters, but that was in 1915 when she was still very far from the serene detachment with which Miss Mitford, in *Parents and Children*, overrides her pupils' objections to her own scheme for going to board with relations:

'You ought not to have to pay relations.'
'Well, the English have no family feelings. That is, none of the kind you mean. They have them, and one of them is that relations must cause no expense.' . . .

'Perhaps they are not near relations.'

'Yes, they are. It is near relations who have family feelings.'

'You might as well live with friends,' said Venice.

'Well, there is the tie of blood.'

'What difference does that make, if people forget it?'

'Other people remember it. That is another family feeling.'[34]

If Ivy had got out of the way of family feelings, so had her sisters. To outsiders, Mr Mowll and Miss Compton-Burnett ('the Oak and the Ivy' as they were known to people obliged to do business with them) made a formidable team, but Vera and Juliet were undeterred by their mentors' united if tacit disapproval of everything from their musical friends to their purchase of a supposedly impractical cottage on the hill above Berkhamsted at the beginning of the 1920s ('If you want my opinion, Miss Vera,' said Rutley Mowll, towering above her on the garden path during a disastrous tour of inspection, 'I think it's a *dreadful* property'). It was Margaret who had advised them to look for something in the country between Berkhamsted and Tring, but things were not much less sticky when she and Ivy came down from London to look over the cottage in turn: 'They arrived from the station by taxi—a good hour and a half before it was possible to have lunch,' said Vera. 'They sat there. I can see them now. Hatted and gloved. They didn't even take their gloves off. Hour after hour. And hour after hour. With rolled up umbrellas. They belonged to a different world.'

So did the five half-brothers and sisters,[35] Dr Burnett's first family, whose very existence Ivy's mother had done what she could to deny. Olive, the eldest and the most unforgiving, earned some sort of living as a journalist and had set up house in 1919—the same year as Ivy with Margaret—with her friend Emily Pope. Iris, who was a nursing sister at the London Temperance Hospital in Hampstead, lived in Stanley Gardens a few streets away from Ivy's flat in Linden Gardens, though her reputation as an active churchwoman in the neighbourhood put her on the far side of an unbridgeable gulf. Daisy, the youngest, retired from the African mission field in the 1930s to run a home called Carfax for other retired missionaries in Bristol. Each received from her half-sisters, in recognition of past injustice, a voluntary allowance of a hundred pounds a year (Ivy's own income in the 1920s was roughly ten times as much). Beyond that the three sisters had dropped out of Ivy's life as completely as the two half-brothers her mother had shipped off to Canada before the First World War: Charlie prospered eventually as a fruit farmer in California but Dick, always considered a dull dog by his half-sisters, was done for by the stock-market crash of 1929 which left him physically shattered, financially destitute and dependent on his brother for support, until he killed himself six years later by jumping off a bridge in Los Angeles.

'You would hardly believe about families. Or many people would not,'[36] as another governess, Miss Hallam, says in *Daughters and Sons*. Ivy's own escape from her family seems to have released, in her life with Margaret, a side her sisters had never seen in the strained and wary creature they had known from infancy. Ivy in middle age allowed herself a gaiety, an ebullience and a humorous teasing affection she had suppressed with everyone save her brothers, Guy and Noel, in her girlhood at Hove. Neither she nor Margaret had nephews or nieces (except for the two children of Margaret's eldest brother Frank, estranged from infancy and both in any case grown up by the late 1920s), but they made up for it with other people's children: there were tea parties for Molly Waechter's two boys and a girl, a trip to the circus for Hester's little brother John Pinney and, later, annual circus outings for Hester's own children at Christmas. It was Ivy who decorated the Christmas tree ('One always went to see Ivy's tree,' said Roger Kidd. 'It was loaded with decorations, like a little sort of flame'), and Ivy who could if she liked turn anything into a treat, from a sea bathe to tea in a café. Between the wars she was said to walk across the park every morning for the pleasure of eating cream buns at Buzzards in Oxford Street; and to the end of her life friends could still elicit a rapturous response, as one might from a child, with a present of chocolates, a pot of jam or a new sort of sweet.

Few novelists have written about children more perceptively than Ivy. They turn up in her books in increasing numbers after the first dim, downtrodden eleven-year-old (Muriel Ponsonby in *Daughters and Sons*), but she is always especially tender to lonely, backward or disabled children, oddities and misfits like Aubrey Gaveston in *A Family and a Fortune* or Reuben Donne in *Elders and Betters*; and Roger Kidd, himself a delicate only child, sensitive and highly strung, remembered being treated in much the same spirit in fact:

Ivy was like a favourite aunt. She showed interest and never patronised. She would often, rather surprisingly, level a direct question about one's life with a searching glance.

She took evident pleasure in things: relish in eating something in a restaurant, glowing fires, sunlight, flowers; I remember her bending over wild flowers in a Dorset wood and saying, 'Oh, you darlings!' She delighted in gossip but not maliciously, and always tempered with honesty. Looking back one is aware of a classical integrity—a dispassionate examination—and not of intellect so much as of perception. Sometimes she would laugh so much while recounting some absurdity that she wept.[37]

When asked if she would have liked children herself, Ivy said no, though she thought she might have managed them better than some mothers did,[38] which was roughly Miss Mitford's reaction in *Parents and Children* when Eleanor Sullivan complained of her children getting beyond her:

'I wish I understood children as you do. It would be such a help to me.'

Miss Mitford smiled in an absent manner, thinking of the shocks that Eleanor would sustain if this could be the case, and wondering if she had forgotten her own childhood or had an abnormal one.[39]

Family life remained Ivy's prime interest, one she pursued with curiosity and compassion like Miss Mitford ('She did not let pity for her employer or pupil mar her interest. Pity had come to be the normal background of her mind, and other feelings arose irrespective of it'[40]), and with sympathy above all. 'She was a friend of my family. Ivy liked families, and Ivy liked us,'[41] said the younger of the two Hesters who had been accustomed to turn to Margaret and Ivy for advice and support at all stages of her own, sometimes stormy married life. Pretty, breezy, rebellious, determined not to conform to the pattern of nice behaviour laid down for girls of her class and background, Hester had always found an ally in Margaret who helped her with odd jobs as a freelance journalist, and generally 'encouraged revolt against parental discipline'.

But Ivy, who never in all her life encouraged anyone to cast off their family (and almost certainly would never have done so herself if things had not got the better of her), was still more receptive. When Hester began walking out with Basil Marsden-Smedley —who came from a family decidedly better off and stuffier than her own—'Ivy used to ask us a lot about our relationship, and particularly the opposition on financial grounds of Basil's parents to me . . .'[42] For the next forty years and more Hester submitted to cross-examination by Ivy as to her job prospects, love affairs ('especially if they went wrong'), professional and marital problems, family conflicts: 'Margaret criticised. Ivy more often sympathised . . . she was always very understanding. Margaret found, quite rightly, many things in my life "regrettable". Ivy wanted to know more about them.'[43]

iii

This impression of Ivy—tolerant, affectionate, inquisitive and understanding—is borne out by practically everyone who knew her well in later life. Close friends after Margaret's death—George Furlong and Rex Brandreth, Barbara and Walter Robinson, Soame Jenyns, Elizabeth Taylor, Sonia Orwell, Madge Garland—all knew this side of Ivy; and even in the years when she most assiduously played second fiddle, there were always friends—some of whom had never opened her books—prepared to lay themselves out for her sake. People who found her perception alarming ('I am often ashamed of understanding them') seldom resented it, for Ivy, unlike Margaret, was not censorious. Reticent, aloof, often constrained in company herself, she could be an encouraging listener just as, when not bored or restive as she tended to be in the grander country houses Margaret frequented, she could be a gentle and ideally appreciative guest. Ivy was delighted with the smallest attention, a little walk down the lane or soft fruit for tea. 'She had to have strawberries from the moment she stepped inside the door until they could not be got for love or money,' said Janet Beresford, who did not care for Margaret at all ('Margaret definitely spoilt Ivy') but always took special trouble when Ivy came alone to stay at the Beresfords' country cottage at Ashwell in Hertfordshire.

So did Margaret's friends, Ella and Dora Noyes, who lived in a long, low, book-lined, wistaria-covered stone house at Sutton Veney, tucked under the Wiltshire downs and surrounded by a rambling, overgrown, secluded and sweet-smelling garden where

Ivy spent hours at a time sitting in the shade of the mulberry tree. The Noyes sisters were among the few, perhaps the only people with whom Ivy discussed her books at all freely. Dora painted, Ella wrote and both, like Dorothy Kidd, set store by Ivy, who came to stay alone or with Margaret every summer between the wars. They would order a trap or a taxi to fetch her from the station, lay in the sort of food she enjoyed, turn her bed to the north, see that her room was just so: 'It was always a big thing when Miss Burnett was coming.'[44]

Margaret was an altogether tougher proposition, more energetic, more enterprising and far more willing to take the rough with the smooth ('I should have been inclined to reject the rough. I don't know why it always has to be included,' says Rosa Lindsay, echoing her creator in *A God and his Gifts*[45]). 'Margaret was determined to know people and make friends. She wasn't pretty and she wasn't rich but she worked away at it,' said Raisley. 'She was interested in *one*, she listened and she asked questions.' But she also toned people up with her sarcasm, her raised eyebrows, what Herman called 'the superior air, as if she knew more than most people, which I believe she certainly did; but also a certain contempt for human beings, as if she despised them'.[46] She was a famous debunker, adept at demolishing other people's pretensions whether they laid claim to fake Chippendale or to a veneer of gentility. Profoundly unconventional in some ways, she attached great importance to keeping up appearances which made her a potentially uncomfortable mentor to her young friends. Adultery or other irregularities might be tolerated but never condoned ('If Bridget has done what one has to do with a man to get a divorce,' she said to Hester when Bridget D'Oyly Carte's marriage was dissolved in 1931, 'one will never feel the same towards her again'[47]). If Ivy hardly needed to know all before she forgave it, Margaret was straitlaced, unbending, apt to quote with approval Mrs Norris's saying, in Jane Austen's *Mansfield Park*, that it was 'a shocking thing for a young person to be always lolling on a sofa'.[48]

For a long time Margaret and Ivy possessed no sofa and when one was eventually purchased—after much teasing on Ivy's part, and reluctance on Margaret's—it was a straight-backed settee with nice legs but a hard, unyielding upholstered seat on which two, or at a pinch three, persons might perch but not loll. Ivy herself had a large, cushioned, black velvet armchair drawn up close to the fire, well stocked with chocolates and magazines. There was another,

smaller armchair for a woman visitor but Margaret, who told
Soame Jenyns that she had never sat in a comfortable chair made
since the Reform Bill, preferred one of the handsome hard-backed
uprights with which male guests had to make do. While Ivy worked
at her ease with a notebook on her knee in the drawing room,
Margaret wrote all her books in her tiny bedroom on a hard chair
pulled up to the dressing table with a litter of notes, cuttings,
jottings on old bills and the backs of used envelopes spread on the
bed.

Her notions of taste and comfort derived from a time when,
though Sheraton had recommended two for a drawing room, sofas
were still widely regarded with suspicion: 'There would often be
but one in a house, and in less luxurious households to lie down, or
even to lean back, was a luxury permitted only to old persons or
invalids,'[49] wrote Margaret, who furnished the flats she shared with
Ivy according to her own characteristically vigorous interpretation
of a whole generation's revolt against Victorian ostentation, fussi-
ness and clutter. Margaret had been a pioneer long before she was
recruited to pass on tips about 'modern design' to readers of Eve.
Barely out of her twenties before she set about rehabilitating
William Kent (on whom she wrote the first book nearly forty years
later), she was one of the first to advocate the return to the eighteenth
century promoted by neo-Georgians like Edwin Lutyens.

Her own highly idiosyncratic style of furnishing was based on
few but fine pieces of Sheraton, Chippendale and Hepplewhite
ranged round walls distempered pale grey (or green, unless the
'hospital green paint' recorded by James Lees-Milne[50] in the early
1940s was simply an illusion produced by the general effect of
starkness and sparsity), and hung with mirrors to emphasize the
sensation of space. Piles of magazines—Tatler, Queen, Country Life,
Eve, all of which both ladies read avidly—stood about on occasional tables but, though two glass-fronted bookcases were installed
later, there were few books to be seen in the 1920s. Ivy did not care
for shop flowers, and Margaret shared Lord Chesterfield's distaste
for building up a collection 'Knick-knackically'.[51] There were no
carpets, no pictures, no colour, practically no soft furnishings. 'I
could not give a house those unmistakable signs of a woman's
presence,' says Ursula Scrope, explaining why she would not have
liked to be married in The Present and the Past. 'I do not even
recognise them.'[52]

Some visitors were exhilarated by the severity of Margaret's scheme ('very elegant with pale oyster walls and superb period furniture'[53]), others dismayed by its comfortlessness. At all events it never varied. Margaret had done up Ivy's Leinster Square flat at the beginning of 1921 and she supervised the decorations when they moved in July 1923 to 97, Linden Gardens—another small, dingy flat, in Bayswater, conveniently close to William Whiteley's emporium where Ivy did her shopping, but still on the unfashionable north side of Hyde Park—and when they eventually settled ten years later in Cornwall Gardens, South Kensington. After this last move nothing changed: 'The same furniture stood in the same positions, in the same rooms, and when the flat had to be redecorated . . . the colour scheme was simply repeated,'[54] said Herman whose own taste ran to artifice and opulence in decor and who found Margaret's 'Gloom Palace' depressing. So did Lady Colefax's partner, the young and afterwards highly influential decorator, John Fowler, when James Lees-Milne introduced him in the 1940s: 'John was amazed by the bareness and austerity of the flat, the uniform stark apple-green decoration and the floor linoleum against which the few nice Georgian pieces looked islanded and insignificant.'[55]

Partly perhaps this impression was a matter of economy ('Ivy wouldn't have thought of forking out money for furniture, and Margaret hadn't any to fork,' said Ralph Edwards). But the pieces islanded in Margaret's drawing room went back to the sparsely furnished interiors of painters like Arthur Devis (another artist Margaret had been among the first to rediscover) at a time when Kent or Burlington could design a 'saloon, large enough to receive a company of sixty or a hundred persons, furnished with six or eight chairs, and a couple of tables'.[56] Even the mirrors were a decorative trick of the Regency. Ivy and Margaret wasted no money on modernization but they had knocked down a wall to transfer an Adam fireplace from Linden Gardens to Braemar Mansions, where another wall had to be demolished to receive it. The bleakness that occasionally disconcerted guests—the linoleum floors, primitive plumbing, unheated bedrooms—went back, according to Hester, to the spartan upbringing of both friends: 'Good food and a warm room with lovely things around were more important than the actual physical comfort of sitting on a soft seat.'[57]

This was the pattern evolved by 'English middling people' in their middling homes from the eighteenth century onwards: a tradition of sobriety, understatement and what Horace Walpole called 'snugness' [58] that went with plain cooking, hard chairs, coal fires, and those other good things prescribed by the housekeeping ladies in *Mother and Son*, 'fine old linen carefully darned'[59] and bone china ('Cracked and mended, but rather rare! That strikes the exact note'). Margaret's forthrightness and Ivy's unnerving honesty belonged to the same tradition, and so did their refusal ever to be carried away: 'I never heard, in forty years, either Ivy or Margaret raise their voices,' said Herman. 'They were flat cultured voices, and they never laughed out loud. Like Fontenelle, they never said "Ha-ha-ha!" . . . I never heard Margaret call a piece of furniture "superb" or "marvellous" or "fantastic" or even "beautiful". Her highest praise was "jolly!" or "very jolly!" And that was that.'[60] By the same token, 'regrettable' was as far as Margaret was prepared to go in the opposite direction.

Naturally there were two schools of thought about the flats and the food, just as there were about Ivy's books or for that matter the ladies themselves. For old friends like the Kings, Beresfords or Noyeses, dinner with Ivy and Margaret might be a tonic but there were others for whom it was more of a trial. Raisley Moorsom remembered a category of what Ivy called 'dripping dinners', which consisted of hangers-on even humbler in the social scale than Raisley and his friend Frankie Birrell, who had disgraced himself, in a celebrated episode at Leinster Square, by falling asleep the first time Margaret asked him to dinner and smashing the arm of his chair:

> I can quite clearly remember the soup . . . Then, I suppose, we must have had fish, because when I woke up there *was* a plate of fish, uneaten, in front of me. As a matter of fact, my left hand was in it, covered with sauce. I was alone in the dining-room; the lights were burning, and when I looked at my watch I saw that it was past midnight. The ladies seemed to have gone to bed.[61]

Birrell found his hat, let himself out and slunk home. There is a similar story told about Ezra Pound damaging a favourite chair on a visit to Gertrude Stein and Alice B. Toklas in Paris.[62] It is the sort of legend often defensively circulated about independent and strong-minded ladies in a position to suit themselves without reference to other people (' "Well, a selfish life is lovely, darling," said Rachel. "It is awful to be of use" '[63]); and it illustrates how completely, at the beginning of the 1920s, Miss Jourdain eclipsed 'her young friend' who had written nothing as yet, and whose presence Birrell barely registered. The next time a similar anecdote went the rounds, it was after the Second World War and the young man who passed out in the soup and woke to find himself alone was Philip Toynbee, invited as an admirer of Ivy's: 'The table, even down to the coffee cups, proved that the meal, as he sat bowed over his plate, had otherwise taken its natural and unperturbed course . . . He crept out from a dark and silent flat. It was Miss Compton-Burnett's habit to retire early to bed.'[64]

Thirty years or so separate these two stories, and it took at least that time for Margaret to recede into the background and Ivy to emerge as the one capable of petrifying apprehensive young men. But already by the early 1930s there were signs that the balance was beginning to shift. When the lease of the Linden Gardens flat ran out at the beginning of 1934, the two friends moved after weeks of energetic 'flatting' to 5, Braemar Mansions, Cornwall Gardens: a gaunt granite barracks ('You'll recognise the house, it looks like Balmoral,' was Margaret's instruction to visitors[65]) with a porter, lifts, a carpeted foyer and large high-ceilinged rooms, a great deal more spacious as well as an address in itself infinitely superior to their previous quarters on the wrong side of the park. Cornwall Gardens had been stuffily respectable when Terence Rattigan was born there in 1911, and it always retained a forbidding aspect although, by the middle of the 1930s, the young and fashionable like Cecil Beaton and Oliver Messel were just beginning to move to South Kensington. T. S. Eliot took rooms in the vicarage opposite Cornwall Gardens the same year as Margaret and Ivy who, with their friends the Kings (established in Thurloe Square the year after) were part of a larger migration: 'Obviously they must have got more money, or inherited more money, for the change from Linden Gardens in Bayswater to Cornwall Gardens in Kensington was stupendous,' said Herman[66] on whom no social nuance was lost.

But in fact Margaret's income, never in any case large, hardly fluctuated during the 1920s and 1930s,[67] while Ivy's had fallen steadily from the beginning of the slump and was still falling at the time of the move. The change, in so far as their circumstances had altered at all, seems to have been moral rather than financial. Ivy's novels never sold in large numbers but by 1934 hers was a household name in households with any sort of literary or cultural pretensions.* She had moved for good out of the ranks of writers —always so feelingly described in her books—who find themselves obliged to pay for their work to be published or, losing hope of finding a publisher at all, to put their manuscripts away in a drawer for reading aloud to themselves in a low tone. 'The judgment of posterity is known to be the only true one. So there seems no point in getting any other. I wonder so many people do it,'[68] says Felix Bacon airily to Jonathan Swift, whose own works were too far ahead of contemporary taste for publication in *More Women Than Men*. It was not a consolation that appealed to Jonathan, or to any of the other aspiring writers in the works of I. Compton-Burnett, any more than it did to Ivy herself. She was, as she freely admitted, always a shrewd judge of property but even so it seems likely that, when she and Margaret held their flat-warming party at Braemar Mansions on 27 March—just over two months short of Ivy's fiftieth birthday—the move had less to do with her business acumen than with her arrival as a writer, or at any rate the satisfaction of knowing that posterity's judgment was not the only verdict she was ever likely to get.

* For instance the Birrells, who received their copy of *Men and Wives* in April 1931 and spent the next few weeks 'snatching it out of each other's hands . . . We all *adored* it. And I thought that it was in some ways the *funniest* book I have ever read. I *howled* out loud . . . At meals we talk about Nothing But Matthew & Harriet & Godfrey and Spong. Your characters have just been added to our lives *en bloc* . . .' (Francis Birrell to I.C.-B., 29 April 1931).

CHAPTER THREE

'No point in being too Greek'

i

MARGARET OF COURSE was still the eminent one of the two, the only one most people they met had ever heard of, and by far the more prolific. Her *Regency Furniture*, published in 1934, brought her score to something like twenty titles since the turn of the century. Admittedly, this included translations, catalogues, collaborations and editions of other people's writings as well as her own original work but they were all indisputably what Ivy's characters call 'serious' books, the sort of thing that occupies Charity Marcon in *Daughters and Sons*:

> I have been up to London to get the book I am writing, out of the British Museum. I have got a lot of it out, and I shall go again presently to get some more; and when I have got it all, there will be another book . . . Mine ought to be quite a success. It will be just like the ones I am getting it out of, and they are standard books.[1]

Margaret was eventually responsible for a dozen or so of these standard books but it was not until the mid-1930s that she finally resigned a lingering desire to write fiction in favour of what Sir Michael Egerton, in *A God and his Gifts*, called 'something more solid and without the personal touch'.[2] Round about the time Ivy's first novels began to appear, Margaret narrowed down her own published output to articles in specialist journals like *Country Life*, the *Connoisseur* and *Architectural Review*, interspersed with scholarly volumes of a kind that need not make sensitive servants like the Egerton's butler (or, for that matter, Ivy's and Margaret's own Jessie) feel even mildly ashamed.

But she seems to have done it reluctantly and with no great conviction. While Ivy was writing *More Women Than Men*, Margaret was at work on a play, *Buchanan's Hotel*, which gives her own straightforwardly naturalistic and rather more detailed version of the circle they both moved in at the time; and, when Ivy's novels attracted attention, Margaret's reaction seems to have been that the sort of reviewer who could call Ivy a genius might surely be induced to do as much for herself. Raymond Mortimer certainly had the impression that she resented his admiration for Ivy,[3] and Rosamond Lehmann, who had published an enthusiastic tribute in the *Spectator* in 1937, actually received a letter from Ivy politely enlisting her help with theatrical managements on behalf of Margaret's play.[4]

Buchanan's Hotel[5] is a perfectly passable, three-act, West End comedy made up in roughly equal parts of topical chat—about the slump and the servant problem, Hitler's anti-semitism, Mosley's British fascists, ominous developments abroad and the predicament of the dispossessed middle classes at home—personal gossip and fairly desultory social and sexual intrigue. Its themes are money and class. Its cast consists of professionally charming, generally well-connected, more or less penniless young men and their patrons, mostly wealthy and much older women: the new poor preying on the *nouveaux riches*, people with taste or breeding or both prepared to trade either for cash. What little action there is—a scheme for marrying money mooted by one of the young men, and another's attempts to secure lucrative contracts for doing up the local big houses—seems to have been largely borrowed from life. There are partial portraits of both Ivy and Margaret in the persons of Miss Wace and Miss Tunstall, indeed the nub of the play, in so far as it may be said to have one, is their mutual friendship with the cheerful, immodest, rising young decorator, Sigismund Siepel, who bears a striking resemblance to Herman Schrijver.

The hotel in which the play takes place has been recently opened in Cornwall by Jim Buchanan ('Before the war hotel-keeping wouldn't have been a possibility for our class'), a consumptive obliged to move south for the climate like Margaret's young friend, Captain Colville. Invalided out of the army with damaged lungs and advised by his doctors not to return to the family home in Scotland, Norman Colville had settled instead at the beginning of the 1920s on the ruined Tudor manor of Penheale in North Cornwall, which was rebuilt over the next decade by Lutyens, laid out with gardens, courtyards, great hall, long gallery and servants' quarters, and done up inside by the grandest of all London decorating firms, Lenygon and Morant. Margaret had worked for years as

Lenygon's adviser, and she rapidly made friends with Norman Colville, who was the soul of hospitality as well as an enthusiastic collector (Margaret devoted a pair of *Country Life* articles to his collections in 1923, and Ralph Edwards another pair to his house two years later), and from now on a staunch admirer of Margaret, who came to stay every summer in the 1920s and 1930s, and clearly based her hotel on Penheale.

The select clientele at Buchanan's, when not absorbed in the delicate art of sizing up one another's social standing ('We don't know anything about Siepel. He's really rather bogus') or currying favour with the local landowner Lord Trevor, are inordinately preoccupied with money. Camp followers like Buchanan himself, and his unemployed, impecunious but otherwise presentable friend Hugh Benton ('one knows his people: he's Trevor's cousin'), discuss with great frankness ways and means of extracting funds from unpresentables like Mrs Simonson:

Buchanan: Simonson—good old non-Aryan name.
Benton: Who are they?
Buchanan: Oh, nobody. Money from jute. She's a widow.

Naturally enough, after various manoeuvres of pursuit and evasion on his part and Siepel's, Benton announces his engagement to the widow in Act III, which calls for some mildly envious sniping from Buchanan ('Well, Hugh, I'm glad you got the job . . . Mind you hold out for your pin money'); and the curtain falls as Siepel is publicly unmasked as a Jew.

The point of this ambivalent ending—whether it was meant to endorse or expose the spectacle of the English upper classes ganging up against a Jewish outsider—remains unclear, though the play gives an accurate if unappealing impression of the manners and assumptions current among Margaret's friends at the time. Certainly she was thoroughly familiar with this world of hard-up, ambitious freelances whose careers depended on manipulating a complicated network of contacts. Her own reputation for disinterested scholarship did not stop her working for dealers like Acton Surgey or Phillips,[6] obtaining pieces on commission from the trade and placing them with her own wealthy clients; and she seems, like so many of her friends, to have had at least a passing connection with interior decoration which, for a single woman of any social pretensions in those days, was often the sole practical alternative to a well-heeled husband. Margaret's famous, encyclopaedic filing system covering all historical aspects of the domestic arts contains also trade addresses ranging from Fabrics, Fringes and Floor Coverings or Porcelain, Plywood and Paint to Glass Panelling for Ballrooms (she had been working on an exhibition in March 1934, the month she and Ivy moved into Braemar Mansions, for Philip Sassoon, whose glass ballroom in Park Lane was briefly the talk of Europe).

She generally relied on at least one steady client or patron whose collections she helped build up and tend: in the 1920s it was the Hon. Mrs Levy whose father had founded the Shell fortunes and who was replaced, after her second marriage, by another rich widow, Lady Assheton-Smith. Margaret also got smaller jobs for and from decorating friends like Herman or Derek Patmore and the architect Basil Ionides (architecture in those days covered anything from garden trimmings to designing maids' uniforms), any one of whom might put work in the way of another. It was Herman who introduced Patmore to the ageing Edwardian beauty who subsequently became his protectress, Mrs Gwendolen Jefferson of High Beech[7] (which Herman had decorated, and where Margaret too was called in for a weekend in the summer of 1933). A few years earlier Margaret had introduced Basil to Nelly Levy, herself by this time a close friend and prodigal source not only of work (Margaret had been employed on and off on the Levy collections in Lowndes Square, and later Berkeley Square, since 1922) but also of gossip, company, entertainment, splendid parties and no less splendid stories like the one of her saying, when someone admired her necklace in the garden at Buxted Park, 'My dear, these are my gardening pearls.'[8]

Basil found himself summoned one day to build a bow window in Berkeley Square, and shortly afterwards married his client. He and Nelly dined on 23 May 1930, the night before the wedding, with Margaret and Ivy who for once both warmly approved Basil's scheme for hanging up his hat in his wife's hall ('I always think that sounds so comfortable,' says Joanna in *A God and his Gifts*. 'And then you will go in to her fire'[9]). Even so, the Ionides and others among Margaret's friends could scarcely have been best pleased to see themselves even faintly reflected in *Buchanan's Hotel*, supposing it had ever reached the stage in the 1930s.

Not that Margaret would have minded. 'Margaret had a wonderful quality of indifference, the same quality which made Boucher call his picture *Le bel indifférent*,' said Herman. 'It was a kind of I-couldn't-care-less; she was so independent, obviously, in spite of her financial poverty, of what people thought or did, and in many ways she was really a French epicurienne . . .'[10] None of the Jourdains had means of their own, a fact which if anything re-inforced their contempt for trade and their faith in the family's im-peccable Huguenot pedigree. Even at the height of her powers in the 1930s, Margaret had small prospect of earning enough to make her comfortably off, indeed for most of her working life she had no regular income at all. 'I can't do collar work,' she would say (meaning the work collar worn by plough or dray horses) to Ralph Edwards, who remembered her in her fifties and sixties still 'stump-ing about for £5 for an article'. After 1923 her financial position had been somewhat eased by a steady arrangement with *Country Life* as secondary sales-room correspondent, a post not unfairly summed up, in Ivy's phrase, as choosing 'to behave in an undignified manner for a pittance' ('That is the best definition of work I have heard,' says Felix Bacon in *More Women Than Men*[11]).

Before that Margaret had been accustomed to get by on very little more—in a bad year decidedly less—than Emily Herrick in *Pastors and Masters* who would 'have had to go on the streets, or even be a governess' if her brother had left her to support herself on her own income (' "A hundred a year," said Emily. "Nicholas is kind and without a true dignity. He calls that on the streets" '[12]). Emily is the first of those shrewd, humorous, sceptical spinsters who were to become one of I. Compton-Burnett's specialities. She is not exactly a portrait of Margaret, more the product of a profound alteration in Ivy articulated, as it were, in the light of Margaret's peculiar personality and outlook. A good many of Emily's views were also Margaret's, not least the horror of teaching that was a natural reaction among women born into a world where even penniless boys, like the five Jourdain brothers, went into the church, the professions or the army as a matter of course, while girls had no choice (failing Nicholas Herrick's alternative) save to marry or teach.

ii

Margaret was the eighth child of the vicar of Ashbourne in Der-byshire, 'a man of little force but considerable charm',[13] who did not believe in education for girls and possessed neither funds nor connections, which put marriage out of the question for his five plain daughters. His wife was Emily Clay, a daughter of the distinguished Manchester surgeon Charles Clay who pioneered ovariotomy and died, embittered by lack of recognition, in 1893 when Margaret was seventeen. What little schooling she and her sisters received had been provided by these Manchester grand-parents, who also paid for the two eldest girls, Eleanor and Char-lotte, to join the first generation of women at Oxford. Margaret's first name was Emily after her mother:

> I believe their mother, Mrs Jourdain, was a charming woman [said Ivy to Rosamond Lehmann]. Eleven children altogether,* the first six almost simultaneously and all the same size. She dressed them all alike and of course it is scarcely surprising that she could scarcely tell them apart. Eleanor was the eldest. Eleanor would have to say, 'Mother, I am now twelve; should not my skirt be let down an inch?'—that sort of thing, you know. She was not at all an intellectual type, the mother, so Margaret told me. She would have preferred something less serious and academic in the way of six daughters—something with more of social grace and lightness. She did not feel at home with them. They were ambitious girls . . .[14]

The boys attended Ashbourne grammar school and the four able-bodied ones (Philip and Melicent, the two youngest Jourdains, were cripples) did at least dance at the Okeovers' balls, which gave them some contact with county society, while the girls were taught at home and asked nowhere. Reticent, tenacious, self-sufficient and starved in childhood of intellectual contact, Margaret and her two celebrated brothers, Francis (called Frank) and Philip, were all afterwards known as much for their personal austerity and biting tongues as for encyclopaedic knowledge in their respective scholar-

---

* The family tree compiled by Margaret's brother, Lt.-Col. Henry Jourdain, gives the number of the Rev. Francis and Emily Jourdain's children as ten, of whom the first six (Eleanor, Francis, Charlotte, Maria Lucy called May, Arthur and Raymond) certainly arrived within seven years, 1863–70; Henry was born two years later and the three youngest—Margaret, Philip and Melicent—were sepa-rated from the rest by a gap of four years so, unless Ivy mistook the number, perhaps there was an eleventh child in this gap who died young or was deliberately expunged (like Philip's wife Laura) for some other reason.

ly fields of furniture, ornithology and mathematics. All their lives they referred to themselves and one another by initials, as 'M.J.' (this was what Margaret was called, even after half a century, by all her closest friends except Ivy), 'F.C.R.J.', 'P.E.B.J.', so that family letters read as impersonally as office memos. A self-contained and critical habit must have been learnt early in the vicarage nursery. 'It was not a very happy household,' said Joan Evans whose mother had gone up to Oxford in 1888 with Charlotte Jourdain, and who had herself been educated by Eleanor and later befriended by Margaret. 'Margaret had no backing at home. Her mother couldn't conceive what intellectual work was; and her father wouldn't have bothered about it in his daughters.' The vicar was remembered by parishioners as 'dangerously high',[15] his wife as uncomfortably prickly, both as too stand-offish to be popular in the village. When the eldest son, another Rev. Francis Jourdain (later the founding father of British birdwatching), became vicar of Clifton-by-Ashbourne and married the squire's beautiful daughter, Frances Smith, in 1896, the Jourdains disowned the bride on the grounds that her family fortunes had been founded by a Smith in the grocery business. Other Jourdain wives were not much more welcome: 'The Jourdains were a very strange family—very brainy, but they lacked other things, such as family affection', wrote Frank's daughter, Violet Clifton-Smith[16] (who took her mother's name in adult life by way of repudiation).

Chronically hard up and short of friends in the neighbourhood, the family 'tended to be centrifugal' in Joan Evans' phrase, and the tendency applied emotionally as well as physically speaking. But, if life under a withdrawn, ineffectual father and a sardonic mother worn down by genteel poverty and twenty years' childbearing inhibited fondness or intimacy between the children, most of them flourished on the family's ruthlessly competitive, sink-or-swim policy of self-help, self-control and self-determination. Margaret's upbringing, in some ways bleak and chilly as the vicarage itself, left her implacably anti-Christian, independent and determined at all costs to avoid the humiliating moral and intellectual compromises involved in being a teacher like her three older sisters. Charlotte and May began life as governesses: May went east with a diplomatic family and died at the age of twenty-six in Persia in 1894; Charlotte ended up in an Anglican sisterhood in Truro (and, again by Joan Evans' account, 'if she'd gone on the streets it couldn't have put her outside the family any more than being a nun, so far as Margaret was concerned'). Their eldest sister Eleanor (called Nelly) became a schoolmistress and eventually Principal of St Hugh's College, Oxford, as well as a bestselling author on account of *An Adventure* which she wrote with her predecessor as Principal, the Bishop of Salisbury's daughter Miss Moberly, describing their encounter with Marie Antoinette and her ghostly court at Versailles in 1901. The book ('My sister's folly' was Margaret's phrase for it[17]) was published under pseudonyms in 1911, causing a good deal of what Miss Mitford called family feeling partly because of its sensational reception in the popular press, partly perhaps because of the faint but perceptible odour of high-minded fishiness analysed by Mrs Henry Sidgwick in the journal of the Society for Psychical Research.* Ivy (who claimed to know Eleanor well, and even once put her into a book) said she could not think of anyone more likely to delude herself into believing *An Adventure*.[18]

Eleanor was thirteen years older than Margaret. She was romantic and not in the least intellectual, a pious, orthodox High Anglican with mystical leanings and scant respect for the sterner exigencies of scholarship: on all these counts the opposite of her sister (though even that unbending sceptic could on occasion be brought to admit that Eleanor had second sight). Both were energetic, ambitious, determined, perhaps faintly French, with the same 'superior air' and the same fondness for feathers and finery. But on fundamentals they were always at loggerheads. Eleanor had gone up to Lady Margaret Hall as a scholar in 1883, five years after it opened, and, when her grandfather died, it was Eleanor (by this time running a small private school of her own called Corran at Watford) who helped subsidize Margaret on a Hall scholarship at the same college in 1894. Their principal was the witty and worldly Elizabeth Wordsworth who publicly subscribed to much the same view of woman's role as

---

* The Society, having dismissed *An Adventure* in 1901 as not worth investigating from a scientific point of view, remained unconvinced by further evidence adduced in 1911 ('I imagine she really understood at the bottom of her heart that she had done a rather fishy thing, and was determined that it should not be exposed,' wrote the Society's officer sent down to interview Miss Moberly: *The Ghosts of Versailles* by Lucille Iremonger, p. 203). Mrs Sidgwick's review was bitterly resented by both authors; what they actually saw at Versailles in 1901 is now generally supposed to have been preparations for a fancy dress party given by Robert de Montesquioux (see 'An End to An Adventure' by Joan Evans, *Encounter*, October 1976).

Mrs Jourdain (and practically the entire Oxford establishment, from dons to the humblest male undergraduate): 'My ideal woman is always graceful and beautiful, better with her hands than with her head, and best of all with her heart,' wrote Miss Wordsworth. 'She is not a bore because she has never overworked her brain . . . She has an income, if a lady, of from £500 to £1,000 a year; if a poor woman, from twenty shillings to thirty shillings a week . . .'[19]

It was an equivocator's ideal to which Eleanor Jourdain had no difficulty in subscribing, but Margaret rejected out of hand the implicit disparagement of learning itself, as well as of girls without a pretty face and a small fortune. 'The education of my generation, especially of girls, was too often fogged and darkened by doctrines of self-sacrifice for the taught, that marked a want of respect for the individual in the teacher,' wrote Joan Evans,[20] whose own education—supervised throughout by Eleanor, first at the Watford School then at St Hugh's—might have been abandoned altogether if it had not been for Margaret. Joan was the youngest child of the archaeologist Sir John Evans, half-sister to his still more celebrated son Sir Arthur Evans, discoverer of Cnossos, who was forty-two years Joan's senior. She had had a difficult childhood: neglected by scholarly parents (her mother was Maria Lathbury, a ruthlessly dedicated intellectual in her own right), wholly dependent for company and affection on her beloved nanny, she had lost confidence in herself so badly by 1910, at the age of seventeen, that she begged her mother with tears to let her off going to Oxford.

Margaret took her in hand, commissioned her while still a schoolgirl to write a book on jewellery, and generally restored her nerve to the point at which she could face going up to St Hugh's in the autumn of 1914; and Joan was only one among a whole series of young people encouraged to flower by Margaret, who took infinite pains to train them up in ways not only of erudition but of self-reliance, scepticism and irreligion (even Joan, reluctant to follow Margaret too far towards atheism, never forgot being helped to shed crushing burdens of guilt and piety in adolescence). Anyone young and in difficulties—especially anyone struggling for independence—could always rely on Margaret's sympathy and practical advice. Joan, at the end of a long and distinguished professional career, felt she had been launched on it by Margaret. So did young Hester Pinney, and perhaps the traveller Freya Stark (who stayed with Margaret and Ivy in London in the 1920s while planning her own rather more drastic escape from the dull, futile, self-denying round of a daughter at home), not to mention any number of rising young men in the furniture world. In a sense Ivy herself was the most spectacular success of a system first evolved to help Margaret's sister Melicent (called Milly), the youngest of all the Jourdains and the only one ever described as having a sweet disposition.

Milly, like Philip, was crippled by a hereditary disease called Friedrich's ataxia, a kind of multiple sclerosis that declares itself generally round about the tenth year and grows worse so rapidly that it is rare for sufferers to survive into their twenties. As children, she and Philip had spent their days roaming the country together, playing horses or shipwrecks, building tree houses, all pastimes that had to be successively abandoned as they found it harder to keep their balance, to walk, eventually even to stand without help. Philip, perhaps the most remarkable member of a remarkable family, so deformed he could scarcely hold a pen, had achieved an international reputation as a mathematician and mathematical historian before he was thirty, while Milly—shy, nervous, imaginative, more than content to stick to the shadows cast by her brilliant next brother and sister—grew up to write two notably original books of her own. The first was *A Childhood* by 'Joan Arden' which came out in 1913 (Eleanor had published *An Adventure* two years earlier under the name of 'Francis Lamont'), with a preface by Professor Gilbert Murray who admired the book both for its own sake 'and because it somehow reads like the proem to something sterner and sadder'. The stern, sad sequel was *Unfulfilment*, a slim volume of verse published in 1924 which records with singular terseness and clarity its author's decline into paralysis and death:

'The Sea Fog'

The fields below me are sodden and grey and the fog has
                                        blurred the line of the hills.
I sit by the hedge and think that every year the darkness
                                        will grow closer round me.
The fog has crept up and all is a sea of whiteness;
My face is wet with its gentle touch and I can only see a
                                        few steps in front of me on the road.

Self-pity was an emotion foreign to the Jourdains. Milly's two short books are unsentimental, unsparing, quite free of imitative or second-hand reactions. There is no mention of her illness in *A Childhood*, which describes skating, tobogganing, haymaking and exploring the dales round Ashbourne with an intensity which is the only indication that the writer could herself no longer run or climb or move at all. The scrupulous accuracy that turned so many of the Jourdains towards scholarship combined with feeling and great sensitivity in Milly to give a piercing sharpness to even the simplest recollections: terror of bogeys under the stairs, the solemn rapture of being lifted on to a drayhorse or allowed to feed worms to the hens by the vicarage gardener (a comforting character called William who was borrowed, along with the hens, by Ivy fifty years later for the opening chapter of *The Present and the Past*).

Margaret, who was six years older than Milly, is called Judith in *A Childhood* and emerges as the figure who counted more to the child than her nurse, her benign distant mother or any of her other sisters and brothers except Philip (called by his middle name of Bertrand in the book). Some of the vividest passages describe her pride and pleasure at being detailed by the daredevil Judith to climb the tallest beech tree, or take part in illicit expeditions up the steep gabled roof, crawling after Judith and clinging to her foot. It is Judith who spurs the child on, always Judith she strives to impress, Judith whose scorn is more dreaded than any adult reproof: 'Judith said contemptuously, "If you are *afraid*, the beech tree will throw you down, but if you climb to the top and are not frightened, he will hold you and not let you fall." I climbed to the top with no fear . . .'[21] The reward for feats like this one was an invitation back up the beech tree to listen to stories of ghosts, devils, tree-spirits, clandestine battles between the noble beeches and the demonic yews ('all evergreens were wicked') whose roots reached down to hell beyond the kitchen garden. This bracing relationship—between the bold, exacting, self-confident elder sister and the younger one, always timid and easily tired—persisted throughout their adult life. When Milly first realized the hopelessness of her condition, it was Margaret who persuaded her to fight despair by attending art classes in Cambridge[22] and, when Milly's hands grew too twisted even to draw, it was Margaret's example that made her turn to writing instead.

But Margaret was always more of a goad than a comforter.

According to Joan Evans, Margaret's debunking instincts—the scornfulness that eventually extended to practically every person or subject she mentioned—went back to earliest childhood when an innate sense of beauty combined with a horror of sham made her reject piety, complacency, insularity, philistinism, all the unthinking orthodoxies for which her family ('*Oh* her family!' said Joan Evans bitterly) stood. Mockery had early provided relief from a harsh and demanding home life for Margaret and Philip, whose revolt against the moral opportunism of their vicarage upbringing made both despise religion as unequivocally as Ivy and her own two brothers were to do a few years later in Hove. 'No good can come of it,' said Ivy long afterwards, discussing Christianity with the novelist Elizabeth Taylor. 'Its foundations are laid in fostering guilt in people—well, that obviously makes it easier for our Pastors and Masters when we are young. Margaret saw that when she was a little girl. She said to her governess, "I don't want to hear any more about that poor man," and walked out of the room.'[23]

The presence of two such cool, humorous, pacifist, atheistical (in Philip's case, downright anti-clerical) rationalists made for tension at home. Never a demonstrative family, tending always to reserve their strongest feelings for things or abstractions rather than people, the Jourdains took no small pride in virtuoso displays of grudge-bearing, will-dangling and the patient tending of feuds. Margaret and her elder brothers and sisters ('She couldn't stand any of them,' said Joan Evans) retained to the end of their lives an outstanding knack of rubbing one another up the wrong way, and Philip, too, quarrelled in the end with them all.

By all accounts it would have been hard to find two more stoutly conservative characters than Colonels Arthur and Henry Jourdain, but they were if anything outclassed by Eleanor, who put paid to attempts to impeach her own and Miss Moberly's testimony in *An Adventure* with the ringing declaration: 'We belong to no new schools of thought: we are the daughters of English clergymen, and heartily hold and teach the faith of our fathers.' Margaret had no more patience with this sort of simple faith than Ivy's characters have with honest worth or true kindness or any other convenient formula appropriated by people attempting to put something over on others (' "Being cruel to be kind is just ordinary cruelty with an excuse made for it," said Evelyn. "And it is right that it should be more resented, as it is" '[24]). Margaret's directness from girlhood onwards had attracted a great many people besides Ivy who, constitutionally circumspect herself, delighted in stories of her friend's reckless disregard for cant or pomposity. 'There's no buckram about it' was one of Margaret's sayings,[25] denoting approval of anything plain, simple and unpretentious. 'Margaret was certainly completely unaffected,' said Herman, 'she would never affect anything; she was herself, standing, as she did, with legs slightly apart and her strange clothes, her hats with feathers, her eyeglass, and raising one eyebrow in that peculiar and inimitable manner.'[26]

It was a stance by no means easy to maintain in the last years of the nineteenth century at Oxford where girls, admitted on sufferance, were expected to keep their heads and voices well down. Conformity, humility, gratitude, hard work and juvenile meekness formed the programme enthusiastically endorsed by Eleanor Jourdain when she reached St Hugh's as Vice Principal in 1901. But Margaret as an undergraduate had insisted on following her own road rather than anyone else's. She read classics, like Ivy, but what chiefly preoccupied her—most unlike Ivy at this stage—was the latest thing in modern literature which, in the 1890s, meant the French symbolist poets. Her closest friend at Lady Margaret Hall was Janette Ranken, a statuesque beauty from a well-to-do Edinburgh family with leanings towards the arts and the theatre. They were both passionately interested in contemporary poetry ('which people weren't at Oxford in those days', said Joan Evans, who had herself suffered throughout her career from Oxford's traditionally disparaging view of the arts). It seems likely that Margaret was not only reading but already translating Baudelaire, José de Herédia, Villiers de l'Isle-Adam and others whose work she interspersed with her own *Poems* in 1911.

She was almost certainly at work on the calendar of nature writings eventually published by Lord Alfred Douglas as *An Outdoor Breviary* in 1909; and it is noticeable that, though the most striking parts of the *Breviary* celebrate monochrome wintry landscapes—bare downland, clear or colourless skies, grey-limbed leafless trees—in the Oxford passages it is always spring or high summer. There are uncharacteristically luxuriant descriptions of the city's towers gleaming through green leaves in Christ Church meadow on May Day, a great spendthrift red hawthorn blooming beside the Cherwell, hedgerows festooned with elder, meadowsweet and dogroses at Iffley where Margaret found, like so many hopeful undergraduates loafing beside the river in June, that 'the passage of the long summer days seems gradually to attune the mind to expect something unusual, to wait for "that expression of hope which is called beauty" '. The *Breviary*, which owes as much to mystical English nature writers like Blake or Traherne as to the French decadents, preaches the contemplation of beauty, especially beauty in its more ephemeral and random aspects:

> The art of life is to accept; to notice without ever going out to see. For the strain of any purpose defeats itself and clouds the charmed moment. But purposeless, in a little we become one with the great and smooth current of existence, and undistracted. It is only in the course of aimless and repetitive sauntering that we can be permeated with the charm of light, and the secret beauty of small things.[27]

It is perhaps scarcely surprising that Eleanor Jourdain disapproved of her sister's conduct at Oxford. The cult of purposelessness, expressed in aimless and repetitive sauntering, was not likely to appeal to one who could imagine no higher goal for a woman than the education of others. Perhaps Eleanor had hoped to recruit a new member for her own school staff at Watford. At all events she took umbrage when Margaret left college in 1897 with a third-class degree in classical mods, and obstinately refused to teach. Their father's death the following summer left Mrs Jourdain impoverished and homeless, with two disabled children on her hands as well as three older, unmarried daughters. Eleanor, keeping her own head above water with difficulty and burdened for the rest of her life with the need to make provision for Milly, could hardly be expected to do anything further for Margaret, who seemed to have picked the worst possible moment at which to embark on a literary career.

   But none of the elder Jourdains was prepared to abandon all hope of independence, as Margaret did for nearly half her adult life, in order to live at home with the two invalids, their nurses and their elderly mother. The household moved in the autumn of 1898 to lodgings in Cambridge so that Philip might read mathematics as an undergraduate under what Norbert Wiener called the Mad Hatter's Tea Party of Trinity: Bertrand Russell (whose pronounced likeness to Tenniel's Mad Hatter was later shrewdly exploited in Philip's *The Philosophy of Mr. B*rtr*nd R*ss*ll*),* Ellis McTaggart, and the philosopher who afterwards exerted a magnetic pull on the Bloomsbury group, G. E. Moore.

Intellectually the most brilliant of all the Jourdains, Philip was also the most outgoing. To the timid and retiring Milly he seemed, like Margaret, always enviably self-assured, 'sociable and talkative and never shy'.[28] He had been an enchanting child, delicate, precocious, bright-eyed and, by Russell's account, he had lost none of his charm when they first met during a course of lectures on mathematical logic in the winter of 1902:

> He is very ill, partially paralysed, and at first sight almost half-witted. But as soon as he begins to talk of mathematics his face shines, his eyes sparkle, he speaks with fire and ability, one forgets that he is ill, or remembers it only in passionate admiration of the triumph of mind . . . I saw his mother for a moment: she pressed my hand, I loved her, and she seemed deeply grateful to me for encouraging her son: it was a deep moment of intimacy, though not a single word was said by either of us, and I had never met her before.[29]

Philip's early years at Cambridge had been shadowed by disappointment and false starts, interrupted by an electrical cure at Heidelberg that cost him his chance of a fellowship at Trinity and quashed all hope of recovery, forcing both Philip and his sister to realize at last that their illness could only get worse. Philip failed his Tripos in 1901, settling instead for a pass degree and thereafter slowly regaining intellectual confidence, becoming runner-up for the coveted Smith's prize in 1904 and winner of the university's Allen studentship two years later. The turning point had been his meeting with Russell, who sponsored him for the scholarship, guided his research into analytical mechanics and the Cantorian theory of transfinite numbers, discussed the problems of Russell's own *Principia Mathematica* and, from 1902 to 1910, traced the slow,

---

* According to Russell, this absurd booklet with its text from the White Knight, frequent acknowledgements to Tweedledee, and set of twenty appendices pointing out correspondences between Russell's philosophy and Lewis Carroll's, was a faithful account of his conversations with Jourdain at Cambridge and afterwards (*Autobiography of Bertrand Russell*, vol. 1, p. 217).

painful growth of that magnum opus in an extraordinary series of long, close, technically detailed letters exchanged with Philip after he left Cambridge.

But Russell's revolutionary mathematical and philosophical discoveries were only part of that intense intellectual ferment at Cambridge at the turn of the century which profoundly affected Margaret, and proved a formative influence on Ivy, captivated by the same heady atmosphere a few years later through her own brother at King's. Philip became the particular friend of Sidney Waterlow (afterwards turned down by Virginia Stephen in favour of Leonard Woolf) who was dazzled, as people commonly were, by the 'vivid, brilliant, boiling over mind'[30] that impressed Philip's sisters' friends as much as his own. He was Woolf's and Lytton Strachey's contemporary at Trinity, and responded as eagerly as they did to the political, social and moral iconoclasm beginning to stir inside the college. 'Margaret was rather on the fringe of the Bloomsbury group,' said Joan Evans. 'Cambridge always counted far more for her than Oxford.' Women were only just beginning to put in a first tentative appearance on the university scene but Philip shared more than most with his mother and sisters ('Philip was so happy in the bit of life he had got, though he must have known how incomplete it was, that he simply overflowed to us'[31]), and in spite, or perhaps because of the effort entailed in coming to terms with the grim future awaiting the two youngest Jourdains, this was a time of achievement, even liberation for all of them. Milly, roused from her initial trance of black misery by Margaret, was absorbed more happily than ever again in her drawing class and her friendship with Charles Darwin's grand-daughter, Frances (who later married a Fellow of Trinity and became famous as the poet Frances Cornford). Margaret herself took up with dons' families such as the daughters of Professor ('Dictionary') Skeat, published her first three books as editor and translator ('No one would have been more surprised than M.J. to find herself in print,' said Janette Ranken long afterwards[32]), and, by the time the family left Cambridge in September 1903, had assumed for ever the sceptical, ironic, characteristically Cambridge frame of mind—so marked in her later that friends found it hard to believe she had been at Oxford—that Ivy found irresistible.

The Jourdains settled eventually at Broadwindsor in Dorset, where this strange, shabby, scholarly household was received with sympathetic amazement by the local inhabitants: 'Their view of . . . mathematical work was expressed by an old woman who used to come and work in the house sometimes: "Mr. Jardeen do and be allus writin': I s'pose it pleases he".'[33] But Broadwindsor, though small, remote, backward and not apt to change its ways for outsiders, was less inaccessible than Ashbourne, and Cambridge ties remained strong. Russell himself stopped off regularly on bicycling tours in the summer for lunch and tea, or to spend the night and sit up talking with Philip. Milly's best friend, Frances Cornford, was also a frequent guest, collaborating on various projects for which she supplied the text and Milly the illustrations (Frances' *Poems* beat *A Childhood* into print by three years, though Milly had already slipped past the post in 1906 with line drawings for Philip's *Topsy-Turvy Fairy Tales* by Somebody-or-Other with Three Illustrations by Somebody-Else). But in these years when Milly's only means of leaving the house was a donkey cart supplied by the Darwins, while Philip chugged round the village in a mechanical wheelchair, Margaret became their chief link with the outside world, undertaking commissions in London, bringing back gossip and news, suggesting outlets, helping Milly place poems with periodicals on which she herself had a foothold such as the *Nation* and *Country Life*. 'Margaret was always very good to Milly,' said Joan Evans; and Margaret seems to have accepted her role in much the same dry, disparaging, eminently practical spirit as France Ponsonby in *Daughters and Sons*, who also chose to sink her own personal resources in the family pool: 'People want some reason for not doing good. Or they would have to do it, as I have to.'[34]

It was precisely this note of contrariness in Margaret that had always infuriated her sister Eleanor, though it found a more sympathetic response in their mother, who was musical and cultivated, if not intellectual, and clearly relished the teasing of her three youngest children: they called her 'Mrs Mouse' (she was tiny) and formed an alliance that was, at any rate after their father's death, far closer and more relaxed than anything their elders had known. Philip contributed a stream of comical and cautionary poems, skits and satires to the Cambridge undergraduate magazine *Granta* (including a popular series, 'Some Unconscious Humourists of the Nineteenth Century', featuring Carlyle, Wordsworth and Mrs Humphry Ward). Margaret, who never made jokes in print, pro-

nounced magisterially in favour of prophets like Shaw and Samuel
Butler (whose posthumous rehabilitation she attributed largely to a
speech by the President of the British Association, Frances Cornford's father, Francis Darwin).[35] Even the devout and peaceable
Milly followed the others' iconoclasm far enough to develop
socialist tendencies ('The Red Flag will soon be flying over Broadwindsor at this rate,' wrote Frances approvingly in 1910).

When assorted Darwins, Cornfords, Murrays and Will Rothen-
stein invented a plan for dividing the entire human race according to
outlook and temperament into pinks and blues, Philip instantly
appropriated the system, becoming expert at spotting rare sub-
species and expounding his general principles in *Granta*: nearly all
artists were blue, along with all dissidents, sceptics and anyone
inclined to line up behind Shaw or Butler, 'while Miss Marie Corelli
and most curates are indelibly pink'.[36] Except that subsequent
opinion has reversed the colour scheme, assigning pink to the
radical party and blue to conservatives, the classification holds good
to this day; and with it went what sounds like a useful adjunct to the
novels of I. Compton-Burnett, 'a Dictionary of Received Opinions
for the use of blue people who find it a tactical necessity to learn the
language of the pink'.

There was no shortage of disapproving, even scandalized pinks in
Broadwindsor when Margaret and Philip set about mounting their
joint assault on Fleet Street and the London publishing houses. The
household income had been drastically reduced in 1904 when the
trust fund set up by their father for his two youngest children was
wound up and his capital divided. Money was something the
Jourdains begrudged one another more fiercely than anything else:
Frank fell out with his family once again over it, Philip afterwards
maintained that he and Milly had been landed with dud invest-
ments, Raymond (a schoolmaster who seems, like Frank, to have
withdrawn from the family under some sort of cloud) was specifically cut off with nothing under the terms of his father's will.
Funds, always tight, now became desperate. Eleanor Jourdain in
her youth is said to have tried living for a time on a working
woman's income of one pound a week, and, up till 1911 (when a
year's retainer from Lenygon provided her for the first time with
something approaching a living wage), Margaret scarcely earned
more. Philip assessed his earnings in 1914 as £200 ('and my total
private income £12'[37]); Margaret's for the same year were £83 8s 1d.

Both sums represented a vast amount of work: on Philip's part, historical, philosophical and mathematical papers in learned journals, a voluminous scientific correspondence, time-consuming duties as English editor of *The Monist* and (after 1915, when he took over from Waterlow on the editorial board) *The International Journal of Ethics*. Margaret (who wrote regularly for both Philip's periodicals, and later succeeded him briefly in both his editorial posts) was steadily acquiring a name as a translator, poet and literary critic as well as expert on decoration. But her best efforts brought in little more than enough to pay for railway fares, and family resentment (which on Eleanor's part at least was intense) must have pressed hard in the twenty years it took her, after leaving Oxford, before she could work up a sufficient income on which to leave home.

iii

Support and encouragement came from friends like Janette, and Alice Dryden with whom Margaret collaborated on a revised edition of Mrs Palliser's *History of Lace* in 1902.[38] Alice, who was ten years older than Margaret, generous, witty, warm-hearted, high-spirited, fond of racing and riding to hounds, was the only child of the Northamptonshire antiquary, Sir Henry Dryden of Canons Ashby, of whom it was said that 'next only to the poet' (John Dryden had died ten years too soon to inherit Canons Ashby, which went instead to his son Erasmus in 1710), 'he was the most famous of the Drydens'.[39] A popular and notably eccentric High Sheriff, an entertaining and controversial lecturer ('he liked to shock people: by him, indeed, they rather liked to be shocked'), Sir Henry was also a learned historian, immensely knowledgeable about his own home and hospitable to interested visitors such as Margaret. Her own expertise seems to have grown, in the wake of the lace book, from a handful of articles on lace extending into stumpwork, whitework, samplers, and so on, via embroidered hangings and Chinese wallpapers to teapots, andirons, card tables and knife cases; and, though she can hardly have envisaged her future as a furniture historian at this stage, it seems likely that, in John Cornforth's phrase, she 'started to get her eye in at Canons Ashby in the 1890s'.[40]

Sir Henry died the year after Margaret's father, and Alice, forced to uproot herself from the home she had known for thirty-three years, settled eventually on Boar's Hill outside Oxford, in a house called Orchard Lee which became a convenient research base for Margaret as well as herself. The lace book proved a success, and the following year they put together an anthology, *Memorials of Old Northamptonshire*, based on Sir Henry's papers and illustrated from the pioneering photographic archive Alice had built up, driving herself and her camera round the country in a dogcart. One of Alice's cousins wrote the chapter on Dryden, leaving Margaret (who was called in on the literary side as a regular thing, whenever Alice edited further volumes in the same series) to cover lesser fry like Thomas Fuller, the historian of *England's Worthies*, a Northamptonshire man who had begun his career as a royalist divine in Broadwindsor vicarage and found himself ousted, during the civil war, by a John Pinney.

Fuller, according to Virginia Woolf's father Leslie Stephen, 'was apparently one of the first authors to make a living by the pen':[41] a point that can hardly have been lost on Margaret, starting out on the same uphill path in the same village with the same Pinney family for neighbours. The Jourdains rented Broadwindsor manor house and insisted on sitting on Sundays in the manor pew on purpose to aggravate the rightful lord of the manor, Lieutenant-Colonel (later General Sir Reginald) Pinney, who had himself taken a house in the village while waiting for tenants to vacate his family home at Racedown. But his wife was not in the least put out: Lady Pinney (born Hester Head and descended from Quaker merchant stock) was a powerful personality in her own right* and agreeably surprised to find a kindred spirit on her doorstep. 'She found in Margaret Jourdain a companion in mind, probably the first and only intimate woman friend she ever made,' said her daughter, young Hester, who was as impressed as her mother by 'Margaret's keen interest in everything, so different from what you might expect to find in a spinster daughter in a small country village, and even more different from the regimental wives who had been the main companions of my mother's married life'.[42]

When Colonel Pinney was posted for four years to Egypt in 1909,

---

* Lady Pinney is said to have told her husband on their marriage that theirs should be a partnership: 'A partnership—my money shall be yours—or let us say rather, a limited company. Six months later, I had to say to him: "When I said a limited company, I did *not* make you managing director."'

Margaret volunteered to keep an eye on the children—eight-year-old Hester, her younger brother Bernard and the baby Rachel —who were charmed with the arrangement. She invented new games, wrote verse plays for them to act, taught them to make up stories, read the tombstones and dance on the graves to the horror of their governess, a Miss Partridge, who complained that Margaret was bad for discipline, unseemly, irreverent, a downright unwholesome influence. The jolly, horsey, hunting Pinneys were, by Jourdain's law, as indelibly pink as Marie Corelli: Margaret and Philip Jourdain were the first professed atheists young Hester had ever encountered, and they retained for her ever afterwards a special aura of pleasure and wickedness. Margaret in particular stood for everything bold, dashing and free: 'Ask Margaret Jourdain' became a Pinney slogan. It was Margaret who supervised the decoration and furnishing when the family moved to Racedown in 1911 or 1912; Margaret who urged the elder of the two Hesters ('who, she said, was the only intelligent Pinney, and that by marriage') to take custody of the family papers; Margaret who chose a boarding school, kept by one of her old Cambridge friends, the Miss Skeats, for young Hester.

Professor Skeat was one of the eminent contributors recruited by Lord Alfred Douglas to write for the *Academy* alongside rising talent in the shape of Margaret herself, Frederick Rolfe, Siegfried Sassoon and Noel Compton-Burnett's friend and rival at King's, Rupert Brooke. Margaret's first, decidedly mannered but not undistinguished sonnet, 'Seleucis of Lesbos', was published in the *Academy* on 16 May 1908, and from then on she contributed a rapidly increasing number of poems, French translations and weekly book reviews, covering everything from Hardy's poetry to *Papuan Fairy Tales*. *An Outdoor Breviary* began serial instalments the following February, and was published by the Academy Press as a book (bound in pale blue buckram with gilt decorations, which suggests that Margaret's taste in her giddy youth was not yet as severe as it was to be later) that autumn, together with Lord Alfred Douglas' own *Sonnets* and his wife's *Poems*.

The *Academy* had been bought for Douglas in 1907 by friends vainly hoping to divert his litigious instincts, for his reputation was still highly unsavoury, though his part in the Wilde trial remained so utterly unspeakable that it is quite likely none of Margaret's neighbours in the village knew exactly what sort of a cloud he was

under.* She herself was often in London, sharing Janette's rooms in
Chelsea, and already more than equal to keeping her editor's
disreputable proclivities sternly in check (Lady Pinney's brother,
Alban Head, remembered Margaret being accosted in the Café
Royal by Douglas with a potentially libellous document from his
latest lawsuit which she refused to read, to her companion's lasting
regret). Her own unconventionality was always strictly functional,
and she disapproved then as later of sexual impropriety and the
desire to shock for its own sake. But General Pinney was not alone
in harbouring misgivings. Margaret's mocking air, her poetry (if
not her Wildean connections) and her trips to London, her evident
penury and complete failure to apologize for it, her irregular
behaviour in the graveyard and still more irregular attendance at
church: all these nettled pink people like the Pinneys' Miss Partridge
and the vicar's daughter, Dorothy Hutchings, who reacted as
ungraciously as the neighbours do in *More Women Than Men* to the
spectacle of a penniless, unmarried, Oxford-educated girl obliged
to work for her living:

> 'Neighbours don't seem to hold the Greek view of the nobility
> of suffering.' ,
> 'Neighbours are English,' said Felix.
> 'There is no disgrace in honest poverty.'
> 'You can't really think that. There is no point in being too
> Greek.'[43]

Margaret afterwards said that Ivy had never known what it was to
be poor, something she herself had known only too well 'as the
hard-up daughter of a hard-up country parson'. Her output,
though not her income, had increased fivefold under Douglas who
persuaded her in 1908 to turn almost wholly to literature. Margaret
in these years was following in the footsteps of William and
Dorothy Wordsworth whom she described scouring the countryside round Broadwindsor for subjects to write about, tramping
the roads to keep warm, growing their own food ('no doubt
for motives of economy almost all the meals consisted of

* Lord Alfred's editorial secretary, the young Alice Head (afterwards editor of
Woman at Home and *Good Housekeeping*, eventually a director of *Country Life*), told
me that neither she nor her mother could make out the exact nature of the scandal
surrounding her editor, with whom she herself remained on excellent terms: 'They
didn't tell women anything in those days,' said Miss Head.

vegetables'[44]), and generally giving rise to gossip in the village. The poet and his sister had lived in the 1790s in the Pinneys' house at Racedown on the slopes of Pilsden Hill where, just over a century later, Margaret and Milly must have spent hours, even whole days at a time, together or more likely alone, immersed in the Dorset countryside both knew and wrote about intimately, especially in its harsher and more frugal aspects. It is always the drab and the dun-coloured that please Margaret best, from the threadbare copses and luminous floodwaters of February to the last shabby garland of an autumn hedgerow ('a tattered and dusty embroidery of humble and graceless flowers, flesh-coloured hemp agrimony, flat-faced yarrow, and ragwort'[45]). The height of delight in Milly's poems is a single celandine or crocus in the grass, the feel of cold stream water, thin sunlight on glittering frost-covered hills. Perhaps she had learnt from Hardy or Wordsworth, perhaps simply from her own constricted life, the deceptive simplicity that matches an unobtrusive verse form with an equally unassuming truthfulness:

> And still I see how clearly shines the light
> On winter branches, and how the dripping rain
> Deepens the colour on the hills, and how
> To draw those horses plodding up the lane.
>
> I know too late; my hands can do no more;
> All powerless upon my lap they lie.
> Only my sense of colour and of smell,
> And biting pain, increases till I die.[46]

There is no way of dating Milly's poems. Some clearly gather intensity from being written in retrospect, after the Jourdains had left Dorset in 1919, but all of them have a musicality, a concentration of thought and feeling, a desolate clarity well beyond the scope of Margaret's *Poems* (published two years before *A Childhood*). Milly's voice, low and faint but true, belongs to an authentic poet; Margaret's verses are accomplished but impersonal by comparison, mannered in the contemporary aesthetic style and heavily dependent on classical or symbolist originals. Her prose in the *Breviary* is another matter: Margaret in those days could hear Pan piping on Pilsden Hill and take messages from the 'vague and speechless voices of leaves', but her most nearly authentic visionary effects come from intent, exultant, minute observation of sun, rain, cloud or the track of the wind rushing up a dry hill pasture. She was to be all her life a byword for scrupulous accuracy but anyone familiar with the relentlessly prosaic style of her later writings will find it hard to account for the fire of, say, this characteristic description of a day on the downs:

> Towards the late afternoon, the blue has dropped away from the lower sky, as a dyed cloth bleaches in keen air, until a pale glass-like colour is left—like the very pale green panes that filled the church windows half a century ago—through which the huge sun soars downward to the shining edge of the pale-coloured world. It is here, in the empty Downs, that Richard Jefferies' worship of the great sun in the heaven becomes fitly explicable . . .[47]

Other entries in the *Breviary* reflect the diarist's knowledge of hangings, embroidery or jewels as clearly as her distaste for Victorian stained glass. But Margaret's habit of comparing the sky to church windows, or autumn leaves to tapestry pictures framed and hung up on hooks, makes it hard to pin down exactly when she switched from being a poetical nature-lover interested in interior decoration to a furniture historian with all mystic tendencies rigorously suppressed; and it is harder still to say whether, if things had not so drastically got the better of her, she would have changed in any case of her own accord. Douglas sold the *Academy* at the end of 1910 which meant that Margaret's contributions abruptly ceased. She scraped together the money for her *Poems* to come out (in a plain paper binding this time) the following year, but a characteristically bracing note from Philip points out that 'M.J.'s greatest possible net gain on this edition of 500 copies, supposing all sold . . . would be about £3'[48] (in fact Philip had failed to allow for the cost of paper covers, estimated by Hatchard at precisely £3 and 'not to be materially reduced by using cheaper paper').

It must have been abundantly clear that poetry would not pay; also, that practically anyone who could hold a pen was capable of turning out the sort of hackwork—pieces on 'Street Noises', 'England As She Is Seen', 'Literature and the Snob'—Margaret produced from time to time for papers like the London *Evening*

Standard; whereas there was little competition to meet the increasing demand from periodicals like the *Connoisseur*, *Queen* and *Country Life* for the knowledgeable pieces on samplers and stumpwork that rapidly became her stock-in-trade. Margaret's services were snapped up in May 1911 by the enterprising young decorator Francis Lenygon (who had just opened his first New York branch —eventually responsible for the Georgian craze in America—and was currently negotiating to buy Morant & Co., cabinet-makers since the reign of George IV).[49] It was a shrewd move on Lenygon's part: his subsequent reputation for expensive simplicity, purveyed with a unique combination of fashionable and historical acumen, owed much to Margaret's work in cataloguing the contents of the firm's premises at 31, Burlington Street in a pioneering book, *Furniture in England, 1660–1760*, which came out with a parallel volume on decoration in 1914. The originality of the Lenygon books lay in their recognizing, long before anyone else did, the importance of English Palladian design while insisting, again for the first time, that furniture should be studied in its decorative context.

Margaret's standing at this stage was still that of a cultivated amateur, called in 'to tidy things up on the literary side' (in Ralph Edwards' phrase) by craftsmen like Lenygon and his colleague, Colonel Mulliner, a bottle-nosed Birmingham coachbuilder whose book, *Decorative Arts in England (1760–1880)*, was also written for him by Margaret. Most of her early work was published under men's names, her own ('Mr. M. Jourdain' was the translator of F. Gusman's *Pompei* in 1900 and editor of Horace in 1904 as well as author of the *Breviary* in 1909) or other people's, for Margaret, who was singularly free from personal vanity, saw no objection to Lenygon and Mulliner taking the credit for books they had hired her to write. They taught her things about cabinet-making that she could have learnt nowhere else, while she supplied them with the cachet essential in a trade so rapidly expanding and so intimately connected with intangibles like taste and class.

In the furniture field, from museums and the great auction houses down to the shadier undergrowth of dealing and faking, much depends on the sort of jockeying for position described in *Buchanan's Hotel*. Mulliner operated from rooms in the Albany on fairly bogus social credentials but he had the sixth sense that can tell a fake from the genuine article by something like divination, which was more than could be said for Margaret's other employer, Edward Hudson of *Country Life* ('the Hudson idiot' was Mulliner's phrase for him in characteristically irascible letters to Margaret[50]). Son of a printer, 'indifferently educated but avid of culture',[51] gruff, inarticulate, outwardly unprepossessing but profoundly romantic at heart, Hudson had evolved the *Country Life* formula from *Racing Illustrated* at the turn of the century when a photographer sent to take pictures of the brood mares at Sledmere is said to have come back with a photograph of the Sledmere library as well. Hudson was the first to exploit a popular craving for glamour and the picturesque that coincided exactly with his own lifelong passion for 'princely mansions and quaint old houses of long-lineaged householders'.[52] He was notoriously churlish towards employees but, though neither he nor Mulliner had any scruples about treating Margaret as a dogsbody, both knew well enough that they were on to a good thing. Her combination of erudition and integrity was a crucial factor in *Country Life*'s development from relatively naive beginnings before the First World War into what Walter Runciman called 'the keeper of the architectural conscience of the nation'.

Though the war effectively suspended Margaret's career as an all-purpose freelance, it gave her a living wage, for she was employed with Janette on government war work in London, submitting for the first and last time in her life to an office routine and staying at Janette's Chelsea boarding house (where they took up with another independent, unmarried blue-stocking, Winifred Felkin, sister to Noel Compton-Burnett's friend Elliott, who eventually introduced Margaret to Ivy). Margaret's attitude to the war was, so far as her family was concerned, a thoroughly provoking detachment. Frank was too old but Arthur, Raymond and Henry Jourdain all fought on the Western front. Margaret and Philip inclined to share Russell's unpopular pacificism,* or at least that prophetic sense of waste and destruction felt by so many Cambridge intellectuals, including Noel Compton-Burnett whose posi-

---

* Philip, who published Russell's paper on 'The Ethics of War' in the *International Journal of Ethics* for January 1915 (also Margaret's account of proposals for a prospective League of Nations in October 1918), sympathized with Russell when he was first imprisoned as a pacifist and later attacked by a jingo, and sent him a set of encouragingly unpatriotic, anti-clerical and non-belligerent verses on 'The War and Christianity'. But Philip and Margaret themselves defended British war aims in strictly rational, anti-jingoist terms in *The Open Court* (January and February 1915).

tion in October, 1914, outlined in letters from King's was neatly summed up by a jingle of Philip's doing the rounds from Trinity:

> '*Gott strafe England!*' 'God save the King!'
>   'God this!' 'God that!' the warring nations shout.
> 'Good God!' says God,
>   'I've got my work cut out.'[53]

But a rational response, strengthened by revulsion from jingoism, only made things harder in wartime for intellectuals not prepared to rate their own safety or comfort higher than anyone else's. Philip's initial reaction in the opening weeks of the war had been to offer his two typists, and his own services as telephonist, to the Cambridge Officers' Training Corps (to which Noel also reported with a heavy heart for military training that autumn). The rejection of both offers, together with a subsequent attempt to give skin for wounded soldiers, plunged him into a depression so black that, even eleven months later, he could still scarcely bear to read a historical account of the outbreak of hostilities in August 1914, because 'it brought back the emotional stir-up'.[54]

Humour and an iron reticence had always been Philip's chosen armour, as they were Margaret's. Brother and sister were perhaps at their closest, professionally and intellectually if not emotionally speaking, in the war, when Philip was estranged from the rest of the family, even in some sense from Milly, whose letters after 1914 were more and more shadowed by suffering, sadness and dread. She and Philip were by now virtually helpless and the Christian submission with which she had struggled for years to contain her illness was beginning to seem to her more like spiritual defeat. But the physical torpor that drove Milly towards a despairing indifference had the opposite effect on Philip, who all his life resisted each fresh depredation with a heroic refusal to dilute or diminish intellectual output combined, at times of particular stress, with a passionate outpouring of feelings he could no longer hold back. All Jourdains suppressed emotion on principle: 'You wouldn't have *scenes* in that family. It was just silence,' said Joan Evans, who had suffered more than most from the obstinacy of hostile and taciturn Jourdains.

A set of melancholy poems written when the family left Cambridge records Philip's attempts to stifle an unhappy love affair; a later attachment to a girl called Eva Loudrun at Broadwindsor in

1911 roused the united opposition of his family, including his mother, whose 'unsympathetic shockedness'[55] sounds much like Margaret's reaction in middle life to any hint of sexual self-indulgence. Margaret was away that spring, working for Leny-gon's in London and no doubt distancing herself so far as possible from an episode that gave the village more than its usual quota of gossip and ended, after a great many painful, sometimes explosive confrontations, with Philip moving out of his mother's house in July, to set up for himself with an attendant called Fred just outside Cambridge at Girton. The forebodings of friends like Waterlow and the Cornfords were as nothing to the commotion three years later when Philip announced his engagement to a beautiful, serious, spirited girl ten years younger than himself, Laura Insull (called 'Queen' because of her regal carriage and bearing).

She was a clergyman's daughter, orphaned, penniless, but not in the least daunted by onlookers like General Pinney who freely declared it was monstrous for a healthy girl and potential mother of sons to shackle herself to a tragic wreck like Philip: the outraged pink party was not mollified by her declaration that patriots who applauded the brides of wounded heroes shipped back from the trenches could hardly object to her choosing a man of brilliant intellect maimed by heredity rather than war. She and Philip met in August 1914, and fell in love almost on sight: they were married the following June in spite of threats, inducements, moral blackmail (Laura's employer, the botanist Ethel Sargant, offered her an allowance of £100 a year together with provision in her will if she would give up the marriage), and stony silence from the Jourdains: 'the absurd meanness of most of my family does make me feel that I have only you,' wrote Philip to Laura on 4 July 1915, eight days after the wedding. 'Except my mother, Milly and Margaret, who have been nice, not a single one has given me a present or even written to me about my marriage . . .'

The marriage proved a success, a source of great happiness and strength on both sides as even Miss Sargant grudgingly conceded, though Philip's family could never bring themselves to acknow-ledge Laura's existence. The sheer obstructionism that made them object to one another's marriages as a matter of course was shar-pened, in this case, by financial anxiety, and a no less pronounced family prudishness. 'I see she is good,' wrote Milly of Laura during the engagement, 'but it shocks me more and more that he should think of marriage. Well, don't bother. I am rather glad there are people like Margaret and me who don't marry.' Margaret explained the position to young Hester: 'Margaret once told me that she had never had any desire whatever for marriage or motherhood . . . She thought this "neuter" feeling might have been a safeguard as the genes of this sad family were probably hidden in her.'[56] Raymond said the same ('Raymond was very embittered towards the end of his life and told me that the Jourdains were meant to die out,' wrote Frank's daughter Violet[57]), and Milly found marriage in general frankly baffling ('I can't really understand it except for the sake of the children, but that isn't enough, do you think?'). Margaret died, like her four sisters, unmarried, and though the five brothers each took a wife—Henry took two—only Frank had children: they were born before the disease affecting Philip and Milly had declared itself fully, and all three died (the eldest as a boy at school) without issue, so that by the middle of the century it was clear that the Jourdains, like the Compton-Burnetts—families of ten and thirteen children respectively—drew the line at reproducing themselves.

Margaret herself sided emphatically with the spinsters in Ivy's books who are apt to reply to any suggestion that marriage might mean a fuller life: 'I don't want the things it would be full of.'[58] But her *Outdoor Breviary* shows signs of a struggle much like Philip's to subdue unruly feelings in the many passages calling for strength, stoicism and self-denial, or—almost continuously in the Broadwindsor sections—celebrating the 'bare and sterile' consolations of age and autumn. The *Poems*, which appeared in 1911, are dedicated 'To Janette' who is said to have paid for them to be published, and an undated note, from Broadwindsor—'My dear Jane, Here are a few last desperate violets laid at your feet. M.J.'[59]—might possibly point to a more passionate attachment. Certainly Janette was generally agreed to have found women more attractive than men, except for her younger brother Willie who was the love of her life as he had been, at one stage, of Ernest Thesiger's: she and Ernest apparently married on the strength of their mutual adoration of Willie and, after the marriage (which was never consummated[60]), Janette ranked high on the list of Margaret's women friends whom Ivy mistrusted.

But, whether or not the *Breviary* records a specific emotional crisis, it clearly reflects the precautionary withdrawal and distancing in Margaret that made Milly and Frances grumble about her heartlessness, her mockery, the strain her presence imposed on Milly's gentler, more pliable temperament. Every withdrawal of stimulus—leaving Cambridge, Frances' marriage, Philip's removal and, still more painful, his subsequent absorption in Laura—had meant a marked physical deterioration in Milly. She had supported Philip's departure in 1911 on the grounds that, as he grew more and more hopelessly dependent, burial alive at Broadwindsor must be unendurable for his adventurous spirit; but she seems to have resigned herself to her own living death by the summer of 1915 when Philip paid his last visit to the family.

She had put away her drawing things for ever the year before and would shortly give up driving her donkey cart. 'My body is triumphing over my spirit,' she wrote to Frances when Henry left England for the Dardanelles in 1915 and, after Rupert Brooke's death at Gallipoli, 'This is a wretched letter but what can you expect from a degenerate mind? Only write to me. Your C.M.J.' Her loneliness, despair and increasing physical pain were met thereafter with a passive endurance that Margaret also fought hard to achieve in the years spent watching her sister slowly turn to stone. Milly felt her spirit shrivel within her, lamenting 'the dried-up state of my mind and body' in her very last letter in 1926 to Frances. Margaret had described the same process in the *Breviary* nearly twenty years earlier in terms that seem by comparison the height of youthful romanticism: 'What a reducing quality there is in subjecting oneself to the open air, until some quality of the spirit seems to die, as a little water dies in the sand, and one becomes passive with a wise passivity.'[61]

iv

A sandy, gritty dryness was one of the first things people noticed about Margaret in middle age when, for all her gaiety and vigour, she struck most of her friends as embittered. So were all the Jourdains more or less, including even Philip who had for most of his life no alternative save to stifle personal feelings in work. Henry did the same when his beloved Connaught Rangers were disbanded,* and so did Frank ('My Father . . . sacrificed his family life

* As the Rangers' last commanding officer, Henry subsequently published a history of the regiment, followed by numerous pamphlets itemizing its medals, decorations, mess plate, etc.

and also his priesthood to ornithology,' wrote Violet Clifton Smith[62]), whose monumental five-volume *Handbook of British Birds* set standards of scientific breadth and accuracy that have scarcely yet been superseded. As for Margaret, she set out quite consciously to eradicate in herself all trace of the romantic girl who had wandered the hills round Broadwindsor, seeing visions and hearing voices, communing with 'Pan of the promontories' on Pilsden Hill and fancying that birds were 'the loosened souls of a tree'. 'She made herself work at documentation,' said Joan Evans, describing the years before the First World War when Margaret had insisted on the need to cultivate flatness and factual precision. 'She trained me. She made me translate French sonnets, and so on.'

Hence presumably Margaret's own French and German translations, her editions of Horace and Diderot, the gradual ruthless elimination from her own style of any flicker of individuality or ornament. Her actual writing in the pioneering books that made her name between the wars is painfully skimpy and dull (most of them consist of a brief introductory chapter or two followed by little more than catalogue lists). Margaret frankly despised the frailty and potential fallibility involved in offering to assess or draw conclusions from original research. Her furniture articles eventually grew so desiccated—'like dry seed cake' said Dorothy Stroud, who began her career as an editorial secretary on *Country Life*—that Christopher Hussey was obliged to ginger them up in the office. He was also called in to add a graceful, explanatory preface to what ought to have been her magnum opus, *The Work of William Kent*, in 1948. But Margaret's text consists of sixty pages in all, stitching together the admittedly meagre documentation with no attempt to interpret Kent's revolution in taste, or relate it to any historical context: one has only to compare the pedestrian prose of this official rehabilitation with the fire and indignation of her original defence of Kent, written almost forty years earlier in the first of the Lenygon books, * to see how far the process of suppression had gone.

---

* 'Had Kent worked in France, instead of England, his name would have been world-wide and examples of his craft would have been almost priceless . . . At the present day Kent is ignored by the many and harshly criticised by the few; one or two modern writers have embellished their pages with illustrations of his work, while at the same time they timidly abuse him for no apparent reason beyond lack of authority for praising him . . .' (*The Decoration and Furniture of English Mansions during the Seventeenth and Eighteenth Centuries* by Francis Lenygon, pp. 36, 43 and 46).

It is the process Ivy described in *Daughters and Sons* when Miss Marcon, encouraging France Ponsonby to take her first faltering steps as an author, ruefully compares her own scholarly achievement with the sort of writing that is done by brains and not training:

> I have trained myself to be accurate and industrious and other low things; trained myself; that is the pity of it, for I began by being as untrained as anyone. I am not one of those people who are born trained.[63]

No more was Margaret born trained. By the time she met Ivy, she had pretty well got the better of the side of herself that survives only feebly and drily in *Buchanan's Hotel*. Twenty years of research and grinding hackwork had turned her into a pundit much in demand to sustain the growing vogue for Georgian furniture and decoration. But it was clearly impossible for Margaret to survive without patronage of one sort or another, perhaps especially in the years immediately after the First World War when she found herself for the first time, in her forties, released from family ties. For a decade and more before that she had relied on Alice and Janette for encouragement, commissions, introductions, somewhere to stay and, especially from Janette, a good deal of financial help 'delicately and unobtrusively given'.[64] But Alice married John Marcon in 1913 and went to live at Highclere near Newbury, while Janette's marriage to Ernest four years later meant that Margaret no longer possessed any fixed foothold in London. She still paid visits and came up on business but her permanent base was Broadwindsor until, in 1919, her mother moved out of the manor house leaving Margaret high and dry—'*sur le pavé*', in Joan Evans' phrase—with nowhere to go and a lasting grudge against her sister Eleanor for the high-handed way in which she had broken up the family home.

What seems to have happened is that Eleanor, always autocratic and growing more so after she succeeded Miss Moberly in 1915 as Principal of St Hugh's, decided without consulting, or even telling, her sister that it would suit her personal convenience to settle the family at Oxford. She had always detested her obligatory, half-yearly visits to Broadwindsor, resenting especially the indignity of being fetched from the station in a farmer's gig, and no doubt depressed by the state of the household she found when she got there. Old Mrs Jourdain was seventy-seven in 1919, Milly by now wholly dependent on her nurse Elsie Barton. They were in no position to protest at whatever plans might be made on their behalf, being largely supported by Eleanor (well off by Jourdain standards on account of *An Adventure*), and by whatever contribution could be extracted from Frank, Raymond and Henry (Arthur, Milly's favourite brother, had been killed in France in 1918, when the family's miserly behaviour towards his widow added yet another black mark to the tally of Jourdain scandal in the village). Eleanor seized the opportunity of one of Margaret's trips to London to persuade Henry, now their mother's sole surviving trustee— classed by Margaret with Frank as the most disagreeable of all their brothers—that it was high time to transfer the family to somewhere smaller and more accessible where they might be kept more easily under her eye. They settled on 24, St Margaret's Road, Oxford, almost next door to St Hugh's: a mean little house only just big enough for Milly, her mother and the nurse with a spare room for Eleanor but none left over for Margaret.

Philip, who might have sympathized, was immersed in trouble of his own that summer. As he lay clenched ever more closely in the tightening grip of paralysis, he had started a wretched feud with Russell that began with editorial misunderstandings over money and escalated when Russell remained unconvinced by a new proof of the multiplicative axiom on which Philip had been working since 1916. The proof (since shown to be faulty) became an obsession. Driven nearly frantic by pain and by the knowledge that he lay dying with what he saw as the crown of his life's work unrecognized, Philip begged Russell to visit him in September 1919, to hear the latest addition to his proof. Russell refused (on the grounds that, even for the sake of a dying man, it could never be right to entertain arguments incompatible with mathematical truth), then relented too late: Philip, who had somehow hung on all summer in hopes of convincing Russell, was already unconscious by the time Russell's telegram arrived and he died five days later on 1 October.[65]

Margaret, who had taken over a good deal of Philip's editorial work in the past year, spent part of the summer travelling between his home at Fleet in Hampshire and her mother's in St Margaret's Road. She must have understood, perhaps shared, the 'speechless desolation of pain' that his death meant to Milly, who was already installed in the narrow room in North Oxford where she was to spend the rest of her life. Many of Milly's poems describe this suburban exile, sleepless nights of waiting for the dawn, days spent gazing through brick walls at the imagined hills and fields of memory. Some are prayers for death, others passionate evocations of the countryside, still others combine both themes:

> 'Death, like a narrow stream, divides
>   That heavenly land from ours.'

> O only once to loose my hold, and slip
> Down the familiar bank, and feel the chill
> Of water lapping round my feet, and hear
> The sounds of distant music in the wind.

> And yet in dreams I know the growing fear
> Of living waves that rise and rise around,
> That grip my throat, and make it hard to bow
> My head and know what I have never known.

> And then I cry that I may see again
> The crocus in the grass of early Spring.

What Margaret felt is impossible to say. Though his comprehensive *History of Mathematical Thought* remained unfinished, and his proof was eventually discredited, Philip had achieved a personal fulfilment and public recognition that neither of his closest sisters had known. For nearly a quarter of a century Margaret stood firm, putting duty before inclination, and now the rug had been pulled from under her feet. She told Hester how deeply she disapproved of handicapped people being shut away, as Milly now was, in concealment and isolation. But Eleanor's intervention meant that Margaret could do no more for Milly; and there are indications that Milly herself found Margaret's unremitting scepticism too hard to take at the end of her life and transferred her allegiance to Eleanor. At all events, Milly's future was now out of Margaret's hands; and though in a sense it must have been a relief to be free, she was also for the first time unwanted, besides being wholly reliant on what she could earn to keep herself off the streets. It meant that she was emotionally as well as practically at a loose end when she travelled up to London in the week of Philip's funeral to move into Ivy's flat.

In so far as the various flats they shared always belonged to Ivy (whose income remained until the slump between four and five times the size of Margaret's), their alliance clearly had practical advantages, like all the other close relationships with comparatively wealthy women who were far more important to Margaret than men in both private and professional life. There was never any shortage of admirers more than happy to finance Margaret in return for what she herself (describing Kent's relationship with his patrons) called 'companionship and services'.[66] One of them even went so far as to make her an allowance of a hundred pounds a year, paid quarterly from the end of 1924, on condition that she made no attempt whatsoever to discover its source.[67] She never did, though rumour variously identified the anonymous donor as one or other of the generous and affectionate friends of whom she probably saw more between the wars than anyone else except Ivy—Lady Waechter, Lady Assheton-Smith and the Hon. Mrs Levy.

Molly Waechter was Irish, large, cheerful, expansive, somewhat disorganized but often extravagantly kind, a skilled embroidress and châtelaine of Ramsnest in Surrey where Margaret frequently stayed before the Waechter divorce in 1924; after which Molly (who moved to Buckingham Gate and was often at the Linden or Braemar Gardens flats with one or more of her three children, for whom Margaret and Ivy organized playgoing and tea parties) was in no position to make provision for others. Sybil Assheton-Smith was the childless third wife and widow of the baronet Sir Charles Assheton-Smith, stepmother of Robin and Lady Juliet Duff, owner of an exquisitely appointed house in Queen Anne's Gate (where meals were served off gilt dishes and even the cushions were medieval): a remote, even regal figure highly esteemed by the furniture trade and genuinely devoted to Margaret, who catalogued her collections, located new pieces for her, accompanied her on visits to Paris and lunched with her generally two or three times a week in the 1930s. Sybil had begun to monopolize Margaret after Nelly Levy married Basil Ionides in 1930. Before that, Margaret had been in the habit of dropping in most days at the large, convivial Lowndes Square luncheon parties served by butler and footman, after which a chauffeur would call to take Nelly on her afternoon rounds of sales rooms and dealers with Margaret, who seemed to the Levy children almost a fixture at home in the 1920s: 'She was always there. A jolly old schoolmistress, frightfully dowdy, hair in a little cowpat—part of the family really. A nice old bun.'[68] Herman claimed that Margaret told him the money came 'from dear Sybil', but in fact her secret benefactor was almost certainly Nelly Levy* attempting with characteristic generosity to lessen the financial discrepancy which seemed to furniture friends to constitute Ivy's sole hold over Margaret.

Not that Ivy's indifference to furniture necessarily precluded her taking a professional interest in Margaret: the frictions and deepening gloom of the Jourdains at home—the tensions surrounding Philip's deathbed and later erupting far more publicly round Eleanor at the close of her life—held something of the lure and lustre of a collector's item for anyone with a connoisseur's interest in families. The Jourdains moreover belonged to the world Ivy wrote about—the isolated, impoverished, small country gentry —as the Compton-Burnetts never had done. In this sense, collaboration with Margaret might be said to have proved in the end as useful to Ivy as Margaret's expertise in another field ever was to Lenygon or Hudson, Nelly or Sybil.

But Ivy, who was two years younger than Milly, belonged in many ways with the much younger girls who had always touched Margaret's heart in time of stress or discouragement. Margaret said afterwards that Ivy looked so ill when they first met it seemed as though she could scarcely survive.[69] Ivy in 1919 had reached probably the lowest ebb of her life. She had recovered from the pneumonia of the year before but was still fast in the grip of that mental and spiritual lethargy Margaret had resisted so hard in Milly; and her invalid state—in the months, even years when she lay about the flat eating sweets, reading Wilkie Collins and silently watching Margaret's callers—certainly puzzled old friends like Janet Beresford and Arthur Waley. It sounds the sort of condition Ivy's father had once diagnosed in her mother when she, too, collapsed in her youth after prolonged strain brought on by 'family trouble' ('People could not think what had come over her. She is one of those human high-breds who will not cave in, but, if duty calls, will go on till they drop: till then, existing on their "go" rather than on their physique . . .'[70]); and something in Margaret clearly responded to

---

* The cheques started arriving in September 1924, before Margaret had met Lady Assheton-Smith, and they continued after her death in 1943, coming via Mrs Levy's solicitors (Raisley Moorsom thought the money came from Lady Waechter, who was said by others to have left Margaret an annuity of £100, but Lady Waechter died four years after Margaret whose annuity—which was £25—came in fact from Lady Assheton-Smith).

Ivy's distress much as James Compton-Burnett had done to his wife's.

In later life when they had settled into the comfortable, often captious intimacy of an old married couple, Margaret always remained the active partner, the forceful, enterprising, in some ways masculine one of the two, though—in a circle much given to well-informed speculation as to its members' sex lives—their oldest friends agreed that it was frankly preposterous to picture Ivy and Margaret as lovers.* Margaret's censoriousness ruled out homosexuality as much as heterosexual frailty. 'She belonged to what my mother used to call the army of unenjoyed women,' said James Lees-Milne: 'Margaret had a very unenjoyed look about her.' If her early life had, as she said, extinguished the faintest twinge of sexual desire, her tastes, as soon as she was in a position to suit herself, ran to feather boas, pretty hats and the attentions of charming young men like Lees-Milne who (as their ranks were thinned by marriage or postings abroad) continued to the end of her life to succeed one another in waves.

But her feeling for Ivy was deep, constant and grounded in that rush of fierce, anxious tenderness that any sign of strain in Ivy —exhaustion after finishing a book, or a return to earlier hurts brought back by the Second World War—could always evoke in her friend. It explains Ivy's unexpected dependence on Margaret as well as the dominance over her noted by so many of their visitors: the fact that, though Ivy was the housekeeper, the one who poured tea and dealt with the tradespeople, she was also the one who needed to be looked after, indulged, even humoured. The protective element in their relationship was strong from the start and still uppermost in Roger Kidd's memories of Margaret twenty years later: 'Her consideration for Ivy was remarkable; tender, self-denying and dignified. When Ivy was demanding, Margaret would say, "She's like a child." She encouraged Ivy to meet new people and introduced her to many of her museum friends.'[71]

Work was always Margaret's remedy for people in trouble. It

---

* Even Willie King, who was adept at coupling the most improbable sleeping partners, admitted that in this case it was out of the question; the only dissenting voice among Ivy's intimate friends came from Herman, who tended, at any rate towards the end of his life, to see homosexuality as an almost universal condition ('The women he knew who he asserted were lesbians, Wembley Stadium would not hold.' Burkhart 2, p. 44).

was presumably at Margaret's suggestion round about 1919 that Ivy first read Samuel Butler, whose *Note-Books* affected her so strongly that she wrote in her copy, underneath Butler's description of people whose life is a partial death ('a long, living death-bed, so to speak, of stagnation and nonentity'), her own terse confession: 'I am a living witniss of this crushing lifless stagnation of the spirit' (sic).[72] Margaret heartily endorsed Butler's exposure, in *The Way of All Flesh*, of 'the glooms and deceptions of the English upper and middle-class households'; and the prescription worked for Ivy as effectively as research into jewellery had once done for Joan Evans, or drawing classes for Milly.

Margaret gave Ivy confidence, and perhaps something more that surfaced in the books she began writing again in the 1920s when, as she put it, 'my brain came back'. Uncharitable characters like Emily Herrick and Theresa Fletcher in *Pastors and Masters*, or their immediate successors Sarah Wake and Caroline Lang in *Brothers and Sisters*, belong unmistakably to Philip Jourdain's blue party. They make short work of received opinion; they vet themselves and each other unmercifully for the least trace of smugness or falsity; they are dab hands at debunking their friends; and they do it in Margaret's voice. 'Margaret talked like a character out of Ivy's books,' said Raisley Moorsom, who had known both ladies before they ever set eyes on each other, and who recognized a familiar tone in *Pastors and Masters*: 'Ivy couldn't do it then. In the end she learnt to talk like one of her own characters.'

Their friends in the 1920s and 1930s all agreed that Margaret's 'quiet biting sparkle of wit'[73] could be far more ruthless than Ivy's. 'She was a very acid type,' said Ralph Edwards. 'Ivy wasn't bad at acidity, but Margaret was rather better.' There could be no more persuasive refutation of Ivy's first novel, *Dolores*, with its almost hysterical insistence on the cardinal importance of sacrificing one's own life to others, than the amiable selfishness first propounded in *Pastors and Masters* (' "Egotism is a gift, like anything else," said Herrick'[74]). Thereafter Margaret's doctrine of self-reliance is elaborated in every single one of Ivy's 'silly little books' as an alternative to the tyrannical excesses of far more dangerous egotists like Hetta Ponsonby in *Daughters and Sons* (or for that matter Ivy herself, in the years when she too had tried to impose her will on her younger sisters at Hove):

'Why is Aunt Hetta getting so much worse?'

'She tried to live for others,' said France, 'and people try to improve what they live for, and that is the end.'[75]

One of the best descriptions of the relationship Margaret eventually arrived at with Ivy came from Rosamond Lehmann, who had not yet met either of them when she set about analysing the work of I. Compton-Burnett in 1937: 'In each novel . . . good is embodied in the persons of independent, shrewd, rather donnish women past their youth: Nature's spinsters, if not actually unwed: for Miss Compton-Burnett does not believe in marriage. An unambiguous respect is accorded to friendships between such women.'[76] Marriage in Ivy's books provides scope above all for the love of power and the horrors that flow from it, a side of family life about which Margaret thought the less said the better. 'It cannot be said strongly enough that Ivy had *genius*, and of course Margaret had erudition —two entirely different things,' said Herman.[77]

It was a verdict Margaret could never accept without some faint sense of grievance ('*That* Mr. Mortimer says Ivy's a genius . . .'[78]). Her teasing, her scorn for things in general and 'Ivy's trash' in particular, gave some indication of the price she herself had paid for her own victory over imagination and feeling, for she came after all of a long line of first-rate raconteurs. Eleanor (who owned to 'psychical gifts' descended from the family's much vaunted Huguenot stock[79]) made what amounted to a professional speciality out of tales of the supernatural; Henry's memoirs are full of tall stories (including several told by their grandfather, a friend of Walter Scott, who claimed to have seen the face of Robert the Bruce before it crumbled to dust when his tomb was opened in 1819, and once to have escaped by the skin of his teeth from an army of homicidal rats); Philip turned out a steady stream of 'Cynical Ballads', 'Dorset Stories', fairy tales and fables like 'The Fate of the Pragmatic Cock' and 'The Bergsonian Hen'. Margaret when young had once peddled a highly superior line in fantasy, rhyming nonsense and ghost stories, and no doubt the family tendency towards romancing reinforced her subsequent determination to stifle all trace of the fanciful in herself.

Certainly Eleanor's inability to distinguish very sharply between reality and illusion twice brought her to grief. *An Adventure* had made her famous, but demands by some few disobliging critics for more scientific standards of evidence had come as a nasty shock (and Mrs Sidgwick's review remained a sore point with both authors to the end of their lives). Far more damaging was the public scandal that terminated her regime at St Hugh's in 1924. She had dismissed a young history tutor, Cecilia Ady, on charges of disloyalty which boiled down to the fact that the two had never got on, whereupon half the college council resigned, together with a number of dons. Accusations of lying, spying, victimization and emotional blackmail were freely bandied about; pupils from St Hugh's were boycotted by other colleges; and, after successive interventions from parents, old students, and the university authorities, the matter was adjudicated by the Chancellor, Lord Curzon, who exonerated Miss Ady while confidently anticipating constitutional reform and 'changes in personnel' at St Hugh's. A friendly don, coming to warn Eleanor of the news, is said to have been greeted with the words: 'We've won, haven't we?'[80] The report was dated 31 March 1924. Eleanor died of heart failure six days later. Miss Moberly maintained that she had been murdered and the *Oxford Magazine* reported her death with the tag from Tacitus, '*Felix opportunitate mortis*' (which might be roughly translated: 'Lucky for her she is dead').

Milly and her mother shared Miss Moberly's bitterness. Feelings ran high on both sides at St Hugh's, and for Milly—impotent, immobilized, tormented by physical pain as well as by grief and loss and the misery of having watched her sister publicly hounded down—the only consolation was that Eleanor had 'died fighting for what she thought right'. Laura Jourdain had used almost identical words about Philip and, whatever else the family may have felt, they might surely take pride in the invincible courage and stubbornness that had sustained both Jourdains to the end. Even Margaret, who had suffered all her life from Eleanor's domineering instincts, remained loyal in public (Miss Ady once stayed in the same hotel as Margaret and Ivy with whom there was a definite awkwardness, according to Nancy Mitford[81]), though invariably caustic in private about her sister's disasters. There was no open breach but Margaret's 'disapproving detachment' seems to have been too much for Milly, watching her own life drain away as Margaret's caught the full tide: she dedicated her poems in 1924 'To E.F.J.' and made a typically Jourdainian will two years later, distributing her minute capital with scrupulous fairness in legacies of £5 or £10 to all her surviving brothers, sister and sisters-in-law with the sole exception of Margaret. She died on 23 December 1926, aged forty-four, after a life that for all its suffering and struggle leaves an impression of singular sweetness, like the robin's song in her own poem, 'September Dawn':

> The pure chill air of dawn blows on my face,
> And in the room the sheets grow white again.
> A robin's song drops in the quiet air
> So sad and fresh and incomplete.

When her mother died, a month to the day after Milly, Margaret had long since cut her losses so far as the past was concerned. It is a moot point if Margaret talked much with Ivy, or in any but the most glancing terms, about her peculiarly sour and rancorous family life; but, if the St Hugh's affair epitomized everything she had always disliked and rejected in Eleanor, it must have confirmed her own decision to come down heavily on the side of objective, verifiable fact. Margaret's mistrust of fiction became thereafter a standing joke between herself and Ivy: 'She said none of Ivy's books made sense,' said James Lees-Milne, who maintained that Margaret's powers of observation were even more frightening than Ivy's. Margaret herself seems to have admitted something of the sort to John Bush, who joined the firm of Victor Gollancz at the end of the 1940s and was reading one of Ivy's novels on top of a bus when a fellow passenger leant over and said: 'I write all her books.'[82] The stranger was Margaret Jourdain. When Hester once asked Margaret if she minded seeing her books published under the names of Lenygon and Mulliner, she said that it never mattered to her whose name was given as author. But presumably just for once, anonymously, to someone she did not know and had no expectation of meeting again, Margaret could not resist claiming credit for having made Ivy—or at least for having set her on the path towards achieving the twin goals admired by Emily Herrick: '"I grow prouder and prouder of you, darling," said Emily. "An author and an egotist, and both of them such lovely things."'[83]

CHAPTER FOUR

'A woman of blameless character'

i

THERE IS NO specific portrait of Margaret in Ivy's books, save perhaps for touches of her manner and looks bestowed on Maria Shelley (in *Two Worlds and their Ways*), who is affectionately known as 'my pretty' by her husband, Sir Roderick: 'With her broad, massive frame, her crumpled weather beaten face, her prominent, greenish eyes and the signs of fifty-three years, she was no one's pretty but Sir Roderick's . . .'[1] Blunt-spoken, good-natured, able, ambitious, industrious, an altogether higher type than her husband (though often too immersed in her work to pay him more than perfunctory attention), Maria, like Margaret, is given to making notes on the backs of old envelopes and turning the table into a haystack with her papers. Nearly all the happiest marriages in Ivy's books started out, like the Shelleys', on a practical rather than romantic footing (romance being generally reserved by the husband exclusively for a first wife who died young): relaxed and restful affairs between non-combatants—sometimes more nearly refugees—who look on, often aghast, at the upheaval and wreckage of other, more strenuous lives. This was very much the case with Margaret and Ivy in the thirty years and more when, though their professional spheres remained sharply distinct, they were otherwise scarcely separated, even at parties. However querulous each might seem on occasion (and there are many stories of Ivy's bossiness, Margaret's boredom and irritation), there can be no doubt that what had begun by all accounts as a marriage of convenience became for both the central feeling of their lives.

But memories of Ivy's first love for her brother Noel remained to the end of her life so strong that few of her friends had the nerve to mention his name, let alone talk freely about him in her presence; she herself could sometimes hardly speak of him at the end of her life without tears welling up. 'Ivy very rarely put into words what was her real feeling,' said Vera Compton-Burnett. 'She put herself into her books and she was a secret otherwise, known only to

herself,' said her sister Juliet. What is certain is that Ivy, who struck
sensitive friends like Janet Beresford as more enigmatic but also far
more emotional than Margaret, had inherited something of her
mother's passionate and demanding temperament. In later life, after
Margaret's death, when she would very occasionally discuss such
things with a woman friend, she talked to Sonia Orwell about
sexual passion with a depth, thoroughness and intimacy that left her
ostensibly more experienced interlocutor greatly shaken.[2] Ivy
made it clear to Sonia that she had never actually made love; and she
discussed with another young married friend, Barbara Robinson,[3]
the cost of the First World War in sexual frustration and deprivation
for a whole generation of women: ' "Men can't do without it, you
know," Ivy said with a bleak look. "Women have to." '[*]

Of the two great affairs of her life, the first had ended tragically
with Noel's marriage and death while the second, for all its apparent
smooth running, seems to have involved some sort of initial
explosion that left a residue still smouldering half a century later.
When Margaret first moved in with Ivy, their mutual attachment
had been keenly resented by Winifred Felkin (who seems never to
have recovered entirely from her sense of exclusion), and also
perhaps by Janette, whose devotion to Margaret remained unim-
paired by a marriage so unexacting on both sides that a great many
of Ernest's friends never suspected him of having a wife at all. But
the friendship was still more trying for Joan Evans, who would
dearly have liked the privilege of providing a flat for Margaret
herself at the end of the First World War. Newly down from
Oxford, far better off than Ivy and still deeply under Margaret's
spell, Joan was miserably lonely in her mother's large, grand,
unfriendly house in North Kensington. With her big black hats, her
celebrated brother and scholarly father, her aura of intellectual as
well as material riches, she seemed wonderfully dashing in those
days to Margaret's other protégée, the schoolgirl Hester Pinney;
and perhaps she seemed something of a menace to Ivy, who shared

---

[*] 'In judging Ivy's sexual proclivities, I should at once make a distinction between
homoerotic and homophile . . . ,' wrote her friend, the novelist Francis King
(who put Ivy in the second category): 'All this would not be worth probing were it
not that Ivy wrote about sexual passion so convincingly—far better than D. H.
Lawrence. This is one of the miracles of her art: she was writing about something
which she herself had never experienced except (where novelists often experience
things most intensely) in her imagination.' Letter to H.S., 26 June 1983.

neither her professional interest in Margaret's fields of decoration
and jewellery, nor her close links with the Jourdain family.

Joan for her part thought Ivy common, nowhere near Margaret's
equal in brains let alone breeding, and almost criminally indifferent
to the beautiful things Margaret prized above all else ('That was the
basis of what I am bound to call the tragedy between them,' said
Joan, who put Margaret's coldness and dryness in later life down
solely to Ivy's stranglehold on her spirit). For a time the three got on
well enough. But Joan, who prided herself on being probably the
only person ever to have made friends with both Margaret and
Eleanor Jourdain, began spending more and more time at St Hugh's
as one of the makeshift tutorial staff hastily assembled at the end of
1923 to tide the college over when reputable dons withdrew their
services (a stink bomb[4] let off in Miss Evans' room signified the
students' indignant rejection of this arrangement).

Always the Principal's staunch supporter, Joan herself came to
think that 'the balance of Miss Jourdain's mind was disturbed' and
tried desperately to persuade her to resign, even providing her in
secret with a substantial sum of money on which to do so. It proved
an unwise move for, when Eleanor died on 6 April 1924, she was
found to have left everything (except her shares which went to
Henry as executor, with instructions to hold them in reserve for her
mother and Milly) to Joan, including the family jewellery. Margaret was outraged: the Jourdain pieces, though pretty, were not
particularly valuable (unlike Joan's own extensive collection which
Margaret had written up in *Queen* that April and which eventually
formed the nucleus of the V&A's holdings) but Margaret, never
inclined to concede Eleanor's superior claims as the eldest daughter,
had always been especially fond of jewellery. 'And this was where
Ivy was so clever—Ivy said I had nabbed the lot. She persuaded
Margaret to write to my mother,' said Joan, who felt herself
hopelessly outmanoeuvred ('I was a sitting bird') by what seemed
masterly tactics on Ivy's part. Harassed, isolated, worn down by
the strain of the St Hugh's debacle, Joan had no one in whom to
confide her own case (which was that the solicitor, having drawn
the will 'in an old-fashioned way', had provided her with a list of
recipients among whom Eleanor had meant her possessions to be
distributed) except Henry Jourdain, who first agreed to explain
matters to Margaret but afterwards thought better of his offer
without telling Joan.

Margaret refused to see her; Lady Evans (whose horror of drawing on capital made it impossible for her daughter to explain what she had done to put Eleanor under an obligation) took Margaret's part; Milly and her mother were unbudgeable on Eleanor's side, and in any case so distraught by this time as to be past intervening with anyone. Margaret was implacable. She never spoke to Joan again, went out of her way to give a hostile review twenty-five years later to her mediaeval volume of the Oxford history of art, and generally saw to it that the feud remained undimmed to the last. Joan detested Ivy—'poison Ivy'—to the end of her life. As for Ivy, her feelings, though never overt, were still palpable long after Margaret's death when Madge Garland inadvertently mentioned a book by Joan Evans: 'Ivy said nothing. But I knew that I had stubbed my toe. I knew I must never, never mention that name again. The temperature dropped to freezing point.'[5]

Ivy's jealousy of Margaret was always intense, and quite distinct from envy (far from resenting Margaret's fame, Ivy went to considerable lengths to play down her own as soon as it gave signs of becoming a sore point with her friend). It showed itself rather in her evident unhappiness whenever a new admirer made a dead set at Margaret, her dread at being left out (hence Ivy's invariable inclusion in all but the most tedious, technical furniture visits), the inner trepidation that made the prospect of even a brief separation from Margaret seem almost insupportable. She made no attempt to conceal her feelings from close friends like Herman, who said Ivy always insisted that jealousy was the dominant motive in human behaviour. He backed vanity himself; and the two would sit together on winter evenings after tea, with the lamps unlit in the bare, high-ceilinged Braemar Mansions drawing room, dissecting their friends in the light of their respective theories and sternly contradicting one another's diagnoses: 'We would sit there like the fates with their scissors, Ivy saying "Jealousy!" and I would say "Vanity!"'[6] It sounds a melancholy scene, borne out by the many other friends who were also well aware by involuntary signs and promptings of the jealous nature Ivy kept firmly in check. It was presumably what Ivy meant when she said that the character in fiction with whom she most strongly identified was Charlotte Mullen,[7] the jealous, tyrannical, eventually murderous heroine of that strange and powerful novel, *The Real Charlotte* (1894), by O. Œ. Somerville and Martin Ross.

It is at first sight a disconcerting claim. Charlotte Mullen is a jolly old Irish eccentric—drab, squat, grasping and almost grotesquely plain, famous in the Lismoyle neighbourhood for her cutting tongue and racy stories, but otherwise widely regarded as a thoroughly amiable stout party: a view shared even by the few who, like Charlotte's pretty young cousin Francie, are uneasily, indeed subconsciously aware of 'the weight of the real Charlotte's will and the terror of her personality'.[8] The book shows how, without in the least disturbing her reputation for harmless goodwill, Charlotte very nearly kills Francie (for marrying the man Miss Mullen had in mind for herself), and actually brings off the death of a previous rival in a scene strikingly like the one in which Josephine Napier also gets away with murder in *More Women Than Men*.

More Women Than Men (last of the four high-spirited early novels, after which Ivy set about coming more seriously to grips with the infinite varieties of human aggression that preoccupied her for the rest of her life) is a work of transition and something of a freak, the jerkiest and in some ways the least satisfactory of all Ivy's novels. For all its rather startling modernity of tone, the plot turns on the machinery of Victorian melodrama—one sub-plot revolving round a tall, dark, veiled stranger coming out of the night to revive memories of an ancient wrong, another round an illegitimate son reunited after twenty years with his long-lost mother ('Oscar Wilde is not so much borrowed from as contributed to,' wrote Asquith's daughter, Elizabeth Bibesco, at the time[9]). It also served as a convenient depository for various still more disparate oddments: its central character, Josephine Napier, for instance, clearly owes much to Eleanor Jourdain. Both are exceptionally efficient headmistresses of flourishing girls' schools worked up from scratch entirely by the prodigious industry of their respective founders (both had started modestly on capital borrowed from a friend, Josephine with twelve pupils, Eleanor at Corran with six[10]). Each attaches supreme, self-congratulatory importance to the education of girls (and hence to her own solemn, even semi-sacred role as its guardian and dispenser), and each is apt to make short work of facts that contradict or interfere with her own sovereign rule. Each functions in her middle fifties on the same inflammable mixture of vanity, touchiness, genuine concern for others shading into authoritarian control, and an appetite for flattery fed shamelessly by the more sycophantic members of her staff: Josephine's wheedling manner, covering a ruthlessness she barely troubles to conceal in private, closely corresponds to first-hand accounts of the almost hypnotic hold Eleanor Jourdain established over her own 'favourites' like Joan Evans.

But, however much Ivy may have amused herself at Eleanor's expense, she did it for fun, in the same casual spirit as she had once by her own account 'made use of' her Uncle Robert and Aunt Lizzie Blackie in *Dolores*, 'just to give a superficial touch to the personalities'.[11] Borrowing so much from Eleanor seems to have been, like the mock Victorian setting, yet another device to distract attention from undercurrents in *More Women Than Men* that remain too close for comfort to its author's own home life. For, at a deeper level and perhaps more directly than any of the other tyrants, Josephine derives ultimately from Ivy herself. The core of the book is its exploration—part humorous, part painfully explicit—of Josephine's passionate, possessive love for her nephew and adopted son, Gabriel Swift, who rouses in his formidable relative a disconcerting girlishness expressed in her constant complacent daydreaming of his masterfulness ('He does not let me forget it. He is my masculine companion, my protector'[12]), his jealousy, her own submission to his lover-like caprices:

> 'You will find it a change when he marries,' said Miss Rosetti.
> 'I must recognise that I have no prospect of such a change. His attitude towards me must keep me a prisoner: I don't know what any young woman would say to it. Well, I must remember that the tie of blood between us is not of the deepest kind. Anyhow, it is put aside by my young gentleman, in determining the basis of our intercourse. I am not his aunt any more than any other woman.'[13]

It is the sort of fatal boast bound, in literature at least, to be taken up by fate. Gabriel's prompt announcement of his engagement to the young Ruth Giffard turns Josephine—with her careful smile and hands trembling beneath her desk—into a monster at once pitiless and pitiful in her successive attempts to bully, override and ridicule the young couple, followed by her resolute refusal to acknowledge or discuss their marriage plans. Bottled-up emotion makes her pick a wretched quarrel with Gabriel on his wedding morning which, in Josephine's subsequent account of the affair to her senior staff, somehow re-emerges as a triumph for herself, with Gabriel ('he . . . fussed and fumed, and almost forgot to go to his own wedding'[14]) cast once again in his old role as jealous lover: 'I might have been the bride instead of her imminent aunt-in-law.' As so often with Ivy's tyrants, there is something irresistible about the sheer impudence of this reversal, whereby Josephine's humiliation is not so much accepted as abolished and her raging jealousy reconstrued as a fond, maternal indulgence towards the luckless Ruth: 'I daresay she found me a great rock to come up against; a formidable bulwark, built out of lifelong feelings; offered to her as an allurement, poor child, when she could only see it as a menace.'[15]

ii

People who knew Ivy well in the First World War, when her younger brother Noel became engaged to Tertia Beresford, used similar terms to describe what happened. 'Tertia found Ivy like a great rock,' said her sister-in-law Janet Beresford; and according to Vera Compton-Burnett, 'Tertia *didn't like* Ivy at all.'[16] 'So far as I remember Ivy made no mention of it [the future],' said Vera, discussing the unhappy months leading up to Noel's marriage and his posting to France in 1915: 'Silence was a weapon.' But Ivy, who played no part in Noel's hurried wedding preparations and did not attend the ceremony, afterwards made the best of a bad job, providing a home for Tertia in London, steadying her alarmingly susceptible nerves, and generally keeping an eye on her for Noel's sake in the dreadful winter and spring of 1916 which he spent in the trenches. Vera described Ivy's attitude to Tertia in these months and later as 'motherly almost'. 'Ivy helped them all through the marriage time,' said the Beresfords' old friend, Eva Fox; and, when Tertia swallowed sleeping tablets on learning of Noel's death, Ivy naturally took charge, finding a nursing home for the half-demented Tertia, sitting with her almost every day for well over a year, gradually pulling her through the breakdown that followed her unsuccessful suicide by an exertion of will for which her sister-in-law 'was not grateful . . . at all'.

When Ruth collapses in *More Women Than Men*, taking to her bed soon after the honeymoon under the strain of a renewed 'contest with Josephine',[17] it is Josephine who assumes control, calls a truce to the hostilities, sends Gabriel away and nurses his wife through pneumonia with tireless strength and devotion, sitting up night after night by her bedside and listening to her 'delirious murmurs' ('I cannot go to meet him now I am ill; but when I am well, I will go to him; and nobody shall watch us. We will tell her not to watch us'[18]). This is the scene in which Josephine, yielding like Charlotte Mullen to a sudden murderous impulse, lifts her half-conscious patient into the icy draught from an open window, relenting —again like Charlotte—almost at once in response to the girl's helpless appeal. In each case the victim dies,* leaving her tormentor appalled, grief-stricken (both Josephine and Charlotte weep copiously at the respective funerals), and rather rapidly reconciled to what comes to seem an unexpected stroke of luck. Neither at any point betrays the faintest sign of either guilt or satisfaction: 'The movements of Charlotte's character . . . were akin to those of some amphibious thing, whose strong, darting course under the water is only marked by a bubble or two, and it required an animal instinct to note them.'[19]

This sort of character movement, caught and pinned in its most intimate, infinitesimal workings, was what interested Ivy above all, though she approached it by very different methods from Somerville and Ross's comparatively conventional, if assured and subtle treatment: where they note the bubbles, Ivy learnt eventually to reproduce the darting course of the subconscious mind itself in the strange, supple, highly charged and passionate dialogue of her mature writing. But the direct authorial intervention and explanation she later almost entirely discarded is still occasionally invoked in More Women Than Men, at moments of crisis such as the one towards the end of the book where Felix Bacon (who has by this time supplanted Gabriel in Josephine's affections) comes in his turn to tell her of his own impending marriage: 'Josephine looked from him to Helen, as if she hardly followed his words. Afterwards she seemed to remember hearing her own voice, coming after a crash and through the ensuing din.'[20]

News of the engagement of a brother or close relative (Josephine calls herself Gabriel's 'aunt-sister'[21]), falling out of the blue with shattering force, is a recurrent motif in Ivy's books. In the next

---

* Charlotte's rival is a semi-invalid with a weak heart who dies of a heart attack because Charlotte denied her the medicinal drops that would have saved her life (The Real Charlotte, Chapter 32).

novel but one, *Daughters and Sons* (1937), it destroys the close relationship between the middle-aged brother and sister, John and Hetta Ponsonby: John's unexpected engagement to a comparative stranger drives Hetta (who has held out against the match in stubborn silence like Josephine) to stage a fake suicide in a last, vain attempt to teach her brother a lesson. In the novel after that, *A Family and a Fortune* (1939), Edgar and Dudley Gaveston find the mutual devotion of a lifetime shattered by Dudley's violent reaction to his brother's marriage to Maria Sloane ('Dudley looked at her and met her eyes, and in a moment they seemed to be ranged on opposite sides, contending for Edgar'[22]). Dudley, who had first proposed marrying Maria himself, had ceded her quite amicably to Edgar. It is the spectacle of his brother's love directed to another that turns Dudley from a tolerant, calm, sceptical observer into a raging fury:

> Maria stood apart, feeling she had nothing to do with the scene, that she must grope for its cause in a depth where different beings moved and breathed in a different air. The present seemed a surface scene, acted over a seething life, which had been calmed but never dead. She saw herself treading with care lest the surface break and release the hidden flood, felt that she learned at that moment how to do it, and would ever afterwards know. She did not turn to her husband, did not move or touch him. The tumult in his soul must die, the life behind him sink back into the depths, before they could meet on the level they were to know . . .[23]

This uncharacteristically explicit passage, describing the emotional shambles of the human heart that was to become Ivy's especial province, is perhaps the nearest she ever came to a manifesto (its language and imagery are closely paralleled in the actual manifesto issued on her behalf in 1956 by that doyenne of the French *nouveau roman*, Nathalie Sarraute[24]); and it sprang from a knot of ideas intimately associated with her own personal experience. The scene between the two Gavestons ends with Dudley leaving the house alone on a suicidal flight through the snow, contracting 'trouble with the lungs'[25] and very nearly dying in an episode based on Ivy's own critical illness in the winter of 1918. The course and circumstances of her pneumonia—the bitterly cold weather, the coughing, fever, delirium, weakness, the frantic attempts to get out of bed, the final crisis following a seemingly endless struggle for breath—are repeated in both Ruth's and Dudley's illnesses, and again in Horace Lamb's at the end of *Manservant and Maidservant* in 1947 (a collapse also precipitated by a jealous contest over a near-sibling*); and there can be no doubt that Ivy's return to health was a matter of emotional as much as physical recovery, as it is for Horace Lamb, and still more for Dudley Gaveston:

> The change was more rapid in his mind than his body . . . The threat of death with its lesson of what he had to lose, had shown him that life as he had lived it was enough. He asked no more than he had, chose to have only this. His own personality, free of the strain and effort of the last months, was as full and natural as it had been in his youth . . .[26]

Ivy's illness, too, marked a kind of release or abdication, the point at which she split her life in two, finally disclaiming any further attempt at domination in that clash of desire and will that had proved so ruinous for all the Compton-Burnetts at Hove. She had loved Noel with the passion and tenacity of an intensely emotional nature that had been denied all other outlet. He never failed her throughout the bleakest period of her adult life, the years of tyranny and isolation that had set in for the whole family with their father's death and closed over them completely when Guy died, a week before Ivy's twenty-first birthday in 1905. For the next ten years Noel had been her only comfort; but however hard it may have been to bear the news of his engagement—harder still to witness, as Ivy did 'all through the marriage time', his exclusive absorption in Tertia—nothing could in the end destroy a relationship far closer at bottom to the mutual security and trust taken for granted, in almost every single one of her books, between brother and sister than to the bullying, rivalrous, overtly sexual domination Josephine attempts to establish over Gabriel.

Whatever her own choice might have been in the matter, circumstances had ensured that Ivy's love for Noel approximated less to the Wordsworthian model (Ivy herself stoutly maintained that

---

* The outsider who comes between Horace and Mortimer Lamb (first cousins, born in the same house and brought up together from infancy) is Horace's wife Charlotte, whose proposed elopement with Mortimer eventually comes to nothing to the undisguised relief of both cousins, each having by this time realized (M&M, pp. 174 and 212) that losing the other is what he minds most of all.

William and his sister Dorothy had been lovers[27]) than to the Byronic, or at any rate to the valedictory mood of Byron's letter to his sister Augusta after their final parting in 1816:

> What a fool I was to marry, and *you* not very wise, my dear. We might have lived so single and so happy as old maids and bachelors. I shall never find anyone like you, nor you (vain as it may seem) like me . . . Had you but been a Nun, and I a Monk, that we might have talked through a grating instead of across the sea—no matter. My voice and my heart are ever thine . . .[28]

Incest remained always a welcome topic for discussion in Ivy's drawing room along with other forms of sexual obsession, transvestism and homosexuality. Lust in her books is glimpsed generally in incestuous or other furtive, illicit couplings—one thinks of Grant Edgeworth seducing his uncle's young wife by moonlight in *A House and Its Head*, Teresa Calderon locked in her father's embrace in *Elders and Betters*—or, among the relaxed and tolerant intellectuals of *More Women Than Men*, in Felix Bacon's sitting on Jonathan's knee, Maria Rosetti nuzzling Miss Luke in the corridor on her way to Helen Keats' bedroom, before finding at last a less casual gratification in Josephine's arms:

> 'I think we might call you masculine, Miss Rosetti,' said Mrs. Chattaway . . .
> Miss Rosetti was silent.
> 'Miss Munday and I can only claim to be neuter,' said Miss Luke.[29]

Miss Munday, the senior English mistress at Josephine Napier's school, is the origin of all the shrewd, watchful, funny-looking governesses in Ivy's later books, a pattern her creator evidently approved in life as well as art; indeed Ivy used Margaret's phrase and Miss Munday's—'We are neutrals'[30]—when discussing sex in connection with herself and Margaret. She explained that a neutral stance gave her greatly increased objectivity, as it does to so many alarmingly observant spectators in her books:

'I have a great knowledge of life,' said Miss Munday.

'If I may say so, I have noticed it,' said Josephine. 'And again if I may say so, I have noticed it increasing.'

'You may say so again,' said Miss Munday.[31]

The drawback to the blameless and contented life of anyone whose interest in human affairs is largely confined to observation and deduction is of course its dullness; and there was perpetual grumbling among Margaret's visitors (and later Ivy's own fans) about Ivy's relentless small talk, her insularity, domesticity, and insistence on a routine unbroken by anything more exciting than a banting programme. Tameness and insipidity are part of the price willingly paid by people in her books who have opted out of, or been worsted in, the power struggle: bystanders like the Scropes in *The Present and the Past* ('We have had such a dear little, narrow life. Will Catherine broaden and enrich it? I couldn't bear a wealth of experience'[32]), or strained and wary survivors unexpectedly released from a tyrant's orbit like the Ponsonbys who find themselves, after Sabine's death in *Daughters and Sons*, contemplating with something not unlike dismay 'a future flat, dim, smooth, without extremes'.[33] The vitality and recklessness of unscrupulous egotists like Sabine Ponsonby or Josephine Napier have a certain splendour acknowledged even by their victims: hence Ivy's own considerable respect and sympathy for her tyrants, her defensive loyalty when horrified reviewers complained that their behaviour was exacerbated by her own apparent readiness to condone it: 'The *New Statesman* wanted wickedness to be punished, but my point is that it is not punished, and that is why it is natural to be guilty of it. When it is likely to be punished, most of us avoid it.'[34]

'People say that things don't happen like they do in my books,' said Ivy, discussing family life with Janet Beresford: 'Believe me, Janet, *they do*.'[35] By 1933, when she finished *More Women Than Men*, Ivy had taken steps to see that things—at any rate unmanageable, explosive things—no longer happened to her; but, if she herself had settled for the flat, dim, smooth future of non-participants like Miss Munday, it was no doubt because she recognized in herself so much of Josephine. *More Women Than Men* is the novel in which she first broached a particularly sharp-edged set of associations—possessive attachment to a brother or other close relative giving rise, when thwarted, to murderous or suicidal impulses followed by a dangerous bout of pneumonia; and it is also the only one that propounds, in its cheerful, comical dénouement, something very like Ivy's own eventual solution to her life.

'"Josephine is built on a large scale," said Gabriel. "She is powerful for both good and bad." '[36] Her dealings with Gabriel and Ruth show her at her worst: passionate, rapacious, grasping, fatally ignorant of the true nature of the predatory instincts that make her a liability to herself and others. The most she will admit, in response to Felix Bacon's shamelessly inquisitive probing on the wedding day, is that people might be pardoned for thinking Gabriel's bride unworthy of him (Felix's reply is characteristically extreme: 'I don't think we ought to be pardoned. My feelings, when I think about it, are quite unpardonable.'[37]). Practically every one of Ivy's books revolves around a protagonist of ferocious energy operating sub- or half-consciously with catastrophic consequences for the weaker or dependent members of his or her household; but none of the later tyrants is put through anything quite like the obstacle course devised for Josephine whose heroics are baulked at every turn by the persistent frivolity of Felix (and, to a lesser extent, Maria).

Felix's brazen curiosity and bland comments, Maria's forthrightness, their evident admiration and no less evident grasp of the squalid tangle of emotions Josephine tries frantically to keep even from herself: all these combine to steer Josephine away from her state of perilous innocence, in which suppressed tensions are always apt to break out in violence, towards the relaxed and conscious concealment practised, in Ivy's books, by those only too well acquainted with their own unpardonable feelings. The change in Josephine is signalled by her reaction to a second crisis that parallels the first in everything except its ending. When Felix (who has consoled her for the loss of Gabriel) himself in turn eludes her grasp by marrying another, the dazed and shaken Josephine for the first time deliberately confronts her inner turmoil, curbing her retaliatory instincts and gracefully relinquishing all claim to Felix in a practical demonstration of his own theory, put forward long before when he followed her out of the school staff room on Gabriel's wedding day:

I could not stay with women who have no sorrow to hide, and not enough to hide of anything else. I am ill at ease with people whose lives are an open book. There is so much in me that must at all costs be hidden.[38]

Josephine was from the start an open book to Felix: his triumph is to make her read it too. Ivy's moral, in so far as she can be said to teach one, is always the same: that anyone who reads him or herself as clearly as Felix and Maria remains thereafter, to other people's prying eyes, a closed book. The division runs invariably between prying eyes—her bystanders, and open books—her tyrants; and the reason *More Women Than Men* is finally a comedy is that Josephine, unlike so many of the later tyrants, is brought to read what in herself must at all costs be hidden.

In so far as any single person might be held responsible for enabling Ivy to do the same, it was Samuel Butler; and the similarities between Butler and Felix Bacon—in their views, circumstances and family background—are too many and too striking to be accidental. Ivy's debt to Butler was immense and, judging by her pencilled markings in the margins of his *Note-Books*,[39] it had been in the first instance personal rather than literary. He had taught her at least as much about her family and herself as about how both might be exploited in her books, and his influence is nowhere so specifically acknowledged as in her humorous variation—in the persons of Felix and his father in *More Women Than Men*—on Butler's relationship with his own notoriously despotic, huffy and resentful father, Canon Butler, the original of Theodore Pontifex in *The Way of All Flesh*.

Felix Bacon, like Samuel Butler, is supported by his father under constant threat of having his allowance cut down or withdrawn altogether:

'My father has written to me for my birthday,' said Felix . . . 'He congratulates me on completing my fortieth year . . . He says it is absurd to be doing nothing at that age . . . Do I realise that he has paid for every meal that I have eaten? I had not actually realised it, meal by meal; he must be always thinking about food. That I have been a daily expense to him? Of course, it is a daily expense to pay for a person's meals; but he does not really consider them; it is a false implication. I don't know anyone who thinks less about his child's meals.'[40]

For twenty-two years Felix has in turn kept his friend Jonathan Napier (the fact that the unscrupulous Charles Pauli lived off Butler for more than twice that long was one of the Canon's many grievances against his son). Sir Robert Bacon, Felix's father, might almost be said to make a third in this ménage with Jonathan, an invisible but far from silent presence registering permanent protest in the name of backwoods conservatism, intolerance and religious decency. Felix's lack of occupation or earnings, his supposed effeminacy and epicurean extravagance in the matter of food and tailor's bills, his thoroughly suspect morals all serve as a constant irritation to Sir Robert who is not above the sort of emotional blackmail the Canon regularly applied to Sam.* It is Felix's successful application for the post of drawing master at Josephine's school that proves the last straw for his father, just as Sam's proposal to adopt drawing as a profession had done for his.†

But the Bacons' likeness to the Butlers sustains a severe jolt when Sir Robert, putting in his first actual appearance at the school speech day, turns out to be more than a match for his son in point of humour, gallantry and charm. Felix's and his father's mutual pride in one another is as fetching as their mutual disparagement (' "He says that in your view he might be a woman," said Miss Munday in a plaintive tone. "A father is disposed to take a hopeful view of his son,' said Sir Robert, bowing as he turned away'[41]); and both are rooted in an affection that surfaces quite openly during Sir Robert's last illness, making their final parting—with its mixture of genuine grief, surprise, tenderness and habitual reticence—among the finest deathbed scenes Ivy ever wrote. Its function, in this most

---

* Both fathers, for instance, make a point of blaming their wives' deaths on inconsiderate or downright callous behaviour by their respective sons (MWTM, p. 25, and *Samuel Butler. A Memoir* by H. F. Jones, Macmillan, 1919, Vol. 1, p. 188).

† 'Dear Sam, If you chose to act in utter contradiction of our judgement and wishes and that before having acquired the slightest knowledge of your powers which I see you overrate in other points, you can of course act as you like. But I think it right to say that not one penny will you receive from me after your Michaelmas payment till you come to your senses . . .' (Letter from Canon Butler, 9 May 1859)

Compare the strikingly similar threatening letter and telephone call from Sir Robert Bacon to his own erring son in the second and third chapters of *More Women Than Men*.

schematic of all her novels, was perhaps partly valedictory (Butler after all had struggled for much of his life in vain to elicit from his father some sign of the fondness and goodwill Felix ultimately finds in his), partly experimental: a practical application of Butler's theory (which Ivy marked with a pencil in the margin of her copy of his *Note-Books*) that 'Virtue has never yet been adequately represented by any who have had any claim to be considered virtuous. It is the sub-vicious who best understand virtue . . .'

Felix, along with his many collateral descendants in Ivy's books, provides a pretty fair working model of what Ivy and Butler understood by virtue. For all his flippancy, shallowness and affectation, his vanity and showing off ('But, seriously, do you not think him a very brilliant and polished man?' 'We could not think it more seriously than we do'[42]), Felix's influence on Josephine is wholly good. His inquisitiveness—the poking and prying that gradually drain off her pent-up vehemence—is a form of tact. His fascination with his own and his friends' appearance, age, tastes and dress (none of Ivy's other novels is anywhere near so clothes-conscious as *More Women Than Men*) helps Josephine evolve a cover as impenetrable as his own, a manner far removed from the reproving stiffness of her very first interview with Felix:

> 'Shall we have a gossip about your staff?'
> 'No!' said Josephine. 'When you have known me a little longer, you will know that my mistresses, in their presence and in their absence, are safe with me. I hope I could say that of all my friends.'
> 'I hoped you could not. But it is interesting that they would not be safe, if we had the gossip. They must have treated you fully as a friend. I almost feel we have had it.'[43]

iii

'Sometimes one takes a real person for a mounting block. Only for a mounting block, that is all,' said Ivy when asked where she got her material;[44] and clearly Samuel Butler provided the same sort of mounting block for Felix as Eleanor Jourdain for Josephine. But if in a deeper sense Ivy herself stands behind Josephine, then behind Felix stands her friend Herman Schrijver. It is not simply that Felix reproduces many of Herman's turns of phrase and mannerisms, his dancing gait, green eyes and penchant for formal Savile Row suits. Herman also gave his gregariousness, social poise and sunny temper, his gallantry to older women (almost a professional qualification in the decorator's trade), the relaxed, teasing, flattering approach that goes so far to disarm Josephine, calming her inner turmoil as effectively as it thaws her external constraint by making her laugh, and let him off small things like going home to dress for dinner:

> 'Stay by all means. Your clothes do not matter at all.'
> 'I noticed that you thought that about clothes; and I see that your clothes did not matter; but I don't think mine can be dismissed like that.'[45]

Exchanges like this one catch the tone of Ivy's London drawing room between the wars much as discussions between the three young Staces in *Brothers and Sisters* (published four years earlier) had drawn on memories of Ivy talking with her two brothers about their mother's tyrannical excesses at Hove. The original in each case supplied what was to become one of the basic patterns of Ivy's fiction. Felix is less an individual portrait ('People are too flat in life to go straight into a book,' said Ivy[46]) than a distillation of all that Herman, and people like him, stood for in Ivy's life by way of diversion, consolation, sympathy and understanding. She prized especially their captivating frankness, and the corresponding skill at side-stepping emotional entanglements that enables Felix to give Josephine the slip as soon as her feeling for him shows signs of heading for the rocks.

He represents perhaps more directly than any other single character in Ivy's books the discreetly homosexual element among her friends and Margaret's, the shrewd, uncharitable, high camp contingent always to the fore among connoisseurs and collectors, dealers and decorators, people who attach the utmost importance to style and artifice (' "I never think about people's age," said Josephine. "I often think about it," said Felix; "and hope they show it more often than I do, and wonder if they can guess mine" '[47]). Herman held that 'narcissism was the basis of homosexuality'[48] just as, in decoration at all times and places, the supreme element was in his view human vanity. He shared Ernest Thesiger's passion for *trompe l'œil* and, though Ivy may not have cared greatly in practice for Ernest's handpainted marble bathrooms or Herman's mania for mirrors ('The eye cannot be deceived too much or too often in a house,' he said[49]), she belonged, like Anthony Powell's Lady War-minster, to a generation that fully appreciated the strategic import-ance of an indirect approach:

> Layer upon layer of wrapping, box after box revealing in the Chinese manner yet another box, must conceal all doubtful secrets; only the discipline of infinite obliquity made it lawful to examine the seamy side of life. If these mysteries were observed, everything might be contemplated: however unsavory, however unspeakable.[50]

Neither Ivy nor Margaret was under any illusion as to the seamy side of Herman's life. Nazi anti-semitism, and its polite equivalent on this side of the Channel, provide a central theme of *Buchanan's Hotel*, culminating in the denunciation of Sigismund Siepel: 'He's just a dirty Polack, a Jew.' Siepel at curtainfall faces the sort of social and professional ostracism still occasionally incurred, in the stuffier reaches of English public life, by anyone unlucky enough to be unmasked as a homosexual rather than a Jew. Any attempt to deal openly with homosexuality in a play aimed at the West End stage between the wars would, of course, have been out of the question. Margaret belonged to a world where it went without saying that marriages like the Thesigers' involved some sort of precautionary element or that a foreigner like Herman, without means or family connections, was particularly vulnerable to prosecution and de-portation. He shared a flat when Ivy first knew him with his sister Elka in Montpelier Terrace: 'We went about everywhere together. Herman took me almost everywhere, and we shared friends to a great extent,' said Elka (who was working for the advertising agency, J. Walter Thompson, while Herman had by 1927 moved on from soft furnishings and second-hand furniture at Peter Jones to an antique shop in Brook Street). 'He told me to be very careful about strange men coming to the door and asking for him. He was *terrified* of being blackmailed. All his life.'

It was only after Elka returned to Holland at the end of 1931 that Herman began moving—by infinitely slow gradations spread over the next twenty years—closer to Ivy. Before that he and his sister had never been parted (except by Elka's three years at a Dutch university) and, after her departure, he sent her regular weekly bulletins interrupted only by the war until he died. He was twenty-seven in 1931, Elka four years older. They came from a frugal, philistine, stiflingly narrow middle-class background in Amsterdam where, being enterprising, inquisitive children in a rigidly conventional and not especially happy family, they had been accustomed from earliest years to turn to one another rather than to either of their parents: 'Herman and I were always great friends from the day he was born,' said Elka. 'We were a great deal together.' Both had detested their father who was something of a martinet at home, perhaps because he cut comparatively little ice outside it: as general manager of M. A. Rozelaar and Zoonen, a fair-sized Amsterdam diamond-polishing works, he had had trouble making ends meet when the diamond market stood still in the First World War, and landed himself in a worse fix at the beginning of the 1920s when he lost his entire capital in a fraudulent enterprise called the National Diamond Company,[51] set up under British government auspices to employ war veterans in Brighton by swindlers supposedly representing de Beers. The factory, which he had agreed against his better judgment to take over in 1920, closed down two years later, the company went bankrupt and, after a brief, unsuccessful venture as a diamond broker in London, Herman's father returned to Holland where he never fully recovered from the shock of having been ruined.

Herman, whose only training had been in the diamond business, set about supporting himself and subsidizing his parents thereafter with characteristic energy and brio, educating himself as he went along from books, museums, sale rooms and friends like Margaret. He rapidly built up a reputation as a talented and amusing youth ('See Maples and die', though often attributed elsewhere, was originally a pun of Herman's), much in demand among hostesses and a growing circle of faithful clients, many of whom went back to his days on the trimmings counter at Peter Jones. In 1932 he took over the prestigious but badly run-down decorating firm of Elden's in Duke Street (when his bid was accepted, Herman, who banked on a gambler's luck and no capital, borrowed the entire purchase price from the Thornton Smith brothers who owned Fortnums); and it was a commission from Mrs Simpson, followed by work for the Prince of Wales, that made his name and gave him for the first time the solid prospect of a comfortable living.

But insecurity could never be kept entirely at bay. For all his luxurious tastes and frequent generosity, Herman was seldom extravagant with money and remained in private life discreet to the point of obsession. Recurrent fever in childhood, followed by a serious bout of diphtheria leading to rheumatism and other complications at Brighton, meant that he seldom felt completely well and, if his infectious gaiety and good humour made his company a tonic to others, their society was for him an essential stimulant. To his sister, his temperament seemed fundamentally melancholy, and his vanity compensatory: he was haunted by the prospect of want as well as the threat of prosecution, 'and he had a terrible fear of the future'. His homosexuality had declared itself very early, round about the time of his father's first financial crisis, when Herman as a child of ten or eleven had begun picking up men in the local park. As a small boy kept short of funds by thrifty Dutch parents on principle, he always had money to buy presents or flowers for his mother whom he adored. He had inherited her inclination to worry and fret but, where his mother was apt to meet disaster with lamentation and tears, Herman kept his own counsel. Stoicism had set in very young, along with the evasiveness Ivy understood so well, and a flair for the sort of gossip that made Boswell say of a friend: 'Lord Lucan tells a very good story which, if not precisely exact, is certainly characteristical.'[52]

This submerged self—unscrupulous, unprincipled and easily dismayed—was a side of Herman familiar to his sister from infancy (Elka had first realized with shock that her little brother told lies to make things more interesting when he announced, at the age of four, that his teacher had told him a pineapple was an animal, not a vegetable, and that it hunted its prey with what people mistakenly thought of as its leaves). Self-reliant like Herman, Elka was always the more dependable, shyer and less wilful of the two. She seems to have regarded him from childhood with something of the admiring, indulgent, protective pride that had coloured Ivy's relationship with her younger brother; and Ivy, like Elka, became expert at detecting how far Herman might or might not be trusted. 'I don't know what Herman had told Ivy. But quite obviously the stories he told her, she hadn't believed. She knew, just as I did, when he was telling the truth.'

Elka, who first met Ivy soon after the war (most of which she had spent interned in Nazi prisons for her part in the Dutch resistance), never forgot being invited alone—in spite of Herman's indignant remonstrances—to Braemar Mansions where Ivy made it quite clear that she wished to know everything about Herman's childhood, upbringing and family background: 'During this solo tea-party, Ivy cross-questioned me, really a kind of third-degree examination, except that it was done in a (to me) fascinating manner and not at all as any SS or MI6 man would have done (I've experienced both). It took her a couple of hours before she was satisfied.'[53] Several other young women have left similar, often rather more unnerving accounts of the interrogation technique Ivy herself described in *Daughters and Sons*:

> 'But if we ask no questions, we have no lies told us. I have subtler ways of finding out the truth.'
>
> 'You mean you have subtler ways of asking questions. If you ask no questions, you have no truth told you either. It is surprising how much truth people tell: I would not, if I were they. And you can get a lot of truth from the falsehoods they tell, when you ask them questions. I admire them so much for telling them so awkwardly: I have a great respect for people.'[54]

Elka never read Ivy's books, never met her again, and certainly never suspected that, in Ivy's life too, the person who had meant most in her formative years had been a beloved younger brother. Herman meanwhile came more and more to fill the role, if not of brother, then of favourite nephew to both Ivy and Margaret. He was infinitely obliging, always on hand to fetch or carry, provide chocolates and flowers, taxis and travelling rugs for a trip to the theatre ('All expense has been spared' was Herman's *mot* on a shoddy West End production[55]) or a stately home in the country. 'Margaret certainly was one of the most remarkable women I have ever come across, and what was fortunate for me was that I liked both Margaret and Ivy immensely,' said Herman;[56] and, whatever her reservations, Margaret for her part appreciated his qualities as keenly as Ivy.

There are clearly recognizable touches of Herman in the easy, unstrained, semi-flirtatious relationship established with the two ladies in *Buchanan's Hotel* by Sigismund Siepel, with his hard-headed determination to make a success in the decorating trade, his endearingly naive delight at having apparently pulled it off, his insistence on rolling up his trousers to prove to Alexia Tunstall that he can at last afford the very best silk underpants, his equally unselfconscious, un-English and over-familiar generosity towards Elizabeth Wace ('Your bag is *almost* bald. I'll get you another with your name in large stones on the snap'). He is the soul of chivalry with both ladies—affectionate, considerate and encouraging towards Miss Wace, a shade more deferential towards the knowledgeable Miss Tunstall who shows him Wyatt's original sketch for her family home, together with correspondence about the new wing in the reign of George II, and receives in return a confidential account of his own misgivings about the English upper classes ('You think me a sort of adventurer? You think me a sort of bum? Quite outside the people you have heard of? You see, I'm a worker. I can be on terms with a moulder or a plumber, anyone with a trade or calling. But *those* people make me uncomfortable, and I can't pass the time of day with them. *Alexia: I'm* one of those people. *Siepel:* You? You're different . . .').*

Herman shared a world of professional concerns exclusively with Margaret, who was in any case inclined to discourage his more irresponsible side, the fibs and rumours he spread in the interests of making life more exciting. Ivy on the other hand led him on to make up more and more outrageous stories: he appealed to her reckless, games-playing instincts—the part of her that sided so strongly with her tyrants—and the private games they played together tended to start from the fact that, in any gathering of Margaret's upper-class friends, Herman was often the only person to have penetrated Ivy's cover as the mousy, innocuous, insignificant governess or companion. Their tacit mutual understanding if anything increased their mutual respect and, as each came increasingly to rely on the other, Ivy grew with time in some ways more intimate with Herman than with anyone else except Margaret. He had recognized her as unique from the start:

> My great attraction to Ivy was that she was perhaps the only human being who made me feel that whatever I said she understood perfectly—unlike so many other friends who gave me the

* Though the resemblance to Ivy and Margaret is unmistakable, it will not be pushed too far: Miss Wace, in her seventies, lives alone with a dog in rooms in Ealing and lays regular bets on the horses, while Miss Tunstall is a local landowner of marriageable age and respectable private means.

feeling that they had no idea what I was trying to say. Sometimes I would complain to Ivy that I understood nothing about nothing —which is true; and Ivy would look at me and say, 'And I understand everything about everything.' She did not say this once; she said it several times; and I wonder what she meant.[57]

Herman was thinking of a time after Margaret's death, towards the end of Ivy's life, when her changed status could hardly have failed to register with even the least observant furniture friends, while her literary admirers—at any rate those apt to write Ivy off as hopelessly out of touch with the modern world—were frequently taken aback by her sharp, disconcertingly well-informed judgments on, say, the contemporary novel or the Wolfenden Report. She would still put on her governess manner from time to time, almost as a matter of form, to amuse herself and her friends; and what she meant by the saying that puzzled Herman seems clear enough from similar claims made by the governesses in her books, for instance Miss Lacy in *Elders and Betters*:

> 'You really know a good deal, don't you?' said Julius.
> 'Yes,' said Miss Lacy in a simple, deliberate tone, keeping her eye on the child, perhaps in compensation for her thoughts being on other people. 'On my own rather narrow line, and in my own way, and according to the standard of human knowledge, I know a good deal.'[58]

Power in the form of knowledge is the compensation awaiting the bystanders and onlookers in Ivy's books, all those who never had, or have preferred to pass up (as in some sense Ivy did herself), any more active opportunity to control or manipulate other people. Ivy, who had switched camps midway through her life, held that circumstances may modify but not change the essence of a personality; and nearly everyone who knew her long enough was struck by the effects of what must have been a drastic modification in her own. 'When I think of the dim woman who poured out cups of tea in 1927 in the Linden Gardens flat, and the delicate, spirit-like creature whom I saw before she died in 1969,' said Herman, 'it is difficult to believe it was the same human being.'[59]

All her life Ivy made a point of misleading people bold enough to inquire about her past, like Herman ('I could never get it straight, because Ivy obviously never wanted to tell the truth'[60]), or Kay Dick, to whom she explained that she had not the faintest intention of giving anything away: 'Well, I think if I wrote an autobiography, a really good one, and put myself into it, I think it would be very interesting, and I think I should do it very well. But I'm not thinking of doing it.'[61] In so far as Ivy ever did touch directly on her own inner secrets, it was via Josephine Napier, who learns to subdue her essential nature, controlling her destructive impulses and beating a retreat thereafter towards the calm, unruffled surface where people like Felix Bacon and Dudley Gaveston lead such pleasant, civilized and entertaining lives.

When Ivy agreed at the end of her life to talk about herself to Kay Dick in the most intimate interview she ever recorded, they discussed whether or not 'people in civilised life'[62] actually do 'real deeds' like the characters in Ivy's books. Kay had recently tried to kill herself, which was what Ivy meant by a real deed ('I think there are a good many more deeds done than some people know. You've done a deed, haven't you?'). Ivy herself cheerfully insisted that she had never done one ('I haven't been at all deedy. Not at all'). But perhaps something akin to the temptation Josephine had failed to resist lay behind Ivy's further mysterious claim to be 'a woman of blameless character', by which she said she meant 'quite perfect morally'. If the springs of action lie, where Ivy's friend Lowes Dickinson located them, 'deep in ignorance and madness',[63] Ivy might be said to have spent the second half of her life exploring those depths in fiction and steering clear of them in fact.

CHAPTER FIVE

'Well, and in Swaffham Bulbeck!'

i

'I HAVE HAD a publisher's account and although I did not look for much from it, I looked for more than is forthcoming,' says the novelist John Ponsonby,[1] beginning to feel the pinch of falling sales in *Daughters and Sons*. The book which came out in March 1937 —Ivy's first to be published by Victor Gollancz—contains much gloomy talk of retrenchment, economy, dwindling royalties, mounting expenses and the impossibility of earning a living by the pen. Ivy could count, like John Ponsonby, on a fairly substantial private income though hers had shrunk in the slump from a comfortable thousand a year to about £750 throughout the 1930s: she told Hester's husband, Basil Marsden-Smedley, that she was ashamed to be so poor. Retrenchment does not seem to have entailed any very drastic cutting back on Ivy's part (she and Margaret replaced Jessie with a grander, starchier and altogether superior maid, Gray, round about 1937, as well as adding an annual winter holiday abroad to their regular travels on the Continent in the late summer), but disappointing sales were said to have been her reason for leaving Heinemann when her three-novel contract ran out with *A House and Its Head* in 1935. Years later she described being accosted at a publisher's party by a man from Heinemann's who claimed that his firm had once had the honour of publishing her: 'Honour?' said Ivy. 'No one would have known it at the time.'[2]

David Higham had by this time left Curtis Brown to set up his own agency, taking many of his best clients with him; but, though he tried to dissuade her,[3] Ivy stayed put which meant that her affairs were from now on in the hands of Albert Curtis Brown's son Spencer, fresh from Cambridge and as yet wholly inexperienced in the ways of the book trade. It was the newly promoted Spencer who had got rid of Higham in July 1935, the month in which *A House and Its Head* was published, and, when Rose Macaulay attracted Gollancz's attention by lending him her copy of *Brothers and Sisters*,[4] Ivy presumably made her own decision to accept his offer for the next three novels. After less than ten years in the business, Gollancz had a reputation for being able to sell virtually anything by what struck staider competitors as hair-raisingly unconventional tactics. Lavish use of advertising space was his trade mark together with gaudy yellow jackets, intensive promotion campaigns and an inimitably flashy line in publicity ('For years the cognoscenti have considered Miss Compton-Burnett one of the finest living novelists . . . Will "the public" now show that it is not without taste and discrimination?' ran one of his advertisements for *Daughters and Sons*, ending on a characteristically scolding note: 'Probably not'). Gollancz raised such a dust in the spring of 1937 that 'the London success',[5] *Daughters and Sons*, was promptly snapped up by the American publisher W. W. Norton, who is said to have confessed years later ('strong men at Norton's still blench at the thought'[6]) to some confusion between I. Compton-Burnett and the highly sought-after writer of Chicago gangsterland thrillers, W. R. Burnett. The bestseller lists that April featured 'Mrs. Virginia Woolf's *The Years*, Miss Agatha Christie's *Murder in the Mews*, Miss I. Compton-Burnett's *Daughters and Sons*' (of the three, only Ivy figured at the end of the year in the *Bookseller*'s Glass Slipper awards for novels that deserved better sales than they got). Reviewers invoked Congreve, Jane Austen, Emily Brontë; and Gollancz went to town with the *News Chronicle*'s obliging claim that Mr Bernard Shaw was the only other maker of comedy in the same class as Miss Compton-Burnett.[7]

Gollancz was the sort of enthusiast who works best by establishing a close personal contact with his authors. Autocratic, didactic, self-confident, forceful and shrewd rather than subtle, he got on famously with Daphne du Maurier and Dorothy L. Sayers, twin mainstays of the firm's fiction list; but it would have been hard to find anyone less likely to hit it off with Ivy, who had so far had no cause to feel much confidence in her dealings with publishers ('I have always thought of Cape as such a good one, and wished I belonged there,' she wrote sadly long afterwards to Robert Liddell. 'But I believe they are all alike in a way, only just different from any other business firm'[8]). Gollancz for his part cannot have relished being ranked by his new client with the accountants and lawyers who still called twice yearly for instructions as they had done in her father's day. He was always a soundly commercial publisher and, when Ivy's sales nearly doubled (from about a thousand copies of each novel to eighteen hundred[9]) but failed for the moment to budge any further, his initial enthusiasm was damped. His loyalty never wavered but in a sense he and Ivy had been at cross purposes from the start. I. Compton-Burnett represented a catch in 1937, at any rate for anyone with an eye on the sort of fiction list being built up by Jonathan Cape, or for that matter by Charles Evans at Heinemann ('They each could spot quality, and Victor only success,' wrote Higham. 'The other two could spot success as well, and that made it the more galling'[10]). Gollancz, having caught the tide the year before with his immensely successful Left Book Club, was very much in the market for new novels; and perhaps the fact that his proselytizing socialism made him almost house publisher to the front, or political half of the *New Statesman* attracted him to an author so highly prized by the paper's literary back parts.

But Gollancz's spectacular coups came from anticipating a popular trend almost before anyone else was aware of it, a brand of originality—eye-catching and effective if relatively ephemeral—that had nothing in common with Ivy's. Both of them clearly hoped for quick returns which perhaps explains why, when 'the public' paid scant attention to Gollancz's blandishments, each tended to blame the other. Ivy was naturally anxious to see her early books back in print to which Gollancz could not agree while he still had unsold copies of those already in hand. She complained that he failed to advertise her sufficiently widely, he parried with her fatal lack of mass market appeal. Ivy grumbled to her friends, Gollancz dined out on his story of Margaret Jourdain turning up out of the blue at the office with a typescript which she plonked on his desk, saying flatly, 'Here's some more of Ivy's twaddle.'[11] The story may well be apocryphal (Ivy's manuscripts tended to arrive, unaccompanied and without warning, by taxi at Curtis Brown) but it gives a fairly accurate impression of their mutual disgruntlement in later years when Ivy's mounting distress continued to be met with waning interest from Gollancz.

But, though it baffled their friends and Ivy herself made at least one attempt to dissolve it, the partnership had its points for both parties. On the one hand, from Gollancz's point of view, I. Compton-Burnett was a name that brought tone to the list (as well as a steady if not sensational profit) while, on the other hand, a hard-headed commercial firm with a rapid turnover and an almost legendary flair for publicity must have seemed the obvious choice for someone who never entirely got over her hankering to write a bestseller. It remained all her life a source of grief and vexation to Ivy that her novels failed to sell in their tens of thousands ('D'you know, I don't think she takes more trouble with her books than I do?' she said once of Daphne du Maurier[12] and, in another conversation about Agatha Christie's worldwide circulation, 'Think of the pleasure she must give—think of the pleasure'[13]). Writers in her books who find themselves forced to appeal to a small but discriminating readership over the heads of 'the public' generally do so as regretfully as Ivy herself: 'Much of the pleasure of making a book would go, if it held nothing to be shared by other people. I would write for a few dozen people; and it sometimes seems that I do; but I would not write for no one.'[14]

Ivy's readers—the sort of readership her characters disparagingly describe as 'the few'—could hardly have been more appreciative. 'I can't resist writing to tell you how I have revelled in every page, every line, every word of your *Daughters and Sons*,' wrote Vita Sackville-West from Sissinghurst on 1 April 1937, in the same week as a letter from the flower arranger Constance Spry (two names carrying so much weight in *Country Life* circles must have given even Margaret pause) hoping it would not seem impertinent or fulsome to say she had taken such delight in the book that 'I am spoiled for anything else for a long time'.[15] If a number of more conservative critics and novelists—especially among Ivy's own generation, like Virginia Woolf—still found her work hard to take, there was no difficulty with the rising generation of writers: Rosamond Lehmann, L. P. Hartley, Desmond Shawe-Taylor, Elizabeth Bowen and Sybille Bedford all wrote about I. Compton-Burnett at the end of the 1930s as one of the most original writers alive. Her growing reputation (and the difficulty of reconciling it with her absurdly incongruous appearance) is nicely illustrated by James Lees-Milne's account of inviting Ivy and Margaret to tea at the end of the war with the young James Pope-Hennessy who brought a French friend, Maurice Gendron: 'Maurice spoke not a word until they left, and then asked in his French English, "Who are these impossible governesses?" J. explained that one of them was the foremost novelist of our time.'[16]

'My books won't live. Yours may, Ivy,' said Rose Macaulay,[17] who was the only bestselling author—indeed for a long time almost the only novelist of any description—among Ivy's close friends.

Rose herself tended to deprecate the light, bright, astringent, topical novels that, from *Potterism* onwards, had made her name in the 1920s. She had been serialized in *Eve*, featured in any number of women's magazines and employed regularly to write for the popular papers but, by 1929 when Ivy first met her, she was already beginning to turn to the more serious, scholarly books on seventeenth-century poetry, or the pleasures of travel and ruins, about which there was no need to feel defensive before even her cleverest friends. Rose's misgivings about her own huge and highly successful output recall Hereward Egerton (in *A God and his Gifts*), another popular novelist inclined to worry about whose books will live and whose won't and apt to need consolation from his family and friends for being despised by the few: 'Well, I am glad you write for the many too. It is natural that I should be. I am one of the many myself. And it gives the whole thing its meaning. The few have too much done for them. To serve the many is the larger aim . . .'[18]

Modesty was an essential part of Rose's charm, together with a deceptive spinsterish primness that Ivy must have understood very well. The two brought out the best in one another from the start; indeed it was typical of Rose that she set about straight away providing practical advice about agents, contracts and terms, recruiting Ivy for Curtis Brown in 1929, as well as eight years later for Gollancz (who, whatever his difficulties with Ivy, remained always Rose's devoted admirer). They were almost the same age and, though Rose's curiosity about human nature found far more active expression than Ivy's, they shared the same delicately derisive view of themselves and their friends. Always eccentric, abstemious and frugal, very detached, very Cambridge (Rose's uncle, W. H. Macaulay, had been dean of King's in Noel Compton-Burnett's day, and afterwards modelled for one of the dons in *Pastors and Masters*), Rose was by all accounts incapable of doing a mean thing or saying a dull one and, for all her austerity, possessed an innate sense of style that made her Herman's favourite of all Ivy's friends: 'I simply adored her,' he said. 'I loved her appearance, her delicious speaking voice, her little curls which covered her rather skeleton-like head, her elegance of movement and her wit.'[19] Ivy too loved Rose's vitality, gaiety, audacity—what Rosamond Lehmann called her 'wit and crackle'—her fearlessness, and above all her integrity ('If, before she died, I had been asked to define integrity to some moral moron . . . or to a man from Mars,' wrote her publisher,

Mark Bonham-Carter, 'I would have arranged for him to meet Rose Macaulay'[20]).

Ivy called her 'the most prominent spinster in England'[21] and said she delighted to see her 'bubble over with high spirits' teasing Ernest Thesiger, or another of their mutual friends.[22] Ivy herself, generally so sparing of repartee in company, would sometimes rise to Rose's challenge and put on a sort of cross-fire double act in which, both parties being evenly matched, neither got the upper hand for long and one or other always ended by bringing up religion (Rose who, after a bumpy start, eventually regained her firm faith in the Church of England, returned with interest Ivy's frank incredulity at an intelligent woman allowing herself to be so sadly deluded). Both were sociable, if to vastly different degrees. 'Rose adored parties,' wrote Gollancz, 'she was one of the best party-goers in London. She liked the glamour and the noise: she liked the talk: but what above all she liked was that parties . . . implied people, and people meant even more to her . . . than words.'[23] Ivy, though never in quite the same class as Rose, had a fair share of parties herself in those days. Her diary for the summer season of 1934, for instance, lists between the end of May and mid-July 'Rosie's party [this was Rosie Bruce, a friend of Margaret's], Pakingtons' party, Herman S.'s party, Nelly's regatta [the Ionides always had a military band on the lawn for summer parties at their house by the river at Twickenham], Soame Jenyns' party, Mary's party, Lady Sprigge's party, Nelly's party [this was a tamer affair in Berkeley Square], Raymond M.'s party', not counting the regular tea, sherry and dinner parties she and Margaret gave at least once or twice a week on their own account.

These gatherings, heavily weighted in favour of furniture friends —scholars, connoisseurs, collectors and a congenial selection of Margaret's wealthy clients—were already beginning to be infiltrated by Ivy's admirers. But, apart from Rose and perhaps Francis Birrell (who died unexpectedly in 1935 to the great grief and shock of his friends), no one on the literary side penetrated anywhere near what remained an intensely private area of Ivy's life. 'She would talk to me about her writing, but always in a mysterious way,' said Herman: 'she would say, "I am writing again," and look happy; or she would say, "I'm not getting on with my writing," and look unhappy . . .'[24] Probably only Margaret realized what writing cost Ivy, who was no stranger to the sense of failure, exhaustion and deprivation described by Hereward Egerton on finishing a novel (" "Well, the book is ended," said Hereward. ". . . I am in a strange solitude. I seem to move in a void. I am without my foothold, my stake in life. I have suffered it before and it is never different. I have had and done what I wanted. But I pay the price" '25]).

Each of the two professional novelists in Ivy's books has his privacy guaranteed by a devoted sister standing ready to repel intruders from the outside world; and possibly some kind of jealously guarded nervous strain connected with her work might account, in part at least, for the rather startling altercations that blew up between the two friends when Ivy insisted on things being fetched for her, or on ticking Margaret off in public. 'We ate lentil soup, white fish with sauce and steamed potatoes, a rhubarb and ginger tart, Morecambe shrimps and biscuits,' wrote James Lees-Milne, describing a memorable luncheon at Braemar Mansions in wartime. 'Margaret Jourdain opened a large bottle of Cidrax, poured out Thesiger's and my glasses and was about to pour her own when Miss Compton-Burnett shouted, "Margaret! Remember at breakfast it was decided that you were to finish the open bottle of flat Cidrax." '26] This was at the end of May 1942, when Ivy was having difficulty with the early stages of *Elders and Betters*. She herself said she felt drained by the time a manuscript was ready to be typed, 'and she even used the stock phrase—not a habit of hers —that virtue had gone out of her'27] (another novelist uses the same cliché after a family row about writing in *A God and his Gifts*: ' "Virtue has gone out of me." "It has," said Reuben. "We saw and heard it going out" '28]).

Ivy felt that producing a book entitled her to a holiday and throughout the 1930s, as soon as she had packed off a manuscript to Curtis Brown (which she did punctually every two years round about Christmas time), she and Margaret crossed the Channel—for two weeks at an English pension in the Swiss Alps in February 1933 (*More Women Than Men*), Rome, Naples and Paris in February 1935 (*A House and Its Head*), and Italy again at the end of January 1937 (*Daughters and Sons*). In between there were countless trips to the country, generally a week at Easter and another at Whitsun in rooms in Dorset or Cornwall or once at a farmhouse near Keswick in the Lake District, and any number of weekends with friends in the country like Nelly at Buxted Park or Soame Jenyns at Bottisham Hall.

ii

But, of all their friends' country places, the only one to which Ivy
went regularly alone, and where she clearly felt entirely at home,
was the Noyeses' in Wiltshire. Ella and Dora prided themselves on
providing complete recuperation and change from her crowded
London life, and Ivy at Sutton Veney made a point of doing 'no
paperwork at all'. She would rest in her room or under the
mulberry tree, picking raspberries or blackcurrants and sitting for
hours at a time in the shady garden which seemed, to the neighbours' children who played in it, a magical place: romantic, mysterious, sweet-scented—'Miss Jekyll's sort of a garden'[29]—full of
hiding places and secret corners, with a fish pond, grassy plots
divided by yew hedges, masses of flowers growing higgledy-
piggledy and lavender spilling out between the paving stones.
Beyond the garden lay the downs which always suited Ivy better
than any other countryside: her father had been born and brought
up forty miles away at Redlynch on the far side of Salisbury Plain,
and, though her grandfather died before Ivy was born (and her
mother had in any case severed all connection with the family's
numerous humble Wiltshire and Hampshire relations), generations
of Comptons and Burnetts had been labourers, farmers and tradesmen on the eastern side of the county and over the border in
Hampshire. Ivy had inherited her father's love of growing things
('It's no good going for more than a week without sticking your
fingers in the earth,' she said once to Sonia Orwell in London), and
villagers at Sutton Veney still remember Miss Burnett's knowledgeable interest in garden plants. But all her life Ivy loved best of
all the small, frail, fine flowers bred by the keen air and thin soil of
the high downland and described so vividly in Ella Noyes' *Salisbury
Plain*:

> The slender cowslips, nodding all down the slopes in the sharp
> wind in April, the blue and white and pink inlay of the milkwort a
> little later, the purple thyme fitting itself closely to the ground of
> the molehills, the bright gold of the bird's-foot trefoil creeping
> along the ground, the yellow rock rose and tiny tormentil . . .
> Knapweed and hawkweed in miniature, starring the ground with
> purple and yellow, and the scabious which spreads an airy blue
> mist over the whole down in autumn; all flowers and herbs up

here are humble and lowly, with a vigour and sweetness bred of
repression. Only the harebells, of all mortal things the most
bodiless, ghosts of blue, swaying upon gossamer threads, inviol-
able even by the roughest gales, belong to the high downs, and
have no grosser selves below.[30]

Harebells had been Ivy's favourite flower from earliest years,
perhaps for the same reasons that made her write so feelingly of the
'vigour and sweetness bred of repression' among the children and
young people in her books. Certainly Ella and Dora found no
difficulty in Ivy's writing: 'They read her books and talked to her
about them, definitely they did,' said Margaret Hawkins, who
had been in and out of the Noyeses' house from childhood on,
and whose education had largely come from their bookshelves.
'That was their life, books. They talked books. They *lived*
books.'

The three sisters (Minna, the eldest, lived rather apart from the
other two, cut off by deafness and a preference for music rather than
literature) read or worked in the mornings, gardened in the afternoons, and read again or sewed in the evenings over the fire in the
drawing room. Ella and Dora were twenty years older than Ivy,
already well into their sixties when she first knew them (Minna was
eighty in 1936) and somewhat withdrawn from the outside world.
They wore strange, beautiful, patched and faded silk blouses and
dresses, all at least fifty years out of date. They lived the traditionally busy, orderly, disciplined lives of English country gentlewomen
except that—highly unusual in a small village—each was an accomplished amateur in her own particular art. Minna played the piano.
Ella had published several historical-cum-topographical books
about Italy as well as her much admired *Salisbury Plain*, all written
in a fine, firm, clear prose style that has the same unpretentious distinction as her younger sister's delicate, Sargentesque portraits and
landscapes. Dora, who painted all the local children from the Sutton
Veney baker's son to the future Marquess of Bath as a boy, had also
exhibited in London and even contributed, like so many of Margaret's friends, to the dolls' house Lutyens designed for Queen
Mary.

She had been roped in to do dolls'-house watercolours by
Lutyens' friend, the painter Sir William Nicholson, who lived in
some state at Sutton Veney manor house with his second wife and

relays of children, stepchildren and grandchildren, the youngest of
whom ran wild all over the Noyeses' house and garden, next door
to their own except for an orchard. 'Their house was idyllic inside,'
wrote Nicholson's stepdaughter, Anne Northcroft: 'I remember a
lot of light-coloured oak and old furniture and floors gleaming with
polish . . .'[31] There were collections of china and 'fine old linen
carefully darned', books everywhere, and texts from the psalms
painted on the drawing-room rafters in gothic letters on green. 'The
whole room had a green feeling,' said Nicholson's youngest daughter Liza, who remembered the Noyeses providing throughout her
childhood a refuge from the comparative formality of home life at
the manor. She and her four nephews and nieces—children of her
half-sister Nancy Nicholson's marriage to the poet Robert Graves,
who lived in the old school house in the village—spent whole days
at the Noyeses', climbing their trees, fishing in their pond, squirt-
ing one another with water or rifling the dressing-up chest in the
attics. 'They really liked children,' said Liza Banks. 'And they were
very, very tolerant. It was such a relief to go there—no sense of
strain—no imprisonment. There was a spiritual wholeness going
there, very much so.'

As they grew older, the sisters were not often seen outside their
own garden; but they welcomed the Nicholsons' many visitors,
especially the younger generation of poets and painters who regularly crossed the orchard to call on the Noyeses for tea or supper.
Graves was often at Sutton Veney until, after a notorious scandal at
the end of the 1920s, Nancy left him to set up house in the village
with another poet, Geoffrey Taylor (with whom Ella discussed
modern poetry as equably as if nothing had happened, to the
consternation of more prurient neighbours). The young Ben
Nicholson also spent holidays with his father, and seems to have got
on well with the Noyeses who owned several landscapes (their
'Foothills in Cumberland' was eventually left to the Tate) done at a
time when his work already verged on abstraction. They had no
family life of their own, being almost the last survivors of a long,
largely clerical and by no means undistinguished Wiltshire line (the
poet Alfred Noyes was a connection,[32] and so was the academic
painter Henry James Noyes; a Noyes had been burnt at the stake
under Mary Tudor and two more sailed for America with the
pilgrim fathers; in 1798 there was even a Robert John Noyes
appointed curate of Barton Stacey where Ivy's Burnett great-

grandfather lived till he left to marry a blacksmith's daughter
named Compton in 1803).

Their father and at least two of their brothers had been London
solicitors but Ella and Dora had returned to Wiltshire some time
after their father's death in 1890, in time to record a world of ancient
rural isolation and self-sufficiency already beginning to break up
even before the First World War. Dora painted the great haywains,
the men in smock frocks wielding scythes and sickles, the lines of
women harvesters in their pink and blue skirts, white aprons and
cotton sunbonnets, whose passing Ella deplored in *Salisbury Plain*.
The book is full of laments for the damage done by 'telephones and
newspapers and bicycles', for the fencing in of Stonehenge and, far
worse, the raising of the monument's great central stone, fixed
upright in 1901 by 'the violent intrusion of modern science'. The
Noyeses were notably free from prejudice when it came to modern
poetry, painting and novels; they were progressive in politics with
socialist and Fabian leanings considered eccentric, if not downright
dangerous, by the retired admirals and colonels who constituted the
Sutton Veney gentry; and they were remembered by everyone who
knew them as inexhaustibly tolerant, whether towards the rackety
Graves and Nicholson children or their elders openly living in sin in
the village. But they looked, dressed and spoke in the 1930s and
1940s as though they belonged to an era nearly half a century earlier;
and part of their charm for Ivy clearly lay in the fact that a visit to
Sutton Veney brought her as near as it was possible to get to the
world of the 1890s in which her books were set.

The Noyeses lived with the utmost simplicity, tending their own
garden, baking their own bread, making jam, doing their own
darning and mending. Minna collected sheep's wool from the
hedgerows for spinning into shawls and seaboot stockings. They
had a maid, Mrs Pink, replaced later by a series of girls who came in
from the village, but, though all their friends remembered the
house as enchanting, its arrangements were spartan and its rooms
often perishing cold ('always rugs on your knees—they had blue
hands from the cold, blue hands and red noses'). Ivy, whose
standards of comfort were exacting if never exorbitant, must have
had much to put up with in the way of plain living, and she seems to
have borne it in something very like Hope Cranmer's spirit of ever
so faintly disparaging forbearance towards the Marlowe sisters in
Parents and Children:

'I always feel that being here is a lesson,' said Hope.

'In rising above disadvantages, do you mean?' said Susan.[33]

The three Marlowes (Susan and Priscilla have a brother, Lester, who lives at home writing books that don't sell) were Ivy's tribute to the three Noyeses and, among all her many partial portraits of friends, theirs was apparently the only one she freely acknowledged, indeed explicitly intended as a compliment to the sitters. 'They knew she was writing about them,' said Mrs Hawkins, who was already working for the Noyes sisters when *Parents and Children* came out in May 1941, and vividly remembered their pleasure on receiving a copy from Ivy. 'They talked about that—that it would be them—and they were very happy with it.' Ella and Dora read *Parents and Children* aloud to one another over the fire in the evenings, and congratulated Ivy on the likeness when she came to stay.

The Marlowes lead lives of great seclusion and contentment, making do in a modest country cottage ('low cramped rooms', 'thin walls and no damp course'[34]) with meagre financial resources, an inadequate coal ration and an elderly Mrs Morris who comes in to do for them. They seldom go out save to gather firewood—after dusk so as not to be seen—in the park belonging to their neighbour at the big house, Sir Jesse Sullivan, a regular benefactor whose rare visits to the cottage are a source of memorable embarrassment (' "I wish he would not keep gazing at the fire," said Priscilla aside to the others. "People are supposed to see faces in it, but I am so afraid he will see wood" '[35]). Like the Noyeses, they have no family besides themselves, no interest in charity outside the home (' "We are the last people to support orphanages," said Susan. "They are fortunate in not having to support us" '[36]), and no desire for any company except their own. Parties made up of the older Sullivan children, or the Sullivans' visitors, slip across the park on more or less surreptitious visits to the cottage, much as the young Nicholsons called on the Noyeses, for a brief respite from the constraints of the big house. But the Marlowes themselves are adept at inventing excuses for not returning these visits (' "We don't wear their kind of clothes," said Susan . . . "We should have to look like other people," said Priscilla, "and that costs money" '[37]), and for turning down Hope Cranmer's repeated advances:

'Books and a fire,' said Priscilla, looking at these things. 'What more could we have?'

'I see you haven't any more,' said Hope with some exasperation. 'But does that prevent your having dinner with a friend? You could have that as well.'[38]

Ella was the only one of the three Noyeses who could on occasion be lured up to London alone, or very occasionally with Dora, to spend a few nights at Braemar Mansions. They had little in common with Margaret's circle, and so little contact with Ivy's that none of her London friends in later life had so much as heard of the Noyeses. No doubt the sisters preferred to keep their distance, and no doubt they enjoyed the note of asperity running through Hope's dealings in *Parents and Children* with the infuriatingly unworldly Marlowes. Hope herself is one of Ivy's most charming variations on a type that recurs constantly in her books, the wry, humorous, observant middle-aged woman whose invariable kindness and tolerance are matched by an insatiable curiosity. Comfortably off herself, and tolerably satisfied with her own domestic arrangements, Hope is consumed by the need to get to the bottom of the Sullivans' family frictions and the Marlowes' no less baffling satisfaction with themselves and their lives. Much of her time is spent cross-examining Susan and Priscilla, who answer her questions as frankly as they discuss her shortcomings—her streak of vulgarity ('there is something second-rate going through Hope'[39]), and her very nearly successful attempts to make it seem better by joking about it—behind her back.

One of the many bones Hope finds to pick with the Marlowes is their contempt for frivolities like 'cushions and flowers and things that shimmer in the firelight' ('"We like the firelight better by itself," said Priscilla. "I can see you do," said Hope. "And I like the things that go with it. I don't even want a mind above material things; I enjoy having one on their level"'[40]). Another is the unmistakable air of serenity which, with their high-mindedness and eccentricity, was always the first thing people noticed about the Noyeses. 'I think they were very, very unusual,' said Liza Banks, which was no more than the Marlowes thought of themselves ('No, but we are unusual. It is no good to say we are not'[41]). Ivy invented a scandalous secret in the family background (it is noticeable that the Marlowes treat the plot's romantic revelations about their past with a fair-sized pinch of salt); but, given that she intended the Marlowes expressly to amuse the Noyeses, they must surely have recognized another of Ivy's private jokes at her own expense in Hope's inquisitiveness, intrusiveness, humorous self-deprecation, her love of comfort and material possessions coupled with a sneaking sense of her own inferiority when set beside the Marlowes' lofty indifference to either:

> 'If you liked me a little better, I should not be so petty,' said Hope. 'What is the good of striving to be worthy of your friendship, when I have no chance of it? You know how I long for your affection; people always know the things that add to themselves; I expect you exaggerate my desire for it. Of course I don't show it in public, when you are so neglected and eccentric . . .'[42]

Hope's friendship with Priscilla and Susan is riddled with this sort of fretfulness: part of the strength and subtlety of Ivy's treatment of friendship in general lies precisely in her never assuming that mutual comprehension and sympathy necessarily rule out a quota of what Hope calls 'normal human discontent'.[43] Ivy herself, secure in the Noyeses' affection, confident of their understanding, had not the faintest intention of abating one jot of her social round of parties, theatres, holidays, foreign travel and visits to friends, nor for that matter her and Margaret's frank predilection for 'things that shimmer in the firelight'.

iii

Parents and Children came out in 1941, by which time the life of ease and plenty had already receded into the past: in retrospect the decade that had opened for Ivy with the publication of *Brothers and Sisters* in 1929, and ended in war, had brought her more settled happiness than any other in her whole life, except perhaps the first. She and Margaret, in their respective fifties and sixties, had achieved a degree of emotional and intellectual as well as material prosperity that neither could have anticipated in her bleak and unpromising youth. 'Well, anyway, we have nothing to dread now,' says the ten-year-old Sefton Shelley, looking back on a peculiarly wretched school term at the end of *Two Worlds and their*

Ways: 'Everything seems to be over.'[44] It is a child's dramatically nihilistic view ('Nothing good, nothing bad, nothing to dread, nothing to hope for. Nothing') of the cheerful adult resignation and self-reliance practised in *Parents and Children* by the Marlowes who, like Margaret and Ivy, 'lived in their interests and their anxieties and each other, with as much satisfaction as most people and more enjoyment'.[45]

For Ivy especially the strain and horror of the past meant always that relief was the keenest form of joy. If she was still vexed at not having brought off a bestseller, she could count on a gratifying amount of attention, especially from the young ('All Ivy's fans are under eighteen, you know,' said Margaret sourly at the beginning of the war when the bookseller Heywood Hill produced yet another young man anxious to meet or hear more about Ivy[46]); and she must have been pleasantly conscious that as a writer she had at last come into her prime. She was steadily deepening and darkening her range with the series of irresistibly entertaining, unsparing and profoundly unsettling family novels that started in 1935 with *A House and Its Head* and continued thereafter, with only a brief hiccup in wartime, at two yearly intervals. In a sense the stable, unchanging, pre-1910 world that became from now on the permanent setting of her novels ('When an age is ended, you see it as it is'[47]) provided a retreat from the perils and uncertainties of the depression, rearmament, Mussolini's Abyssinian invasion, civil war in Spain, and the rise of Hitler's National Socialism. In another sense, the collapse of civilized values was Ivy's especial subject: 'In the age of the concentration camp when, from 1935 or so to 1947, she wrote her very best novels, no writer did more to illumine the springs of human cruelty, suffering and bravery,' wrote Angus Wilson when she died.[48]

A Family and a Fortune, published in February 1939, had been finished towards the end of the previous November,[49] two months after the Munich crisis. Herman had a story that on the day war was declared Ivy, alone in the flat at Braemar Mansions, telephoned to say she was terrified and beg him to come at once and sit with her.[50] In fact this happened a year earlier on Wednesday, 28 September 1938, the day on which a declaration of war was widely expected and only narrowly averted in the late afternoon by Chamberlain's announcement of plans for his last-minute dash to Munich. The first air raids on London were confidently anticipated that night. Mar-

right: Margaret Jourdain on the steps of the Manor House, Broadwindsor, in 1910, at the time of her first success in London as poet, visionary and literary critic

below: Philip Jourdain: '. . . as soon as he begins to talk of mathematics his face shines, his eyes sparkle, he speaks with fire and ability, one forgets that he is ill, or remembers it only in passionate admiration of the triumph of mind . . .' – Bertrand Russell. (see p. 79)

below right: Eleanor Jourdain *c.* 1910, the year before *An Adventure* was published and five years before she became Principal of St Hugh's

right: Herman Schrijver between the wars: 'But, seriously, do you not think him a very brilliant and polished man?' 'We could not think it more seriously than we do' – *More Women Than Men* (see p. 121)

below: 'Nothing is more terrifying to me than to see Ernest Thesiger sitting under the lamplight doing this embroidery' – Beverley Nichols (see p. 35)

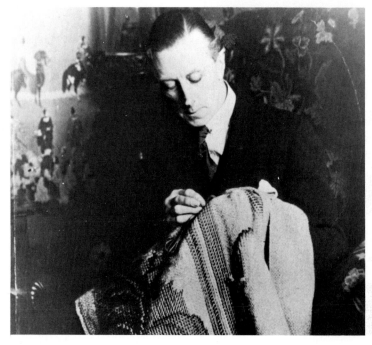

above: Ivy and Margaret taking tea in 1942 (a photograph taken during a session with Lee Miller arranged by Jane Stockwood for *Vogue*)

left: Rose Macaulay: 'My books won't live. Yours may, Ivy' (see p. 133)

right: Victor Gollancz at a meeting of the Left Book Club

below: Dorothy Kidd in the 1920s

above: Ivy with Vita Sackville-West, photographed by Vita's friend Edith Lamont in the White Garden at Sissinghurst on the day of the expedition described by Madge Garland: 'Once Vita received us wearing a Persian coat in vivid colours and crimson silk pants . . .' (see p. 236)

left: Madge Garland round about the time Ivy first met her at the beginning of the 1950s, photographed by Cecil Beaton in the ballroom at Londonderry House

Ivy photographed by Cecil Beaton after the Second War, a portrait that went far towards establishing her austere public image in the last two decades of her life (see p. 191)

above left: Ivy photographed by John Vere Brown in a characteristic pose that seemed to her friends to express both her stoicism and her loneliness at the end of her life in the empty flat

above: Ivy photographed at the end of her life by Hans Beacham: 'I am old. I have seen and heard. I know that things are done' (see p. 261)

left: Robert Liddell soon after he first met Ivy in the 1940s

left: Elizabeth Taylor drawn by Rodrigo Moynihan in the early 1950s at the beginning of her long triangular friendship with Ivy and Robert

above: The Liddell family at tea; from left to right: step-aunt with dog, Robert, Donald, their half-sister Betty, their father, step-grandmother and the step-mother in whom Ivy took such particular interest

garet had been away all week with a newly acquired young man, Peter Wilson (afterwards chairman of Sotheby's), touring stately houses in Leicester, Derby and Chesterfield. 'That *was* a dismal time,' said Sir Peter who remembered Margaret's sardonic reply, when asked what her brother Frank might be doing: 'Burying his great auk's egg, I should think' (if Frank's marrying money still rankled with his family, worse still was the frivolous way he chose to disburse it on birdwatching expeditions and his celebrated egg collection). When Herman reached Cornwall Gardens, Ivy, who had washed her hair, was sitting in front of the fire with a towel over her shoulders looking 'really quite yellow with horror'.

It was a widespread reaction. Herman had Jewish parents and a sister in Holland; Ivy's maid Erna Gray was German (widow of an English husband, she decided to throw in her lot with 'her ladies' and later supplied the English war office, via Margaret's friend Soame Jenyns, with maps and details of factories in her German home town). People all over the country were trenching their orchards, laying in supplies, and blacking out windows. Ivy and Margaret must have known, when they spent a week in Provence at Easter 1938 and another fortnight just over the Channel in Normandy at the beginning of September, that this was likely to be their last glimpse of abroad for some time. 'I am perfectly convinced,' said Hester, 'that these two non-political, rather apart women, living in their comfortable flat with their good maid, their good food, their fascinating work, were quite certain that Munich was not the end of war threats, but the end of life as they had known it for ever.'[51]

Arrangements were put in hand for evacuation and storage. Gas masks had to be fitted ('The girl said to Margaret: "Don't you write? Didn't you have *The Adventure*?"' reported Ivy, describing the scene at the depot. 'And Margaret said no, it was her sister, but she also wrote. Then she came to me and said, "I think you write?" I felt thankful that the maid didn't write'[52]). The V&A was in turmoil throughout the following year, even Kensington Gardens, where Ivy walked as she worked on scenes from her current plot, had men digging trenches against bombardment. When the war did eventually break out, Ivy and Margaret were staying at Lyme Regis in Dorset ('I don't think that they were in the country to run away from the bombs,' said Hester, who was herself hoping to be posted as a war correspondent to Holland, 'but because they went to the country in August and early September'[53]). On Sunday, 3 September 1939, they took a bus along the coast road to Seatown near Chideock, where Basil and the three little Marsden-Smedleys were staying in a row of black-painted coastguards' cottages known as the Watch House, arriving just in time for family Bible-reading and hymns in the garden overlooking the sea before Chamberlain's broadcast at 11.15. Official evacuation of London refugees began that afternoon and once again the first air raids were expected that night. Ivy and Margaret stayed on in their lodgings for a week or so and, by the end of the month, were installed with their maid as paying guests of Soame Jenyns' widowed mother at Bottisham Hall just outside Cambridge.

It was a rash and, as it turned out, unsatisfactory arrangement on both sides, but there was ample room at the hall for two maiden ladies with their own maid, and no doubt Soame's highbrow friends struck his mother as a more hopeful proposition than the parties of unwilling, unwanted and often completely unhouse-trained London evacuees liable to be billeted on anyone with room to spare in the country. There had been Jenynses at Bottisham ever since 1700 when it belonged to the father of the first Soame Jenyns, the writer, theologian and M.P. for Cambridge who never forgave Dr Johnson for laughing at his pretensions to serious scholarship ('What Soame Jenyns says upon this subject is not to be minded,' said the doctor when someone brought up Jenyns' belief in disinterested benevolence: 'he is a wit'[54]). Margaret's friend Soame was considered an odd fish in the village on account of his London job and literary leanings; but he cut quite a dash in a generation of memorable eccentrics at the British Museum by deliberately cultivating something not unlike his namesake's reputation as a country squire dabbling in matters a gentleman would hardly take seriously. He specialized in Japanese ceramics, and claimed to be frightened of Ivy's old friend Arthur Waley who would lie in wait in the museum's corridors and courtyards to jump out and stun him with learning, much as Dr Johnson had stunned his ancestor.

Soame got on better with Margaret's other friend, Willie King (the two were connected through Bulwer Lytton on the Jenyns' side whose grandson married Byron's daughter Ada, wife to the eighth Baron King), another celebrated wit who looked like an unfrocked eighteenth-century abbé and was, from a very different standpoint, as great an expert as Ivy on the ravages caused by the struggle for power down several generations in an English upper-class family. Willie's unexpectedly successful union with the lovely but decidedly raffish Viva ('As if a Daumier drawing had married a Toulouse-Lautrec,' said Margaret with disapproval to Soame[55]) had been so strenuously opposed—and Viva so contemptuously treated—by his parents that the young Kings relieved their feelings (like Horace Lamb's wretched children in *Manservant and Maidservant*) by sticking used gramophone needles into a wax effigy of Willie's father who died, shortly followed by his wife, 'one happy day in 1934'.[56] Whereupon the pair ran through Willie's inheritance with phenomenal speed, fury and splendour, leaving Willie once again rich only in the fund of anecdote he supplied to colleagues like Soame, and the young Angus Wilson, who shared air-raid duties with him at the museum (' "Oh God," groaned Willie, stumbling about with Angus one night in the blackout through a sculpture gallery of Great Assyrians, "why *do* they let the public in here?" '[57]). He walked to work every day from Thurloe Square via Piccadilly Circus to Bloomsbury, and said when the amiable Soame proposed an alternative route: 'Walk across Hyde Park? My dear Soame, I *hate* the country.'

Ivy and Margaret, though nowhere near so extreme as Willie, took the Londoners' view of the country as all very well for holidays so long as you were not expected to live in it. But they were both fond of Soame who returned their liking, admiring especially Margaret's habit of speaking her mind no matter whose toes she trod on, and seeing straight through Ivy's small talk: 'She was one of the very few women I've ever met, whom one just used to sit and listen to.' Even with Soame, Ivy never discussed anything much beyond housekeeping—the vagaries of refrigerators and the new gas boiler, varieties of biscuit and gentleman's relish—but 'the things she said were strange, mysterious, illuminating'. Though still very much one of Margaret's young men, Soame came eventually to see Ivy as by far the more remarkable of the two, and the seeds of a lifelong affection were sown during the three months she spent at Bottisham in the autumn of 1939. This was her first and only stay of any length in the kind of country house she generally wrote about, and Bottisham was everything she and Margaret liked best: a severely simple, small, elegantly proportioned Georgian brick house with a flagged hall and a lovely square stairwell, pierced by long windows which give the hall and the principal rooms that 'sensation of light and space so perennially dear to East Anglian builders.

The hall stands in its own park, approached by a long, curving gravel drive, backed by stable yards and service wings, encircled by lawns, glades and woods, formal walks and alleys full of daffodils and violets in spring, as well as two great walled gardens (where Ivy in happier times picked soft fruit, and apricots trained round the walls with roses, japonica and a border of espaliered apples). Bottisham, like Sir Roderick Shelley's ancestral home in *Two Worlds and their Ways*, is surrounded by trees sighing in the wind and by 'flat green land'[58] stretching as far as the eye can see. Like Horace Lamb's house in *Manservant and Maidservant*, it is 'fifty miles from the east coast of England'[59] with the same 'wide bleak rooms' where water froze on the windowpanes (the winter of 1939–40 was the coldest for more than forty years), and the same once despised Georgian furniture newly restored to fashion. Like so many of the impoverished estates in Ivy's books, the place was no longer self-supporting (there had been an indoor staff of six, including a boy whose time was almost entirely spent trimming lamps, before death duties when Soame's father died in the 1930s had entailed drastic cutting back); and its occupants suffered, like the Lambs and the Shelleys, from the difficulty of heating, maintaining and repairing the fabric in time of fuel restriction and staff shortage.

Admittedly, Ivy's country houses are as artificial and inconsistent as her arbitrary period settings: their primary purpose is to provide a sealed environment as isolated and enclosed as Kafka's castle or Beckett's dumping grounds, another sector of the twentieth-century no-man's-land designed for exploring man's inhumanity, inadequacy and infinite resilience in face of both. As a writer, Ivy was no more interested in nuances of class than in other inessentials like her characters' looks, clothes or taste in furniture. In so far as she bothered about domestic detail at all, she drew on the comparatively rootless, suburban, rising professional or self-made middle classes to which she herself belonged (Andrew Stace and Godfrey Haslam, the first two landowning squires in her books, share her own family background of nonconformism and trade respectively) as much as on the quite different ethos of the landed gentry. Supposed country squires like Duncan Edgeworth, Horace Lamb, Cassius Clare and Miles Mowbray—or for that matter John Ponsonby with his goatee beard and his life of 'service to the pen'[60]

—would all ring a great deal more true as masters of the grander sort of residential villa, standing in its own shrubbery instead of a park, and staffed by servants recruited from the local employment agency rather than from a village dependent for generations on its big house. What is missing is any sense of continuity, of the network of responsibilities and obligations binding the manor to its surrounding community: it is a discrepancy easily overlooked since the upper classes, never in any case great readers, were almost by definition debarred from tackling any writer as unorthodox as Ivy, while her admirers were generally not much concerned with social niceties. 'Margaret showed her the first butler she ever saw,' said Willie King,[61] who was one of the few (Hester's cousin, Michael Pinney, was another) in a position to note that Ivy was not in fact writing at all accurately about his own, largely obsolete social caste.

Nonetheless it is noticeable that, after her visit to Bottisham, a slightly more practical note creeps into her writing on the rare occasions when it touches on the routines of estate management ('"Bailiffs, tenants, gardeners," said Cassius . . . "Accounts," he said in a just audible voice'[62]), or the successive stages by which people's grounds go to pot ('"Your gravel wants attention, Chase," said Gaunt . . . "And the road through the park needs repair"'[63]). Ivy always had pleasant memories of Bottisham: she found the low-lying, windswept countryside sad, but the park with its sheltered gardens and walks was a consolation, and, since she kept all her life the knack she had learnt as a child in the schoolroom of being able to work anywhere in spite of distractions, she was almost certainly beginning to think about her next novel. 'We would often see her about the village, usually too absorbed in her thoughts to notice us,' wrote Dulcie Pendred,[64] who had read Ivy's books and been invited to meet her at the hall by Mrs Jenyns (whose attempts to amuse her guests were not always so well received).

Soame, working for the Admiralty in London, came down only at weekends, leaving his mother, who was wholly without intellectual or artistic leanings, to cope as best she might with what was proving a trying visit. Several people noticed at the time that old Mrs Jenyns—a kind and punctiliously attentive hostess, devout churchwoman and solid subscriber to the conventional morality of her generation—was rather puzzled by Ivy, and remained puzzled until out of politeness she read one of her books, when she was appalled. The book was thought to be *Pastors and Masters*, which takes Dr Johnson's line, rather than the first Soame Jenyns', on doing good (' "The sight of duty does make one shiver," said Miss Herrick. "The actual doing of it would kill one, I think" '[65]). Soame's mother, who came of Quaker stock (she was one of the formidable Yorkshire Peases, descended from the Gurneys and Elizabeth Fry), had the ingrained Quaker horror of passing judgment, though she could not help complaining, to Ivy herself as well as to Soame and Mrs Pendred, about the wickedness and oddity of the people in Ivy's books.

But, if she was flustered by Ivy's characters, she had far more to put up with from Margaret, who did not trouble to hide the fact that for her there were no compensations at Bottisham: her friends were nearly all scattered, called up or seconded, social life was a desert, the sale rooms were out of reach, professional outlets were drying up, even the long-postponed book on William Kent seemed uninviting at close quarters. Mrs Jenyns had hoped that having Margaret in the house would help loosen her hold on Soame, or at least increase his mother's share in the professional, intellectual and social side of his life which Margaret at the end of the 1930s had looked like monopolizing; but in fact, far from making headway with his London contacts, Soame's mother found her position in her own house made steadily more uncomfortable by Margaret's critical looks, scornful laughter and mocking tongue. Bored and restless, Margaret disapproved of practically everything her hostess did, disliking especially the sight of Mrs Jenyns setting off down the drive on her regular rounds of the cottages, to distribute largesse in the village and see to the school.

Mrs Jenyns for her part had always taken her duties as the squire's lady seriously. She was well liked on the whole by the villagers, who relied on her support, helped themselves to her services, applied to her with their problems and knew all about her own troubles at home ('To some extent she was a brass serpent,' said Ivy's friend Anna Browne, meaning that, like Moses' followers in the Temple, the local people found it handy to have someone set up on show as a figurehead: 'There was a lot of brass-serpenting in those days'). When Mrs Jenyns had first come as a bride to the hall there had been soup at the lodge gates for the poor, and to the end of her life the schoolchildren still touched their caps; before the war, some of them even wore the Jenyns' charity clothes—green suits for the boys, and purple frocks for the girls.

It was all too much for Margaret, who had always drawn the line at organizing anything beyond Shakespeare readings for the Broad-windsor villagers. Perhaps this whole encounter with a way of life that struck her as intolerably overbearing and interfering brought back painful memories of conflict in the schoolroom at Ashbourne; certainly her friends were astonished when news leaked back to London that Margaret and Ivy throughout their visit to Bottisham had been obliged, by the sheer force of Mrs Jenyns' personality, to become regular churchgoers for the first and last time in their life together. The visit lasted in mounting mutual uneasiness ('I don't know if Ivy had ever been inside a church before,' said Soame, marvelling with mixed consternation and pride at his intrepid parent) until Christmas, when Mrs Jenyns thankfully packed her bags and left to stay with another son for the holiday: Ivy and Margaret went back to London and wrote, no less thankfully, cancelling plans to return on 8 January.

Churchgoing had been one difficulty, bearing the burdens of the village was another, the dogs made a third (Margaret, who, like all the Jourdains, loathed domestic animals, had not hesitated to object to the Jenyns' dogs coming to be fed by their mistress after meals in the dining room instead of being kept, if at all, out of sight in the servants' quarters). An already exasperating state of affairs was not improved, from Margaret's point of view, by the fact that Ivy had fans in the neighbourhood. Young Mrs Pendred, married to a carver teaching at Bottisham Village College and living a mile away in Swaffham Bulbeck, vividly remembered being tackled by Margaret in private after tea on the first day they met: ' "You haven't really read her books, have you?" she said brusquely. "Almost nobody reads them, and she only sells about 250 copies." ' Mrs Pendred, who had worked for the *New Statesman* and 'dutifully followed the avant-garde tastes of the literary editor', replied firmly that she had, and could if required prove it by producing her copy of *More Women Than Men*. 'Miss Jourdain was silenced. Then she said, "*Well*, and in Swaffham Bulbeck!" '[66]

CHAPTER SIX

'When war casts its shadow, I find that I recoil'

i

MARGARET BEGAN THE new year, January 1940, with a tag from Spinoza at the front of her diary: 'A free man thinks of death least of all things, and his wisdom is a meditation not of death but of life.' The war having apparently got off to a false start, evacuees had been steadily trickling back all that winter to London. 'Ivy had no courage, I mean no physical courage at all,' said Herman. 'Margaret on the other hand was splendidly brave.'[1] It was Ivy who had insisted on fleeing the bombs in the first place and, when none fell, presumably Margaret who determined that the time had come to return. It meant that she could work again, and go back to lunching with Soame, Willie, Herman or Sybil Assheton-Smith; while for Ivy there was a new admirer, the young novelist Robert Liddell, who had sent her a critical essay on her work and was invited to tea in April to collect his manuscript. He was one of the small army of readers recruited by the *New Statesman*, having first heard of Ivy five years before when Raymond Mortimer identified her as the single most powerful force at work in the English novel in the generation following James Joyce and Virginia Woolf:

> At first sight her work strikes you as clumsy and heavy-fisted; her figures, though solid, are not what is called 'life-like', and she composes her books on highly defined and artificial designs. In fact, she is open to all the reproaches laid upon the founders of post-impressionism. And it is still as useless, I think, to put her work before the general public as it was to put that of Cézanne a quarter of a century ago . . .[2]

Robert had immediately ordered a copy of the book under review which was *A House and Its Head*: 'It filled a weekend when I was alone . . . I read it twice, my hair (like that of Henry Tilney in *Northanger Abbey*) standing on end . . . I thought I should go mad if my brother did not come home at the appointed hour, for I longed to thrust it into his hands.'[3] Robert and his younger brother Donald were themselves only slowly recovering from damage inflicted in their formative years by a tyrannical stepmother. Robert, having got away from home to go up to Oxford, had been joined by Donald in rooms in the Banbury Road where, to their own content and their relatives' considerable annoyance, they set about leading the peaceful, unmolested life of seclusion and self-sufficiency so often enjoyed by survivors or non-participants in Ivy's books. Her novels (Robert sent for the four early books as well as writing to Blackwoods for a copy of the 1911 edition of *Dolores*) supplied them with a map of a landscape which they already knew intimately. It was a double shock of recognition and revelation: the two brothers spoke and wrote to one another thereafter in the manner of Ivy's books.

Robert, who worked in the manuscript department of the Bodleian Library, hunted in vain for traces of Compton-Burnett family history in directories, Burke, Crockford's and back copies of *The Times* (which yielded only Noel's obituary, and a cursory report of the inquest on Ivy's two youngest sisters); and the search was not much helped by Spencer Curtis Brown, who became Robert's literary agent in 1937 and justified Ivy's dim view of anyone connected with publishing by saying, quite untruthfully, that she was 'very deaf and very slow'. The Liddells' curiosity remained unappeased and their admiration intense. Their own experience of persecution and cruelty in a thoroughly respectable, upper-middle-class household in South Kensington, only a few streets away from Cornwall Gardens ('my brother and I were her predestined readers. And so often we passed under the windows of that Sibyl who knew everything'[4]), meant that they grasped sooner than most that Ivy's apparent clumsiness was not so much unlifelike as, on the contrary, an attempt to pursue reality itself well beyond the currently accepted limits of literary realism.

A friendship sprang up at once on Robert's first visit to Braemar Mansions: 'Ivy opened the door to me; she was small, neatly dressed in black, and rather surprisingly jewelled; her greying corn-coloured hair a little reminded me of the "blond head" in the Acropolis museum in Athens.' Robert had hopes of placing his article on Ivy with Cyril Connolly's highly fashionable *Horizon* (in the event Connolly published long essays by Mortimer and Eddie Sackville-West, so Robert's was published as an appendix to his

Treatise on the Novel in 1947). Ivy was pleased and grateful. No one else had yet attempted to assess her work at anything like this length, or for that matter had the nerve to submit a manuscript beforehand for inspection; and, though she often met and sometimes made friends with people who had written appreciatively about her work—Mortimer himself, Rosamond Lehmann, Vita and Eddie Sackville-West, Elizabeth Bowen and Mario Praz are obvious examples—she treated none of them as frankly, and with as little constraint, as she talked that afternoon to Robert about her books.

> I was seated on a hard sort of sofa covered with worn black velvet, and tea (as in *More Women Than Men*) went 'through all its stages'. 'Water-cress? Very wholesome,' offered Ivy. 'Home-made gingerbread, very good. Cheese straws.'

She asked him to emphasize the goodness of her characters, especially the sensitivity and generosity evinced on occasion by her tyrants (' "It's because they were intelligent," she said, and for her there was no greater virtue than intelligence'). Before, during and for two or three hours after tea they discussed tyranny, virtue and sex in her novels, the influence of Greek tragedy and the gap in her career after *Dolores*, before moving on to the strengths and failings of other authors in a long, comfortable talk about books interrupted only when conversation got on to Margaret's sister's *Adventure* (one of Robert's jobs at the Bodleian had been to catalogue the contents of the box—'Miss Jourdain's baby'—containing all the original documents), and 'would not easily get off it'.

A few weeks later Robert was up again in London, bringing his brother on 4 May for a hasty tea before all four left to catch the 4.45 p.m. train at Paddington, for Margaret and Ivy were on their way to spend a week at the Bear in Woodstock, just beyond Oxford, with Herman, who had eagerly accepted Margaret's invitation to go over the furniture at Blenheim Palace. Apart from the food—even more frightful than usual in English pubs in wartime because it came out of tins—the visit was a success, especially for Ivy, who cheerfully consumed her own and the others' daily dose of stewed prunes and never so much as set foot in the palace, giving her attention instead to the bluebells carpeting the grass and woods in the great park: 'Ivy was in her heaven. She would walk among the bluebells and sit down and look at them and admire them and was altogether very happy.'[5] Ivy saw to it that the stay included an excursion down the Banbury Road for tea with the Liddells, another hurried occasion (the ladies were en route for Margaret's brother Henry, also settled in North Oxford) when Margaret, whose social manner was a good deal more impressive than Ivy's, monopolized the conversation.

> Donald afterwards a little reproached me (and justly); he felt Ivy wanted to be more intimate, and that I held her off, and let Margaret dominate [wrote Robert]. He liked Margaret, but loved Ivy. I think it was when I took him to Braemar Mansions to tea that Ivy tapped on Margaret's head with the teapot, to stop her talk, and get down to tea.[6]

Nothing was said, then or later, about either party's family background. But Robert had sent Ivy a copy of his second novel, *Kind Relations* (1939), based on his own and his brother's experience as bewildered and unhappy small boys after their mother's death: 'You mean to go on?' she asked at their first meeting,[7] and at their next two she certainly saw enough to understand very well what the brothers meant to one another, and why. When Robert himself came to write about these years in a second autobiographical novel, *The Last Enchantments*, he described something very close to the special bond of intimacy and affection common between siblings in Ivy's novels.

Books and a fire—the Marlowe's refrain in *Parents and Children*—are also the sign and embodiment of happiness, blocking off the outside world, sealing in everything pleasant and companionable, in *The Last Enchantments*. The book was published in 1948, four years after Donald's death, and celebrates the two brothers' brief, peaceful respite together in Oxford between leaving home and being engulfed by a war that, in the spring of 1940, barely seemed to have started. 'None of us spoke of the War, in which (I think) none of us much believed; but it was there all the time, like a nagging pain,' Robert wrote afterwards of this afternoon in the Banbury Road, which neither he nor Ivy ever forgot. 'Soon, my brother and I knew, it must separate us, and we lived these last months together in the mutual kindness that (I hope and imagine) commonly exists between deeply attached people of whom one has been condemned by the doctors—but we might both be condemned. Such a time seems happier than it was in recollection, for anxiety, its chief torment, is over. Anxiety may be replaced by loss and intolerable grief, but at least it does not in itself last forever—not even in Hell, where there is no hope.'

Ivy and Margaret returned with Herman to London on 10 May, the day on which Hitler invaded Holland and Belgium. Hester, stranded as a press correspondent in the Netherlands, caught the last boat home three days later with help from Herman's sister Elka in Amsterdam, arriving in time to be struck by Margaret's courage in the terrifying weeks leading up at the end of the month to the fall of France and the evacuation of Dunkirk ('I remember Basil telling me he had never seen her so moved as by the invasion of the Low Countries and France . . .'). Herman's parents, who had gone into hiding when the Nazis reached Amsterdam, were persuaded like many other Dutch Jews to give themselves up of their own free will to the Germans, and both died in Auschwitz; Elka joined the resistance, was arrested and disappeared into German prisons; Herman himself, called up to join a contingent of the exiled Dutch army in Wales, suffered some kind of breakdown and was discharged as unfit to serve. Ivy and Margaret spent the summer in London, apart from a fortnight at the Marsden-Smedleys' seaside cottage in July, just before the first waves of German bombers began daily flights across the Channel. The London blitz started in earnest in the first week of September and, by the twenty-eighth of the month, Ivy and Margaret had left for the country just as Ivy had fled from the sound of guns on the Somme nearly twenty-five years earlier in the First World War.

This time they returned to the Noyes sisters in Wiltshire, putting up briefly at the Manor House Hotel in Warminster before taking refuge on 15 October with the Noyeses' niece, Joan Hadden, on Calves Hill at Chedworth in Gloucestershire. It was an experiment that turned out in its own way quite as badly as Bottisham. Miss Hadden was between the two friends in age, an old-fashioned gentlewoman with a pleasant, grey stone Cotswold house and a garden which she cultivated with that flair for colour and design —amounting in her case almost to genius—no other art so readily brings out in the English. But she was not popular in the neighbourhood (according to Ivy, who told this story 'laughing so much that she could barely get the words out',[8] their hostess's only social intercourse with the local colonels, vicars and doctors took place at innumerable blood transfusion parties where 'they all lie prone on sofas and the floor in most intimate positions, and are publicly "cupped" in turn, and refreshed with tea afterwards'); and she was not kind to her aunts. Minna was by now eighty-four, Ella and Dora fast approaching their eighties. All three had made wills leaving everything to Joan, who was for all practical purposes their sole surviving relative, and who made no secret of finding them a burden. Her apparent heartlessness, both behind the aunts' backs and on visits to Sutton Veny, disturbed others besides Ivy and Margaret who reacted, as the helpless, horrified bystanders do in Ivy's books, by covering pity with humour. 'The two were very entertaining about their refugeeing with the niece of an old friend near Chedworth,' wrote James Lees-Milne, describing in his diary the first time he met Ivy and Margaret in 1942. 'They hated the niece, who tactlessly referred to her aunt's impending demise from senility, and let them know what she would do with her aunt's furniture and belongings.'[9]

Asked afterwards what she had made of her visitors, 'Miss Hadden was a bit reticent about them but she did say that Miss Jourdain had been difficult about her food.'[10] Food was by no means the only difficulty, and Margaret got away whenever she could, making trips to London or Oxford, fetching clothes, possessions and papers from the flat for disposal in parcels up and down the country—a mahogany occasional table with Henry in North Oxford, silk dresses and manuscript files with Alice Marcon (who had settled there too, after her husband's death in 1929), a fur coat with Elliston and Cavell in St Giles, and a hatbox full of oddments with Frank's son Seymour at Worth. War news grew worse, air raids heavier, future prospects more disheartening and, at the beginning of February 1941, Margaret came up to Braemar Mansions to supervise the storage of furniture at Frank Partridge's depository in South Mimms. Homelessness, falling incomes, food shortages, fuel and petrol rationing, uncertainty about where or how to get through the next year—the general physical and mental dislocations of War—all posed in acute form the problem, so vividly brought home to dependents in Compton-Burnett novels, of 'having to be housed and clothed and fed and provided for' ('When people have to be provided for, death is the only thing').[11]

Work became increasingly difficult, either to do or to manage without. 'As you say, it was an effort to write it in these days,' Ivy admitted to Robert about her next novel, 'but my reluctance to disappoint the few hundred people who were looking for it, held me to my purpose.'[12] She must have put in much time at Chedworth on the final stages of *Parents and Children* (' "Sir Jesse says we must continue to practise economy," said Priscilla Marlowe . . . "He says it need not interfere with our comfort. I could see he knew it prevented it" '[13]). Ella and Dora knew she was writing about them and, if Ivy disliked her hostess's bullying, grasping attitude to the Sutton Veney household, she could hardly have chosen a more delicate or cheering consolation than the portrait of the three Marlowes, which gave such particular satisfaction to both artist and sitters in the bleak spring of 1941.

The manuscript was acknowledged by Curtis Brown, writing to Ivy at Chedworth on 18 March,[14] but by the time Gollancz published the book two months later, the friends had packed up and moved on, as thankfully as they had left Bottisham, to stay with the Marsden-Smedleys at Hartley Court near Reading. This was a large house with its own staff and grounds, poultry yard and kitchen garden (priceless assets in wartime), which Hester had taken on the autumn before from her uncle, the neurologist Henry Head, and promptly turned into a sorting house and transit camp for friends and relations, their children and nannies. Margaret and Ivy, staying there for a few days at the New Year, had been relieved to find the Thames valley full of evacuees like Janette Thesiger (living with her sister at Farley Hill Place, Reading), and the Graham Rawsons with whom they had dined regularly in London. Basil, always a particular favourite with Margaret, found her company more of a comfort than ever at weekends when he left the Ministry of Economic Warfare in London to join his wife's cheerful but noisy household with its floating population, improvised meals and miscellaneous collection of extras. Hospitable by nature, loving bustle and change, Hester had even found a new and appreciative young man for Margaret in the shape of her cousin, Michael Pinney, billeted with his family at Hartley while serving as a gunner nearby. But it says much for Ivy's relationship with the Marsden-Smedleys—or rather for the way in which, with old friends, she was still completely overshadowed by Margaret—that *Parents and Children* was published on 19 May, and reviewed at length with considerable enthusiasm in all the national newspapers, without anyone at Hartley Court taking the faintest notice. 'We knew absolutely nothing about it till long afterwards,' said Hester[15] who, like Basil, never entirely saw the point of all the fuss people later made about Ivy.

Ivy herself worked or read in her bedroom at Hartley, emerging to walk in the garden or compete for oranges at meal times ('I don't know if you remember Ivy eating an orange,' said Hester. 'She would attack it almost fiercely, but very neatly and sometimes eat several after quite a big meal'). Ivy's craving for fruit (hardly ever obtainable in wartime, even for ready money) grew sometimes so sharp that she told Michael Pinney she had once been reduced to raiding the larder for raw rhubarb, and her insistence that, when oranges were in short supply, she needed her share at least as much as the children rankled for years with Michael's wife, Betty. Margaret, too, found the little Marsden-Smedleys (the eldest, Luke, was her godson), their cousins, second cousins and small hangers-on hard to put up with en masse. There was a dispute over oranges, another about the discipline and upbringing of children. The children themselves looked on Margaret as a fixture, part of the furniture, the sort of honorary aunt who could always be relied on to throw up a sandcastle or, when you got older, sympathize about school and propose a holiday outing; while Ivy was still very much 'the poor relation', assigned in their minds to that vast army of dim, depressed spinsters tagging along in the wake of more fortunate relatives.

The friends spent the month of May at Hartley, searching meanwhile for a roof of their own which they finally found by the twenty-third and to which they moved ten days later. 'Our wartime activities compare most unfavourably with yours,' wrote Ivy to Robert in Egypt. 'We are lurking ignobly in a little furnished bungalow at Thatcham, three miles from Newbury, and about ten miles from Reading, for the simple reason that we are afraid of bombs.'[16] The bungalow, called 'Zealand', stood on the Elmhurst housing estate, conveniently close both to the Pinney headquarters and to Janette, who seems to have relied a good deal on Margaret when Willie (also sharing their sister's house at Farley Hill) died suddenly of a stroke on a trip to London in March. Rose Macaulay, whose flat had been reduced to rubble in the last great raid on London in May, paid them a visit at Thatcham, and so did Elizabeth

Bowen, one of the reviewers who found *Parents and Children* more than a match for the enormities of life itself that spring ('. . . an icy sharpness prevails in the dialogue. In fact, to read in these days a page of Compton-Burnett dialogue is to think of the sound of glass being swept up one of these London mornings after a blitz'[17]). Marion Rawson took them to call on Louis and Mary Behrends who had commissioned the painted chapel at Burghclere from Stanley Spencer, kept open house for friends like Benjamin Britten and generally cultivated the contemporary arts with an enthusiasm that cut no ice with Ivy and Margaret, who would have preferred more conventional country-house comforts.

Heywood Hill came down from London with his wife, Lady Anne, both enthusiastic admirers of Ivy's, already beginning to recruit a steady stream of new readers at their bookshop in Curzon Street. Soame also brought his wife, Anne, soon after their wedding in April, so that Margaret might help them choose chairs. Herman arrived, aggrieved and affronted to find Ivy, Margaret and Gray carrying on business as usual in a modern 'monstrosity' furnished with fumed oak, frightful paintings, reproduction dining and living room 'suites', but otherwise greatly reassured by their comforting air of serene and resolute triviality:

> I don't think that on the whole, and apart from fearing the dropping of bombs, the last World War meant a thing to either Margaret or Ivy. They simply looked upon it as unspeakable, and it did force them to change their habits and live in various and different forms of discomfort until it was over and they could resume their pre-war way of life, and that was all it meant to them.[18]

ii

Certainly this was the effect Ivy desired at all costs to produce, though there are indications that it was not always easy to preserve a calm front over what people in her books call 'inner tumult'.[19] When the seventeen-year-old Francis Wyndham (who had sent Ivy a fan letter from Eton) came to tea at Thatcham in the critical period after the German invasion of Russia in June, he was intercepted at the bus stop by Margaret who warned him that neither the bombing, nor the fighting on the Russian front, must on any account be mentioned in Ivy's presence.[20] War brought out the protective instinct always uppermost in Margaret when Ivy struck other people as being, however obscurely, in distress. Ivy herself told Robert a few years later that her ability to read the news had been exhausted by the shock and strain of two world wars ('I turn my eyes from the reconstruction of 1914,' she wrote to another friend when a spate of war memoirs flooded the papers in the 1960s: 'I have had enough'[21]). At the time she did not discuss her own state of mind in this war any more freely than she had in the first. When Jack Beresford was killed on duty with the Home Guard in the autumn of 1940, Ivy resorted to the same formal, guarded tone she had used to contain her desperation after Noel's death in 1916:

> October 22, 1940
>
> Dearest Dorothy,
>   There is so much courage about us today, and so much feeling that any demand upon it must simply be met, that the normal thoughts and feelings seem out of place. And yet I can't help seeing it all as tragedy. It is a rough piece of road for you. May you be able to push on. Let me have a word to say how you are.
>   With all my love and sympathy,
>   Ivy.

Jack was the person to whom Noel had confided his hopes and fears without reserve, as he never could to Ivy, from the trenches in the First World War. His death brought back feelings reinforced a year later when Hester's closest brother, Bernard Pinney, was killed in Libya at Christmas 1941. Hester, supported as always by Margaret (who had first known Bernard as a small boy jumping on the gravestones in Broadwindsor churchyard), found great gentleness in Ivy at this time as well as strength and practical realism. Matter-of-factness was always Ivy's strategy against grief. 'I hope that your brother is quite well and not in any danger, a thing I can't help hoping about my friends,' she wrote on 5 January 1942, ten days after news came of Bernard's death, to Robert whose brother was serving in Bomb Disposal: 'I am a very bad war-time subject.'

She and Margaret had decided once again to return to London, encouraged by the respite from bombing and constrained by shortage of funds (Margaret's bank, more than usually restive about her permanent overdraft which now stood at £316—as much as she had earned in any one year even in her palmy prewar period—had written ominously in December to remind her 'that the Bank is now only lending money for essential War purposes'[22]).

> The problem of meeting two rents on an income sunk below the level of one, has proved impossible of solution, and we are soon returning to Kensington and whatever risks there must be—many less than there were, I should think [wrote Ivy in her letter to Robert]. We are looking forward to rescuing our poor flat from its plight of shattered windows and fallen ceilings and deluge of water from a burst cistern on the roof. The enemy attentions stopped short of an actual hit with a bomb, but bestowed this on so many adjacent houses that we got a good share of the results, and on more than one occasion it was a good thing we were not at home . . . we shall be glad to be back in sad and battered London, and among the stoic and battered friends who are held to it by work or poverty or sheer liking for the city in all her moods.

They returned on 17 February. Braemar Mansions remained intact ('Well, Miss, we had a bomb drop in Cornwall Gardens and broke nearly every window in the Gardens. There was only one in your dinner-room so do not worry as I have had it fix,' wrote Gray,[23] who seems to have gone on ahead at Christmas to clear up). But the porter of the Thesigers' block of flats just round the corner from Cornwall Gardens had been killed in the street while Ernest himself, hanging out of his window one Sunday morning, had watched a dogfight over the mansions which ended with one plane shot down in flames; another time a house almost next door disappeared in front of his eyes, carrying with it a friend who had run out to help.[24] Ernest, having sent Janette to the country, was one of the friends held to the city by work throughout the blitz: he spent evenings at the theatre, days making a comprehensive record in watercolour of London's bombed churches, nights camped out under the stairwell with the only other two remaining occupants of the flats. Ivy and Margaret took to this makeshift version of London life with alacrity and relief. Gaps left by friends evacuated, bombed out or posted abroad were filled by newcomers like James Lees-

Milne, invited to join the Hills after luncheon at Braemar Mansions on Saturday, 28 May 1942:

> I arrived for coffee. This is a great occasion. Margaret Jourdain is patently jealous of Ivy Compton-Burnett, whom she keeps unapproachable except through herself, and even when approached, guards with anxious care. This is evident from the way in which the former diverts one's attention if she thinks one is talking too much to the latter. It is a selfish kind of affection, to say the least. The two have lived together for years and are never parted. They are an Edwardian and remarkably acidulated pair. The coiffures of both look like wigs. The hair is bound with a thin fillet across the forehead and over a bun at the back. Thin pads of hair hang down their foreheads unconvincingly. Miss C.-B., whom I consider to be the greatest living novelist, is upright, starchy, forthright and about fifty-seven to sixty. There is a bubbling undercurrent of humour in every observation she makes, and she makes a good many, apparently hackneyed and usually sharp, in a rapid, choppy, rather old-fashioned upper-middle-class manner, clipping her breathless words. She enunci-ates clearly and faultlessly, saying slightly shocking things in a matter-of-fact tone, following up her sentences with a lot of 'dontcherknows', and then smiling perceptibly. She has a low, breasty chuckle. She has not unpleasing, sharp features, and her profile is almost beautiful. But she is not the kind of woman who cares tuppence for appearances, and wears a simple, unre-memberable black dress (I guess all her clothes are unremember-able), which she smooths down with long fingers.
>
> . . . We talked chiefly of country houses. Miss Jourdain looked rather wicked and frightening, when she peers through her quizzing glass. Miss C.-B. says that Miss J. has too little occasion to use it these days, now that there are so few houses available with furniture to be debunked; that she lost a lens in the train, and it has hardly mattered.[25]

James Lees-Milne, historic-buildings secretary to the infant Nation-al Trust (it had a staff of six in those days, and about half a dozen historic houses open to the public), had been recently invalided out of the army and was to spend the rest of the war inspecting properties that eventually formed the basis of the Trust's collection ('I knew at once he was the sort of young man you would rope in,' said Ernest Thesiger to Margaret, who cordially agreed: 'He is quite a new acquisition'[26]). But it must have been disconcerting to find someone who might legitimately have been supposed to fall well within Margaret's sphere of influence regarding her as scarcely more than an adjunct to Ivy. Michael Pinney, charmed and flattered by Margaret's interest in him as a young man, had the impression from the start that Margaret felt herself cold-shouldered by the literary admirers who did not bother to conceal their low opinion of the furniture faction. The war had reduced Margaret's income to vanishing point and severely cramped her professional scope: she had not even found a publisher for her last book, an anthology called *Fantasy and Nonsense*[27] which she had spent much time compiling at Chedworth and Thatcham. Ivy's sales meanwhile were beginning to increase sharply, and so were her letters from fans ('I think I should hardly have ventured to write to you but for the war,' wrote one who thought 'the wit, the restraint, the balance' of *Parents and Children* 'almost perfect: superior even, if I may say so without impertinence, to the wit, the restraint, the balance of Jane Austen'[28]). Her critical reputation had never stood higher, and she herself enjoyed on occasion playing something other than second fiddle. Accounts of Ivy in the early 1940s show her as generally more forthcoming, talkative, even assertive than ever before: these were the years when for the first time people who met her—Robert Liddell, James Lees-Milne, Anne Hill, Robin Fedden—began noting down things Ivy had said as soon as they got home:

She makes very acid comments in a prim, clipped manner, enunciating sharply and clearly every syllable while casting at one sidelong glances full of mischief [wrote Jim Lees-Milne in his diary on 28 May 1942]. We talked about servants. She agreed that today fewer servants managed to get through double the work, doubly efficiently, to what a greater number did a generation ago. They are better fed and housed, she said. Her parents took care to have excellent food themselves, whereas their children were thrown the scraps . . . For supper she used to be given the crusts cut from her parents' toast. She has an insatiable appetite for chocolates, and Ernest Thesiger told her she was intemperate in some of her habits. Miss Jourdain gave us cherry brandy, but did not offer any to Miss C.-B., who took some for herself. She swigged it all in one gulp instead of sipping, declaring that it was excellent and she would have some more. Miss J. intervened and would not allow it. [29]

Clearly some sort of realignment was going on between the two friends now that Ivy's subsidiary status was no longer a matter of course. She still went nowhere alone, but it was not always easy to tell who was whose consort, at any rate for onlookers faced for the first time with this majestic and arresting couple, sitting side by side bolt upright on a sofa at somebody's party, or arriving for dinner dressed in their full prewar fig of long satin evening dresses with matinée coats ('Look, Margaret, do you see?' said Ivy one night at the Kings' when Viva, who had been cooking, wore a Viyella frock and Anne Hill came straight from working all day at the bookshop in a shirt and skirt: 'When we get home we shall have to chop a foot off our dresses'[30]). When they went out these days, it was as likely to be to a literary as a furniture function. They were among the notables assembled at the Aeolian Hall for the Sitwells' celebrated poetry reading on 14 April, along with the Queen and the two princesses and the poet Dorothy Wellesley, who was tipsy and had to be forcibly restrained from reciting by Vita Sackville-West and the programme seller, Beatrice Lillie. 'Ivy Compton-Burnett ate half a pot of raspberry jam, and I was shocked to see her surreptitiously wipe her sticky fingers upon the cover of my sofa,' wrote Jim Lees-Milne, with whom Ivy seems to have behaved at times less like the governess than the naughtiest girl in the school: 'Both she and Margaret ate like horses. This time Miss C.-B. talked a great deal more than Margaret. Her description of the Poetry Reading and Lady Gerald Wellesley's antics was very funny. They are a wicked pair.'[31]

They dined with Jim and John Pope-Hennessy before a charity concert given in Whistler's house by the young Peter Pears and Benjamin Britten in November. Ivy still kept herself to herself so far as the literary establishment was concerned, presenting an impregnable front more often than not to other writers like Lytton Strachey's niece, Julia, at a christening party for the Hills' baby daughter on 2 December 1943:

Miss Compton-Burnett looked handsome, not unlike Elinor Glyn. She stood, a solid blockbuster or blockhouse whichever way you look at it, in a navy Bradley's coat embroidered with winding strips of astrakhan like the carefully-designed paths in a municipal garden. Her portcullis, drawbridge and visor were all down too. After an hour's hard work, I elicited only two things from her that interested me, one that she never felt guilty about anything, and the other that she had no set working hours—'Oh no, nothing like *that*.'[32]

But in this shifting, erratic, oddly mixed wartime social scene, Ivy and Margaret belonged undeniably as they never had before to the London intelligentsia, or, in Ivy's phrase, what there was of it ('Let us shut the door to keep the heat in. What there is of it,' was one of her sayings, part of the ritual recorded by John Pope-Hennessy of 'going in to lunch on a freezing draught ridden day' at Braemar Mansions[33]). They saw a good deal of Richard Aldington's ex-wife, the poet Hilda Doolittle (always 'Mrs Aldington' to Ivy as Rosamond Lehmann was 'Mrs Philipps' and Elizabeth Bowen 'Mrs Cameron'), and her friend Bryher in Lowndes Square; also of John's austere and erudite mother, Dame Una Pope-Hennessy, who lived with her two clever sons at 48 Ladbroke Grove in North Kensington (opposite St John's church which Ivy's half-sister Iris attended, on the wrong or north side of the park). Dame Una's was one of the houses where Margaret found herself underrated, now that Ivy was beginning to cut a figure in her own right and clearly enjoying it no end. 'I went to tea with Ivy Compton-Burnett and Margaret Jourdain. Anne Hill was there; also Dame Una and Rose Macaulay. Again I was the only man among blue-stockings,' wrote Jim, who must have felt he took his life in his hands in the highly competitive atmosphere engendered whenever Dame Una began trading intellectual snubs with Margaret: 'Ivy C.-B., I noticed, when she did condescend to speak, shouted everyone else down.'[34] Chitchat about the weather, prices, or servants was out of the question at Ladbroke Grove—'Dame Una wouldn't countenance small talk to a degree that was really terrifying'[35]—where Ivy politely discussed Greek tragedy instead with her hostess.

When they first met round about the winter or spring of 1943, Dame Una was writing her life of Dickens, John (the art historian, later head of the V&A) was at work on a book about Domenichino, while his younger brother, the brilliant and wayward James, had just finished his *West Indian Summer*. 'Can't you write a book and join us?' said Dame Una to John's and Jamesey's friend Jim, who felt he would need more than a book to his name as a passport to this hopelessly exclusive, united and mutually protective society of three.[36] If Ivy's literary credentials were by this time unimpeachable, Margaret's barely passed muster:

> My mother was not much interested by Margaret Jourdain, but admired Ivy's books and was fascinated by her whole identity [wrote Sir John Pope-Hennessy]. For me Ivy was an acquired taste, but the more often one saw her and the better one got to know her the fonder of her one became . . . Sometimes I think the most important thing in life is how one tends one's talent, and she tended hers with marvellous disinterest and conviction and consistency. B.B. [Benjamin Britten] once said that if Giacometti sculptures could talk, they would speak like the characters in her books, but face to face one was conscious of a great wealth of humanity which was never, or scarcely ever, articulated.[37]

People who met Ivy in the 1940s or later were often aware of the unspoken sympathy and understanding flourishing alongside the rocklike endurance that had carried her through what had seemed unendurable in the First World War. Her attitude to the second was resigned, and thoroughly practical: the worst that could happen might dismay but could not surprise her and, in the meantime, she took the only available precaution which was flight ('We are such cowards. We both hate air raids and are frightened to death of bombs' were her opening words to Eddie Sackville-West on a visit to the National Trust's headquarters at West Wycombe in June 1942[38]). But if Ivy had learnt early to count on nothing, she had also developed to a fine point the survivor's art of extracting pleasure from small things: a dish of prunes or an illicit lump of sugar in wartime, little tins of blackcurrant purée hoarded to give to her friends at Christmas 1942, a sunny afternoon spent with Dorothy Kidd in deckchairs in Regent's Park or exploring a country garden. 'The day with I. C.-B. and M.J. in the country was full of Visions Spiritual and Physical, we spent much time in Arabian Fruit and Flower Gardens, ripe Raspberries literally dropping about our feet—' wrote Dorothy on 18 July 1943, when Ivy and Margaret were staying for ten days at Uckfield in Sussex. The three saw much of one another that year when Roger Kidd was up at Cambridge: 'What a good vacation it was—Hampton Court in blazing sun,

Kew Gardens, the Rooftreeites, all the readings behind these "magic casements", the list is endless but to be run through often if a dismayed moment comes,' wrote Dorothy to Roger on 8 October ('Another Keats like day after our rather gunfired night'), and again two days later: 'So glad I pulled myself together to meet the Rooftreeites in the Orangery [Wren's orangery in Kensington Gardens] this morning—M.J. and I sat warmly in the sun while Miss I. prowled about the Round Pond—Walpole is tiresome but the saying of one of his characters "It isn't life, it's the Courage you bring to it" rings in my head—certainly M.J. has a goodly stock.'

Margaret's courage buoyed Ivy up, perhaps especially in the long, hot, gunfire-ridden summer and autumn of 1943 which the two spent in London, until a warning from Elliott Felkin that the Germans had invented some kind of flying bomb made them pack up once again just after Christmas to take refuge in Dorset. But Margaret had none of the gift Ivy was beginning to cultivate for cherishing her friends, and making them feel how much they meant to her. Raisley Moorsom remembered Ivy, some time in the 1920s, contradicting Elliott when he looked forward to escaping from all human claims in a shamelessly selfish old age: 'Nonsense, my dear Elliott, you will need all the love and affection you can get.' The saying—so unlike the cheerful cynicism Ivy generally conveyed in those days when she seemed neither to ask nor expect anything from anyone—startled Raisley so much that, even fifty years later, he remained at a loss to account for it. But it explains much about Ivy's own old age when she drew more and more on a side of herself she had long and severely suppressed in life, though never in her writing. Bertrand Russell describes a comparable readjustment when he summed up his position, in June 1931, by saying that he had always 'believed in the value of two things: kindness and clear thinking'[39] and that as he grew older he found the two things almost impossible to separate.* It is the philosophy invariably adopted in Ivy's books by characters like Dudley Gaveston, who explained, when asked what he meant by saying it was always a mistake for people to try to see themselves as others see them:

* At first these two remained more or less distinct; when I felt triumphant I believed most in clear thinking, and in the opposite mood I believed most in kindness. Gradually, the two have come more and more together in my feelings. I find that much unclear thought exists as an excuse for cruelty, and that much cruelty is prompted by superstitious beliefs. The War made me vividly aware of the cruelty in human nature, but I hoped for a reaction when the War was over.

'I think I only mean . . . that human beings ought always to be judged very tenderly, and that no one will be as tender as themselves. "Remember what you owe yourself" is another piece of superfluous advice.'

'But better than most advice,' said Aubrey, lowering his voice as he ended. 'More tender.'[40]

The fourteen-year-old Aubrey in *A Family and a Fortune* (1939) was the first of those enchanting, mercurial, tender-hearted and hard-headed children whose strangeness corresponds (as one reviewer remarked of the pair in *Elders and Betters*[41]) more to what it was actually like being a child than to any conventional, external, grown-up's eye view of childhood. After Aubrey, there were nine young Sullivans—including the tyrannical three-year-old Neville, surely one of the most accurately observed infants in literature—in *Parents and Children*, two Calderons and a Donne in *Elders and Betters*, six little Lambs in *Manservant and Maidservant*: dependent, vulnerable, alert and unsentimental, they live precariously in an unpredictable, often violent world which seemed perhaps more readily recognizable in wartime than before or since, as Elizabeth Bowen was the first to point out, reviewing *Parents and Children* in the *New Statesman* on 24 May 1941:

> Miss Compton-Burnett, as ever, makes few concessions; she has not, like some of our writers, been scared or moralised into attempting to converge on the 'real' in life. But possibly life has converged on her.

Ivy never wrote directly about wartime conditions, unless you count the austerity regime imposed on the household in *Manservant*

Russia made me feel that little was to be hoped from revolt against existing governments in the way of an increase in kindness in the world . . . I have not found in the post-war world any attainable ideals to replace those which I have come to think unattainable. So far as things I have cared for are concerned, the world seems to me to be entering upon a period of darkness. (*Autobiography of Bertrand Russell*, Vol. II, p. 158)

Russell, spurred by personal unhappiness in 1931 to articulate a pessimism widespread among people of his and Ivy's generation, was appalled by the 'very sober philosophy' she took for granted: what interested her was not the metaphysician's unending search for attainable ideals but the ways in which people actually function without them.

and Maidservant (published in 1947, when food, fuel and clothes
rationing became, if anything, stricter than ever) by Horace Lamb,
who skimps on ‥ ‥ children's shabby, frayed, shrunken and handed-
down clothes, docks them of sweets and toys, doles out economy
rations to the adults (' "Six cutlets would have been enough,"
said Horace. "They know we do not eat seven" '[42]) and prowls the
house snatching live coals from the grates (' "Fire piled right up the
chimney! Who is responsible?" said Horace'[43]). When *Parents and
Children* came out in May 1941, Ivy told Douglas Muir (a young
R.A.F. officer invited as an admirer to meet her at Hartley Court)
that she did not think she would be able to write anything more
during the war.[44] Eighteen months later she complained to Jim
Lees-Milne that she could not get on with her book because the war
was drying her up, and *Elders and Betters* was indeed a year behind
schedule when it finally appeared in January 1944. 'Not a cheerful
tome,' wrote Dorothy, who was staying with Ivy and Margaret at
Lyme Regis when *Elders and Betters* was published. 'Reviews of
Ivy's book are too good, encouraging this devastating analysis of
the evil in human nature.'[45]

Dorothy's was the common complaint of romantics defending
down the ages the importance of being ignorant ('Of all his lovable
qualities there was none so nobly potent . . . as David's white
innocence, his utter want of curiosity about all that was filthy,'
wrote E. F. Benson,[46] who had fought to the last against the
novelist's right to deal openly with matters much better kept dark,
like homosexuality). But it was an attitude less prevalent in wartime
when Ivy's hard line seemed on the whole as exhilarating as it was
alarming. Vita Sackville-West told Ivy that reading *Elders and
Betters* was like sucking a lemon ('She writes that she often felt
inclined to hurl the lemon to the far end of the room but was aware
that she would have to get up and pick it up again!' reported
Margaret from Lyme to Heywood Hill[47]); and for once Ivy's
astringency appealed to a public accustomed by this time to fear and
privation, unable any longer to bank on the future, unimpressed by
official evasiveness or easy sentiment, increasingly inclined to feel
with Vita that the only answer was a lemon. Ivy's sales had risen
steeply with *Parents and Children* in the early part of the war;
Gollancz started with an initial three thousand copies of *Elders and
Betters* on 24 January 1944, followed by two thousand more, then
another thousand, all of which had sold out by April without

satisfying the demand (the eventual print run came to more than double that amount[48]). 'The effect out here is quite astonishing,' wrote Captain Muir, whose copy reached him that summer on a posting in Malaysia with South East Asia command. 'If it has been difficult to write in wartime, I assure you that the extra effort has at least brought an extra reward to us.'[49]

What might be called the moral economy of Ivy's books had always been organized on a war footing. The rigorous honesty and irony that so often strike detractors as heartless, uncalled-for and cold will be familiar to anyone acquainted with soldiers' letters from the front in both world wars. The frame of mind underlying Noel Compton-Burnett's letters to Ivy and Jack in the first war was analysed in the second by the poet Keith Douglas, explaining his own lost innocence as a writer shortly before he was killed in Normandy in 1943:

> I suppose I reflect the cynicism and the careful absence of expecta-
> tion (it is not quite the same as apathy) with which I view the
> world. As many others to whom I have spoken, not only civilians
> and British soldiers, but Germans and Italians, are in the same
> state of mind, it is a true reflection . . . To be sentimental or
> emotional now is dangerous to oneself and to others. To trust
> anyone or to admit any hope of a better world is criminally
> foolish, as foolish as it is to stop looking for it. It sounds silly to
> say work without hope, but it can be done; it's only a form of
> insurance; it doesn't mean work hopelessly.[50]

This form of insurance, too costly and painful to be generally recommended for long, was essential to Ivy, whose humanity had grown from the complete lack of illusion with which she had emerged from the First World War. It was a policy that paid handsomely in the second, as L. P. Hartley reluctantly acknowledged, reviewing *Elders and Betters* for the *Sketch* on 23 February 1944: 'Anti-realistic, careless and even defiant of probability as it is, Miss Compton-Burnett's work sometimes seems nearer to reality than that of any living novelist.'

iii

At the beginning of 1944 when *Elders and Betters* came out, Ivy once again turned her back on the war, embarking with Margaret on a

final period of what she always called 'exile' at Lyme Regis where
they had often spent holidays before the war. Lyme lies a few miles
along the coast from the Marsden-Smedleys' cottage at Seatown,
within easy reach of Pinneys' at Racedown and Michael's family
home at Bettiscombe, as well as Margaret's old haunts at Broadwindsor, but low spirits, high prices and petrol restrictions made
for isolation. Dorothy and Roger had travelled down with them at
the New Year ('How lovely it is to feel that we know this place of
Peace to be found with Persian Carpet ease—unfettered sea and
coast'[51]) for five days spent exploring the precipitous little town
with its harbour, cliffs, Tudor tea shops and sheltered sea walks, its
prospect of sky and sea which Ivy and Margaret admired from
deckchairs in wintry sunshine or, more often, from behind the bow
windows of the Royal Lion overlooking the front. The Lion ranked
high on Margaret's list of 'possible pubs'[52] for its '*ample* food' and
willing service, but cramped quarters and fairly hit-or-miss housekeeping meant that, by the middle of the month, when heavy
regular bombing had begun again on London, the two friends were
looking for cheaper rooms of their own.

> Yesterday M.J. and I turned to Lyme (Upper) as I have on one or
> two evenings after tea, having walks along lanes where the
> evening birds seemed certain of primroses and white and purple
> violets [wrote Dorothy on 18 January to Roger (who had started
> his Cambridge term while his mother returned for a further week
> to the Lion)], but yesterday we just called on a delightful old lady
> who'd apartments and a bureau like the one Anne received the
> letter from (here I went off for your *Persuasion* to find that
> Captain Wentworth was seated at a table so it was only in the
> room, *how* inaccurate one's mind is even about Jane Austen . . .).
> How grateful I am to you and the Rooftreeites for making me
> return to this unbelievably blissful place.

Jane Austen was always much in mind at Lyme, where she herself
had stayed with her family and where she set parts of *Persuasion*.
Hester remembered once driving Ivy to the far end of the sea front
for a walk along the famous breakwater called the Cobb: 'I can see
Ivy standing on the Cobb with her gloves on, her hair neat, but a
rather flimsy scarf blowing in the wind, which is never very far off
at Lyme Regis.' When they reached the place where Louisa Mus-

grave slipped in *Persuasion*, Ivy looked down, 'saying how much more important in the long run was the twisted ankle of a young girl than all the clamouring of leaders in far off countries . . .'[53] This, or something very like it, was Jane Austen's response when urged to turn her attention to foreign affairs;* and she crops up repeatedly in the dialogue Ivy and Margaret composed in the spring of 1944 for *Orion*. This was a new literary magazine founded by Edwin Muir (long an admirer of Ivy's), Denys Kilham Roberts, Cecil Day Lewis, and Rosamond Lehmann who had boldly asked Ivy to explain her astonishing technique and received a rather dubious response ('She said she had not known she possessed a technique "until I looked and found that it was so" '[54]). 'In the end we compromised by writing together a "Conversation in Lyme Regis" in the manner of George Moore's *Conversations in Ebury Street*,' wrote Margaret on 22 June 1944, to Heywood Hill. 'I rake up all the absurdities of criticism and she answers them, and tells us why she writes as she does—It has its points.' This 'Conversation' was the nearest Ivy ever came to a considered public statement about her work, and for once it was Margaret who gracefully played second fiddle:

> M.J. I should like to ask you one or two questions; partly my own and partly what several friends have asked. There is time enough and to spare in Lyme Regis, which is a town well-known to novelists. Jane Austen was here, and Miss Mitford.
> I.C.-B. And now we are here, though our presence does not seem to be equally felt. No notice marks our lodging. And we also differ from Jane Austen and Miss Mitford in being birds of passage, fleeing from bombs. I have a feeling that they would both have fled, and felt it proper to do so, and wish that we could really feel it equally proper.[55]

Apart from this brief aside, apologetic but firm, current events hardly enter the 'Conversation': 'When war casts its shadow,' Ivy said, when asked why she never wrote about modern life, 'I find

* By the Prince Regent's librarian (*Jane Austen's Letters*, ed. R. W. Chapman, O.U.P. 1952, pp. 451–2). Ivy, pressed by John Bowen in a radio interview in 1960 to explain why her characters steered clear of politics and the Irish question, replied that public affairs never bore on their lives in the same way as personal experience: 'and I think that must always be so with everyone in all countries and at all times, and in every case—don't you think so?' (Burkhart 3, p. 168).

that I recoil.'[56] So do the bystanders in her books whose civilized, restraining voices prove so ineffectual against the explosions of primitive feeling that grew if anything fiercer as she steadily reduced overt contact with the contemporary world. Her four early novels, each in some sense experimental, had each maintained at least a nodding acquaintance with the life of the 1920s and 1930s, culminating in the cheerful modernity of tone, stylistic jerkiness and loose, gossipy structure of *More Women Than Men*. Thereafter, from *A House and Its Head* (1935) onwards, she narrowed her focus on the self-contained, heavily controlled and monitored, closed society of the high Victorian family. 'You write of the family as being a destructive unit,' said the novelist John Bowen in his 1960 radio interview with Ivy, who answered austerely: 'I write of power being destructive, and parents had absolute power over children in those days. One or the other had.'[57] Concentration brought greater technical control, and with it the greater emotional pressure banked up, in *A House and Its Head*, behind Duncan Edgeworth's repressed and withering rages or, with *Manservant and Maidservant* (1947), the nervous tension licking out of control round the edges of Horace Lamb's voice in repeated, hysterical attacks on his two defenceless small sons. Nothing in the early books matches the great family gatherings in *A Family and a Fortune* (1939) where passion seems to swell between the lines, scenes which are closer to a play than a novel in their surge and beat of feeling, the tumult of voices juxtaposed and interwoven so that the reader is successively aware of up to eight or nine characters reacting, collectively and individually, in a richly orchestrated whole.

The political aspect of Ivy's novels was not lost on contemporaries: 'Apart from physical violence and starvation, there is no feature of the totalitarian régime which has not its counterpart in the atrocious families depicted in these books,' wrote Edward Sackville-West immediately after the war.[58] But less was said about the emotional generosity always present and, as her plots grew harsher and more constricted, increasingly prevalent in her work. Admiration and pity—mixed feelings evoked as much by those who inflict suffering as by those who endure it—came in this middle period of her life as a writer to be the normal background of her mind, as they were of Miss Mitford's in *Parents and Children*. Ivy's tyrants, by their very destructiveness, breed little pockets of resistance. Courage, tolerance, sweetness, sanity and understanding spring up everywhere in holes and corners of nursery, schoolroom and servants' hall. Romantic love may be outside her compass (though never the misdeeds committed for love's sake). But no writer has made more of the affections that bind people across the generations in the same family (children, grandparents, quite often one or other parent as well as sympathetic uncles and stepmothers), young or middle-aged friends, and the convivial old married couples who flourish so cheerfully behind the front lines—or beyond the closed front doors—of her 'atrocious families'. Persecution is not the less palpable because its victims are adept in the ancient and honourable British tradition of bearing the unbearable by joking about it ('"It is true that tragedy arouses pity and terror," said Nance. "In me, terror is getting the upper hand"'[59]). *A House and Its Head* and *Daughters and Sons*, two chilling tales of domestic oppression and exploitation, contain between them half a dozen of the funniest proposals in fiction; and, if comic relief was always a speciality, so is the long, slow return to equilibrium after havoc and ruin at the end of books like *A House and Its Head* and *A Family and a Fortune*, or the knack of extracting sympathy even for monsters like Horace in *Manservant and Maidservant*:

> 'Is there something in Horace that twines itself about the heart? Perhaps it is his being his own worst enemy. That seems to be thought an appealing attribute.'
> 'The trouble with people who have it,' said Charlotte, 'is that they are bad enemies to other people, even if not the worst.'[60]

Elders and Betters, the book Ivy and Margaret discussed in 'A Conversation', has less of these grace notes than most ('In no other novel does Compton-Burnett allow such a consistently low standard of behaviour to prevail among the principal characters,' was Violet Powell's verdict in *A Compton-Burnett Compendium*[61]), perhaps because it was conceived, written and published in wartime. But neither Ivy nor Margaret felt inclined to raise the wider implications of this or any other book (Margaret had still not got round to reading *Elders and Betters* the month after publication,[62] though she had mastered the plot by the time they came to write 'A Conversation' in March). Their dialogue stuck firmly to the concrete and particular. Ivy began by politely and airily endorsing Margaret's belief in the intrinsic absurdity of critical theorizing: 'I cannot tell you why I write as I do, as I do not know. I have even tried not to do it, but find myself falling back into my own way.'[63] Questioned about sources, she declined to acknowledge any debt to other writers, saying no most emphatically to Henry James and the Russian novelists, less so to the Greek dramatists, least of all to Jane Austen ('I have read Jane Austen so much, and with such enjoyment and admiration, that I may have absorbed things from her unconsciously. I do not think myself that my books have any real likeness to hers. I think that there is possibly some likeness between our minds').

Margaret's prosaic style of questioning clearly suited Ivy better than the more formal, literary approaches of later interviewers. Margaret was accustomed to treat a novel much like any other historical source, itemizing points of interest[64] like the little modern tables cluttering an old-fashioned parlour in *Persuasion*, the sybaritic sofas in *Mansfield Park*, the mahogany wardrobe in *Northanger Abbey*, the Pembroke tables in *Emma* and Jane Austen's unfinished fragment called *The Watsons* ('Once I thought I should go mad because I couldn't finish *The Watsons*,' Ivy told Robert Liddell at their first meeting[65]); and Margaret's professional eye for incidentals perhaps pushed Ivy further than she might otherwise have gone towards defining and defending her own condensed and abstracted kind of reality ('I hardly see why the date and style of the Gavestons' house should be given,' she said, faintly nettled by Margaret's only comment on *A Family and a Fortune*, 'as I did not think of them as giving their attention to it, and a house of a different date and style would have done for them equally well'). Though she would not waste her time or Margaret's on questions of novelistic innovation and theory, Ivy's part of 'A Conversation' returned explicitly, again and again, to her preoccupation with those mysterious, submerged, subconscious depths where human beings function without inhibition well below any visible, external level, which was why people in general gave her no help at all: 'They do not say or do things that are of any good. They are too indefinite and too much alike and are seldom living on any but the surface of their lives. Think how rarely we should ourselves say or do anything that would throw light on our characters or experience.'

Certainly Ivy and Margaret gave nothing away, either publicly or to their oldest and most intimate friends. 'Dear I.C.-B. and M.J. I *am* so thankful we bring cheer to an, at the moment, rather

overcast existence for them though I don't exactly know why,'
wrote Dorothy to Roger on 18 January 1944, when advance copies
of *Elders and Betters* reached the Royal Lion from Gollancz. Ivy had
been especially edgy and tiresome that week, as she so often was
when she had finished or was on the point of bringing out a book,
while Margaret found herself probably for the first time in her life at
a loose end with no work on hand save a single French-furniture
article, Ivy's 'Conversation' and the Kent book (a prospect beginning to look up at last with the discovery of various Massingberd
and other papers, including five unpublished letters from Alexan-
der Pope). The last two were projects she would never have
undertaken, as she told Heywood Hill, if it had not been for 'the
breakdown of our ordinary life'.[66] Margaret was getting on for
seventy in the spring of 1944, Ivy would be sixty in June, and
neither welcomed the thought of living hand-to-mouth out of
suitcases again, very likely for months on end. Exile seemed
drearier than ever the second time round. Both missed London
sadly, and their friends even more. 'I.C.-B.'s letter this morning is
most amusing,' wrote Dorothy, back in London on 19 April, 'a
description of the party from Bettiscombe; a criticism of her and
M.J.'s dialogue from *Orion*; saying they miss you and me! and
ending "May we soon all gather on the pavements"—'

They had hoped to return to London themselves with the slack-
ening of air raids at the end of March but Elliott's warnings of secret
weapons meant that they were still in Lyme ('It isn't amusing but it
is safe'[67]) when the new and terrifying V1s began falling in June,
after the allied fleet landed in Normandy. Ernest, playing Malvolio
in Regent's Park, reported flying bombs several times cutting out
overhead, once so close that he was blown off the stage by the blast.
'I hope you have got Anne and the baby away?' wrote Margaret
anxiously to Heywood on 22 June. '. . . It sounds unpleasant
writing from a safe place to anyone in London and I feel apologetic
about it. I hope this chaos won't last long.' Left to herself, Margaret
might perhaps have settled, like Rose Macaulay, for braving the
destruction in London, though she admitted that flying bombs
—and later the even more alarming V2s or explosive rockets
—made the capital 'impossible for the moment to idle people like
ourselves, who are so used to safety that we feel like soft-shelled
crabs!'[68]

Not that Lyme proved an ideal refuge. Money was a problem

(they split the proceeds when Heywood sold one of Ivy's letters, supplied by Margaret in response to a request for manuscripts: 'Many thanks for the £1 which Ivy and I divided,' wrote Margaret, 'It will encourage her to write more letters'[69]). Where to stay was another problem. They moved at least half a dozen times at Lyme—from the Royal Lion to rooms at 'Cliff Bank' on the Sidmouth road in February, and on a month later to the Victoria Hotel, where they were staying when their Braemar Mansions flat 'had all its main windows blown in, so that it is a cave of the winds and uninhabitable'.[70] Margaret went up at the end of May to inspect the damage ('She says Ivy will not come back to London, she is so afraid of bombs'[71]), followed briefly a month later by Ivy: 'Our flat is blasted but the structure stands,' she wrote to Heywood on 3 August from the Victoria Hotel. Forced to pack up again, when the Victoria closed for a staff holiday in November, they shuttled to and fro for the next few months between the Royal Lion ('dearer and worse'[72]), the Clarence ('a smaller and cheaper hotel') and their old rooms at Cliff Bank. 'It is awfully harassing being driven from pillar to post, and it develops an acute longing for London,' wrote Margaret in an afterthought on the back of a letter to Jim Lees-Milne on 5 November 1944, and again, in another muddled, uncharacteristically wistful postscript five months later, 'I wish I was in London, and could see one's friends again.'

Friends were supremely important in these years to both Margaret and Ivy. Margaret made her will at Lyme in 1944, leaving everything to Ivy and, after Ivy's death, to her godson Luke Marsden-Smedley, in spite of Basil's best efforts on behalf of Frank Jourdain's son Seymour (cut off with £100). Seymour was by this time, with her brother Henry, Margaret's sole surviving relation. Frank had died at the beginning of the war (a will-dangler to the last, he too had explicitly disinherited Seymour, leaving his still considerable fortune to his daughter Violet, who promptly seized her chance to drop the hated name 'Jourdain'). Iris Compton-Burnett died in November 1944: 'It is sad news indeed. My sister was only sixty-three, and did a great deal for other people, and will be missed by many,' wrote Ivy diplomatically on the twenty-second to Mr Mowll: 'I had not seen her for over a year, as I have seen no one.' Family feelings had by this time ceased to trouble either Ivy or Margaret but, of all the deprivations of exile, the loss of friends was perhaps the hardest part.

Margaret was once again bored and restless, making plans that autumn to move nearer London ('for Dorset is a barren and dry land'[73]), to settle in Alton, Oxford, Winchester, anywhere within reach of a library, at the very least to get away from the seaside with its bad train service and dearth of congenial company, its want of any furniture to speak of, its stubborn resistance to diversions like the architectural exhibition put on by a friend 'to enlighten the people of Weymouth (who are a tough and refractory lot)'. Her *Georgian Cabinet-makers* sold out, like *Elders and Betters*, on publication in November ('I certainly did not think it was the book the world was waiting for!' reported Margaret fondly[74]), and the long-postponed first number of *Orion* was enthusiastically reviewed in the New Year. War news grew steadily more encouraging. By March, Ivy and Margaret were beginning to contemplate going home; on 4 April they left Lyme for the Swan at Alton (afterwards a favourite pub), and on the twenty-seventh they left Alton for London. 'We are returned from exile,' wrote Ivy triumphantly summoning the Hills to tea on 4 May, three days before peace was formally declared.

The tea party to which the Hills were invited was the first of many, for Ivy and Margaret had no notion of surrendering to postwar austerity which—in a phrase Margaret quoted in *Regency Furniture* about the Napoleonic campaigns—had 'doubled the cost and trebled the difficulty of genteel living'. Her diary shows that they spent the spring and summer of 1945 seeing their friends, renewing contacts, exchanging visits and generally picking up where they had been obliged to leave off. They scarcely left London save for a few days with Alice Marcon at Oxford and a weekend at Cambridge in June, followed by brief sorties later to Lyme Park, Kelmscott and Shillingford. Robert Liddell was back in England in August to dismantle the Oxford flat he had shared with his brother:

I went to tea with 'the ladies' (as their maid called them). 'Marge?' said Ivy, in a frank, open tone.

She asked after Donald, and I had to tell her that he had died of wounds in the Normandy invasion.

Ivy knew that it was the worst thing that could have happened to me, but she was, rather nicely, awkward. 'Oh, that is bad news; I didn't know, I hadn't heard.' Margaret was far more

socially adequate. She helped us both. Ivy (I now know) minded
too much.[75]

Nothing more was said. They changed the subject, swapping
literary gossip, discussing Robert's new book, *The Watering Place*,
and his efforts to help an elderly aunt, the sole survivor of his
mother's family, who was giving up her house in Tunbridge Wells
after losing her sister as well as her nephew the year before, and who
kept addressing Robert by his brother's name as 'Don':

> I mentioned that my mother, having died young, was canonized
> by her. 'And you are canonized too,' said Margaret.
>   'But she wants to live,' I said—it seemed extraordinary to me.
> 'You lack imagination,' said Ivy sternly. 'Death is the end.'[76]

This was as far as Ivy was prepared to go, then or later, with Robert
or anyone else, towards deliberately breaching the surface of life
which, in her view, afforded such precarious protection against
what lay below. But she had read *Kind Relations* in which Robert
and Donald reappear in the persons of Andrew and Stephen Faring-
don; and, though she never mentioned her own brother, she knew
that Donald had been to Robert what Noel had once been to herself,
'the beginning and end of life'.[77] Robert left England at the end of
the summer, returning for the last time in August 1947, when he
called again at Braemar Mansions and found Ivy briefly alone.
Margaret arrived late for tea, bringing ice cream ('for which Ivy and
I were insufficiently grateful I am afraid'[78]) and the latest news of
Dame Una's dissatisfaction with a reviewer who had cast doubt on
her qualifications for writing a book about jade (' "I don't know
about jade," said Ivy. "Except that it's that green stuff you get from
China." "I know a lot more about it than that," said Margaret in a
full, satisfied tone.'[79]) They talked about religion and relations and
whether or not Edith Sitwell ought to sue a critic whose views
might damage her sales ('we thought it had merely been his duty to
his readers to discourage them from buying a book he thought
bad'[80]). Margaret, with her scornful air, her superior poise, her
unstoppable flow of wickedly funny gossip, had again taken
charge, steering all three of them over deep waters which Ivy, for
once, was determined not to ignore: 'Ivy caught me alone in the
passage to say how much I must miss Donald. "Dreadfully," I said,

and it was very much worse when I was in England. This she well understood, though she did not think much of "Abroad".'[81]

Robert was one of the very few people Ivy freely forgave for settling abroad; and, though they never met again, they continued to share a side of her life firmly closed to friends who still saw her regularly at home. His book on the novel was published just before he left England for good in 1947, and she wrote on 14 October to thank him in Cairo 'for the part about myself', ending with a gentle reminder: 'I am still hoping for another book about the two boys, but know that your time must be full.' A year later he sent her *The Last Enchantments*, which tells how Andrew's and Stephen's story ended in Oxford (called Christminster in the novel):

July 9, 1948

Dear Mr. Liddell,

I returned from a month abroad to find *The Last Enchantments*.

And I was indeed enchanted, and find it a great pleasure to tell you how *much* I shall like to carry it with me as a companion.

It recalled to me the day when the two of us had tea with the two of you in your flat in North Christminster, and it even gave me the measure of what you have had, and what you have lost, and of the courage you must have needed to press on.

And there is still the gap in the history of Andrew and Stephen, that I want to be filled, though it is indeed ungrateful to ask for any more at the moment.

Yours very sincerely and gratefully,
Ivy Compton-Burnett.

Over the next twenty years and more, Ivy kept a close, benign, almost motherly eye on Robert and his activities through letters and reports from mutual friends, asking after his work, urging him not to write too fast, not to move house, not to draw on capital or tamper with his domestic arrangements (all problems with which Ivy found herself forced to contend in the 1950s and 1960s), always maintaining her delicate, insistent pressure on him to write what she called '*my* book'—'the further enchantments, and my especial ones'.[82] This was to be the middle instalment of the story of Andrew and Stephen, describing what happened after their father's second marriage when, under their new stepmother's rule, the two had no one but each other to turn to for comfort or affection. Robert's experience had been essentially Ivy's own and, for all their mutual reticence, it drew them together as nothing else could have done. In the aftermath of Donald's death, she offered what help and encouragement she could: 'We were sorry to hear that you are not thinking of coming to England for some time,' she wrote on 26 July 1950. 'But I see that the past must become the past and leave the present before you can wish to do so, and in your place I should feel the same. I hope you are writing, or will do so when the mood returns. It is subject to fits of wandering . . .'

Another ten years were to pass before 'my book' was written (whereupon publication was delayed for almost a further ten): years in which the two grew steadily more at home with one another's work, writing appreciatively whenever a new novel appeared, exchanging consolation when one was held up, discussing the contents of Robert's *The Novels of I. Compton-Burnett* ('I should be grateful indeed for this book to see the light'[83]). *The Last Enchantments* had contained an implicit tribute to Ivy,[84] and *Stepsons* (when it eventually appeared in 1969, after the second Mrs Liddell's death and only a few months before Ivy's own) brought them—as Ivy said—'very near'.[85] Robert wrote directly about an experience that Ivy had broached with no one, probably not even with Margaret, though it acquired in her work, in distilled and abstracted form, a universal application not accessible to a more strictly naturalistic novelist. Their literary methods could hardly have been more different but morally, emotionally and intellectually they were at one as Ivy had not been with anyone since Noel died. Both before and after the 'Conversation at Lyme Regis', Margaret in private scarcely let up in her derisive attitude to Ivy's (and by this time practically everybody else's) books; and, after Margaret's death, Ivy looked to Robert for a sympathy and comprehension that grew stronger with time.

> I feel that in many ways I was closer to her mind than anyone [he wrote after Ivy's death]. I am told she never gave a hint of this, and that does not alter my view. We started off with a similar (though no doubt different) experience of family life, and an adoration of Jane Austen, and . . . a profound feeling for Samuel Butler. And we knew a similar love and loss. It was a tragic accident that the pattern of our lives should have so followed each other. Of her goodness to me, if I tried (ineffectually) to fill the gap and her charity, I don't wish to speak . . .[86]

CHAPTER SEVEN

'Truth is so impossible. Something has to be done for it'

i

MANSERVANT AND MAIDSERVANT was finished at the beginning of March 1946,[1] which means that it must have been written over the previous year, in London, after the end of the war. It was one of the books Ivy most enjoyed writing ('I quite missed it when it left my hands,' she wrote to the novelist Elizabeth Taylor[2]), and the one she afterwards singled out whenever anyone asked for her favourite. Its publication marked a high point in her reputation with reviewers on both sides of the Atlantic who responded to the richness, complexity and emotional warmth of her mature work, set off by a return to something very like the buoyancy and high spirits of twenty years before in humorous, hopeless Mortimer Lamb (variously interpreted by Ivy's friends as Elliott Felkin and/or Ernest Thesiger, mixed on a base supplied by Goldsworthy Lowes Dickinson and topped off perhaps with an astringent dash of Roger Hinks) and his friend, the magisterial butler Bullivant. The book is unsparing on Horace Lamb's cruelty to his deprived and defenceless small children ('I am so glad you think I am a compassionate writer,' wrote Ivy in another letter to Elizabeth Taylor when Manservant and Maidservant came out, 'as I always feel myself so very pitiful'[3]). But it ends leniently all round, and the general impression is light, gay, airy, full of energy and good humour, a marked relief after the cramped and wintry world of Elders and Betters. 'It is as if the author has turned a corner in a dark tunnel and emerged into a brighter landscape,' wrote Violet Powell in her Compton-Burnett Compendium.[4]

This was very much how Ivy felt at the time. She and Margaret had emerged intact from a second round of violence and upheaval ('After living in mature awareness through two wars,' she wrote to Robert Liddell a few years later, 'that side of me is worn out, and can do no more'[5]); and both were only too thankful to settle back with their maid, their flat and their friends into the 'dear, little, narrow life' so highly prized by Elton Scrope and his sister in The

Present and the Past. 'I tolerate nothing that looms ahead,' says Ursula Scrope, explaining why she preferred at thirty-two to take no further active part in human affairs: 'I will not be threatened by life.'[6] Ivy, who had been not so much threatened as systematically assaulted by life between her seventeenth and thirty-second birthdays, wholeheartedly endorsed the Scrope plan thereafter; and she managed to make the most of it again for a few years after the Second World War.

An abundance of gossip and visits made up for much that was missing from bombed and blackened London. The flat had been restored, its furniture retrieved and ranged round the walls again between the tall windows of the bare, high-ceilinged drawing room instantly recognizable, to a visitor seeing it for the first time, from Ivy's description in *Manservant and Maidservant*: 'large and light and chill, and furnished with few and stately things . . . good to look at, less good to live in'[7] (a rather gloomier view was taken by Raymond Mortimer, whose memories of Ivy's various London flats clearly lay behind his impression of her fictional country houses: 'We feel that the rooms are sombre, the furniture massive, the food too plentiful and too plain'[8]). Entertaining was possible again with the help of food parcels sent from abroad by friends like Robert: it was round about this time that cucumbers, bowls of lettuce and radishes with home-made curd cheese and white and brown loaves began to appear on Ivy's tea table in place of the buns, cakes and enormous sugary meringues no longer obtainable in time of shortage and sweet coupons.

Rationing is a running joke in *Manservant and Maidservant* where scones, puddings, stale cake and lamb cutlets are all parsimoniously counted out, the children steal sweets and raid store cupboards, while the servants pass disparaging remarks in private about 'labour-saving', mass-produced 'factory stuff' and substandard redcurrant jam (' "I prefer jam that is not all pips; that is all," said George, routing in the pot as though for some substance distinct from these'[9]). The stern line taken below stairs in the Lamb household was by and large Ivy's own in an age of austerity. Sonia Brownell (Cyril Connolly's very young and extremely pretty assistant on *Horizon*, afterwards George Orwell's second wife) came to tea for the first time immediately after the war, when Margaret apologized for having run away to the country—'You must have suffered a great deal, my child, in London during the bombing'—and was teased for it by Ivy: 'Nonsense, Margaret, you remember how we suffered from that butcher!'[10]

Sonia belonged to a younger generation of Ivy's admirers with whom it was Margaret's turn to register, if at all, as the funny old companion who kept the conversation going, fielding awkward questions and plugging gaps with social protocol of the most banal kind. At this first meeting, when Margaret asked after 'dear Mr Connolly', Sonia replied without thinking: 'Oh, he's getting frightfully boring—only interested in *furniture*'. Even before the publication of *Manservant and Maidservant*, life at Braemar Mansions was beginning to fall into the postwar pattern set by increasing numbers of newcomers who found Margaret affable enough but officious, interfering and, by comparison with Ivy, decidedly dull. Of course there was still a furniture faction, generally friends of much longer standing who continued to write Ivy off to the end: 'If you went to their flat, you'd never have thought she had anything to do with the world of letters,' said Ralph Edwards. 'Literature was a topic you hardly raised. She was very strong on charwomen. And patum peperium and radishes and whether this was a good biscuit. She hadn't read *anything*. If Ivy didn't wish to be communicative' (and in his experience she never did) 'you couldn't do anything with her.'

Ivy had always adopted a protective carapace with people like Ralph Edwards but it changed a good deal after the war. For one thing she was no longer inconspicuous. Her unfashionably long dark dresses had ceased to serve their original purpose of deflecting attention, and she wore her delicate, Georgian diamond brooch and ear-rings (chosen by Margaret, when Ivy—who had inherited her mother's love of diamonds—lost all her jewellery in a burglary at Christmas, 1945[11]) with simplicity and distinction.

Her jewellery managed never to look like jewellery but, on her, seemed hieratic insignia [wrote Robin Fedden, describing their first meeting at tea in 1946]. I do not recall seeing her out of black. She wore it like a uniform, with care but with the disregard for mode proper to uniform. A sense positively of the Services attached to a black tricorne, vaguely reminiscent of an eighteenth-century quarter-deck. There was also the long black umbrella. This she would carry to dinner a mere two hundred yards from Braemar Mansions on a halcyon evening . . .[12]

Strangers like Fedden, who had read Ivy's books with astonished delight since the 1930s, seldom had much difficulty in recognizing the classic integrity of her writing in Ivy's erect carriage, firm features and humorous expression:

> For me, the physical impression was recurrently of a Roman head, a soldier-emperor, perhaps Galba. The rolled hair and the ribbon sometimes seemed like a laurel wreath.
>
> The moral impression was of sanity and principle. Level-headed, in the best sense of the word, was an adjective that she evoked. If I have met a human being whose values were not blurred, it was Miss Compton-Burnett.

Others found both the author and her books altogether more off-putting. Several observers remembered the striking figure she made in her black tricorne town hat (she had a brown straw, with brown coat and gloves, for the country, and a parasol for sunny days instead of the umbrella) at a party given by the Edwardses a few years after the war to watch the Oxford and Cambridge boat race from their house on the Thames in Chiswick Mall. 'She looked formidably severe. I think she was severe,' wrote Anthony Powell, whose introduction to her at this party induced 'the sort of constraint experienced as a child talking to an older person, whom one suspected could never understand the complexity of one's own childish problems'.[13] She produced the same reaction in a good many people of Powell's generation, and it grew more pronounced with age:

> I think the explanation of my sense of unease was no more and no less than what has been said; Ivy Compton-Burnett embodied in herself a quite unmodified pre-1914 personality, so that one was, in truth, meeting what one *had* encountered as a child . . . No writer was ever so completely of her books, and her books of her.

Ivy's 'pre-1914 personality' was, as Powell went on to point out, an illusion or rather an invention, as artificial in its way as her period settings and providing, like them, a formal context which could preclude or permit intimacy at will. There are many accounts of the consternation Ivy caused by hitching up her long dress far above the knee and splaying her legs as she sat down to table (a habit left over, according to Fedden, from days when the legs of both table and diners would have been modestly concealed by a floor-length damask cloth), sitting back afterwards with her legs comfortably stuck out in front of her like a man, or—most disconcerting of all to nervous subjects—rummaging around under her capacious skirts in a slow, methodical search for the handkerchief tucked in her knickers ('I always stuff mine in the elastic of my breeks,' she explained frankly to Elizabeth Taylor[14]). She shared with Margaret a trick of ducking her head to look down the front of her bodice, 'as though she had detected something surprising there, and not altogether pleasant'[15] (Margaret blew down hers as well, so often that friends used to wonder what on earth she kept in her bosom —Herman suggested perhaps a white mouse). For all her insistence on propriety and manners, Ivy's conventionality was never more than skin deep: 'In her life as in her novels,' wrote Fedden, 'she used the framework of her Victorian–Edwardian background as a convenience to be discarded when it suited her.'

Powell and Fedden had both been formally presented to Ivy and both remained afterwards on decorous, dinner-party terms, but 1946 brought another admirer who scrutinized her with great affection and shrewdness from a quite different angle. Ivy marked the completion of *Manservant and Maidservant* by spending a fortnight in Cornwall with Margaret, returning on Tuesday, 26 March 1946, in good time for the Edwardses' first postwar boat-race party the following Saturday, and sending on the twenty-seventh for a new typist to replace the agencies who had typed her manuscripts up till now. This was Cicely Greig, who had discovered Ivy's books at a very early age through David Garnett in the *New Statesman* and knew them by this time well enough to recognize almost immediately the rules by which she was expected to play: 'I was of the governess class, I decided. Once I had solved this little problem of our relationship I was quite happy and content to "keep my place" . . . I enjoyed my part, and our relationship was always a smooth one.'[16]

Cicely, starting out on a freelance career after the war, with ambitions as a writer herself, had simply sent postcards care of their publishers to favourite authors, including Rose Macaulay and I. Compton-Burnett ('I would love to type one of your novels. I have read *A House and Its Head* seven times'), and thought no more about it until Ivy's summons, arriving out of the blue many months later, filled her with amazement and disbelief. Ivy saw to it that their first interview kept to a strictly business footing. Effusiveness was in any case ruled out under the terms of their tacit agreement but Cicely was rapidly accepted as a regular visitor at Braemar Mansions—'To Ivy and Margaret I was a creature from another world: I worked for my living'—becoming something of a favourite with both ladies, and one of their principal informants on strange, new postwar anomalies like the welfare state and the National Health Service.

She typed for them both, dropping in at least every two or three months, often stopping for tea or coffee after lunch when she called to fetch or deliver work. Ivy's manuscripts came in batches of cheap school exercise books, neatly written in pencil, twelve or fourteen to a novel, with red or blue covers and multiplication tables on the back ('I remember thinking this last detail quite a fitting decoration for a book of Ivy's'). Margaret's articles, or later the loose chapters of her book on William Kent, were stuffed into bulging untidy parcels and had to be pieced together from scribblings on the backs of old coal bills, circulars, used Christmas cards, letters and their flattened-out envelopes (these were naturally read with care on both sides by Cicely, who found her employers' lives as fascinating and as hard to imagine as they found hers). From 1946 onwards, Cicely was the first person to set eyes on each fresh novel as it left Ivy's hands and, though she had started with no intention of being Ivy's permanent typist, it became a satisfaction she could not give up:

> Her writing never changed. And her wit remained sharp, the knock of her sentences as powerful, the same strong beat and rhythm throughout. And the pleasure I got from typing those sentences can't be put into words. Their beauty slowed me down. I would read the sentence I had just typed again, and stare at the finished page.

Cicely's enthusiasm, however carefully subdued and ineffusive, made a change from the comparatively blank if deferential reception Ivy's manuscripts got elsewhere. She tried for the last time to change publishers in 1946 when the novelist Graham Greene, then working for Eyre and Spottiswoode, persuaded her to let his firm republish the three Heinemann novels together with *A Family and a Fortune*,[17] the second to come out from Gollancz who had sold two thousand copies and let the book go out of print—to Ivy's surprise and chagrin—less than four months after publication. She had remonstrated at the time, holding that Gollancz should have either printed a larger edition in the first place or preserved the type long enough to meet the demand for another impression. Gollancz remained adamant, preferring in the end to relinquish rights over *A Family and a Fortune* sooner than agree to reprint it or any other of her novels. Ivy saw no alternative save to accept Greene's proposal, promising him her next new novel but one when Gollancz's second three-novel contract ran out with the book after *Manservant and Maidservant* (her confidence in publishers was so shaky that she seems to have taken it for granted Gollancz, like Heinemann, would drop her at the end of the first contract, and had been pleased and taken aback by his prompt acceptance when Curtis Brown's wife Jean offered him refusal of *Elders and Betters* in 1943).

But nobody mentioned the shadier side of this deal to Gollancz, who was first alerted two years later by Eyre and Spottiswoode's advertisement for the first volumes of their handsome new Compton-Burnett *Collected Works*. A telephone call to Douglas Jerrold, the firm's managing director and Gollancz's longstanding publishing rival, erupted into heated accusation and recrimination, sharpened on Gollancz's part by an acute if not wholly justified sense of personal betrayal. By this time—the beginning of September 1948—the two-year period stipulated for Eyre and Spottiswoode's republication had expired which meant that their contract was technically cancelled: Graham Greene wrote at once to Ivy, explaining that all four novels were already at the printers and apologizing for the delay ('You know my own feelings about your work, and that there is no living English novelist whom I would rather publish'[18]). Spencer Curtis Brown washed his hands of the whole affair, disclaiming any further responsibility to Ivy and executing a rapid volte-face in favour of Gollancz. Ivy herself sent Gollancz a series of letters in her loopy, black, illegible handwriting setting out her own position from the start: her anxiety to see her books in print, her repeated discouragement at his hands, her reluctance to leave him ('I have never had a wish to make a change of publisher, only a very strong one that my books should be made available'), and her current disappointment with Eyre and Spottiswoode, ending with a confession of helplessness and a still more disarming apology ('I am sorry indeed to have discussed the matter on a wrong basis. But you will see that I am more sinned against than sinning').

The upshot was that Gollancz, who had apparently published Ivy's books for over a decade without ever meeting her, took her out to lunch on 6 October 1948, when they settled that Eyre and Spottiswoode should go ahead with the four old novels while Gollancz got the new ones on condition he republished *Daughters and Sons* and *Brothers and Sisters* (which left only *Pastors and Masters* outstanding). Both parties emerged from this affray with mingled relief and dissatisfaction: Ivy cannot have felt entirely sanguine about forcibly extracting Gollancz's consent to an arrangement he roundly denounced as bad publishing while, though Gollancz had held on to his author, he must have felt her behaviour legitimately discharged him from any further pretence at enthusiasm. He turned down Jerrold's last offer to take Ivy off his hands altogether or, failing that, take over her back titles in April 1951; but he never shared Jerrold's view that each new novel built up overall sales or that her reputation might be enhanced by keeping her books in print. His correspondence with Ivy settled over the next two decades into routine complaints from her about the handling of her current book, automatically parried by his insistence that prominent advertising would damage her sales while the reissues to which he had so reluctantly agreed were in his view pretty well bound to prove a glut on the market.

But relations, though cool, were still cordial when *Manservant and Maidservant* came out on 11 February 1947, after Ivy had decided to leave Gollancz and before he suspected her intentions. Publication was celebrated by a party in Ivy's honour given by the Hills with Robin McDouall (gourmet, bon vivant and later a convivial secretary to the Travellers' Club) who had met her through Heywood and remained ever afterwards a faithful friend. The critics were almost uniformly appreciative, and mostly a good deal more discriminating than Ivy was inclined to allow ('I have never had such superficial reviews on the whole as I have had this time, or had so far,' she wrote ungratefully to Elizabeth Taylor on 28 June). Other novelists—Elizabeth Bowen, P. H. Newby, L. P. Hartley, Anthony Powell ('this new one is in the top class'[19]) and Pamela Hansford Johnson—were especially generous; Daniel George went so far as to lay a public curse in *Tribune* on 21 March on Compton-Burnett fans—'I hope their water freezes again'—who made off with his first editions; and several writers recommended her to the redoubtable Blanche Knopf of New York, making her first publishing sortie after the war in search of fresh talent in Europe that summer.

'My books do not take in America, and this one will need all the help it can get,' said Ivy,[20] writing to thank Elizabeth Taylor for negotiating on her behalf while she was abroad, spending June with Margaret in France. *Manservant and Maidservant* sold nearly five thousand copies in six weeks, easily overcoming the token resistance put up by Mrs Knopf—'I daren't take home any more prestige'[21]—whose firm became the third (after Harcourt, Brace and Norton) to try to get Ivy to take with the American public. Knopf published her next three novels, beginning with *Manservant and Maidservant* which came out as *Bullivant and the Lambs* in 1948, and was generally felt by reviewers to have won the season's New York novel stakes by a short head from Norman Mailer's *The Naked and the Dead* ('Miss Compton-Burnett is increasingly unfair to most other contemporary British novelists . . .' reported the *New York Times*. 'They seem to be breathing too hard by comparison'[22]).

ii

The tide of celebrity showed signs of washing over Ivy again as it had done twenty years earlier and this time, though she did not ask it in, she made no move to shut it out either. Cecil Beaton, arriving to take her portrait for *Vogue*, found his wheedling professional charm assessed by an eye as stonily expert as his own: 'He was more interested in the furniture, I think,' Ivy reported to Cicely. 'He asked me to sit in that chair . . . I told him it was broken, and might give way. He just said, "Yes, but you will sit in it for *me*, won't you?"'[23] According to Jim Lees-Milne, it was Margaret rather than Ivy whose vigilance rivalled Beaton's own ('I don't know anyone who approached Cecil Beaton for being observant. His eyes were fixed on every blemish. Margaret wasn't quite like that, but she came damned close'); but he and Ivy summed one another up pretty well. He photographed her in black with a diamond brooch and a touch of white at the neck, enthroned on the rickety chair, gazing squarely at her photographer with hands clasped and eyes level, framed beneath a gilt mirror by two small, ornate, fan-shaped eighteenth-century firescreens on tall, slender stands. Between them, she and Beaton had arrived at an image—formal, hieratic, the extreme simplicity, severity and firmness of the pose emphasized by the delicate straight lines and curves of the furniture—that did much to fix the impression Ivy and her work were from now on to make on the public.

Beaton's pictures were of course specifically designed as public portraits, which did not please people like Cicely who thought he made Ivy look old, sinister, unlike herself and uncomfortably close to her own tyrants. But what Beaton saw is borne out by another trained observer, Cecil Gould of the National Gallery, who also met Ivy for the first time in 1948 or 1949 when he wrote about the paintings in Sir Malcolm Stuart's collection which Margaret was cataloguing:

She was something which I hadn't met before, and haven't since. Her attitude to life was that of an intellectual, but she had the minimum intellectual interests in the academic sense. Almost the only one was contemporary English fiction—of which she had read, and immediately on publication, everything that anybody ever claimed might be any good, and of which she was a penetrating and never wholly favourable critic . . .

The object of her intellectual curiosity was almost exclusively people's behaviour, their habits of life, their reactions under temptation, and particularly the minutiae of their lives. The latter linked with the only material thing which really did interest her—money. She was passionately interested in the price of everything, particularly of indispensable things, food, domestic appliances, rents, rates and servants' wages. She was also much interested in sexual aberrations. 'He's getting married, like so many homos one knows,' she remarked once in my hearing . . .

She had very little overt vanity to the extent that she never led the conversation to her writing, and tended to kill it quickly if anyone else did. Some of this may have been due to another kind of vanity—the idea that no one was equipped to give her work its due. She undoubtedly thought highly of it herself. She took a very low view of people in general, always imputing the worst and most selfish motives until the contrary was proved . . .

She seemed with all this very cold. Hard—but not impossible —to be fond of, and hard—but not impossible—to have her fond of one. Most people in addition were a little frightened of her. She depended on her friends to constitute a circle and much resented it if they defected. Undoubtedly some of them were drawn to her by her celebrity value. To me the attraction initially was as a survival of a very interesting form of life—a Victorian intellectual of an unusual kind. And of course entertainment value. Though the cracks were not nearly as thick off the ground as in her books, one was not bored.[24]

This is a retrospective portrait, based on a friendship of twenty years during which Ivy changed a great deal in private as well as becoming to the public one of the legends of literary London. Even so, estimates of her coldness varied wildly, generally corresponding quite closely to what the observer found in her books ('One had a gruesome feeling that, for the moment, one had *become* one of her characters, and not a favourite one at that,' wrote Pamela Hansford Johnson, whose first nightmare visit to Braemar Mansions in 1951 bore out her view of the novels as on the whole brilliant but heartless[25]). Ivy was, as she said, always pitiful in her books to the maltreated and weak, young or old, from the elderly Miss Griffin brutalized by her employer in *A Family and a Fortune* to the seven-year-old Avery Lamb who can't sleep in *Manservant and Maidservant* for fear of his father (' "Is Father gone now?" said Avery. "I don't want him to come here. He is always in all the places. I don't want him to come where I sleep. I don't like to think he might look at me in the night" '[26]). But she was scarcely less sorry for their tormentors, caught in a situation they can no more control or resist than their victims; and what made people nervous of Ivy was often this impartial distribution of feeling, coming from someone who hardly needed to know all before she forgave it. If her friends preferred on occasion to avoid exposing their problems to Ivy, it was not so much for fear of what she might do, or even what she might say, rather for fear of how much she might understand ('I wonder people are not afraid of the truth,' says Charity Marcon in *Daughters and Sons*, discussing death with her brother, who answers: 'They are afraid of it, terrified, as you are. You have put their fears into words. You are much bolder than most people; I think you are too bold'[27]).

'Where everyone says what he thinks, and thinks much, it is as if everyone were clairvoyant,' as an American reviewer said of

Bullivant and the Lambs[28]; and visitors to Braemar Mansions—at any rate those who had read her books attentively—were often painfully aware of Ivy's clairvoyance. It explains her insistence on talking about prices and plumbing, which grew steadily more perverse after Margaret died when Ivy, who could not say what she did not think, was seriously short of innocuous small talk. 'To me Ivy and her books were inseparable,' wrote Cicely. 'If you loved one you loved the other, and you understood Ivy from reading her books and enjoyed her books more from having met her.'[29] But even for Cicely—easily flustered by Ivy, and too close to the workings of her inner mind ever entirely to shake off an initial trepidation—it was often a relief to be relegated to the governess class. Though Margaret's casual, friendly manner eased the strain, Cicely remained acutely aware of how much a slow or insensitive reaction grated on Ivy, who marked her displeasure with withering silence or a cutting aside, very rarely an open rebuke: 'At such times Ivy's grey-green eyes could take on a fierce, cold glint, and she made me think of some of her old tyrants . . .' But Cicely bore Ivy's occasional sharpness ('and even her sharpness was worth having') meekly in silence; and no one has left a more persuasive picture of Ivy's private face, the hospitable and encouraging side of her nature that played no part in her public image:

> Photographers like line and bone structure, and wanting this they made her tilt her head upwards, some of them, so that her chin appeared to jut menacingly. She had a strong face, but her chin was not at all the jutting kind, and there was no hardness in the lines of her mouth. Her small, arched nose was not arrogant but suggested the classic austerity of her thought. Her mouth, on the other hand, showed a great sweetness and gentleness of character. Her humour was in her eyes, wonderfully expressive green-grey eyes. I never heard her laugh, but I have often seen laughter in her eyes. At other times they were watchful, wary, sometimes hostile . . .

Probably only Margaret knew Ivy well enough to understand what lay behind her wariness, and Margaret to the end of her life protected, even pampered Ivy as she had done since they first met more than thirty years earlier. Cicely describes a curious incident in the summer of 1948 when Margaret was so stirred by a review of

Bullivant and the Lambs in *Time* magazine, fixing her eyes on Ivy's face with an expression of such rapt pride and intimacy, that Cicely made an excuse and left ('there was an urgency in her look that fairly drove me away'[30]). Certainly the general impression was that things were going well between the two, now that Margaret was also securely back in the top class as a pundit. Vere Watson-Gandy, a contemporary and close friend with whom they often stayed at Buckland Newton in Dorset after the war, remembered Margaret treating Ivy with the sort of indulgent, amused affection a man might keep for a silly little wife, especially the 'wonderful snort' with which she greeted each fresh absurdity of Ivy's, like not knowing which end of a train was the front or how to fix stamps and string to a parcel. Mrs Watson-Gandy's son, Jim Brandreth (the name was changed to comply with a relative's will), arranged a visit to the Marquess of Blandford's place in the country where Ivy infuriated her hostess by first politely declining to admire the magnificent formal borders and beds, then being captivated by a stray daisy the gardener had failed to pluck from the lawn. On a second trip with Jim to Maple Durham (unknown and generally inaccessible even to connoisseurs in those days), Ivy mesmerized the entire party, when four o'clock came and there was no tea, by retreating once again to the centre of the lawn, sitting down and refusing to budge, a small mutinous black dot ('she was the very picture of revolt') in matching coat, hat and gloves.[31]

To people like the Pinneys and the Watson-Gandys—members of old county families, descendants of hunting squires, the last generation still clinging to the pleasant, well-appointed lives of the cultivated country gentry in a world that knew nothing of the novels of I. Compton-Burnett—Ivy remained always 'Margaret's shadow': retiring, inconspicuous, comical, even derisive, but more than content for all her teasing to follow where Margaret led. Ivy's constant complaint in these years was of being abandoned in London while Margaret flitted round the country escorted by one or other of a fresh supply of young men ('Bobbie' and 'Robin' and 'Keith'—Bobbie Heath, Robin Ironside, Keith Miller-Jones—had replaced the married men, Soame and Peter Wilson, in Margaret's postwar diaries) on furniture jaunts or lucrative consultation jobs at fifty guineas a time. Being left alone was what Ivy dreaded more than anything. She was, as she said, 'a very sociable person'[32] but, apart from a handful of old familiars—Rose, Herman, Ernest,

Roger Hinks when he was at home, the Kidds and the Marsden-Smedleys—she could never feel entirely comfortable in company without Margaret to bear the brunt.

> Margaret was quite unselfconscious [wrote Elizabeth Taylor, who met Ivy for the first time through Robert in 1947]. Would stand stock-still in a restaurant surveying the tables through lorgnettes. Had bitter feuds, bore rancour, took umbrage (*her* phrases). She stuck out her legs in theatres, so that people who had annoyed her couldn't pass, & prevented some poor creature from pursuing his studies at the V&A because they seemed to encroach on her territory.[33]

If Margaret struck most people as the man of the party, there were others who found something essentially masculine in Ivy's strength and reserve; while, to young women like Cicely and Dorothy Stroud, Margaret (who had given generous encouragement to both in the early stages of their respective careers after the war) seemed the embodiment of feminine charm and warmth, all feather boas, pretty hats and voluminous Edwardian drapery. 'I remember seeing her once in the Library of the Victoria and Albert Museum,' wrote Cicely. 'She rustled and flowed between the bookshelves, a harmony of soft pinks and greys and E flat, so that heads were turned . . . Margaret was languorous-seeming, with a charming graciousness.'[34] The fact is that Margaret and Ivy were both, as Ralph Edwards said, *sui generis*, unique, outside ordinary categories. 'Their drawing room might have been a man's room,' said Soame Jenyns. 'If you'd gone into that flat, you wouldn't have known it was inhabited by women.' 'Yes,' said his wife, 'but then, on the other hand, you wouldn't have thought it was lived in by men either.'

At all events, Ivy and Margaret in those years were both at the height of their form. The young writer Kay Dick, commissioned by the B.B.C. French service to write a script about Ivy, met them for the first time at tea in October 1950:

> Ivy welcomed me with grace and some amusement. I felt at ease—this was a trap—because physically she reminded me of a patrician step-aunt I had known in childhood. She was tiny, yet unequivocally imposing. Her physical quality was neat and

precise. Her eyes were beautiful, and most appealing. They reminded me of someone I loved, who had a similar perceptiveness. Her ringed hands were small, delicate, sprightly and suggested gentleness . . . So enthralled was I with my experience of tea with Miss Compton-Burnett, that at first I failed to notice that I was the one who was being questioned. In fact, with a sparse directness I was soon to recognise as her forte, Ivy was fast discovering everything about me, and I was lamentably failing to discover anything about her.[35]

It was not till much later that Kay Dick, who had not then read any of Ivy's novels, realized her mistake in thinking she had concealed the fact from her hostess. But her growing confidence at the time was strengthened when Margaret, arriving late, brought her own charm to bear alongside Ivy's:

I felt quite stunned as I sat between the two ladies and was amiably interrogated by both of them—about my reading, not, happily, about Ivy's novels. 'What would you advise us to read?' they innocently asked. I fell right into it, and gave my act of young, up-to-date reader advising two quiet elderly spinsters what titles they should add to their library lists. I was being quizzed and had not the wit to appreciate it until I was outside the flat. Their smiling faces and dutiful nods impressed me—with my own knowledge . . . 'You must come and see us again,' they said, I feel certain, in chorus.

Margaret was by no means always so benevolent to Ivy's callers; but on a good day in the right company when she and Ivy were both in the mood, they were expert at tending, coaxing and firing a conversation much as others might stoke coals in a grate. They capped one another's witticisms with a vigour and skill that made their perpetual scoring off one another almost a spectator sport for their friends, and they had a very funny antiphonal style of telling stories, taking it in turns, for instance, to describe the frightful fix they found themselves in at a French convent (Ivy always strongly recommended convents for holidays, as being cheap, quiet, clean and free from strong drink), when they set out along a cloister, making for the bathroom with soap and sponge bags, only to be met head-on by a procession bearing the host.

After the tedium, isolation and hardship of England in wartime, even Ivy admitted that abroad had its points ('We had a perfect month in France,' she wrote on 16 July 1947, explaining to Elizabeth Taylor that people who didn't drink could manage quite well on the government's meagre £75 travel allowance: 'Of course, *Paris* is ruinous'). They spent June 1948 in the Savoy, returning the year after for another month at St Gervais within easy reach of Elliott, who came over from Geneva to walk, talk and explore with Margaret while Ivy gave her full attention to the Alpine flowers. It was probably on one of these holidays that Joan Evans, sitting in a slow train from St Moritz in the Alps down to Macon, saw Margaret standing with Ivy on the platform at Bride-les-Bains (one of only three treasured glimpses of Margaret after the breach in 1924—once Joan caught sight of her from the top of a bus in Sloane Street, and once they were in the same room but did not speak on the day women were admitted to the Society of Antiquaries[36]). Later plans for a holiday in Greece, to see Robert Liddell and admire the wild flowers, were successfully scotched by Roger Hinks, who said there was nothing to look at and nothing to eat except things cooked in oil. Roger's career at the British Museum had been abruptly terminated before the war by a notorious scandal over cleaning the Elgin Marbles, and a subsequent stint as British Council Representative in Athens had given him no cause to revise his low opinion of Greece. He looked like the National Portrait Gallery's bust of the poet Gray and excelled at the quick, dry, glancing wit Ivy practised herself: 'He and Ivy were made for each other,' said Cecil Gould to whom Roger once said, when told about a ski resort with the great attraction for bored or indifferent skiers of easy access to Innsbruck: 'Rather a homoeopathic cure, I should have thought.'

These Alpine visits were as it turned out Ivy's last sight of abroad, since she and Margaret settled on a Yorkshire tour in the summer of 1950, taking in various great houses, stopping at Leeds and the Watson-Gandys' old family home, Heaves, by then run as a luxurious ('though too expensive') hotel near Clitheroe. Here they listened to themselves reading their old 'Conversation in Lyme Regis' (recorded for the B.B.C. Third Programme the previous February and broadcast in June): 'The bangs and bursts caused by the disturbance from the hills in Yorkshire rendered our hopes of hearing our own voices null and void,' wrote Ivy, back in London, to Vere on 4 July. 'In London the talk seems to have come through fairly well, though some people heard Margaret's voice better than mine. One critic, favourable otherwise, complained that my voice was too high and light, as though I had purposely ordered the wrong one . . .'

There were country weekends with old friends like the Ionides and new ones like the Watson-Gandys and the infinitely hospitable Charlotte Bonham-Carter ('She never will say a single disagreeable thing about anyone,' reported Margaret. 'A most tiresome woman to be with'[37]). People with gardens invited Ivy down to raid the soft fruit, but people with pets kept them dark if possible on pain of both ladies' disfavour (Ivy's dislike of cats was so pronounced that their owners—several of whom had seen her push, if not kick, an offending animal out of her path with a small, firm, neatly-shod foot—found it hard to credit her intently observed and by no means unfeeling portrait of the cat Plautus when she came to write *Mother and Son*). Ivy spent a few days each summer in the strawberry season with Janet Beresford at her cottage near Ashwell, while Margaret went to Alice Marcon at Oxford, and they paid separate visits to Sutton Veney again after the war, though the three Noyes sisters were growing increasingly frail: Ella, always closest to Ivy, died in 1949 within a few months of Minna, leaving Dora alone, too old and infirm either to pay or receive further visits.

Life at Braemar Mansions ran smoothly in spite of minor vexations—'a change of landlord, a dishonest porter who made away with all the coal in the mansions, a painter to do over the kitchen, all sorts of irritating household jobs,' wrote Margaret to James Lees-Milne on 29 May 1948—and an accelerating postwar turnover of maids:

Frightfulness has fallen on us in the shape of the loss of our valuable Jayne, who is taking a long-wished-for chance of leaving 'sleeping-in service' and going out to work from a home of her own. She has found good quarters in a horrid, coal-mining place called Pontefract in Yorkshire, and I expect will be miserable [wrote Ivy gloomily to Vere] . . . We have engaged an elderly superior woman for the simple reason that we could get her, as 'her lady' had died, and hope for the best . . . Jayne, on hearing of our prompt action and its outcome, broke into tears.

Did she expect us to keep her place sacred to her and look after ourselves?[38]

Ivy, who could no more cook or clean than work a typewriter or drive a car, continued to get on well with her housekeepers long after the last of the stern, starched maids who kept visitors at arm's length and spoke only when spoken to (Gray had left after the war and Henrietta Day, Jayne's successor, belonged to a breed already almost extinct), and who were in turn replaced by a procession of untrained helps and companions in coloured nylon overalls only too pleased to pass the time of day. Both Ivy and Margaret also depended increasingly on Basil Marsden-Smedley, a tall, thin, dry, patient, immensely kind man chiefly devoted all his life to good works and municipal affairs in Chelsea (it was Basil who, as mayor of Chelsea at the end of the 1950s, insisted on trees in the streets and a fountain in Sloane Square). Basil was generally invited alone ('He used to say he appreciated being "a loose man" at their parties,' said Hester), having long since been adopted by both ladies as a cross between father-figure and favourite nephew: 'Ask Basil', 'Ring Basil', 'Send for Basil' was always their cry in time of trouble. His mistrust of Ivy's writing was balanced by a boundless admiration for Margaret whose company he enjoyed, according to Hester, more than anyone else's not excluding her own: after the war the two had a craze for exploring golf clubs together, buzzing about all over the Home Counties at weekends, casting a critical eye over the greens, sampling amenities, quizzing the members and lunching quite irregularly in the club houses.

The nearest Ivy came to these country jaunts was wooding, or 'faggoting', with Margaret in Kensington Gardens, expeditions for which she wore thick brogues, an ancient Burberry and a battered pork-pie hat (these were her casual clothes, for rough or heavy work, and she put them on again whenever she stepped out to water the flowers in her balcony window boxes at Braemar Mansions). Marketing in the Gloucester Road occupied part of every morning, and Ivy took pride in the frugal art of stretching and saving three sets of 'points', or ration coupons: 'I was brought up to think it was wrong to waste anything,' she said. 'And what was worse, it was vulgar.'[39] Food at Braemar Mansions was once again, points permitting, good and plentiful and in season (too plentiful for fastidious visitors like James Lees-Milne, who was regularly taken aback by the staggering quantities of depressingly plain cooking put away by his hostesses). Both Margaret and Ivy ate hugely, but they also enjoyed themselves hugely and saw to it that others did too: 'I dined with Margaret and Ivy,' wrote James on 2 December 1947. 'Charlotte Bonham-Carter and Soame Jenyns the other guests. It was the greatest fun, although there was only cider to drink, and it was perishing cold. Ivy and Margaret were at their best, playing up to each other and making strikingly pertinent and lively observations . . .'[40]

Ivy had been approached about writing her memoirs by Knopf's English agent that autumn, but claimed (as she invariably did to pokers and priers) that it was out of the question because a life as uneventful as hers supplied no biographical material ('There just is none'[41]). She was working instead on *Two Worlds and their Ways* in which Cicely (who typed the manuscript in the summer of 1948) recognized touches of Margaret in the large, plain, cheerful person of Maria Shelley with her great good nature, untidiness, industry and habit of jotting things down on the backs of old envelopes. *Two Worlds and their Ways*, published in June 1949, while Ivy was on holiday at St Gervais, was also the first and only one of her novels centred on a happy family (the tolerant, loving and united Shelleys find their days darkened only by the parents'· decision—taken reluctantly, and for purely disinterested motives—to send their children to boarding school). Work was going well for Margaret too. *The Work of William Kent* came out in 1948, together with a highly successful revised edition of *Regency Furniture* and, in the intervals of journalism, she was running up a history of interior decoration for Batsford, revising another seminal furniture handbook by the cabinet-maker John C. Rogers, and collaborating with Soame on *Chinese Export Art*. Ivy, unlike Margaret, liked to let each book settle for nearly a year before starting another, as she told an interviewer from *Books of Today* in April 1950:

> 'And then,' she says, 'I do not go so slowly as you might think.'
> 'It flows?' I said.
> 'I do not think it comes more slowly than it has to,' she corrected. 'I do believe it seldom flows for anyone.'

iii

The book that was flowing as fast as it could at the beginning of 1950 was *Darkness and Day*. 'I did some work in the winter and spring and am now giving the book a rest, as it needed it,' Ivy wrote to Robert Liddell on 26 July. 'London is pleasant and peopled again; and food is easier, but life grows in expense.' In fact Cicely had already collected the manuscript (which Ivy feared might prove too short, though it turned out to be the usual length and in no need of what she called 'interpolations') three weeks before this letter was written, on 3 July, when the signs of strain Ivy generally showed on finishing a novel were more marked than usual. She had barely spoken ('Now and then a slight whispering sound escaped her, as though she was talking to herself'[42]), seeming withdrawn, exhausted and so frail that she could not walk properly and had to be helped to stand.

It was Margaret who kept the conversation going over glasses of sherry and escorted Cicely to the front door, reacting sharply to a polite hope that Ivy might feel better after a holiday:

> 'I thought she seemed not very well,' I said.
> To my surprise Margaret looked at me with a sort of anguish, and cried: 'She's *very well*,' with bitter emphasis on each word.
> She turned and rushed back into the sitting room.
> It was the last time I saw her. She died the following April.[43]

Since the war Margaret had had what she called a smoker's cough without smoking, and her heart was tired ('This was a medical description and she said it was a very apt one'[44]). She consulted various doctors but otherwise carried on much as before, though Cicely was by no means the only person aware of fierce undercurrents between the two friends in the last year or two of Margaret's life, when Ivy was preoccupied with *Darkness and Day*. This was her variation on an Oedipal theme (in which Bridget Lovat, having caused her mother's death and supposedly married her father, stops short at putting out her eyes to her family's great relief—'Anything like that would make it very public'[45]); and the absurd, outrageous, tragi-comic inventiveness of the plot, combined with its strictly classical machinery of reversal and revelation, to some extent distracts attention from a more mundane, secondary theme of old age, infirmity and death.

Sir Ransom Chase, a widower of eighty-eight, spends much of the book anticipating with various degrees of gloom and reluctance the death that finally claims him in the last chapter; while his neighbour, Selina Lovat, refuses out of hand to admit the possibility that she will not live for ever though even her small grandchildren feel pretty confident that her days are numbered:

> 'Could anyone be older than Grandma?'
> 'Yes, of course,' said Rose. 'She is only seventy-eight. People can be ninety and a hundred.'
> 'But then their days are but labour and sorrow. Are her days like that?'
> 'No, I shouldn't think so. Other people's may be, when they are with her.'[46]

Other people's days were often labour and sorrow at Braemar Mansions during and after the writing of *Darkness and Day*. Pamela Hansford Johnson, invited to dinner in the winter of 1950–1 when she was working on her British Council pamphlet about Ivy, mistook the time out of nerves and spent thirty minutes walking round the square, arriving frozen cold on the doorstep only to be told that she was half an hour late and the others had started without her. She was shown into the dank, dark dining room and narrowly cross-examined as to her unpunctuality by Ivy—'ivorine, sharp-featured, with eyes green as peeled grapes'[47]—before being offered a chair on which she sat in mutinous silence for the rest of the meal ('I do not think the dinner could have been utterly spoiled since the main course was corned beef'), while her hostesses talked to one another and a nameless third party without addressing a further word to their reprobate guest. Robert Liddell had another hair-raising report from his friend, Peter Duval-Smith, who went to tea armed with an introduction and a big box of Turkish delight from Robert, and ended up making sticky conversation with Margaret about Rose Macaulay's *Pleasure of Ruins*:

> Ivy said: 'She's writing not only about ruins, but about things people built to look like ruins. I don't know what she sees in them.' Margaret developed the theme and Peter (a South African)

did his best. Then suddenly Ivy began talking to herself aloud. 'I can't think why Margaret is showing off like that; she can't think how silly she sounds. And this young man obviously knows nothing about it whatever.'

Margaret showed him out, and helped him to find his umbrella or what not. At the door she said: 'What do you think about Edith Sitwell's poems? We think they're bosh.'

Peter said that was much his own opinion. Margaret then called: 'Ivy, Ivy, come here! This young man says Edith Sitwell's poems are bosh!'[48]

There were similar incidents with other visitors, several of whom realized unhappily that something was up. The last winter of Margaret's life was bitterly cold, and she would sit crouched over an oil stove supplied by Hester, or quite often take to her bed. Altercations with Ivy grew sharper, and not funny at all. Elizabeth Taylor remembered a tea party at which the two nagged one another about fetching the jam ('Margaret, there's no gooseberry jam.' 'There isn't any apricot, either.' 'If you fetch the apricot, I'll fetch the gooseberry'[49]) for what felt like hours while the guests hung their heads and stared at their plates. Margaret's cough grew worse. She suffered from catarrh and had such difficulty in breathing that, at the beginning of December, she had X-rays taken of her heart and throat.[50] Ivy, always delicate, accustomed from childhood to taking care and wrapping up warm, accepted bad throats, chest complaints, bouts of quinsy or influenza as a matter of course in the winter. But Margaret had never needed nursing before, and Ivy reacted with panic-stricken protest, misery and rage. She could not stand the sound of Margaret's cough, or stop herself punishing Margaret for it. Friends grew increasingly worried, strange stories began to circulate, a rumour reached even Joan Evans about a distinguished colleague who had dropped in at the flat to find Ivy engaged in teasing Margaret till she cried. Things got so bad in the end that—after another distressing public scene over jam, with Ivy refusing to pass the pot unless Margaret first submitted by fetching a handkerchief from Ivy's bedroom—Herman and Peter Wilson of Sotheby's decided to tackle Ivy together in private but, courage failing, applied instead to Basil Marsden-Smedley who said there was nothing to be done.[51]

Trouble was apparent even to comparative strangers: the Jungian psychotherapist Margaret Branch, meeting the pair at a party, heard Ivy turn on Margaret with such oblique, wounding cruelty that she could hardly believe her ears and consulted the friend who had introduced her, the poet Stevie Smith, who explained that Ivy was beside herself at times with terror of being abandoned.[52] Ivy's behaviour went back to the years immediately after the First World War when old friends, seeing the two together for the first time, were embarrassed at the way Margaret gave in to the much younger Ivy, fetching her bag or her book or her handkerchief, and saying mildly when Janet Beresford protested: 'You see, she's like a child.'[53] What seems to have happened is that the tyrannical streak that had dropped from Ivy completely in time of mutual happiness surfaced again after the Second World War, when Margaret first showed signs of failing her, and mastered her more and more as ill health wore Margaret down. 'Margaret wanted to go, and she didn't want to go,' said Margaret Branch, who thought that Margaret fought against encroaching weakness less for herself than because she, too, was appalled at the prospect of Ivy being left on her own: 'But I think she had had enough.' Certainly Margaret responded generously for as long as she could to Ivy in trouble, bearing her thrusts in silence, setting aside her own jealousy ('Ivy had always been in the background of her fame, as it were, but she was only on the outskirts of Ivy's,' said Hester loyally), coping with the literary admirers who otherwise got short shrift in those days at Braemar Mansions. Margaret took to escorting Ivy's ruffled or indignant visitors to the front door so as to mollify their feelings with a change of subject or, for Pamela Hansford Johnson after that disastrous dinner party, an outright apology: 'She said to me kindly, "You mustn't mind. Ivy isn't at her best tonight" '[54] (Miss Hansford Johnson was by her own account more graciously received at a later visit for tea on 26 February 1951, the afternoon before the two friends left for a few days at the Eardsley House Hotel, Worthing, in the vain hope that sea air might do Margaret good).

It was not simply that Ivy, like her mother before her, needed someone permanently on hand to smooth her path, to support and shield her from 'a world which' (in Ivy's phrase from *Dolores*) 'had shown itself unloving'.[55] More than that, by enabling Ivy to remain in some part of herself 'like a child'—with a child's uncontrolled egotism, helplessness, fear, resentment and anger—Margaret had also enabled her in another sense to grow up. Perhaps Ivy's childishness was the price she paid for her rare and discomforting maturity. Margaret after all had not only made it possible in the first place for Ivy to write, she had supplied the tone of voice that allowed Ivy's characters to comprehend, if not master or modify, their own and other people's emotions in the light of that 'great wealth of humanity' that many friends sensed in Ivy's presence, though it was fully articulated only in her books.

Margaret's death and the reactions it provoked provide perhaps the clearest and strangest example of the two levels on which Ivy worked. As Margaret's illness gradually declared itself, Ivy began talking more and more under her breath, a habit Cicely first noticed on the day she came to collect the manuscript of *Darkness and Day*. Cicely wondered at the time whether Ivy might be repeating snatches of conversation from her novel, and perhaps she was, for—whatever sort of mess Ivy and Margaret made, or seemed to their friends to be making, of their last months together—their general predicament is explored with great delicacy and feeling in a series of conversations running through *Darkness and Day* between the dying Sir Ransom Chase and his much younger friend, Gaunt Lovat. The pair cover the ground pretty thoroughly, ranging from practical details like the reading of Sir Ransom's will after his funeral (a gathering pictured by Gaunt with disobliging alacrity: '"You can imagine me sitting there, having my curiosity satisfied . . ." "I shall do no such thing. I shall imagine you weighed down by grief" '[56]) to the metaphysical question of which of the two deserves the more pity:

> 'I never see why people should have it for being old,' said Gaunt.
> 'Everyone else does. You want some reason for not giving it.'
> 'We are supposed to like to pity people.'
> 'We only like to look down on them for needing pity.'
> 'Well, why should I not do that?'
> 'You are too attached to me. It would have to be real pity, and people do not like that. They are not equal to it.'[57]

Darkness and Day begins with this tentative exploration and ends, after the more spectacular upheavals of the main plot have subsided, with the eventual acceptance by these two deeply attached friends of the elder's forthcoming death. They start in the first chapter discussing, to Sir Ransom's steadily mounting irritation, his failing powers, his will, his well-spent life and his determination at all costs to hang on to it. The same themes crop up repeatedly—the disparity in their ages, the empty place Sir Ransom will leave, the annoying way Gaunt keeps harping on the future—and are majestically resolved in two long, lucid deathbed conversations in the last chapter:

'You cannot have much to regret.'

'There is not much that I do regret. I have done much that I ought to have done. Much that I ought not to have done, I would do again . . .'

'You will leave a great blank. I shall never find things quite the same.'

'But you will find them nearly the same? Life will not be over for you?'

'I do not believe in not taking people on equal terms until the end. Your mind is not failing. You are as much a man as I am. You would know if I distorted the truth.'

'Truth is so impossible. Something has to be done for it. If you had said you would find life quite different, I should have believed it. I think I do believe it.'

'I think I do too,' said Gaunt, in another tone. 'I shall be a lonely man when you are gone.'[58]

Of the two, Gaunt is perhaps the more touching, certainly the more ignoble, his genuine grief tinged with the insatiable curiosity and the deferential, self-deprecating, ill-concealed confidence of the survivor. Sir Ransom on the brink of the grave is a model of stoic composure: humorous, sober, regretful, even faintly tetchy but dry-eyed, issuing instructions, directing the mourners, and still with his last breath firmly proclaiming his irreligion (' "I believe I shall be as I was before I was born." "It is interesting to see that a man can face that, when he is actually confronted by it." "It does not sound as if he had much choice," said Sir Ransom'[59]).

Margaret of course cannot have read *Darkness and Day*, which was published ten days after she died. Her cough and catarrh had eased a little after Christmas, though her breathing was no better, and she kept up the usual round of luncheon and tea parties until well into the New Year, 1951. But entries in her diary peter out towards the end of January, leaving a blank that suggests she scarcely saw anyone or went anywhere in February save for four days' sea air (Dr Compton-Burnett's sovereign remedy for bronchial trouble) at the end of the month. She and Ivy were back in London on 2 March, and on the thirteenth Ivy's doctor, Stephen Pasmore, arranged for Margaret to be admitted for a five-day course of drug treatment to a nursing home in Knaresborough Place. Dr Pasmore, called in because Margaret's own Dr Landor was not available, thought her condition ominous—'I didn't like the look of her at all'[60]—and Ivy's evident distress almost equally worrying. Margaret, exhausted by pain and anxiety and attempts to conceal both from Ivy, seemed by this time to have accepted the end, perhaps even welcomed it ('She feared Ivy might come to a full stop,' said Margaret Branch. 'But I think she herself was glad enough to go. And no wonder'). Whether or not she talked openly to Ivy, Margaret's mind was certainly moving in the same direction as Sir Ransom's. 'People do not always run consistently true to form,' wrote Ralph Edwards, describing the only time in their long and close association that the formidable M.J. showed him another side of her character: 'That staunch atheist was badly rattled by the fear of death . . . & told me shortly before her end that she thought the odds are on personal survival!'[61] But Margaret was still quite sufficiently herself to make a Roman exit: her last words (widely circulated later in a variety of versions among her friends) as she left by ambulance for the nursing home were, 'Ivy, don't let Day eat all the Elvas plums.'[62]

This flash of the old scathing Margaret served perhaps in some sort as a signal to Ivy, in much the same way as Sir Ransom's tart pronouncements forestall any possible inclination on Gaunt's part to lapse into self-indulgence or sentimentality. Ivy had refused, almost to the end, to acknowledge a catastrophe she was powerless to prevent. She had suffered, and watched Margaret suffer, and made things worse for them both; but, with another part of herself, she had been preparing for the worst, exploring and charting the process of mourning, at least since the end of 1949 when she started writing *Darkness and Day*. From now on she retreated again into her old resolute courage, dignity and reserve ('I had to follow my nature,' said Dudley Gaveston, explaining his own iron restraint after an emotional explosion in *A Family and a Fortune*: 'It may be my second nature in this case. It would be best to hide a first nature quickly, and I was very quick . . .'[63]).

Ivy visited Margaret in Knaresborough Place, complaining freely about having to go up and down in a narrow, box-shaped lift designed in her view for coffins. Margaret came home the week before Easter on 17 March (two days before *Darkness and Day* was published in America by Knopf), and seems to have rallied briefly, judging by a final entry in her diary on 27 March—Easter Tuesday —recording the various heart treatments prescribed since December in a memorandum at the front, and marking the day itself, 'End of fortnight bedridden'. Ivy clung to hope and disbelief even now: 'Margaret was certainly better on the Sunday,' she wrote later to Robin McDouall, 'and the doctor had no idea she was in any danger.'[64] But Joyce Felkin, Elliott's wife, who had a flat round the corner and called every day for news, reported that Margaret was seeing imaginary people at the foot of her bed.[65] On 3 April she collapsed, and was taken to the Charing Cross Hospital where she died of a blood clot on the lungs on Friday, 6 April.

Joyce, ringing the bell on her way to work that morning, learned what had happened from Day, who opened the door and brought a message from Ivy asking her to come in. They sat together, saying very little, and later drove to the crematorium at Golders Green, to make funeral arrangements. Ivy was not demonstrative, then or later, with Joyce or anyone else, but she did need company. An old friend of Margaret's, Helen Rolleston, stayed for a while at the flat, and Basil Marsden-Smedley also came, bringing his two teenage children, Luke and Henrietta, to whom Ivy gave tea ('I don't think she was in such a state then,' said Henrietta, who remembered Ivy calmly passing plates and filling cups), while Basil, as executor, hunted in Margaret's room for her will. 'I have never been in Margaret's bedroom,' Ivy said, when Basil suggested she might find the will there, 'and I don't mean to start now.'[66]

Ivy sent a great bunch of Margaret's favourite violets, but did not herself attend the funeral, which was large and well-patronized and not without the sort of incident that might have appealed to its chief protagonist. 'This is the happiest day of my life,' a distinguished museum official was heard to say to a colleague. 'Margaret Jourdain is dead, and you've got the sack.' Margaret's nephew, Colonel Seymour Jourdain, who presided (his offer to escort Ivy as chief mourner having been turned down), amused the Marsden-

Smedleys by rashly 'doing the relative' without knowing—as they did by now—that his claim as the last of the Jourdains had been passed over in favour of Luke's as heir. Herman hurried home by taxi to give Ivy lunch at his flat in Mulberry Walk, claiming that he heard her say under her breath, as she struggled up his stairs, in her clearly audible triple aside: 'I have lost my man, I have lost my man, I have lost my man.'[67]

Certainly she struck a great many people at this time, and for months, even as much as a year afterwards, as lost, depleted, physically and morally shrunk. 'Ivy seemed to wither. She shrivelled,' said Vere Watson-Gandy. 'We thought she was going to die.' To the many friends who wrote in condolence, Ivy replied at once, tersely and often in a variant of the same phrase: 'I feel that my life has been torn away, and do not try to face the future.'[68] She made no attempt to conceal a misery that appalled her friends ('I was so upset by Ivy Compton-Burnett's letter that I wrote again saying that if she wanted a refuge she could come here for some days,' Vita Sackville-West wrote from Sissinghurst to her husband on 16 April. 'I really cannot bear to think of people's sorrow and grief and loneliness. I cannot bear it . . .'[69]). But Ivy had shut herself up, seeing hardly anyone and refusing invitations, offers of help, suggestions, advice and proposed visits with the same polite formula. 'You are kind indeed, and some day I would like to,' she wrote on 5 May to Elizabeth Taylor, and to Robin McDouall on 14 April: 'I am going to the country for a week on Tuesday, and a little later I should like to see you. I shall have to depend on my friends.' Like people dreadfully bereaved in her books—the widowed Sophia Stace and Duncan Edgeworth, both of whom demand constant reassurance on the score of their own dealings with the dead—Ivy turned in the first few weeks to friends prepared to talk about Margaret, people who had loved her like Basil and the New Zealander, Helen Rolleston, whose visit was not a success. 'Ivy said she was "horrible" to her [Helen], because she could not forgive her for not being Margaret. Nor could she forgive herself for ever having been impatient with the latter—she really suffered from remorse—but most of all she could not forgive Margaret for having left her.'[70] To the end of her life, Ivy could never be reconciled to living alone. 'Every minute of every day,' she said fifteen years later to James Lees-Milne, who had asked if she still missed Margaret, and to Olivia Manning: 'I miss her more with every day that passes.'[71] For nearly twenty years, Ivy mourned Margaret in the phrases she had used at the end of *Darkness and Day*, when Gaunt first learns of his own loss:

'I shall miss him day by day. Not an hour will pass, but I shall miss him . . . I see for the first time the place he held in my life.'

'He always saw it. Do not fear. There is nothing for you to regret.'

'I can only regret being myself. I suppose all regret comes to that.'

'It is the last thing that he regretted. It was always a refreshment to him, your difference from other people.'[72]

For a while 'the various duties incident to these times' took, as Ivy said, all her energy.[73] With Basil she set about winding up Margaret's affairs ('The letters about everything are almost too much for me'), answering queries, dealing with publishers, sorting belongings, going through the vast jumble of papers that had somehow to be raked into sheaves and stacks, crammed into folders and files, stuffed into tea chests and hat boxes for eventual dispatch to the V&A. Ivy had no talent whatsoever in practical matters: 'Her helplessness in a crisis was truly pitiful,' wrote Cicely, who found her, well over a year later, still defeated by even the simplest domestic chore which seemed to rear up against her in token of how much she missed Margaret (' "She did so many things I find difficult to do—like doing up a parcel, for instance," Ivy told me . . . pointing to an arrangement of brown paper and string she had been struggling with when I arrived'[74]). Ivy learnt in time to cope with the Post Office, receive admirers, give interviews, go to parties, even travel on her own, but she never got over the great trouble ('the greatest I could have had'[75]) symbolized by these lesser ones: 'Three years after she [Margaret] died, as we parted one evening, she [Ivy] said: "I begin to get a little organised, but it is very difficult being alone." '[76]

It is perhaps scarcely surprising if her disorientation in those first months resulted in various uncharacteristically impulsive gestures, all of which were more or less promptly withdrawn. Ivy, always derisive about the scientific pretensions of psychiatry, many of whose secrets seemed to her an open book, nonetheless made—or seemed, at this time of desolation and overwhelming defeat, to make—tentative, indirect inquiries as to the possibility of therapeutic help from Margaret Branch[77] (who replied that, on the contrary, she advised her students to consult Ivy's novels as practical textbooks—a compliment Ivy accepted with some small satisfaction). She retreated while Day was on holiday for three weeks in June to a country hotel in Tilgate Forest, near Pease Pottage in Sussex, from where she sent an equally startling suggestion to the Principal of Somerville College, Oxford:

June 11th, 1951

Dear Madam,

I hope you will forgive my broaching a personal matter.

I have lately lost a friend who had lived with me for many years, and I now have accommodation in my flat for another woman, and should like to meet one who would like to live at a moderate cost in London, and who would up to a point share my life and interests.

I am myself in the sixties, and am a novelist, in so far as I have a profession; and I thought the arrangement might perhaps suit some don who is retiring, and does not want living expenses on a large scale. I would make the expenses about £3 10. 0 a week, for anyone who would take the life in my flat as it is.

Yours sincerely,
Ivy Compton-Burnett

My own friends are settled in homes of their own.[78]

Ivy thought better of this rash proposal almost before any answer could reach her ('Dear Dr Vaughan,' she replied on 20 June to the Principal, '. . . I am afraid I have made the mistake of solving my problem along too many lines, and have become rather involved at the moment. But I hope I may write to Mlle Aline Lion later, if my way is clear. And thank you so very much'). In the end she gave up hope of filling Margaret's place because, as she said to a decorating friend, Ivo Pakenham (who moved in briefly with Ivy himself a few years later, while his own flat was being refurbished), it was no good settling for less, 'once you've lived with someone with a first-class brain'.[79]

Ivy was made a C.B.E.—along with Peggy Ashcroft, Margot Fonteyn and the soprano Isobel Baillie—in the Birthday Honours on 7 June 1951, but the congratulations forwarded to her at the Tilgate Forest Hotel came, as she wrote to her cousin Katie Blackie on 14 June, 'at a time when things have little meaning for me'. Critical acclaim must also have seemed a painful irrelevance when *Darkness and Day* was published in April. All that spring and summer reviewers took particular pains to emphasize that the glittering sharp points and cutting edges of I. Compton-Burnett's dialogue ('Within the last few days one has counted rapiers, axes, stilettos, knives and grenades,' wrote Elizabeth Taylor, reviewing Ivy's reviewers in the July *Vogue*) should not make the reader overlook the glitter of tears between the lines of her talk. Stevie Smith, in the June *World Review*, insisted on the power and truth of Ivy's tragic vision; and so did Francis Wyndham, defending her in the *Observer* on 6 May against the old charge of being too cold and too clever by pointing out that the sole aim of her dazzling, destructive wit was to clear a way to the naked feeling beneath —'for the writer's air of detachment covers a sensibility to suffering that responds to the subtlest social embarrassment as well as to deep passion and pain'. Ivy herself copied out in her own hand Raymond Mortimer's magisterial accolade in the *Sunday Times* on 15 April, nine days after Margaret's death, which began by comparing her to Sophocles and Plato ('Though often she makes me laugh aloud, she must be read with the same unhurrying vigilance as these pithy, formidable Ancients'), and ended by declaring her immortal.

All these people knew Ivy (the acquaintance being based in each case on admiration for her books), and all of them knew what had happened to her. It is hardly possible at this stage to establish how far what they wrote reflected a new profundity and compressed feeling in *Darkness and Day*; how far her admirers had simply got used to a way of writing that seems difficult only when it is unfamiliar; or whether their understanding was quickened, with this particular book, by a sense of personal pity. Probably the answer lies in some mixture of all three elements. But, whatever the reason and whether the effect was intended or not, there can be no doubt that Raymond Mortimer's tribute to *Darkness and Day* may be applied equally well to what its author had recently gone through in fact:

Everyone in it is either protecting himself from the truth or unearthing it. 'What we ought to be is not what we are.' If all the characters blaze with wit, this is in order to illuminate the most unlovely recesses of the human heart: in none of the fashionable prophets of despair do we find a blacker view of human nature. Yet here the reader is exhilarated—by the author's iron courage and by her austere diction, which can rise to poetic grandeur . . .

CHAPTER EIGHT

'The English Secret'

i

'I KNOW THAT you, if anyone, can measure my loss, and understand how hard it is to look forward. And it is true indeed that work is the last thing that can be done,' Ivy wrote to Robert Liddell on 28 April 1951, three weeks after Margaret's death. 'I find I can only live from day to day, and do not look forward; and concentration of any kind seems impossible . . .' she wrote a month later to Cicely (who had recently moved to Sussex). 'I am glad that you like the country, and that your work progresses. I must try to get back to mine before long, but so far the effort seems too much.' Visitors to Braemar Mansions privately feared that Ivy might never be equal to the effort again, for her loneliness that autumn was dreadful to see. Furniture friends, never for the most part enthusiastic about Ivy, still less so about her books, stayed away in large numbers. People who had put up with her for years as Margaret's appendage naturally looked on Ivy alone as a liability, while others who were genuinely fond of her hesitated to intrude on a grief that even outsiders could see was literally crushing. Ivy relied on old friends and neighbours like Herman, Basil, the Thesigers and Kidds, and a few persistent new ones like Carol Rygate who had first met her with Margaret and afterwards spotted her one day in Kensington High Street, dressed all in black, looking so small and so sad that she went up and asked her to tea. The flat itself seemed as mournful as its mistress: 'When the maid opened the door on the dark brown hall, one felt "Oh, help,"' said Sonia Orwell, who also said that in all the years after Margaret's death her only moments of comfort or intimacy with Ivy came when two or three friends, gathered round the fire, could turn their backs on the high, chill, dismally empty drawing room beyond.

Ivy confided in no one and nothing, unless perhaps in the novel she was writing that winter. *The Present and the Past* was finished on schedule the following summer, two years to the day after *Darkness and Day*, and it, too, begins and ends with death. Chapter One starts with the Clare children watching a dying hen tormented and trampled by its companions in the hen run (something Ivy said she had seen herself when she and Margaret kept poultry at Zealand in the war[1]), which leads to a long, unflinching discussion as to whether or not the sick bird will be better off dead (' "It won't go to another world," said Henry. "It was ill and pecked in this one, and it won't have any other" '[2]). The same theme is taken up later in the funeral service for a dead mole conducted by the three-year-old Toby ('Dearly beloved brethren. Let us pray. Ashes and ashes. Dust and dust. This our brother. Poor little mole! Until he rise again. Prayers of the congregation. Amen'[3]). Toby's foibles—his captivating self-confidence and bids for attention—are less endearing when they reappear, barely modified, in his father, the jealous, demanding and highly competitive Cassius Clare who is the book's tyrant. The second half is given over to Cassius' fake suicide, staged in a bid to pay out his family, who retaliate with an uncomfortably acute analysis of his motives, only to be overtaken by genuine compunction when the book ends with Cassius actually dying ('I wish he had been happier. I wish he had had more. I wish I had given it to him. I had the opportunity day by day. I had it only a few hours ago, and to the end of my life I shall wish it'[4]). It is a plot expressly designed to give death a second thorough going over in all the aspects that currently interested Ivy—its squalid physical reality and posthumous ennobling effect, its finality for the deceased and mixed effect on the survivors. The children's ruthlessly logical speculations—frightening to both themselves and their elders, whose own reactions are clouded by pain and pity—are developed on a more detached level by the bystanders, Elton Scrope and his sisters, who pick up where Gaunt Lovat and Sir Ransom left off discussing immortality, religious faith or the lack of it, parting, grief, loss and extinction:

'Cassius was not of an age to die,' said Catherine.
'What is the age?' said her sister.
'About seventy,' said Elton, 'when we have had our span, and people have not begun to think the less of us.'[5]

Ivy was sixty-eight in June 1952, the month when she finished *The Present and the Past*. She wrote asking Cicely to type the manuscript on 2 July, and turned to reading Robert's new novel, *Unreal City*, which is the story of Charles Harbord, teaching in Caesarea (Robert himself taught at the universities of Cairo and Alexandria) and learning slowly to live with his grief at the death of a beloved sister.

> I have just come to the end of *Unreal City*, and though I do not think it suits either you or me quite as well as the real one, I wanted to tell you what great pleasure it has given me, and how I look forward to reading it again [wrote Ivy on 1 August]. Its unrealness is of course its real nature, and it could not be better given. And Charles's situation, essentially yours and mine, gives me the sense of fellow-feeling that perhaps one should not welcome as much as one does . . .

Ivy by this time seems to have been ready to surface again from the long seclusion and unreality of mourning; also perhaps to note with satisfaction that, though she was only two years short of her span, people clearly thought more and more of her.

She was known as 'the English Secret', a phrase coined by the aesthete Brian Howard on account of the fact that, though I. Compton-Burnett had been a name freely bandied for years by the literati of London, New York and Paris, precious few had actually set eyes on her.[6] But Ivy in the mid and late 1950s became steadily less of a secret. She gave interviews, sat for photographers, attended functions, appeared on television; and she might be said to have marked a fresh start in the spring of 1952 by readily agreeing to help with the radio adaptation of *A Family and a Fortune*, which was broadcast by the B.B.C. in November ('They are giving me £90,' she said flatly, 'so naturally I accepted'[7]). This was the first of a good many radio, stage and television plays, about which Ivy took a characteristically deprecatory line to her friends, though people who worked with her found her a cooperative and surprisingly flexible colleague. She got on at once with the young radio adaptor, Peter Mellors; and the producer, Christopher Sykes (who made later adaptations himself, when Mellors moved to Canada after his highly successful, pioneering versions of *A Father and his Fate*, *Men and Wives* and *Pastors and Masters*), found her from the first a pleasure to do business with: 'Of all distinguished writers with whom I worked in radio, this severe character was the most harmonious collaborator. The reason was simple. She had no vanity. Absolutely none.'[8] She was practical, easy, encouraging, never moody or shy, and flustered—to the point almost of 'panic rather than embarrassment'[9]—only when Sykes made the mistake of saying how much he admired her work. This remained always tricky ground for Ivy, now that she entertained increasing numbers of admirers herself and could no longer ward off any mention of her books by an automatic reference to Margaret's. But she grew more resourceful at negotiating the difficulty, chiefly by a technique of diplomatic forestalling: 'People always say the wrong thing about the books,' she said sweetly to a young painter, Barbara Robinson, who had invited her to a private view, 'so I shan't say anything about the paintings.'[10]

She used similar tactics when Sybille Bedford sent her a fan letter in the shape of a long, subtle, highly polished and knowledgeable survey of her work and its revelatory effect on the writer over the past fifteen years. The letter is dated Rome, 3 July–10 August 1952. It was prompted by the excitement of reading *Pastors and Masters*, available for the first time in nearly thirty years in Gollancz's reissue that spring; and perhaps parts of it too vividly evoked memories of the start of Ivy's career, when her early happiness with Margaret leaked over into her writing in the persons of Theresa Fletcher and Emily Herrick, whose company cuts—in Sybille Bedford's phrase —'like a breath of air' across the rancorous, claustrophobic confusions of self-deception, greed and desire ('Theresa and Emily are admirable women, perhaps they are great, with their minds, their honesty, their sadness, their deprecations and their wit. And how agreeable they are, how well-bred, how articulate. There are not many of their kind'). Ivy's laconic response to a tribute that had taken nearly six weeks and ten thousand words to compose ran simply: 'Dear Mrs Bedford, Thank you so much for your letter. I shall treasure it always as a possession. Yours sincerely, Ivy Compton-Burnett.'[11] She used the identical formula four years later when writing to thank for Sybille's novel, *A Legacy*. Her polite reserve, maintained for years after Herman arranged an introduction, cracked only once, when Sybille was working on her life of Aldous Huxley at the end of the 1960s, and Ivy—who had never before permitted conversation to stray beyond trivialities—gave her 'a straight look' as they sat together in the twilight after tea at Braemar Mansions: 'She knew what he was, and what he'd been, and what I saw. And she said, "You love virtue, don't you?"'

Other young writers who made less daunting approaches to Ivy after the war, and more easily made friends—who might indeed be said in due course to have constituted a kind of court round her after Margaret's death—were Olivia Manning, Francis King, Kay Dick and Kathleen Farrell. Nancy Spain (who had never heard of Ivy in those days, nor Cyril Connolly either) heard Elizabeth Bowen complain mysteriously at a literary party: 'It's really too bad of Cyril to say that Ivy is the only one of us all that will live.'[12] Readers, would-be acolytes, devotees and prospective hangers-on had comparatively little trouble finding people prepared to point out, or even present them to the English Secret, who was herself to be seen on occasion, looking memorably fine in her black velvet and diamonds, at select London parties. Madge Garland, an admirer ever since her days as a junior on *Vogue* when its readers were first alerted by Raymond Mortimer to *Pastors and Masters*, met her at the beginning of the 1950s at a Christmas luncheon party given by the Vere Pilkingtons in Hamilton Terrace (Vere was chairman of Sotheby's but generally rated, at least by Ivy's friends, rather lower than his wife, the brilliant and fascinating Honor, who said she had only to think of *Pastors and Masters* to shake with laughter).

Ivy unwrapped Honor's presents so enthusiastically, clearly giving herself and others such a good time, that Madge rashly invited her a few years later to another Christmas party at which Nancy Cunard was a rival guest of honour. Nancy, whose stylistic allegiance to the 1920s and 1930s was as intransigent in its way as Ivy's own to a period thirty years earlier, was another of the extraordinary women to whom Herman paid homage ('Please, darling, please; no Compton-Burnettry for me,' Nancy would say firmly whenever he showed signs of wanting to mix his two great devotions[13]), but only Madge ever attempted to bring them together: 'Nancy Cunard decked out in all her corals, with spit-curls on her cheeks, together on a sofa with Ivy in black velvet was quite a sight.'[14] Ivy was mesmerized, Nancy scarcely less so by every detail from the conspicuous tea-cosy hairdo to the neat bows on Ivy's black, pointed shoes, and, like ships in the night, they passed and parted in silence: 'I don't suppose they exchanged a word all evening,' said Madge. 'The only thing I could do as hostess was go into the kitchen and get drunk.' Angus Wilson witnessed a similar confrontation a few years earlier at a party given by another intrepid London hostess, Cara Harris, and presided over—this time

on strategically placed separate sofas—by Ivy and Norman Douglas (a close friend of the Kings, then staying near them in Thurloe
Square and enjoying the kind of social amnesty conferred by great
age on even the most scandalous of prodigal sons). He and Ivy
seemed to divide the drawing room, 'like a lion and a hippo sharing
space at the zoo',[15] each well aware of and perfectly impervious to
the other's existence. The only acknowledgment either made was
when Douglas recited from time to time an obscene or irreligious
limerick: 'Ivy would perk up and send one of her young men "to see
what that old gentleman is saying"—she'd a sense that something
blasphemous was being said at the far end of the room.'

Ivy had always sensed undercurrents as anyone who ever met her
gaze will confirm ('it was a very peculiar gaze, round-eyed, repti-
lian, she might be talking and seem to be thinking of prices,' said
Sybille Bedford, 'but not when you saw her eyes'). But it was only
after Margaret's death that she found she could also negotiate quite
well for herself, socially speaking, on the surface as well. Within her
own strict limits, Ivy in her seventies would go anywhere, see
anyone, fall in readily with any suggestion whether it was for a
quiet tea-shop lunch with a woman friend or to go on after dinner to
a party of Lord Kinross's at which Ivy (who had been dissuaded by
Madge at the last moment from going home to bed) put on a star
turn with Rose Macaulay: 'She and Ivy had one of their heated
arguments with a circle of admirers egging them on . . .'[16] Ivy
spoke evil of Rose to her face as easily as behind her back, and she
was often sardonic in private about celebrities like Douglas ('They
always said he was up to snuff,' she told Angus, 'but he *wasn't quite
up to it*, that was the trouble'), but in public, with people she did not
know or disliked, she was almost unscrupulously loyal. Though
she held no great opinion herself of Virginia Woolf as a novelist,
Robin Fedden was struck by her indignation when Angus Wilson
argued (in a notably fair and sensitive review of *A Writer's Diary* in
the *Observer* of 1 November 1953) that Mrs Woolf's reputation had
been overestimated—'Ugly behaviour,' said Ivy, 'I trust it will do
him some harm':

> In the previous year she had been hardly less incensed by Harold
> Nicolson's paragraphs in the *Spectator* at the time of Norman
> Douglas's death, with their allusions to noisy drinking and boast
> of sexual triumphs. 'A most improbable thing,' she said. 'I do not

recall that he boasted of his sexual triumphs to me.' She was not well-disposed to Harold Nicolson and found in him a streak of comformity and a tendency to go along with the times, a tendency which she saw reflected in his Labour sympathies. 'I dislike progress,' she said. Thereby meaning, I believe, the thoughtless acceptance of contemporary ideas and attitudes.[17]

Ivy's own judgments, at least on literary matters, were always informed and unorthodox. 'Dr. Leavis's bad criticism, which is so very bad, takes from the value of his good criticism, which is so very good,' she wrote to Robert Liddell at the beginning of the 1950s, when the literary establishment was seething and splitting under the impact of Leavis and his critical crack troops: 'One feels the truth is not in him, and anyhow the whole truth is not.'[18] She held no brief for Leavis' popular opponent, Charles Snow ('I am wading through the C. P. Snow novel, The Affair,' she wrote to Barbara Robinson on 26 April 1960: 'It is able only in a way, and I hardly recommend it'), who rose to fame in the great imagination v. science debate that raged at the start of the next decade: 'I can see Ivy now,' said Herman, 'chuckling as she read out a bit where Dr. Leavis said that some people had feet of clay, but Mr. Snow . . . was entirely made of clay, particularly his head.'[19] Snow's wife, Pamela Hansford Johnson, had given Ivy no cause to revise her unfavourable initial impression: 'She works in such haste that her words cease to have a meaning, and a mind seems to be going to waste,'[20] Ivy wrote of Miss Hansford Johnson's British Council pamphlet, which turned out a dashing affair, full of enthusiasm if at times inaccurate and understandably nervous in tone.

Ivy herself, in the opinion of a good many friends, would have written trenchant criticism, and she certainly never slackened her scrutiny of current intellectual trends. She thought Rupert Brooke as unjustly neglected after the second war as he had been overrated after the first;[21] she greatly preferred Charlotte to Emily Brontë, sharing Anthony Powell's unfashionably moderate estimate of the latter ('Posterity has paid its debt to her too generously,' she wrote to him, 'and with too little understanding'[22]); she granted E. M. Forster a pleasing talent but no genius long before the general verdict supported her;[23] and she found Henry James' revaluation by Leavis and others exaggerated, even exasperating, perhaps because her work was so often compared to his ('Of course Henry James had talent, but he makes one work too hard for such a small result,' she said to Barbara Robinson, and to Lettice Cooper: 'A curious talent. One has to respect him. But how one would like to give him a push'). Shakespeare was, with Jane Austen, her comfort and joy: 'I should say that I have heard her talk about Shakespeare more than any other writer,' wrote Anne Hill. 'I think she must go to nearly all his plays that are performed, and read him constantly.'[24]

She told Robin Fedden in 1953, when *The Confidential Clerk* had its premiere at the Edinburgh Festival, that naturally she admired T. S. Eliot, 'but perhaps not as much as one is expected to do', and, when Dylan Thomas died in the same year, she said how much she had enjoyed his poetry ('At the time the qualification on the one hand, and the appreciation on the other struck me as unexpected').[25] Among contemporary novelists, she rated Anthony Powell and Henry Green highly, also Elizabeth Bowen, though again perhaps not quite so highly as other admirers did ('People are always writing to tell her about the death of their hearts,' said Ivy sarcastically when *The Death of the Heart* proved yet another of Gollancz's bestsellers: 'I suppose her publisher sends her peaches'[26]). Elizabeth Bowen was one of the friends who seems to have dropped out of Ivy's life after 1951, perhaps because each found the other's growing celebrity hard to take, or simply because Ivy made heavier weather than ever after Margaret's death of the more penetrating critics of her own work. But she saw more and more of many younger novelists, all of whom regularly sent her their books, which she generally acknowledged by return in the encouraging but noncommittal formula used to Sybille Bedford, for even—perhaps especially—with friends she came to cherish greatly, such as Olivia Manning and Rosamond Lehmann, Ivy could not write or say the word she did not think. She mystified Rosamond, when they first met at the publisher's party for *The Echoing Grove*, by saying kindly: 'I've read your book, oh yes, I've read your book, and I've decided that one of us cannot be a woman.'[27] But she could not resist being more explicit when Cecil Gould asked afterwards what she had thought of the novel: 'If it had been half as long—which would have done no harm—and if she had taken out half the characters—which would have been an improvement—' Pause. 'Well, there wouldn't have been much left, would there?'

Ivy's friends in the 1950s and 1960s relied on her implicitly in the matter of literary merit. 'Ivy educated me,' said Madge Garland.

'For seventeen years she was my guide. I read what she read; and she read *everything*. And that is why I have never come to grips with the contemporary novel since she died.' But Ivy would only discuss other writers freely, or even àt all, with people whose judgment and discretion she could trust: 'One remembers . . . those rare discussions about the contemporary novel,' wrote Sir John Pope-Hennessy, 'when one would ask whether it was worth reading a new novel by Iris Murdoch, and she would reply: "I don't think you need trouble." '[28] Ivy made short work of anyone classifiable as a literary snob or a bore, or simply too keen on her own work for comfort, and admirers who begged to meet her were apt to find the introduction going disastrously wrong. There was the famous wartime encounter arranged by James Lees-Milne when Ivy successfully baffled Eddie Sackville-West with 'Do you know Manchester?' and, when he hesitated, 'You get excellent teas there.'[29] At the very first tea party to which Madge invited her, the unfortunate admirer—a charming and up-to-date lady, intellectually fashion-conscious to a fault—chatted civilly about the latest reviews, plays, modern novels ('Nothing Ivy liked better than talking about modern novels,' said another old friend,[30] 'but not with someone who hadn't read any'), until cut short and left gasping by Ivy politely but coldly asking after her weekly butcher's bill, and what she made of the shocking price of meat.

Invited by the editor of the *Times Literary Supplement*, Alan Pryce-Jones, to meet the Duchess of Buccleuch (later apocryphal versions of this popular story substituted the Duchess of Devonshire), Ivy obstinately refused to volunteer information about anything except her window box and her new refrigerator, saying plaintively when Herman reproached her afterwards: 'I wish people would *tell* me when they want me to be literary. I don't think it was a great success.'[31] But perhaps the most memorable of all the parties reduced, at any rate in the host's view, to a shambles by Ivy was an intimate luncheon given for the French ambassadress in the early 1960s at which 'Ivy pretended—I think I may say pretended—that she had forgotten who Mme de Courcel was . . .'[32] Offended as always by Herman's exquisitely un-English food ('Ivy . . . despised a *cuisine raffinée*,'[33] said Herman, who was used to her pointedly scraping off sauces and leaving her wineglass untouched), further affronted by his lapsing momentarily into French, Ivy cross-examined her fellow guest severely and in impertinent detail on the running of the embassy in Kensington Palace Gardens, popularly known as Millionaire's Row ('Aren't they rather large houses? . . . How do you get staff? Don't you find it difficult to get someone to clean the front doorsteps?'). But the ambassadress, who later melted Herman's heart by calling him '*notre M. Swann*', proved socially quite equal to the crankiness of eminent old British authors: 'A *déjeuner*,' she said, 'with Miss Compton-Burnett . . . is rather like a *déjeuner avec le général de Gaulle*.' Silence. '*Ce n'est pas facile*.'

With Herman Ivy was always at liberty to behave as irresponsibly as she liked, and she saw no reason to oblige strangers who came to marvel at her like sightseers at a monument. But with people who lacked social confidence, anyone diffident or at a disadvantage, Ivy was altogether different: 'She had charming manners, she was the perfect guest,' said Olivia Manning, meaning that Ivy could be counted on to take her fair share in the conversation and—unlike some literary lions who turned up only to be admired—would always help out in a sticky patch. She loved style in friends like Madge Garland (who became the first Professor of Fashion at the Royal College of Art after the war), and the novelist Theodora Benson, a 1920ish figure of great charm, chic and dramatic, angular beauty whom Ivy came to love dearly after Margaret's death. Theodora and Madge would always dress up for Ivy's tea parties —'And what fun we have all had in that Stygianly gloomy dining room,' wrote James Lees-Milne,[34] remembering the years when tea at Braemar Mansions turned into a ritual rather far removed from the constrained and conventional occasion it had been in Margaret's day.

The tea table drawn up between the drawing-room windows was abandoned in favour of a more substantial meal announced by a handbell—'school-room tea' said Angus Wilson—with everyone sitting up to table in the dim, cheerless dining room, lit only by a curtainless window opening on a fire escape and a single electric light bulb dangling on the end of a wire, absurdly out of scale and character with its pretty little fancy shade of blue Bristol glass and crystal teardrops. These occasions—'Braemar gatherings' in Roger Hinks's phrase—might not be cosy but they were often uproarious, with gossip rising and flying round the table alongside clouds of white sugar as the guests bit into outsize meringues specially supplied by a local bakery. 'The fare, as tea goes, was perfect,' wrote Robin Fedden. 'Everything was home-made: the oat cakes, the large iced cake, the jams, the cheese and cress, or cucumber, sandwiches, and not least the brandy snaps which were referred to as "jumbles".'[35] There was always something hot—muffins, crumpets, at worst toast—generally a loaf of bread with a honeycomb or gentleman's relish, possibly potted shrimps as well, and 'once,' said Robin McDouall, 'there was ice cream on glass plates'.

The company was mixed, old and new, the sharper or more tenacious of Margaret's upper-class friends eyeing and eyed by the literary contingent, recent acquisitions jumbled up with old standbys like Rose and Roger Hinks, even one or two who, like Arthur Waley, had first known their hostess in the Compton-Burnetts' original, shabby schoolroom at Hove half a century earlier. Anyone might be invited since Ivy, unlike Margaret, seldom if ever dropped people on grounds that they were too dim or too dull (some who found the conversational standard too high or the going too strenuous fell out of their own accord); and anything might be discussed, especially friends ('I like to hear about them,' as Hope Cranmer says in *Parents and Children*, 'and the different ways in which they have gone downhill'[36]). Ivy looked on smiling as she used to do at Margaret's parties, only now she took a more active part, stirring up the talk from time to time with a fresh subject, putting in a word or a story, occasionally convulsing the table with laughter but mostly watching and listening, as amused as her guests, who went home often exhausted but always amply entertained. 'Ivy's parties were totally unlike other people's,' said James Lees-Milne. 'Walking away from Braemar Mansions one had so much to think about. *What* had she meant by that?'

People who knew Ivy before and after Margaret's death all agree that she emerged transformed from her period of mourning. 'She changed and flowered,' said Carol Rygate, 'she became enchanting to her friends.' 'She began to blossom,' said Vere Watson-Gandy, 'she seemed a different person.' The change was obvious even to newcomers like Olivia Manning, who had been very young, nervous and practically unknown when she first set eyes on Ivy standing with Margaret at a party of Rose Macaulay's, observing everyone, talking to no one—'As a pair they gave me the impression of close self-sufficiency'[37]—and looking so forbidding that, when Olivia actually met her a few years later, 'she seemed totally different from the Ivy I had seen at Rose's party'. They made friends at once though Olivia remained always faintly dubious, like Rosamond Lehmann, about Ivy's cryptic compliments on her own novels. 'It's an organic book,' Ivy said approvingly of *Friends and Heroes* and, when Olivia complained of her reviews, 'The trouble with you, Olivia, is that you *deserve too much.*' To Olivia, who suffered more than most from unfriendly criticism, Ivy was always consoling, affectionate and understanding. 'Once you pick up a Compton-Burnett, it is hard not to put it down again,' Ivy said encouragingly; and another time, when Olivia stormed out of a tea party at Braemar Mansions, infuriated by 'Ivy's rich friends' lamenting the plight of one of their number obliged for tax reasons to retire in idleness to the South of France, she overheard her hostess explaining that she was a writer. 'Has she had much success?' someone asked coldly as Olivia trod noisily down the passage. 'Oh yes, indeed,' said Ivy enthusiastically, 'yes indeed, she has had *much success.*' Even in private with the discreetest of confidantes Ivy's loyalty scarcely faltered: 'It really is full of *very* good descriptions. Quite excellent descriptions,' she said when Elizabeth Taylor asked about Olivia's latest novel. 'I don't know if you care for descriptions? I don't.'[38]

The B.B.C. producer Norman Wright was another who approached Ivy in some trepidation and was surprised to find how easily she dispelled his constraint. He met her at dinner at Theodora Benson's flat in Sloane Square where he found himself scrutinized, interrogated and so shrewdly summed up that he was beginning to wonder how he would get through the evening when Ivy abruptly changed and took charge of the conversation, producing, pursuing and switching topics—religion, life, art, sex (this last being the only one that dismayed her: 'She said she could not understand it, had nothing to say about it, she got quite worked up about it'). It was a brilliant display, 'as though, every so often when enough had been said, she tossed in a firework or threw up a whole lot of coloured balls', and the whole party sat up talking till two in the morning when Ivy—who had by this time closed up again as suddenly as she had opened out—stoutly refused to allow anyone to escort her home.[39]

This sociable, expansive side of Ivy recalls her father, and still more her brother Noel who would also sometimes startle his Cambridge contemporaries by abandoning his habitual ironic reserve to dominate a whole dinner table with irresistible energy and wit. Accounts of Ivy in the last two decades of her life suggest that she came closer than ever before to disclosing something very like the sensitive, responsive, deeply emotional nature that Noel had always shown to his friends. 'She was ruled by her heart,' said Vere Watson-Gandy who, like a great many others, came to love Ivy and know her intimately only after Margaret's death when old friends realized for the first time how much she craved their affection, and how surprised and glad she was to find she had it. Both Watson-Gandys thought it was realizing she had not in fact been abandoned that changed Ivy, who made an art at the end of her life out of cultivating her friends. 'Why did we love her so much? She had a gift for friendship,' said Carol Rygate. 'After Margaret's death I learned to love Ivy, for she was lovable, like a child is lovable,' said Herman. 'She would look up at me, and her eyes would twinkle, and she looked so mischievous, and you felt that she had done something that she shouldn't . . .'[40]

Ivy never lost her mischievous air, nor the infectious pleasure she got like a child from a treat or an outing, but the tyrannical childish urge to hurt or wound dropped from her again after Margaret died. To people who knew her well in those years, she was gentle, considerate, patient, often protective:

> I remember . . . thinking as I went to sleep that night that really everything had passed off quite well [wrote Madge, describing her first encounter with Ivy], when, with a blinding flash of insight, I saw a remark of mine pinpointed by a counter-remark from Ivy—but too politely said, too understated, to be immediately apparent . . . Yet, in spite of her famed wit and repartee, I never, in all our seventeen years of friendship, left her presence feeling diminished, or with any barb planted in my sub-conscious. Her generosity of friendship was extraordinary, her interest in one's life and surroundings never-failing. She was the most tender of friends.[41]

No one has left a more intimate portrait of this private Ivy than Elizabeth Taylor, who saw her only intermittently on trips up to town from the country but described each meeting to Robert Liddell in letters often written the same night from notes made on the train going home to Buckinghamshire. It was Robert who had given her an introduction to Ivy in the spring of 1947: they shared the same initial delight and amazement over her books, and

Elizabeth came gradually to feel as deeply attached as Robert to Ivy herself. From the start the two speculated furiously—as Compton-Burnett readers commonly did—about mysteries on which no one had the nerve to probe Ivy herself: who she was, where she came from, what dark secrets had lain 'through long lives and on death-beds'[42] concealed in her past, above all who had supplied her with first-hand experience of the cruel patterns of tyranny and exploitation in her books. Elizabeth was inclined to rule out Ivy's mother, if only on the grounds that someone had certainly mothered Ivy, who sensed Elizabeth's nervousness and 'knew what to do' ('She wouldn't have known if someone hadn't done the same for her'[43]).

Robert pooled his researches. Elizabeth put in a little light detective work on a fruitless visit to the village of Compton in Wiltshire with her husband John (a manufacturer of fine chocolates who greatly appealed to Ivy). Both acknowledged themselves hopelessly outclassed as investigators by Ivy, who serenely asked questions and gave advice, eliciting all she needed to know about Elizabeth's domestic affairs, making occasional tantalizingly casual references to her own family and still airier pronouncements about families in general. 'What about that murder?' she asked suddenly one day in 1955, when a neighbour of the Taylors was shot dead (killed by Ruth Ellis, afterwards notorious as the last woman to be hanged in England): 'I saw the young man came from Penn. Did you know the family?' Elizabeth admitted that she did: ' "Such dreadful things happen in families nowadays," she said. (I liked "nowadays".)'

Elizabeth's writing is at its very best—clear, pure, almost transparent on the surface, full of ambiguities of humour and feeling below—in this correspondence from one novelist to another about a third regarded by both recipient and sender with admiration bordering on awe. 'The dialogue is as fresh as a water-ice . . . ,' V. S. Pritchett had written of Elizabeth's fourth novel, *A Wreath of Roses*, in 1949, 'a water-ice from those brilliant refrigerators of family utterance, Virginia Woolf and Miss Compton-Burnett.'[44] In a sense Elizabeth's position at the time paralleled Ivy's own twenty years earlier, when she was introduced at the start of her career to Virginia Woolf on the peak of hers. Though the letters to Robert show a relationship that grew steadily warmer and more relaxed, it had begun formally enough with constraint on both sides, quickened on Elizabeth's part by apprehension and pity in the early 1950s when Ivy had only recently emerged from grief and isolation. The first letter describes a luncheon on 9 June 1953, a week after Elizabeth II's coronation, three months after Ivy and Elizabeth had respectively published in March *The Present and the Past* and *The Sleeping Beauty*, while Robert, having just brought out *Some Principles of Fiction*, had also sent Ivy five draft chapters of his forthcoming book on her novels:

10 June

Dear Robert,

I think this will be a long letter. I even think you may wish it to be, for it is Reporting Back. (I need not say for you alone). I was in a fine state of disintegration when I arrived for luncheon. It is impossible in these Coronation days to judge how long it will take to get from place to place and I asked the taxi-driver not to be too early. He put me down in the Brompton Road—very kind & understanding—saying 'If you walk from here you'll keep him waiting just a minute like all you ladies do.' I made him take me on a bit further at the risk of him thinking I lacked the right sexual tactics. Then I was afraid I was late & began to run, with my arms full of flowers from the garden—people stared. 'The Servant' looked me over contemptuously. *She* was reading *The Daily Telegraph*. The room looked the same. She was pleased with the flowers & said, as I remembered her saying before—'Before I do anything I will give them a drink'.

She looked smaller but not much changed. Do you remember the dusty black velvet chairs and the sofa with too many cushions? There were no Coronation decorations. ('We seem to have been crowning her for a whole year. I was bored with it long ago, and so relieved to know it is really done at last.') We were alone. The longest time I have ever been alone with her. We had sherry ('Do have some more. There is only a bottle of beer in the dining room'). She obviously waited for me to prove myself an old toper, but I did not. She talked incessantly, her head averted towards the window boxes. She seemed much gayer, much less strange, younger (but not in appearance), rather mischievous. We could talk about anything, but not the Five Chapters. This was made clear.

Luncheon: Hot gammon, cabbage, sauté potatoes. Raspberry

fool—with dollops of cream. And then, oh dear, a Camembert of mahogany colour. I do not know how I ate it. It had gone through all its stages. Not helped by: 'So delicious to eat, but it makes the whole flat smell as if the drains were wrong.' She was wonderfully kind & maternal to me, as she has once or twice been before. She gave me all the blobs of cream on the raspberry fool, as if I were a child.

We discussed you—'Robert'—and your works. How once she & Margaret had tea in Oxford with you & your brother and —again—how cut up you were at his death. She was very nice about this. Of your books—'I liked the last novel [*Unreal City*] very much. That old homosexual really *was* one—not like Angus Wilson's—he just says they are and we must take his word for it.'

'I wish writers would not write such annoying letters to me. Joyce Cary wrote a very kind letter . . . I was quite glad to have it . . . sending a copy of my book to be signed, & saying he would like to have it back quickly, as at least a dozen people were waiting to borrow it . . . such a dreadfully stupid thing for one author to say to another. I always write my friends' books on my Harrods list, even if they give me a copy, and then I keep it out for quite a time so that other people can't have it. Another thing is the way others think they can have free copies. One has to pay two thirds, and Mr. Gollancz only gives me six (How many does Mr. Davies give you? Exactly!). One has one or two friends who must be given a copy, and there it must end. And of course, one must keep one or two clear copies for an emergency.' (I loved this.)

(I hope I remember her words correctly. I am not a good Boswell).

We talked about horses quite a lot. How they always love her and keep nudging her. ('Of course, one falls over, unless one is standing against a wall.') 'I used to ride but I can't afford it now, naturally.' Cats she hates—all domestic animals—cannot bear a house where there is a dog—'Parrots are jealous'. She loves pigs. (A wonderful categorical conversation.)

Literary: Reading life of Gorki—all Russians are brutal, except Tchekov. 'People dislike his plays as they are all about nothing. *I* like them very much.' She also likes Aksakov—& that beautiful Chronicles of a Russian Family.

Rosamond's novel[45]—(She called her Rosamond but was only introduced to her once at a party). 'Little bits of it very well-written.' Over coffee we discussed Blanche Knopf. 'I went to see her at Claridge's . . . they are always so obsequious when one asks for her . . . I think I caught her on the hop for she was wearing trousers and sandals and . . . no, I cannot remember what else . . . whatever one wears with trousers . . . she must have worn something . . . a blouse, do you think, or a jumper? Yes, I think I caught her on the hop. I imagine she was resting and over-ran her time. I do not understand Americans, and she is a Jewess as well, so there you are. She said: "I think I am making a mistake about Liz Taylor (her name for you, not mine). Do *you* think I am making a mistake?" I told her she must make her own mistakes in her own way. She said: "I would never ask *you* or Elizabeth Bowen to alter a comma, but Liz Taylor's only a baby."' (This amused her very much.)

All this time, she was staring at my legs, & suddenly asked: 'Are those nylons you are wearing, or are you wearing no stockings at all?' I said they were the last pair of nylons, memorial to my relationship with Blanche. 'Oh, she didn't ever give me nylons. I daresay she thought I was too frumpish' . . .

Blanche had summoned her to Claridge's to make impossible suggestions about *The Present and the Past*. Either she didn't want to publish it this year, or not at all, but wanted her not to go to another publisher all the same. 'I could not understand what she was trying to say, because it was too preposterous *for* her to say.' She has followed my example (which she kindly applauded), & gone to another publisher.

She remembers her reviews and quotes them, knowing long passages by heart . . .

I hope I have remembered the things she said. I am writing almost at once, in case I forget. I am glad she was so alert and gay. She only mentioned Margaret twice—once tenderly—'the beautiful curtains Margaret and I chose together'—and once tartly—'Margaret would never prepare her lectures . . . just gather a few notes together and wonder why she was nervous at the last moment. In the end I urged her not to do it.'

It seems a grim, uncosy life there, but it appeared (yesterday at least) not to be having that effect upon her. She is thinking of her new novel ('letting it germinate for a period') and seems busy and hungry. She wasn't quite as neat as she used to be. Hair the same

grey tea-cosy streaked still with gold. The same diamond ear-
rings. The same interest in money. Knowing the price of everything. That intense love of flowers—a window box with flax and
fuchsias. 'People say the earth must be sour, but it has been there
eighteen years & still grows plants. What *is* sour earth?'

I was not quite sure, though confessed to having used the
expression. 'Then very honest of you to say so.' 'I love,' she said,
'to see a seed push out of the earth & crack in two. That is quite
enough for me. I should not want many flowers.'

She gave me much advice about the children, whose ages she
remembered precisely . . .

She took some old flowers out of a vase—'You can see what a
poor way we were in'—to make room for the new ones. When
she had gone to get water I put this one in my handbag for you.
The only one not dead.

Do not bother to answer this. I hope you are having a nice
holiday.

Aren't you glad you are not Joyce Cary?

With love,

Elizabeth.

She asked why Blanche did not like my book and kindly suggested that perhaps it was the woman being scarred from a motor
accident which she didn't like. (It was really the book itself.) 'But
a very real modern problem it is, as being injured in war is, too.'
She said this with energy and emphasis and I was astonished
('When war casts its shadow I find that I recoil', etc.). She kept
her eyes lowered to make sure she did not look at me at this
moment, at my own quite irrelevant scars.[46] I kept my hands
tightly clasped, to avoid the habitual gesture of hiding myself
from sight. The room froze with self-control. I wished I could
say: 'This is nothing to do with my book. Definitely not.' I so
dreadfully wanted her to know that, although I am sure it is not
really important either way. I think she felt awkward, because
she quickly helped me to more raspberry fool. The hand shook
and she spilt a bit into my glass.

Mrs Knopf, who gave Ivy flowers done up in cellophane ('I thought
she was going to give me a doll,' Ivy reported to Angus Wilson,
'and of course, I was very fond of dolls. She'd put them into

a—what should I say?—a receptacle. Strange, wasn't it?'[47]), had in fact written the previous December declining to publish *The Present and the Past*, on the grounds that Ivy's sales—satisfactory to start with—had failed once again to rise in America in spite of consistently enthusiastic reviews.[48] The book was published instead by Julian Messner of New York, and Ivy much enjoyed describing the various prevarications advanced by Mrs Knopf who thanked her, according to Ivy, for behaving like a lady ('What did she expect me to do?' said Ivy tersely to Francis King. 'Hit her?').

The new book that was germinating in the summer of 1953 was *Mother and Son* in which a brisk plot (comprising missing documents, long-lost parents, a strong line in discreditable personal revelations) is constantly held up by a placid, leisurely flow of talk about housekeeping, and more particularly hospitality: food, drink, menus, what to order and how to serve it, all the domestic minutiae that fascinated Ivy are discussed in detail, down to the finer points of laying a table, getting out special china and opening wine only for guests. Rose's *Pleasure of Ruins* was finally published in 1953, the year in which Ivy signalled her return to vigour and spirits with *Mother and Son*, which is, incidentally, the closest she came to compiling her own *Pleasure of Entertaining*. More to the point perhaps is the book's main theme of companionship: the two neighbouring households in *Mother and Son* are both largely preoccupied by questions of how and on what terms to live with other people, whether or not to stay single, the vexations of sharing a home with strangers, and the impossibility of managing alone. Companions of various sorts are engaged under more or less gloomy auspices ('"Are you proof against insult, Miss Wolsey?" asked Francis. "Because, if not, this is no place for you"'),[49] though all but one of these rash engagements, marital and otherwise, are broken off in the end. There is a congenial couple of spinsters running an eminently civilized ménage together, and Miranda Hume, the mother of the title, dies of heart failure, leaving her unprepossessing, unmarried, elderly son plaintive and, as he says, partnerless. But in so far as the book gives an authentic glimpse of its author at all, it is in Miranda herself, who probes candidates for the post of companion with such shameless personal questions about their age, sexual aspirations and financial circumstances that the rest of her family are appalled:

'Where is Miss Wolsey, Mother?' . . .

'Well, where is she?' said Francis. 'Not fled the house so soon?'

'Gone to her room,' said Rosebery. 'A most natural thing to do.'

'In a state of collapse?' said his cousin.

'Why, what should be the reason for that?'

'I thought she had had a talk with Aunt Miranda.'

'You will have one yourself, if you are not careful,' said his aunt.[50]

Young women commonly emerged shaken, if not in a state of collapse, from cross-examination at Ivy's hands. 'Had I known what it would be like I should *never*, *never* have attempted to see her again,' said Elliott Felkin's daughter, Penelope Douglas, who emerged from cold storage after her marriage some time in the 1950s and wrote to Ivy only to find herself invited alone to Braemar Mansions, seated facing the light and interrogated at length about her own and her family's affairs: 'I remember being jolly well looked over and gone into. She was very fierce. And I know that I was determined never again to have a tête à tête with Ivy (though of course I did).' Ivy had known Penelope's parents, her unlucky Aunt Winifred and both her grandmothers; and there was an impersonal intensity about her curiosity that impressed Penelope, as it had done Herman's sister Elka, but not everyone had the stamina to stand it. 'Though she lacked Margaret Jourdain's eye for works of art, nothing where human beings were concerned escaped her,' wrote Robin Fedden. 'There the eye and the intelligence never slept. She sometimes seemed to watch people as intently as a predator watches its prey.'

This was precisely the impression Ivy produced over the next decade or so on strong men as diverse and distinguished as Lord Goodman (who claimed to have found her so daunting that he would leave any house sooner than risk being placed next to her at dinner[51]), and Tom Matthews of *Time* magazine (a man unaccustomed to fear but said to have been visibly cowed nonetheless by a simple enquiry from Ivy as to how many pairs of shoes he possessed[52]). The philosopher A. J. Ayer, finding himself seated beside her at table, could think of nothing to say until he nerved himself to ask if she minded people discussing her books, and was reduced to silence again by her civil reply: 'Not if they have something interesting to say.'[53] But Professor Ayer, nerving himself a second time, said something interesting about the immorality of her characters, after which the two got on splendidly for, however short she might be with over-confidence or pretentiousness, Ivy was seldom discourteous. 'I was always surprised when someone whom I was taking to meet her admitted to fear, because there was nothing formidable about her . . .' wrote Kay Dick. 'To anyone who was inordinately shy Ivy was enormously kind, and took great pains to put him at his ease.'[54]

Now that Ivy's life was no longer shaped and run by Margaret, she laid herself out to comfort and amuse her friends, who looked out for anything that might please her in return, whether it was a scrap of gossip, a cutting from the *Spectator* about the Sitwells' latest raid on its letter columns or the first spring violets packed in moss and posted straight from the country. She went often to the theatre with Herman or Madge or Carol Rygate, preferably meeting for lunch and going on to a matinée. She kept an eye on her friends' books, and an equally sharp lookout on their children: the Braemar Mansions Christmas tree was given up after Margaret's death, its decorations packed away and given to the Hills' small daughters (who were charmed one tea time, as they were saying goodbye, when Ivy ran them up and down several times for fun in her lift), but Ivy, who never forgot names or ages, always asked affectionately after other people's children and got on exceedingly well with quite a few of them, sympathizing particularly strongly with anyone in trouble at boarding school. She made a spontaneous hit with Rosamond Lehmann's teenage daughter Sally who found Ivy's jokes killingly funny (pressed to another slice of Fuller's walnut cake, Ivy said it was so good 'it might almost be said to eat itself', whereupon she and Sally collapsed in giggles on the sofa), and she surprised the Feddens by asking specially to see their small children ('To what depths I wondered, as she considered my own children, was she penetrating? The disturbing children in her novels provide the answer . . .').

Gardening was another great pleasure. Besides her own balcony window boxes—running the whole length of the flat on two sides, stocked with flowering thrift and thyme, old-fashioned granny pinks, petunias, little roses and fuchsias, even a tiny hydrangea —she helped plan and plant the neglected, junk-filled wilderness that eventually became an exquisitely groomed town garden at the back of Madge's new house on Clarendon Road in North Kensington. Ivy sat on the grass to make a daisy chain the first time she visited Madge's prospective property, and later the two made expeditions to choose flowers and shrubs, striped grasses, lilies of the valley, spring bulbs, roses, viburnums and clematis, always single and simple, as far removed as possible from the frilly, fancy florist's blooms that Ivy deplored ('She particularly disliked chrysanthemums with their heavy towelled heads and heavy, damp smell, but liked dahlias if they were single,' wrote Madge,[55] who even agreed to reprieve a few daisies in her lawn on Ivy's account). If museums and the great country houses no longer detained her, gardens remained Ivy's delight. She and Madge would meet at the bus stop in Kensington High Street for a trip to Kew Gardens (once with lunch at the pub on Kew Green), and they made annual outings to Vita's magical garden at Sissinghurst Castle, choosing a different season each year, hiring a car and driving down for lunch, first at the Royal Oak in Sevenoaks which Ivy approved for its plain cooking, rambling garden, and the photograph in the hall of Lord and Lady Sackville entertaining royalty, with Vita as a little girl in a frilly dress, lace hat and black boots:

> Only the boots (brown riding ones, not black buttoned) were visible when we met the adult Vita who, in her mannish clothes and with her dark, cropped head, was the antithesis of the small Ivy, dressed in brown tweed, matching brimmed hat, and brown lace-up shoes and gloves to tone. Vita did not usually bother much about tea but she always took special care that a large and proper meal was offered to Ivy, beginning with toasted buns and a cake made specially by the cook . . . Once Vita received us wearing a Persian coat in vivid colours and crimson silk pants —her exotic appearance was marvellous in the all-white garden, sitting at the end of a path lined with lilies, with Ivy, small, neat and darkly-clad beside her.[56]

There were still regular country visits each spring and summer to friends such as Janet Beresford at Ashwell, the Kidds (Roger was now married with small daughters of his own) at Eastbourne, the Jenynses at Bottisham (Soame had fallen into the habit of calling at the flat every three weeks or so after Margaret died, for lunch or tea and a talk) and the Watson-Gandys at Buckland Newton in Dorset (where Vere drove her all round the country, stopping now and then to admire the cowslips or buttercups or for Ivy—who loved riding about in a car—to go behind a hedge and be cheerfully and expeditiously sick). She had become a notably easy guest, quite free from the stiffness and boredom that used to afflict her on furniture visits, entertaining, appreciative, always ready to amuse herself with a flower or a book or a little light brain work: *Mother and Son* was finished at the beginning of June 1954, and typed ('It is short, but it will want some care, as it is rather smudged and interrupted by interpolations'[57]) by Cicely at once so that Ivy might take it away with her to correct in the country. 'I had a happy summer with a good many country changes in the houses of my friends, the kind of holiday I like best, now I am alone,' she wrote on 20 October to Robert, whose *The Novels of I. Compton-Burnett* was scheduled for publication by Gollancz with *Mother and Son* the following spring. 'It was good news that your book and mine were to appear on the same day, and I wish the novel was good enough to hold its place at the moment, and that there were four of us, instead of two, to await it.'

One of Ivy's favourite stopping places for work or rest in the country was Broome Park in Kent, a large, plain but palatial, pink brick house between Dover and Canterbury, built in the reign of Charles I and done up by Lord Kitchener ('He was a bachelor *or something*, wasn't he?' Ivy said sweetly to Robin McDouall), who ransacked the empire to furnish it but died in 1916 before finding time to move in. It was acquired between the wars and opened after the second as a retreat—part country house, part hotel—by Dennis Jell and his wife, the painter Pauline Jell (née Konody), who provided precisely the sort of surroundings that suited Ivy: good plain food, pleasant service, spacious rooms, a secluded untidy garden and wild grounds where she might pick tiny posies of the inconspicuous woodland and hedgerow flowers she had loved best from girlhood. 'Cowslips are out in front of my window, and the blackthorn, my favourite of the prunuses—or is it pruni?—is out in clouds,' wrote Ivy,[58] who made a point of going each year 'to Broome to see the spring', as well as spending two or three weeks there each summer. There were long drives, short walks and huge fires on a hearth big enough to burn whole branches of trees on a great mound of white wood ash, with a tea trolley drawn up in front and a fireside armchair reserved specially for Ivy.

She had first come to Broome in the mid 1950s with Helen Rolleston for Christmas (a festival increasingly hard to bear without Margaret in London), and sometimes she invited another friend—Carol Rygate, Vere or Madge—with whom she would explore the park and the deep flowery lanes round about that had once been smugglers' tracks, or catch a bus at the end of the drive to ride into Hastings for a blow on the front. She questioned Dennis Jell closely on the management of the estate, helped choose a riding school—interviewing the owners, going over the curriculum, inspecting the bedrooms—for Madge's teenage Parisian goddaughter, and once she took Madge to lunch with Mr Mowll at his house in a pretty village outside Dover (Ivy told Pauline Jell that the original Mowll, her parents' solicitor, had been the tyrant who darkened the days in her childhood).

But mostly she was alone, walking by herself, reading or working in her room: 'She had a staggering power of concentration,' wrote Mrs Jell. 'She would go on writing, without any feeling of irritation, while the chambermaid made her bed and tidied up her room.'[59] Other guests noticed her talking incessantly even at her table for one in the dining room—'apparently she was rehearsing a couple of sentences over and over again, rearranging the order of the words until she got it right'[60]—and so did Mrs Jell:

> Sometimes one would find oneself walking behind her along the main corridor, and would overhear a lively dialogue as she was on her way to the bathroom, which one could hear continuing in full spate through the closed door. Occasionally this oral trying out would break into ordinary conversation between us; she would slip in a sentence that had nothing to do with what she was saying, but was obviously something that had come up in connection with her current book—this without any change of voice or expression. She would then resume the conversation as if nothing had happened.[61]

Other people reported strange behaviour in Ivy when she seemed, like Charlotte Brontë, to be what Mrs Gaskell called 'possessed' by her novel. Charlotte Brontë, too, was adept at putting up with interruptions, carrying on with her ordinary domestic routine 'even at those times when the "possession" was on her', only hurrying through the housework 'so as to obtain leisure to sit down and write out the incidents and consequent thoughts, which were, in fact, more present to her mind at such times than her actual life itself'.[62] Mrs Gaskell's description sounds very like Hereward Egerton, the last of Ivy's novelists (in *A God and his Gifts*), emerging from his room 'dazed and dumb and vacant-eyed'[63] to find his actual family vague and insubstantial compared to the fictional characters 'who have lived with me and made my world. More deeply than mere flesh and blood.' Ivy seldom discussed her own methods, and then only with fellow professionals like Christopher Sykes or the painter Barbara Robinson ('I get an idea and start writing and the book seems to have a life of its own, and takes twists and turns I hadn't foreseen,' she told Barbara. 'The characters develop and change and then the beginning has to be altered'). But she did once say to Kay Dick that writers were hard pressed for material to work on—'We have to dig it out of our insides'—compared with painters who have theirs laid out before them: 'I think I feel on the whole that something's there trying to get out . . . It's sort of trying to get out and wants help.'[64]

She also said what so many other writers have said about the difficulty or impossibility of writing, the impossibility of not writing ('What a difficult kind of work to choose! But of course one did not choose it. There was no choice'[65]), and how much easier life would have been as an interior decorator or a furniture expert, 'because their artistic instincts are satisfied without too much effort. Producing something is rather an effort.'[66] Cicely Greig has described how coming to the end of a book drained Ivy, so that lunching with her to collect a newly finished manuscript was always a strained and edgy affair compared with the convivial occasion a month later when she called to deliver the typescript. 'They are hard matters and take their toll,' Ivy warned Robert when he contemplated a travel book at the same time as a novel.[67] She herself left comfortable gaps—'at least they seemed comfortable to her'[68]—between books, insisting sternly to Barbara that any artist must learn to endure what she called 'a blank time', which might in any case produce results in the long run.

Ivy had met Barbara and her husband Walter Robinson through Arthur Waley, who brought them to tea at Braemar Mansions in 1956. Walter was charming: a classical scholar and orientalist specializing in fourth-century Japan because it possessed, or so he said, 'no human interest', he was also a devoted and exceedingly knowledgeable admirer of Ivy's books, which suited his own subtle, complex, profoundly ironic temperament so well that he might have stepped out of one himself. Both Robinsons were presently adopted as part of the growing circle of honorary nephews and nieces whose doings in the 1950s and 1960s Ivy followed with inexhaustible interest, pleasure and concern. Walter touched her intellectually, Barbara (brave, forthright, determined, until comparatively recently an art student at the Slade School) stirred the generous sympathy Ivy felt increasingly for young women struggling to make an independent career in the arts: by way of encouragement she talked a great deal to Barbara about technical problems common to both writing and painting, such as composition ('The plot is not very important to me, though a novel must have one, of course. It's just a line to hang the washing on'[69]) and pruning ('One must do it,' she said emphatically, many times).

With other novelists, she tended to stick to the drab, concrete, mercenary terms in which writers generally discuss their work among themselves, swapping hard-luck stories, girding at publishers, grumbling about sales, commiserating over reviewers ('Their verdicts are always so incalculable that it is best to take them as amongst the vagaries of the spring,' she wrote to Robert on 6 March 1955, when their books came out together). She was invariably a comfort to writers in trouble, urging them on, sympathizing in blank times, enquiring solicitously whenever there was too long a gap between books, tending her own talent meanwhile as steadily as she tended her garden ('Ivy was strict about dead-heading, weeding, watering and general tidying-up. All had to be done regularly. She disliked disorder'[70]). 'Writing is not breaking stones,' as somebody says in *A God and his Gifts*, and one can almost hear Ivy's voice behind Hereward's, answering that the saying is only partly true: 'Everything is breaking stones up to a point.'[71]

ii

All this was of course far removed from Ivy's normal conversational method which was to round up and head off her guests until she had reduced the most unlikely people to discussing the price of refrigerators at the Army and Navy stores, whereupon she would say with mild surprise: 'Here we are—some of the best-educated people in England, I suppose—and all we can talk about is the price of refrigerators at the Army and Navy.'[72] An outstanding partner in this particular game of skill was T. S. Eliot, who moved into a house round the corner from Cornwall Gardens with his new wife in 1957, and met Ivy at a party in Knightsbridge. She came home with the Eliots in a famous taxi ride when—according to Alan Pryce-Jones and Christopher Sykes as well as to various enthusiastic accounts put about by Ivy herself—they talked about nothing but the forthcoming Rent Act, cake shops, fishmongers, greengrocers in the Gloucester Road and where to go for the best fillet steak. 'Ivy roared with laughter at this visit from one of the leading literary figures alive at the time,' said Herman. 'Somehow it rather emphasised her poor opinion of married life.'[73] The Eliots for their part had been chiefly 'tickled by the fact that she was complaining bitterly both at the party and in the taxi at having to pay the porter five shillings for bringing up her coals!'[74]

But observers could not help suspecting that behind their respective impenetrable façades, the two illustrious neighbours were by no means displeased to display their critical expertise in debate over shopping lists and scones rather than literary theory. They continued to glimpse one another on their rounds of the Gloucester Road ('I don't see very much of him, you know,' Ivy told Barbara, 'but I like to know he's there'), while 'Mr Eliot's bride' remained a source of much friendly and fruitful speculation in Ivy's drawing room:

Apparently she's always adored him, although she was his secretary for years. I am sure if I had been his secretary for a fortnight I should have wanted to poison him, not marry him . . . [Ivy said to Elizabeth Taylor]. Yes, I should have run round to the chemist's for threepennyworth of poison after a very short time. John Hayward, with whom he used to live, is keeping on the old flat, and Eliot has apparently paid up the rest for another two years. There was a great deal of talk about that . . . no, I don't think there was really much talk. I think I just asked a lot of impertinent questions. People say that if you don't ask, you get told more, but I have never found that to be true. I have found that one gets told nothing at all.[75]*

Ivy's idea of an impertinent question naturally varied according to whether it was put to or by her. She might question her younger friends singly and in private as to their family or financial circumstances ('There is no point in discussing furniture if you don't know how much it cost,' as she said to a couple of collectors, 'and no point in discussing incomes if they won't tell you how much theirs is'[76]). But she gave no quarter herself to pokers and priers like the Frenchman who, having come to England expressly to meet her and prevailed on the Hills to arrange it, rashly raised the question of stylization in her work: 'She said a little severely, as if he was blaming her: "One can't help *that*. One talks in a certain way, and one writes in a certain way; one certainly can't *help* it." '[77]

Ivy's standing among intellectuals in Paris in the 1950s was high if still somewhat mysterious. Five of her novels had been published by Gallimard and hailed with enthusiasm by those manning the barricades of novelistic theory in places like *Critique* and *Les Lettres Nouvelles*. For Sartre's contemporaries, immersed on the literary front in the upheaval that issued in the *nouveau roman*, Ivy seemed to have surmounted precisely the difficulties with which they were themselves still struggling.† Where English critics have tended to see her achievement in painterly terms, mostly French—she has been variously compared with the Post Impressionists, Cézanne and the Cubists, Bonnard, Picasso, even Mondrian, all radical innovators who changed the face of painting this century—for Nathalie Sarraute, Ivy plainly stood in direct line of descent from

---

* Compare Ivy's comments on the Eliot marriage in 1957 with the neighbours' reaction to the Ponsonby marriage in *Daughters and Sons* (1937), p. 182:

'You are not going into the house?'
'Yes, of course I am going in. But we can't arrive in a body to ask questions.'
'No, no, not in a body, no. But we want to ask some questions; yes, I think we do.'
'To find out about the marriage we have seen in the papers. How else are we to know about it? It is a wonderful and startling thing and fraught with bitterness for others . . .'

† '*La solution absolument originale, à la fois élégante et forte, qu'elle a su leur donner, suffirait pour lui faire mériter la place qui lui est attribuée depuis quelques années par la critique anglaise unanime . . . : celle d'un des plus grands romanciers que l'Angleterre ait jamais eus.*' Nathalie Sarraute, *L'Ere du Soupçon*, p. 119.

Proust, Joyce, Kafka and Virginia Woolf. Ivy's writing became the central framework round which Mme Sarraute erected her own theory of the novel: if Ivy's originality struck readers on the far side of the Channel as heroic, so did her courage, stamina and clarity of purpose ('For nothing could be . . . more astonishing than . . . the monotonous obstinacy with which, during forty years of labour, and throughout twenty books, she has posed and solved in an identical manner the same problems'[78]).

Ivy for her part received their homage with a majestic, indulgent, ironic indifference which suggests that, though she had no intention of mentioning it, she did not entirely reject their conclusions ('I am sometimes rather complacent about my writing,' she said once to Robin Fedden). Mme Sarraute was taken to tea at Braemar Mansions by Sonia Orwell (which vexed others among Sonia's Parisian intellectual circle, who saw no reason to underestimate their own claims to be presented to 'cette Ivy'): 'She did not seem to have the slightest idea as to what I might be doing in life. Neither did she seem to know that I had written anything about her books. I believe that if she had known, she would not have cared,' wrote Mme Sarraute,[79] who was enchanted by her visit and everything about it from the hostess's long black dress and velvet hairband to the coal fire and the maid in cap-and-apron, the buttered buns and the silver teapot, the demure conversation about rising prices, and not least by Ivy's parting shot: 'Do you girls want to go down the passage?'

Literature was a topic not raised at all, or only far enough for Ivy to slip in a complacent account of the Eliot encounter and to describe Virginia Woolf as a snob. Mme Sarraute went away feeling much like Alice waking up after her trip down the rabbit hole —'maybe all this was just one of my delightful dreams about England?' Ivy must have made a similar impression on the Frenchman Roland Cailleux, invited to meet her by the Hills at a luncheon when their mutual imperviousness so impressed their hostess that she made notes afterwards, describing how M. Cailleux doggedly developed his views on the novel ('The Frenchman said that Ivy, Céline and some South American writer whose name I've forgotten [presumably Jorge Luis Borges] were the only really modern writers quite uninfluenced by Jam Jars. We were surprised and puzzled until he referred to Jam Jars' *Ulysses*') which Ivy, primarily interested in the food on her plate, doggedly countered with remarks about her maid, her rent and her holiday plans, how to patch holes in a carpet and 'the devotedness, as parents, of swans'.

What struck Mme Sarraute and other visitors to Braemar Mansions was the sensation of stepping into a Victorian novel, much the same misleading impression Ivy had long since perfected in her books: 'The old-world atmosphere is so important, and I pay it strict attention,' as Felix Bacon said in *More Women Than Men*.[80] As the 1950s wore on, Ivy complained fiercely about the accelerating winds of change which she disliked even more than ordinary winds ('Death to me draughts, death to me draughts, death to me draughts,' she said once under her breath when Janet Beresford asked if she minded an open window at Ashwell). ' "Don't speak to me," she would say, "about the 'age of affluence'. How I loathe the age of affluence." '[81] She made no attempt to fathom the workings of socialism or the welfare state, steadfastly blaming all ills on a Labour government even when Labour was not the party in power. 'I don't know *what* Margaret would have said' became her standard response to rising rents, rates, bills and wages, falling standards of service, tall buildings, increased immigrants and thickening traffic ('The roads are like a dangerous sea,' she wrote to a cousin[82] as old and infirm as herself at Christmas 1959). She seemed at times so cut off from the modern world that her younger, naturally leftish, intellectual friends were constantly taken aback by her vigorous approval of changes like the liberalization of the censorship laws, and the Wolfenden Report which so greatly eased the lives of friends like Herman in 1957. 'I remember her also saying that it made her smile to see what ridiculous precautions young people took when they spoke to her about homosexuals,' wrote Mme Sarraute, 'as if that could have shocked her . . .'[83] It was Rose who had been shocked when Ivy said of an old friend's marriage eleven years earlier: 'He's homosexual, so of course he had to get married.' '*Ivy*,' said Rose, 'you really can't say things like that—think of all our friends.'[84]

1957 was also the year of the Rent Restriction Act, a prospect which filled Ivy with gloom and foreboding for months beforehand. 'I feel nervous, too, about the new, short BBC novel,' wrote Elizabeth Taylor to Robert (the novel was *A Father and his Fate*, due to be broadcast in Christopher Sykes' adaptation on the Third Programme in June before publication in August). 'She has to have the money, though, because goodness knows what her rent will be, & Rose Macaulay says *she* will not pay a penny more but Rose will do exactly what everyone will have to do, & pay what she is told. Ah, naughty, headstrong Rose.' Tea parties at Braemar Mansions grew loud with the sound of protest, alarm, appeal and lament. 'I live under the sword of Damocles in that my rent may soar after the revision of the Rent Act in the autumn,' Ivy wrote on 12 July to her cousin Katie Blackie, and on 17 September to Robert: 'The Rent Act is looming over everything here, and it has fallen on me with thunderous force.' Her friends were disturbed and full of advice. Robin McDouall suggested they might buy a house together and share it: Ivy had always had a soft spot for Robin because, as she said, he would have made such a wonderful butler—'I suppose you mean I look as though I'd been at the port,' said Robin. 'No. I don't mean you've been at the port,' said Ivy laughing, 'but you look as though you knew about the port.'[85] But she had long since discarded the notion of living with anyone ('It is a kind idea, and might be such a useful one, if I were not past the age for moving and moving alone . . . ,' she wrote on 21 August, adding prudently: 'If you are not providing for possible marriage, would not a flat be better than a house? Houses produce so many unforeseen expenses, and have roofs and drains and outside painting and dry rot, and people never know where they are').

In the event Ivy's rent was almost tripled to a stupendous £512 a year, which she paid with incredulous outrage ('It would be of little good to move as the same thing is happening everywhere and there is nothing to be done but suffer it, though in my case not in silence,' she told Robert on 25 June 1958). Ivy responded to what struck her as a shocking piece of opportunism on the part of her Polish landlord by breaking her generation's ingrained taboo against drawing on capital, arranging for herself and her sisters each to receive £3,000 from trust funds[86] and confessing the deed ('I've done something wicked') to Jim Brandreth. 'These are hard days and we are the doomed class,' Ivy wrote grimly to Katie. Tea parties grew stormier—'We all in London talk only of Rents'[87] —servants harder to come by and their wages steeper as their services became more essential to Ivy, whose last maid went mad[88] in the mid 1950s and had to be taken to hospital:

Poor Ivy alone in the house with her & sudden strange conversations about spiritualism & the stars [Elizabeth reported to Robert] . . . Ivy found 'a very strange library' in her room. 'So very peculiar. I didn't know that kind of book existed, but I have since learnt there is quite a demand for them. Horribly unpleasant. Quite a shock to me.' I hope I didn't look too anticipatory, or too disappointed when she said they were all about horoscopes & 'Find Yourself Through the Stars', etc. 'A very unhealthy lot. When she recovered, I advised her to get rid of them & so she did. It was distressing to hear her talking like that. When people are upset I always say I have a headache & that takes their mind off their troubles. But she only said, "I *knew* you had. I always know about you, because we are both under the same star."' This is carrying the democratic attitude too far. I said in a careless laughing way: 'What star is that?' 'I am afraid I don't remember,' she said coldly.

Towards the end of the 1950s more and more friends with private incomes left the country to lead a roving life in continental hotels like Jim Brandreth, or settle like the Robinsons in the South of France. Ivy, whose horror of dislodgement and dispersal went back at least to the time when her sisters had dismantled the household at Hove nearly half a century earlier, was deeply indignant. She refused to accept or even listen to the Robinsons' reasons for going, and they felt themselves disgraced ever afterwards. 'I am sorry you have gone to make a corner of a foreign field for ever England,' she wrote on 9 April 1958 to Barbara and Walter, who grew accustomed over the next decade to the mixture of disapproval, grief and reproach in Ivy's letters which grew wilder and sadder as she neared the close of her life: 'Yes, it is long since we met, but not, I think, longer than it tends to be, when people live under different skies,' she wrote to Barbara on 3 December 1968. 'I have quite a number in my life; and expect long partings and unfamiliar young faces . . . When you barter your heritage, you will have great wealth, but perhaps cannot even think you need it.'

Ivy spoke often and openly to London friends of her loneliness ('Living alone is unspeakable' was another regular refrain), to which she was by this time resigned. 'My life goes on in the same groove since Margaret Jourdain died, always with its roots in the past,' she wrote to Peter Mellors (who had emigrated to Canada by this time, in spite of all Ivy could say): 'I wish you had met her, and so met more of me.'[89] She still missed Margaret constantly, at times—on what Cicely called her 'Margaret days'—with palpable, angry vehemence. Cicely describes a dreadful occasion when she and her sister with a woman friend entertained Ivy to lunch at the National Book League in Albemarle Street where, the Regency staircase having first called Margaret to mind, Ivy retreated into herself with freezing dignity. Cicely referred to her as 'Miss Jourdain' by mistake, the rest of the party seized up with nerves and, all through the meal, 'Margaret seemed to come like a ghost between us'.[90] This was 12 January 1956, when Ivy was working on *A Father and his Fate*, which perhaps had something to do with her state of strain. A year later Margaret's spirit presided in altogether more sardonic and humorous mood over the tea party Ivy gave for Lucille Iremonger, whose latest book, *The Ghosts of Versailles*, attempted to get to the bottom of the various adventures of Eleanor Jourdain and Miss Moberly, beginning with their respective upbringings and ending with the public debacle at St Hugh's. Though Margaret is nowhere mentioned by name, the book's patronizing and somewhat inaccurate account of the Jourdain family—especially its unfairness to Eleanor ('She was, in sum, a sneak and a spy, with uncanny powers to boot')[91]—made Ivy feel that family loyalty on Margaret's behalf, together with curiosity on her own, might be served by meeting the author:

> She asked me to a cocktail party to which I didn't want to go . . . And then I thought I would write and suggest that she should suggest herself to tea one day & not only did she have the effrontery to do so ['Gave me pause to think myself,' Elizabeth wrote in the margin of her letter reporting Ivy's words to Robert], but she brought her husband. As soon as Rose knew that she was coming, she said that she must come too, & challenge her statements about Margaret's sister. For so much was untrue, & Margaret never had doubted her sister's integrity; they really believed, poor things, that what they said was true, & Miss Ironside or whatever her name is seems to have had some grudge against her. Then everybody wanted to come to tea. They swarmed in, & I had to have a cup which didn't match the saucer. Lots of people had to be refused. I couldn't just have them standing up at the back. It became out-of-hand & I had to stop Rose, for after all Miss Ironside was my guest & she was getting very angry & upset. I believe she has written other books, you know, though I am sure I don't know what they are.

But Ivy, for whom the art of conversation was always a matter of drama, movement and friction rather than academic discussion, had organized this affair with rather more care than her casual account to Elizabeth suggests. She had taken pains with the guest list—besides Rose, there was Carol Rygate who had been an active undergraduate member of the anti-Jourdain faction at St Hugh's in 1924, together with a strong detachment of Margaret Jourdain's supporters: Cecil Gould, Ivo Pakenham, Jim Brandreth and Basil Marsden-Smedley (Hester had begged to come too but been forbidden by Basil—'we had the worst row of our married life over this'[92]—on grounds that she knew too much about the Jourdains and was bound to get over-excited). All had been primed beforehand with copies of the book—'Have you done your homework yet?' Ivy wrote on a postcard to Jim Brandreth—and required to come armed with pertinent questions. The general verdict was that in the event the party had been spoilt by Rose's heckling, but retrieved after the Iremongers left by Ivy saying expectantly: 'Now, let's all say what we think of them,' which they did, to everybody's satisfaction. But it casts an interesting light on Ivy's stance as neutral observer that—whatever her other guests may have supposed to the contrary—she had privately contrived to give Mrs Iremonger the impression beforehand that she fully endorsed her view of Eleanor Jourdain[93] (and the Iremongers remained on Ivy's visiting list for years afterwards).

Ivy had a revenant of her own from the past round about this time in the shape of her long-lost cousin, Anthony Compton-Burnett, a distinguished amateur cricketer and science master at Eton, whose parents made contact by chance in 1957 with Ivy's sisters (they shared a radio repairer in Watford), and who subsequently turned up himself at the flat of his illustrious relative. His great-grandfather, William Compton-Burnett, had been the brother of Ivy's grandfather Charles; the first inkling either set of descendants had of the other's existence had been when Ivy's half-sister, Olive, herself a cricketing enthusiast, came across Anthony playing for his prep school on the south coast between the wars; and, though the connection was distant, both sisters must have been struck by the family likeness, for Anthony had the broad open brow, massive frame, curly hair and square-set eyes they had known in their father and their brother Noel. Ivy naturally warmed to him at once, and continued to see him regularly, asking in due course after his children (Anthony's sons, Richard and Nicholas, were, after all, the last of the Compton-Burnetts in a position to pass on the name), and enjoying his company on a much less impersonal footing than her sisters', or the Blackie cousins' who were her only other surviving relations.

These Blackies were the children of Ivy's Aunt Lizzie, her mother's favourite sister; and the strenuous rivalry between the two forceful sisters that had loomed large in Ivy's childhood might be said to have found a peaceful solution at last in herself and her cousin, Margery Blackie, who was by this time well on the way to succeeding Ivy's father as the country's leading homoeopathic physician (the official recognition of homoeopathy for which James Compton-Burnett fought all his life was eventually achieved under the new National Health Service in 1948, thanks largely to a campaign organized by Dr Blackie who followed her uncle as senior consultant at the London Homoeopathic Hospital in 1957, afterwards becoming dean of the Homoeopathic Faculty and personal physician to the Queen). Dr Blackie practised in Kensington but, being profoundly religious, exceedingly busy and in any case twenty years younger than Ivy, left contact with their cousin chiefly to her older sister Katie.* Another devout churchwoman (Ivy's relations clung to religion as staunchly as she repudiated it), Katie had been as a girl the closest of all the Blackies to Ivy, who found cordial conversation about parish activity hard to sustain in later life ('My congratulations on the church garden' was a characteristically truthful compromise: 'I think it is a very good work'[94]).

But Ivy was growing less strict about keeping people in separate compartments. 'My own circle seems to come from several different worlds, one of them hardly literate,' she wrote to Robert ('Perhaps we . . . are really her hardly literate world,' wrote Elizabeth darkly on hearing about this letter) on 20 February 1962, at a time when she was beginning to let her friends edge open the door so firmly slammed on her past after the First World War. She invited Herman (always faintly resentful about her family having

---

* The late Katharine Blackie was the cousin who preferred to be identified only as 'Katie' in *Ivy When Young* for fear of possible damage to her own and her sister's reputation if the family's Wesleyan background ever became common knowledge ('It must never come out, oh no,' she told me Dr Blackie had said, in dismay at the thought of her connection with Ivy being made public: 'Even the Queen—*even the Queen* who has done so much for homoeopathy—would think the less of me').

been, as he said, 'deliberately kept from him') to tea to help be nice
to Katie: 'She believes,' Ivy said by way of warning, 'and'—another
of her favourite sayings—'people who believe in the resurrection
will believe in anything'.[95] She responded generously out of the
blue after fifty years' silence to a fund-raising appeal from her old
college, Royal Holloway; and, when Basil was elected mayor of
Chelsea in 1957, the two set off on a jaunt in the mayoral car to call
on his friend, the principal, Edith Batho (Miss Batho apparently
had happier memories of this occasion than her guest, who was
frankly appalled: 'The library crowded, the dining hall also, the
roses gone, the principal housed in a first floor flat instead of the
ground floor rooms that were rightly her own . . .' Ivy reported
gloomily long afterwards to a long-lost college contemporary[96]).
She produced Elliott Felkin, by this time almost her oldest friend,
also out of the blue one day at tea with Madge, who was charmed
and disconcerted by his evidently extensive but unexplained links
with Ivy. Elliott's daughter, Penelope Douglas, went to some
trouble to bring about a reunion with Raisley Moorsom which
—since neither he nor Ivy was prepared to stand host to the
other—took place in a tea shop, and turned out a great success: 'I
have never seen her so relaxed with anyone as with Raisley.'

Though never exactly forthcoming on the subject of her early
years, Ivy talked more freely about her family in the last decade of
her life than ever before. *A Father and his Fate*, published in
September 1957, contains incidentally Ivy's first direct portrait of
her mother since *Brothers and Sisters*,[97] but its central concern is a
fuller working out of the theme of the present and the past already
propounded in the novel of that name. In each case, a missing wife
(divorced and supposed dead, respectively) returns home to con-
found a disgruntled husband anxious to exchange the drab reality of
unromantic middle age and an unappreciative family for a more
glamorous role (an heroic fake suicide for Cassius Clare and, for
Miles Mowbray, a clandestine affair with his son's fiancée); both
husbands find themselves back where they started from, only
appreciably worse off; and both try with the same dauntless in-
genuity to carry off the impossible. But, where *The Present and the
Past* ends painfully with death and recrimination, *A Father and his
Fate* closes on something very like victory for the jaunty, unscrupulous, irrepressible life force embodied in Miles Mowbray (it is not
for nothing that Miles' first grandchild, expected at the end of the

book, is in fact his own bastard), and subsequently taken a great deal further in Hereward Egerton, hero of the next novel but two. *A Father and his Fate* is full of energy, vigour and the determination not to look back:

> 'It is the future we must look to,' said Constance. 'It is useless to pursue the past.'
> 'It is needless,' said Audrey. 'It will pursue us.'[98]

The book might also be said to have the last word on that wave of feeling flowing like a receding tide through Ivy's work since Margaret died, in a passage where the orphaned Verena Gray talks about the death of her mother:

> 'Do you miss her very much?' said Audrey.
> 'I miss my life with her, and am still strange in the new one.'
> 'Do you not enjoy your freedom at all?' said Ursula.
> 'I might, if I had it. But I do not enjoy the things that go with it, the homelessness and the feeling that I matter to no one.'
> 'You can have that feeling no longer.'
> 'No, I have lost it. I can be myself. I have ceased to be a leaf tossed on the wind. I can look to the future.'[99]

Ivy too could look to the future by this time. She abandoned the strict black she had worn for years in favour of occasional grey, and even a touch of pale colour, with advice and encouragement from Madge (who had once been asked by Virginia Woolf to choose clothes for her, when success as an author in 1925 was followed by a greatly increased social life[100]). Though Ivy said that her fame meant little without Margaret, and even the most enthusiastic reviewers seldom earned a kind word ('I have had on the whole "a good press", but many of the comments were, as usual, incomprehensible,' she wrote on 17 September 1957, to Robert), she clearly enjoyed the wider recognition that came in the 1950s. *Mother and Son* won the James Tait Black prize in 1955 and throughout the decade her name was a household word increasingly popular with cartoonists and the compilers of literary competitions. Interviewers came thick and fast (one of Roger Hinks' favourite pastimes was enumerating 'the delicacies and indelicacies with which journalists would say that Ivy's tea table was "literally" groaning'[101]). Entertaining grew more and more lavish: 'Wine crept in, and sherry, especially in the evenings,' said Robin McDouall, though drink at Braemar Mansions remained for the most part deplorable, supplied in job lots by admirers, served too cold or too warm, and frequently corked in spite of remonstrances from Robin himself and Ernest Thesiger ('He was most impertinent about my wine,' said Ivy, dropping lumps of ice into her glass of sweet Graves overheated in front of the electric fire: 'I am not very wine-wise, you know'[102]). But the food was copious in time of austerity, and generally good (though not everyone cared for the rum-flavoured blancmange —'cornflour shape with hair-oil'—to which Ivy herself was so partial). Soame looked in often with a box of chocolates or occasionally a brace of pheasants, Robin could be relied on for 'a rich gift'[103] of butter, the Robinsons sent supplies of quince paste, friends in the country brought fresh eggs, soft fruit and garden flowers.

Ivy made probably more friends on her own account in the 1950s than she had ever had before, and her old friends drew closer. She saw Herman at least once a week at his house or hers: 'He flirts with her & flatters her. It is rather like being at the court of Elizabeth I,' wrote Elizabeth to Robert. 'He teases her. She answers him sternly and literally, but talks a great deal more, and more fluently, than usual. "And you will not repeat what I have said, Herman."' Ernest was always on hand for shopping or sewing, sorely missed when he left to play Jaques in As You Like It ('Ernest Thesiger is back from America, successful and in funds, but looking absolutely worn out. What a bad thing work is'[104]), or Polonius to Paul Scofield's Hamlet in Moscow in 1955 (when Ernest borrowed a pencil at a party to write on the pristine wall of a Muscovite gents': 'Burgess loves Maclean'[105]). Roger Hinks returned from running the British Council in Athens in 1957 to Ivy's great pleasure ('I am sorry you have lost him,' she wrote generously to Robert: 'It is hopeless the way life has to change and become less than life. It just has to be accepted'). She had always loved Roger's charm, erudition, his inability to tolerate humbugs (to whom he could be immensely and wittily rude), and, best of all, his fantastical, far-fetched stories like the one about a Roman Catholic friend who said, when asked if that morning's mass had been quite as she liked: 'Well, not exactly perhaps, it was rather Hail-Mary-well-met.'[106] Roger immediately joined the Braemar Mansions regulars, keeping Robert posted by letter and becoming indispensable to Ivy until he annoyed her again by a posting to Paris two years later.

Basil was her standby in all practical matters, supplying advice, assistance, invitations to mayoral parties (Basil said 'Ivy was the best thing that happened in Kensington'[107]), and support at her Saturdays—'it isn't as if the others have a wife to leave behind' —from which Hester was banned, as she freely admitted, for talking too much. As often as not, in these years of fame and self-confidence, Ivy's parties consisted of men only ('her attention in any group was always for the men,' said Rosalie Mander, another of the young writers Ivy met and made friends with after the war). Her closest women friends were probably Madge, Theodora and most of all Rose, whom she had known on and off, through thick and thin, good reviews and bad, for nearly thirty years ('Once at lunch with Ivy Rose Macaulay said, "I'm reviewing your book for Sunday." "That will be very nice," Ivy said complacently'[108]). They still teased one another with great delight and vivacity, and Ivy was not above shamelessly misrepresenting Rose when it suited her ('Quite sane friends of mine whose opinions I respect over other things, believe in this terrible religion,' she told Elizabeth Taylor. 'Well, it is something I can't understand, and Rose Macaulay can't either'). Their perennial debate was if anything more heated, as each grew older and more set in her allegiance:

> Almost the last time I saw her [Rose] [wrote Alan Pryce-Jones], we were both sitting in Ivy Compton-Burnett's dining room and she was carrying out a firm inquisition on her hostess's beliefs. 'I cannot understand you, Ivy, a clever woman like you. You have never got the hang of it. Of course, you may perfectly well be right. There may be nothing to believe *in*. Though I don't lose hope.'[109]

Rose died in October 1958. 'She was a unique person, and I feel a light has gone out, and that the world gets more and more grey,'[110] wrote Ivy, perhaps unconsciously echoing the butler who prides himself on his pessimism in her current novel ('Yes, ma'am, it adds a touch of darkness to the greyness of life'[111]). 'I shall miss Rose Macaulay to the end,' she wrote to Katie that Christmas, and to Cecil Gould: 'I am utterly deprived by losing Rose.'[112] Ivy's grief at the deaths of friends was always sharpened by indignation. Life without Margaret, whatever its compensations, could never be acknowledged as anything but a poor substitute. 'I never thought to enjoy a book about a foreign country so much, as I am an insular person, and essentially at home only in my own land, and perhaps chiefly in the past in that,' Ivy wrote on 2 June 1959 to Robert, thanking him for *The Rivers of Babylon*. '. . . I have enjoyed having Roger in England, and wish you were coming, though it is empty to you now, as indeed it is to me, though it is the only foot-hold I have and can have at my age.' She still urged Robert to write about his brother, talking often about him to Elizabeth ('He was very much cut up about Stephen dying. They were so happy together'), responding enthusiastically when the book was at last begun in 1955, unwillingly resigned two years later to further delay ('It must not be spoilt by being adapted to the sensibilities of living persons . . . It may live beyond their lives, and it should not suffer from them'[113]). She herself came in some ways close to the position taken up in *A Heritage and its History*, the novel she was writing in 1958, by Walter Challoner who barely exists save in his capacity as intellectual observer: a character disabled by early misfortune ('"I am grateful for the compulsions of my boyhood." "I am not," said Walter. "They rise up before me in the night. I might have been a less bitter poet without them"'[114]), but unresentful, indeed thor-

Ivy in the drawing room at Braemar
Mansions by Feliks Topolski
(see pp. 264–5)

oughly appreciative of the past, and in any case amply compensated by interest in the present: '"I wish Shakespeare were here," said Walter, to lessen the tension. "I mean, I wish I was he. I could make so much of this scene . . ."'

A Heritage and its History was finished at the end of October and published the following September (Julian Messner, who had brought out Ivy's last three books in America, now handed her in turn to Simon and Schuster, who published this and the next two). Ivy agreed to be interviewed by Alan Pryce-Jones who arrived on 8 September 1959 with a television crew and cameras at Braemar Mansions. She herself missed the programme on television, 'as even my friends who had it had not the Independent, and the only person who saw it seemed to be the greengrocer, who naturally had everything'.[115] But Elizabeth watched it, and described what she saw to Robert:

My heart was knocking wildly. The camera hovered in a sinister way over Cornwall Gardens, the grim outside. It looked like the beginning of a murder film. Then, once inside, I felt better. The high, light, pretty voice, the mouth pursed yet smiling. The eyes . . . sometimes looking bewildered, even desperate, but I think it was the horrible bright lights which are the worst part of all . . . She was most amusing, & described how much she had been abused by reviewers & how one man wrote to her asking her to explain what on earth her books were all about, & enclosed a stamped and addressed envelope for her reply—'I used it when I was paying a bill'. When asked which was her favourite of her books she said: 'Well, I do really rather like *Manservant and Maidservant*.' 'I'm very fond of *A House and Its Head*,' said Mr. Pryce-Jones. 'Yes, I like that very much, too,' she said enthusiastically. 'I rather like them all, in fact. After all, they are mine.' . . .

I feel now more that it was her *father*. You know what I mean. Mothers would never speak of workhouses. And someone has. I almost dare suggest myself again and take a stiff brandy and ask a lot of questions we want to know the answers to. Stake everything. She would at once understand the motive and, however coldly she dealt with me, she would understand the necessity.

CHAPTER NINE

'One of nature's Dames'

i

THE FIRST PERSON to come anywhere near asking the questions Elizabeth and Robert wanted answered was probably Kay Dick, who had felt thoroughly at home with Ivy from the day they first met:

> I felt that I was somehow established as one of those near-impossible children in her novels who might do and say anything. She assumed a favourite maiden-aunt quality for me, and vaguely, I felt adopted. In fact, I suspect, she regarded all my generation as children, and she watched our antics with a sort of measured anticipation. She expected us to behave as we did, and indeed, she was not slow to encourage us in our behaviour.[1]

Kay had recently emerged from hospital after a very nearly success-ful attempt at suicide when Ivy agreed to an afternoon of what she called 'note-taking' on 9 October 1963. The interview, intended ultimately to form part of a book of conversations with writers, was in the nature of a consolation prize for Kay—'it was her present to me'[2]—with compensatory advantages for Ivy, who was intensely curious about what had happened ('I was her raw material, she was sniffing me out'), as well as deeply sympathetic.

Her manner was gentle, cooperative, even eager throughout: the tape-recording of their conversation is punctuated by little exclamatory flurries of encouragement from Ivy and the involuntary low laugh she gave, almost under her breath, whenever things were being said that generally go without saying. She answered clearly and copiously, interrupting every so often to ask for a question to be put more definitely, held back apparently less by her own reticence than by the nervous delicacy that prevented her interrogator from probing too hard in what might have proved sensitive areas. Ivy talked freely about the process of writing itself, about her observation of people, her view of human nature in general and, in particular, her own childhood, upbringing and early life. She protested emphatically, with a great deal of humorous, deprecatory umming and erring, only when asked about her own reputation for wisdom: 'Wise, in what way? Well yes, perhaps one does think one is wise. One thinks one knows, of course. Perhaps that is thinking one is wise?'[3] When Kay admitted that she herself hardly ever thought she knew, Ivy rapped back in a flash, laughing at herself, with impeccable comic timing and intonation: 'Then perhaps I think I'm wiser than you think you are.'

The interview changed their relationship. 'Ivy grew fonder,' said Kay, 'after the interview, really—you felt her affection when you went in. She was so pleased to see you.' Always interested in her friends' private lives and prepared, as she said, to give any human problem her full attention ('Some people don't. They give it a very casual attention, and then tell you about an antique they've bought'), Ivy had questioned other people closely about Kay's present crisis. But it was characteristic of both her tact and her generosity that she mentioned it only once—'You've done a deed, haven't you?'—submitting instead to being questioned herself about matters she had scarcely permitted an interviewer to touch on before. The information she volunteered about her family was matter-of-fact, and perfectly accurate so far as it went (spreading confusion among inquisitive friends had always been a pleasure to Ivy, who made no move whatever to contradict the belief—almost universal by this time in her literary circle—in a mythical Compton-Burnett family 'place' in the country). Clearly the afternoon spent 'note-taking' with Kay was part of a general relaxation and loosening in Ivy towards the end of her life; and she went a good deal further a few years later with the writer Julian Mitchell, who pressed her as no one else had dared to do on tricky points like her feeling for her mother, her attachment to the nurse who had been 'the real mother', the influence of her peremptory and tyrannical maternal grandfather, and her love for her brothers. These conversations were probably the closest Ivy ever came to broaching the compulsions of her own childhood: 'She knew what she wanted known,' wrote Julian after her death, '. . . and no biographer is ever going to be able to explain what Ivy didn't want explained.'[4]

Julian was half a century younger than Ivy ('I'm afraid I may once or twice have come into her category of "a gaping boy" '), who had been all her life peculiarly susceptible to the sort of charming, sensitive, intelligent, humorous young men she had first met in Noel's company at Cambridge. In her books, they occupy what even Pamela Hansford Johnson recognized as a soft spot ('It was the adolescent boys who touched her heart the most'[5]), and she grew fonder than ever in her eighties of what she called 'a nice lad'. Ivy by this time was apt to make fairly arbitrary age distinctions, referring airily to anyone under fifty as 'young'. She entertained Herman's guests like an elderly aunt unbending in spite of herself to a hopelessly flighty younger generation ('She was at her best and talking as she writes, and trying not to smile when she made us laugh,' wrote Elizabeth Taylor of a luncheon in 1963 at which the other guest was Lesley Blanch: 'We kiss now. Even in the Brompton Road, saying goodbye'); and she treated Herman himself on occasion as a delinquent youth—'Herman, how can you stand there telling me such lies?' To which he stoutly replied, 'I can, and I do.'[6]

But Ivy always knew who was lying, and who not. 'People have a way of not coming out well in a temptation. They generally behave quite as ill as they can, don't they?' she said to Kay. 'Well, not any worse than I should expect them to behave. I mean, people have to consider themselves before anyone else, don't they, and one wonders what would happen to them if they didn't.'[7] Her comprehension came from self-knowledge—'I don't think there is such a thing as self-deception'[8]—and it made her inexhaustibly lenient. Ivy's friends at the end of her life felt very much what Noel and Rupert Brooke had once felt about Lowes Dickinson, that nothing they might do—no matter how shameful, squalid or actually criminal—could ever be too much for such patience, humour and tolerance. Her support was unfailing, though often ironic. 'She asked me about your novel,' wrote Elizabeth to Robert (who had posted her the manuscript of Stepsons—the book for which Ivy had waited so long—in the summer of 1960): ' "It's all about his stepmother, isn't it?" And then she made a noise that sounded like Ho-Hum.' Sonia Orwell, grumbling one day about the drudgery involved in her meticulously documented, four-volume edition of George's letters and journalism, was surprised by Ivy's reaction: 'It's your plain duty,' she said gently but firmly.

Ivy congratulated the Robinsons on news of an impending first baby, advising Barbara to make the most of her last few months to herself ('You will never be so much your own person again'[10]), recommending a second child a year later which was the interval between herself and Guy (the Robinsons took Ivy's advice and stopped short at two), and later sending her sympathy to the supplanted elder child ('You will have to show great tact, and continually asseverate your preference for him in open words. "Love me best" he will say, and you will say it'[11]). She gave Barbara much domestic as well as professional advice in these years ('It is much better to have only one maid. More than one either hate each other or hate *you*. And anyhow they have tea together all day, cementing one hatred on the other'[12]). She treated Elizabeth, for all her two children and lengthening list of successful novels, as an irresponsible girl, urging her to wear warm underclothes, eat more ('I think she is trying to console me with food for not being a very good writer. When she fills up my glass with water—for there is not always wine—it is a protective and consoling gesture'), and avoid unnecessary risks, especially in the perilous winters when Ivy herself suffered more severely each year. 'I had a letter from her [Ivy] this morning in which she said she had a bronchial chill and hoped I fared better. "But still take care. The evil days are on us. I hope we will meet when they are over." It is like the Ides of March and we had better all stay indoors . . .'

When Herman asked Ivy on her eightieth birthday—5 June 1964—what she had learnt from life, 'she thought for a long time, and then said: "That people are morally the same, and intellectually different." '[13] Now that she herself was no longer sufficiently attached to a single person to be emotionally in anyone's power, Ivy watched her friends with a truly disinterested affection. 'That marriage won't last,' she said, after a somewhat sticky luncheon given by Herman to meet Sonia Orwell's prospective second husband, Michael Pitt-Rivers (who had only comparatively recently emerged from prison after one of the most notorious homosexual scandals of the 1950s): 'That young man won't like all this bookish talk.'[14] For Sonia, installed as châtelaine of the Pitt-Rivers family home in Dorset, one of the memorable disasters of her short married life was an evening at the Watson-Gandys, with Michael loudly expounding the folly and misery of marriage to Jim, while Ivy (on one of her annual summer visits to Vere) carried on stolidly passing the potatoes and saying that a little more cauliflower would be acceptable. It is the attitude philosophically explained by Oliver Shelley in *Two Worlds and their Ways*:

'We have done our best, and must leave it. No one can do more.'

'We have done nothing,' said Maria.

'Well, that is usually people's best,' said her stepson. 'Their worst is something quite different.'[15]

Ivy made no comment to Sonia, beyond making her welcome again when the marriage was over ('I can't imagine her in a country life,' Ivy wrote diplomatically to the Robinsons on 15 September 1962: 'I am sure London is her home'). She had taken much the same line nearly ten years earlier over the equally painful and public collapse of Madge's brief marriage to Sir Leigh Ashton, then head of the V&A. 'After the break with Leigh, when I was once again alone in the little house, Ivy came to tea,' wrote Madge, 'and, as soon as she entered, went directly to the glass doors which opened on to the garden, turned to me and said, "You have the garden, you have the house, there are worse things than loneliness." And never spoke of the matter again.'[16] The certainty that Ivy, who understood everything, could be relied on to say nothing was often a comfort: 'You know, I think that my friendship with Ivy was one of the happiest things in a long and troubled life,' said Madge. 'It was because nothing was said. *Nothing*. We didn't have to say anything. There was complete trust on both sides.'[17] Ivy seldom gave advice unless on practical, tangible matters like which novel to read, or where to go for the best brand of stockings ('I always swear by Harvey Nichols'). But her general policy is clearly formulated by the aged Selina Middleton in *The Mighty and their Fall*, comforting her grand-daughter Lavinia at a moment of crisis, despair and public humiliation:

'What am I to do?'

'What people do, who have been found out. Wait for the trouble to subside. Suffer it when it arises. Fight it, if it is too much. There is nothing else for you. And the worst is behind. You have little more to dread.'[18]

A hard person to surprise, Selina, like Ivy, is grimly disillusioned about both human and religious affairs ('I don't believe in a future life, or want to. I should not like any form of it I know. I don't want to be a spirit or to return to the earth as someone else. I could never like anyone else enough for that'[19]). She is watchful, unyielding, a tartar to her grandchildren, who find themselves unaccountably fond of her, and no less unaccountably consoled to discover how well she knows them: 'I am old. I have seen and heard. I know that things are done. Temptation is too much for us. We are not always unwilling for it to be.'[20]

The Mighty and their Fall was begun in the autumn of 1959, finished by 10 February 1961, and published on 18 September.[21] The Robinsons and others were immediately struck by the twenty-year-old Lavinia's likeness in looks and character—she is described as an 'autocrat' and an 'intellectual'[22]—to the young Ivy; and certainly Lavinia belongs with the many brave, spirited, vulnerable girls, more or less ruthlessly exploited by their elders, who might be said, from Dinah Stace onwards (*Brothers and Sisters*, 1929), to contain a touch of Ivy—more than a touch in the case of France Ponsonby (*Daughters and Sons*, 1937) and the eleven-year-old Clemence Shelley (*Two Worlds and their Ways*, 1949). But Selina represents an older, less innocent Ivy. Admittedly, there are repressive, tyrannical grandmothers elsewhere in her books—Sabine Ponsonby in *Daughters and Sons* is the first of a line that ends only with Jocasta Grimstone in the posthumously published *The Last and the First*. It is a type that owes something to stories of Ivy's own maternal grandmother—Sophia Sabine Rees—and great-grand-mother, more perhaps to a number of fierce, domineering, big-chinned old women she and Katie Blackie had known as children among their Rees and Pudney relations in the Methodist connection round Clacton, most of all no doubt to the stubborn Rees will passed down by both Ivy's mother and Katie's.

But Selina combines an autocratic temper with for the first time another side of Ivy—the alert, neutral intelligence previously embodied in governesses like Miss Mitford, outsiders like Hope Cranmer, non-participants like the Scropes or Walter Challoner. This is Ivy in her professional aspect, so to speak, and there could hardly be a clearer definition of the writer's relationship with society than Selina's account of herself: 'my presence makes no difference. I am on no one's side. I see with the eyes of all of you. It is as if no one was here.'[23] Selina is eighty-seven, ten years older than her creator when *The Mighty and their Fall* was published, and strongly reminiscent of the sardonic, self-contained, grimly humorous spirit of *The Real Charlotte*. But Selina's influence, unlike

Charlotte Mullen's, is wholly benevolent (as she herself readily
concedes when told that her grandchildren consider her bark worse
than her bite: 'That is an empty saying. There is no opportunity to
bite. I have wished there was'[24]). As a self-portrait, this is far from
flattering though perhaps not wholly dissatisfied, since anyone as
familiar with her own faults and as frank about them as Selina is
clearly on reasonable terms with herself. 'I think people know
themselves. I am sure I know myself,' Ivy said to Kay,[25] and the
knowledge brought with it—as it always does in her books—a kind
of peace, or at least release from the intensity of feeling that had
caused such misery in the past.

Ivy in her seventies and eighties had many close friendships with
women, quite a few of them lesbians ('Come to tea on Saturday,'
she would say encouragingly, *my lesbians are coming*[26]). Margaret's
death had laid her open for a while to anyone anxious to establish a
larger stake in her life, but even in what she called 'the difficult days'
Ivy made short work of unwelcome advances ('And weren't they
surprised young women,' said Margaret Branch, who had watched
several of Ivy's more proprietorial friends firmly shown off at this
time). She herself told a funny story about an unknown woman
who sent long and persuasive fan letters, backed up by rich gifts of
butter and eggs and invitations so pressing that in the end Ivy agreed
to a rendezvous on Brighton Pier. She told Madge that she thought
it best to avoid inviting her new admirer to the flat; and she told
Renée Fedden that, when she eventually spotted the lady bearing
down behind a huge bunch of red roses, evidently less interested in
Ivy's work than her person, it had seemed better still to leave her
standing and flee. Even Herman, who delighted in arranging his
friends' affairs as much as in fixing their flats, could not persuade her
to reconsider this decision, though he never entirely abandoned his
hopeful view of her lesbian proclivities.[27] If Ivy got on better with
women, in the sense of being generally more relaxed in their
company, it was in much the same spirit as Hope Cranmer, who
also preferred her own sex: 'Most people do. It is a thing that has not
been noticed. People know too much about their own sex to think it
possible to prefer it, when really they find it familiar and
congenial.'[28]

But Ivy, like Hope, was strikingly partial to men, and not only
nice lads. 'We've got a bit of your mother, all of us, in us,' she said
once to Kay, who was the illegitimate child of a dashing and

romantic parent—'my mother was a very feminine woman, adored by men, a great flirt and a great liar'—with no very obvious likeness to Ivy. If Margaret had settled for celibacy by choice (and seems in any case always to have found her emotional fulfilment in women), Ivy liked to imply that it had been forced on her by the war that had taken Noel and so many of his friends, who were the only young men she had known as a girl. She often said she belonged to a generation that had had to do without marriage; and she was clearly thinking of herself when she explained to Kay about the preponderance of women novelists between the wars:

> Well, I expect that's because the men were dead, you see, and the women didn't marry so much because there was no one for them to marry, and so they had leisure, and, I think, in a good many cases they had money, because their brothers were dead, and all that would tend to writing, wouldn't it, being single, and having some money, and having the time—having no men, you see.[29]

Not that Ivy in later life ever slackened her mistrust of married couples, however much she might like each partner singly:

> The same food *of course*—the boiled bacon and parsley sauce and white pudding [wrote Elizabeth in the autumn of 1962, of a luncheon at Braemar Mansions with Herman and John Pope-Hennessy]. She carved up Muriel Spark and Iris Murdoch at the same time as the bacon. Marriage and religion were discussed and deplored. I felt guilty to be married and to have stayed married so long, and was almost thankful not to be religious. Rose Macaulay has never been forgiven. To have such a thing happen—when for a lifetime she had been a perfectly sound agnostic like everybody else.

Marriage was a blight for anyone who prized her friends' company as highly as Ivy. If she and Margaret had once consigned newly wedded couples to cold storage, it was for much the same reason that made her so stern with expatriates like the Robinsons and Jim Brandreth. Marriage, which removed people, was a malign influence, like 'abroad', and must be as stoutly resisted. 'So dangerous, these fusions of personality, don't you think?' she said softly one day at tea,[30] when Hester arrived late from a wedding at the

House of Lords; and she strongly advised another woman friend[31] against accepting a late, last proposal: 'Don't ever get married, unless you absolutely have to.' Naturally, as her fame spread, people labelled Ivy a lesbian or even an androgyne just as others liked to think she had had a lover killed in the First World War, or that she had been all her life incestuously in thrall to her brother. A façade as impenetrable as Ivy's, coupled with writings so violent, bred a rich crop of rumours ranging from Sybille Bedford's story that Ivy's father had burnt the manuscript of her first novel to the legends proliferating about her two youngest sisters, who were said to have been found drowned in a pool or hanged in a cupboard, to have been murdered, or surprised illicitly in bed together by their parents—alternatively, accused of being lovers by a half-brother —and to have killed themselves from remorse (being discovered, in one version, hanged at intervals in the same room). All these stories, all false, were circulated in her lifetime (and several printed after her death) by friends driven wild by Ivy's inscrutability.

The truth behind an image as imposing and unusual as Ivy's can perhaps only percolate slowly. Her public face, in the last decade of her life, was itself something of a legend. She seemed austere, unapproachable, positively regal when she travelled up to Leeds University to receive an honorary doctorate on 19 May 1960: 'Ivy and the Princess Royal (who was Chancellor of the university) got on splendidly,' wrote Madge, who went too as companion. 'They sat beside each other at tea, after the ceremony, and there was something about the basic honesty of those two women which made them immediately sympathetic to each other. Luckily for me the Princess's lady-in-waiting was now Mrs Seaton Dearden, the wife of a friend, so that the real and the make-believe ladies in waiting got on just as well as their superiors.'[32] Ivy, who had been dissuaded by Arthur Waley from her initial 'idea of having flu instead of Leeds',[33] afterwards confessed to Robert that, in spite of the ruinous expense (hotel charges of £3. 10s a day), 'actually I rather enjoyed it'. Actors presented to Ivy during radio or stage adaptations of her work—'She came like a queen with Rosamond Lehmann as lady-in-waiting'[34]—found the experience very much like being lined up to meet royalty. Photographers, following Beaton's example, show her majestically composed, often enthroned, though she emerges from the characteristic birds'-nest tangle of Feliks Topolski's drawing in the early 1960s as a slightly hunched, pensive, sad but not at all stern, and very old sibyl.

Herman was her escort on a first visit to Topolski's studio, recorded in a passage that nicely catches his own and Ivy's respective brands of vagueness and obstinacy: 'One day at tea time she said, "Do you know Krassovsky, the painter?" I said, "Yes, Ivy, but he isn't called Krassovsky; he is called Balthus." "No," she said, "he is called Krassovsky." She meant, of course, Feliks Topolski.'[35] As she grew older and frailer, Ivy seldom went anywhere without a faithful attendant, very often Herman or Madge, with an extra supporter for serious occasions such as the matinée of Samuel Beckett's *Happy Days* at the Royal Court Theatre in November 1962 (Ivy had enjoyed Nicholas Bentley's cartoon, in the wake of *Waiting for Godot*, of one tramp saying to another as he fished a dilapidated book out of a dustbin, 'Look! An Ivy Compton-Burnett!'[36]). 'This should be a rather unusual outing,' wrote Elizabeth, and so it proved in her detailed report to Robert:

Well, then, we went to the theatre. (I am sorry to make such a letter of it, but is it not like going to one of the Basingstoke Assemblies with Jane Austen?) It was a sparse audience, & Ivy took a great interest in it. 'Would you call this an *intellectual* audience, Herman?' (Too distinct voice in an empty auditorium.) 'One or two look that way inclined,' he whispered. 'Do you think they are staring at us, because they think *we* are intellectuals?' 'Of course they don't think that,' she said scornfully. 'We are far too well dressed.' 'Would it help if I took off my tie?' he asked. 'Not very much,' she—I think I will say 'retorted' for the first time in my life, 'for I daresay Elizabeth will have to take off everything.' So much for my intellectual underwear. The play —just the middle-aged woman buried in a mound—was to me quite unexpectedly wonderful. I went for Ivy, & found myself forgetting her. She watched it keenly, through opera glasses, from the third row of the empty stalls, & I don't know how that poor actress carried on under the circumstances. '*Not* a play to miss,' she said in the interval, while Herman had gone running round Sloane Square to buy her a box of chocolates. *He* had dozed off in the first act, but always does after luncheon wherever he is, he explained. But I am sorry to say that, however alert Ivy's attention was & no matter how much Herman admired Brenda Bruce, they both seemed to miss the point. It is really devastat-

ing, & as much as one can bear—a middle-aged woman's gallantry (I see so much of it) signifying the human tragedy—the
terrifying attempts at optimism & the Molly Bloom nostalgia
—heart rendering! [A word coined by Robert's Oxford servant.]
'Now is the crucial moment,' Ivy said, her hand wavering over
the opened box of chocolates. 'One hopes for a ginger one.' 'I
wish your husband would make some good, *cheap* sweets,' she
said, & then said—almost tenderly—'he was very good to me in
the difficult days.'

I am glad—as you must be—that she has her adoring courtier,
to take care of her in old age, to give her gallantry & flattery &
sweets. Not many women reach her years & have as much—for
everything he can imagine her wanting, he hastens to provide; &
it is bestowed as if she were a young & lovely creature at her first
ball, & when he helps her down the stairs or into a taxi—for she is
getting frail—he turns her into Gloriana.

If Herman brought with him the atmosphere of a court—at any
rate, something of a court's bustle and intrigue—so in his own way
did Ernest, growing at the end of his life more and more like Queen
Mary with his pursed lips and bolt upright bearing, his censorious
dowager's air and crushing line in regal retorts. He would startle his
colleagues by turning up at rehearsal in the drab 1950s wearing a
pink linen coatee, and was once reproached for extolling the past
glories of the stage by a young actor who said that sort of thing was
considered by modern standards distinctly ham: 'I am well aware of
it,' said Ernest grandly, 'but you may as well know that I consider
the type of acting that you advocate as definitely "spam".'[37] Ernest
was five years older than Ivy who had for years been aware of his
growing exhaustion, though he showed no obvious sign of it. He
died without warning in his sleep on 14 January 1961, to her great
distress ('He was a very old friend and his loss is a real grief, and I
feel I have had enough,' she wrote to the Robinsons on 21 January.
'And the suddenness made it a shock, though it was good fortune
for him'). His death left Janette blind and bedridden, confined to the
flat with her housekeeper, but it was years since Ernest had been
able to offer her consolation, or even company. Her form of
stoicism, a certain massive simplicity and nobility of nature, was
altogether foreign to her husband who—like Mortimer Lamb and
other unreliable jokers in Ivy's books—had always given more to

people who needed less: he is aptly commemorated, as his obituary in the *Journal of the Embroiderers' Guild* pointed out that spring, on one of two kneelers he stitched for Chelsea Old Church in honour of 'Henry Patenson, Sir Thomas More's Jester, "a man of special wit", pictured in the costume of the time with cap and bells . . .'

Ivy was also by this time a performer in her own right. Alone with one other person, or with at most two or three old friends ('She was always an *intimiste*,' said the publisher George Weidenfeld, who often made the third at Herman's luncheons), Ivy made absurd, inimitable play with her murmured asides, her flat throaty chuckle and the impossible truth that occasionally shot past her guard. 'Dreadful, absolutely dreadful,' she said once when Ivo Pakenham asked her what she thought of his latest fake-Adam interior; and, when Ivo protested that she ought not to say such things to his face, Ivy said sternly: 'You asked a question and I gave you the answer. If a question is asked and no answer is given, no communication of thought is possible and all conversation ceases.'[38]

Ivy had spent the great part of her life devising stratagems —inconspicuousness, evasiveness, unstoppable small talk or an equally impregnable stonewalling—to cope with the truthfulness that made her writing so startling, and her life at times quite impossible. She deplored other writers' compromises—'I read *Prelude and Fugue*, Joan Evans' autobiography,' (which makes barely a reference to the St Hugh's affair, and no mention of Ivy), 'and enjoyed it, but found it too discreet,' she wrote to Barbara Robinson on 21 November 1964. 'It is no good to write about things, and then *not* write about them.' Her own books of course were widely held to go too far in the opposite direction; and conversation at Braemar Mansions, on occasions when Ivy spoke her mind, could take on a hair-raising edge—'part prize-giving, part disciplinary hearing', as Proust's illustrator, Phillippe Jullian, wrote in *Les Nouvelles Littéraires*,[39] describing a tea party with Robin McDouall, Francis Wyndham and Arthur Waley. M. Jullian had been suitably primed beforehand by Robin ('*Il vaut mieux être voltairean que religieux, réservé que banal*'), who was horrified afterwards—as Ivy was too—to find his friend publishing without permission this uncensored sample of her deft, backhanded disposal of the various writers put forward in turn by her guests. Asked what she thought of Lawrence Durrell—invariably the first question put by a Frenchman discussing the English novel in the early

1960s—Ivy said she had not read him: 'Is it essential nowadays to
turn a novel into a travel book?—He is greatly admired in France.—
But then, you admire Charles Morgan in France, don't you?—
Angus Wilson?—I like him very much. Especially the short stories
you find tucked away in his great long novels.' Ivy used a more
scarifying technique on Rebecca West, who had told her friends she
could make nothing of Ivy's books, and whose request for an
introduction had been wisely turned down by Elizabeth Taylor:

> Madge Garland, however, fell for it and, although scared, invited
> them both to lunch. Rebecca was apparently at her most scintil-
> lating—brilliant talker as she has the reputation of being. She put
> everything into it, and Ivy simply lopped off everything she said
> and left it lying there, dead. Feverishly she went on, and coldly
> Ivy felled her. Gaps grew in the conversation—unimaginable in
> Rebecca's presence. Poor hostess! She should have known how it
> would be . . .[40]

ii

This formidable streak had long been familiar to Victor Gollancz,[41]
who confessed to the novelist Lettice Cooper in the 1960s that he
was afraid of Ivy. Perhaps Spencer Curtis Brown was too, for the
pair spoke and wrote of 'the Compton-Burnett' behind her back in
much the same terms as the ill-used younger generation banding
together to bait one of the tyrants in her books. 'Dear V.G., I hope
you have taken Ede's advice [Chuter Ede, Home Secretary in the
postwar Labour government] and not destroyed your air-raid
shelter for I have heard from Compton-Burnett . . .' wrote Curtis
Brown on 25 July 1949, when Ivy protested as usual about
Gollancz's failure to advertise *Two Worlds and their Ways* ('Will you
ask him what his reasons are for not wanting my books to sell?').
Curtis Brown's procedure, on receiving a confidential complaint
from his client, was to forward her letter with a request for
instructions as to what sort of reply Gollancz would like sent. 'I
know you realise as well as I do that whatever arrangement is
mutually satisfactory to you or Douglas will be equally satisfactory
to me,' he wrote on 1 May 1951, enclosing Jerrold's last, unsuccessful proposal that Eyre and Spottiswoode should take over all the
back titles that were proving such a burden to Gollancz, 'but it is

extremely unlikely that it will be satisfactory to Miss Compton-Burnett. As you know, her aim is to have all her books published every day.'

Spencer Curtis Brown was nearly thirty years younger than Ivy, who seems to have cast him from the start as a sort of solicitor's clerk—an inexperienced and not particularly promising junior in constant need of reproof and supervision—a role he apparently accepted, making little effort to protect Ivy's interests and tending to side against her, or wash his hands of the affair altogether, whenever a fresh altercation blew up with Gollancz. From Curtis Brown's point of view, Ivy meant trouble—'Curtis Brown is indeed sadly in need of the goad,' she wrote when *Manservant and Maidservant* was published, [42] and his letters to her are understandably cautious and wary in tone. Gollancz for his part threatened to retire and write a novel in the Compton-Burnett style, with Ivy herself as the central character. Admittedly, others doing business with Ivy also found her on occasion a trial: she behaved with peremptory, high-handed courtesy to her accountant who was not in the least put out, rather amused than otherwise, at being kept in his place in the 1960s exactly like his father and grandfather who had served her father before him; and, though she scrutinized every transaction in detail, Ivy in return approved and generally accepted his professional advice about stocks and shares. But the handling of her books was another matter. Dealings with Curtis Brown and Gollancz had none of the pleasant air of family tradition and mutual respect that enlivened the twice-yearly luncheons with the accountant and Mr Mowll ('She talked like her characters, you know—we had great fun, the three of us' [43]). But, if Ivy acted tyrannically, she got as good as she gave for the scolding note in her letters bred, in both agent and publisher, a stubborn resistance to even her most reasonable demands.

Much of Ivy's grumbling went no further than the normal dissatisfaction of authors with publishers ('Their ways are not as our ways,' she wrote to Barbara [44]), disappointment over sales being after all an almost universal grievance. Ivy was more open than most about her feeling that she had done all that could be expected towards producing bestsellers ('good plots, interesting characters and plenty of sex', as she explained encouragingly to Curtis Brown [45]), and been let down by others. 'Nowadays one's agent, and one's solicitor, and one's bank manager only do the irreducible minimum,' she said to Lettice Cooper, 'but unfortunately it is the minimum one cannot do oneself.'[46] Commercial success fascinated Ivy. 'I have always wanted a portrait of a real, bestselling novelist, done honestly and ably and with understanding,' she wrote on 9 June 1957, describing her *great* and *lasting* pleasure' in Elizabeth's new novel, *Angel*: 'You have served your theme well, and to my mind it was a theme that both needed and deserved the service' ('I should love to read a reference written by her for a maid leaving her employment,' wrote Elizabeth, complacently forwarding this testimonial to Robert). A few years later she met a real bestseller when Soame bravely arranged a dinner for Ivy and Angela Thirkell, which turned out a great success (one of the college books Ivy kept all her life was her *Epigrams from the Greek Anthology*, edited by Angela's father, Professor Mackail): 'She's got plenty of go,' Ivy said admiringly afterwards, 'plenty of go.'[47] She attended the celebrations for James Pope-Hennessy's life of Queen Mary, which included a film of the royal progress: 'At the stage of the funeral procession there was hardly a dry eye in the audience of publishers and other sinister men!' Ivy reported to Barbara. 'He is reaping a fortune.'[48] Rose's fortune (assessed when the will was published at almost £90,000) became a source of extreme chagrin to Ivy, who was only partially mollified by repeated assurances that the money had not come from books. 'She had some bestsellers,' said Ivy gloomily. 'I have never had bestsellers. I don't sell.'[49]

Her sales figures after the war remained steady, at about seven thousand copies for each new novel[50] with back titles also in regular demand, though Gollancz's thrifty reissues of never more than a thousand at a time were perpetually running out. It was seldom easy to obtain any given Compton-Burnett, and readers' confidence was further diminished by the fact that even the new novels, with their cheap paper, garish wrappers and drab bindings, were got up—as Raymond Mortimer pointed out[51]—to look like school textbooks (reviewers were almost unanimous in congratulating Eyre and Spottiswoode on the good looks of their abortive Collected Works). Gollancz had never believed in spending money on appearances, and his advances were generally frugal. 'My last book brought in £60, and it took two years to write,' said Lester Marlowe in *Parents and Children* (1941);[52] Ivy's last book at the time of writing was *A Family and a Fortune* (1939) which had netted her £62 (including £50 advance on royalties[53]) in the four months before it went out of print. Her first novel issued by Gollancz in 1937 had apparently failed to cover its £50 advance in the year of publication, and at that time Ivy had no other income from writing ('It is awkward that I am assumed to earn so much more than I do,' says Lester. '. . . I am ashamed to confess how poorly my work is paid'). It was only with *Darkness and Day* in 1951 that Ivy's advances went up to £200 on publication, and her contracts stipulated that earlier titles be returned to circulation.

But money was never Ivy's prime complaint of her publisher, nor did she mind much what her books looked like. What she wanted always, more than anything, was for her books to be read; and, though there can be no doubt that Gollancz was in his way proud of her, it was not only Ivy who noticed the contrast between his lavish advertising of authors in whom he believed, and the brief box announcements of her novels. Publicity in her case was in his view, as he frequently assured her, worse than useless just as reissuing old novels would almost certainly damage her sales. He was consistently disparaging about the 'highbrows' who had been 'wildly praising her for years'; he was among the first to detect a potential falling off in praise from the rising, resentful, young generation of critics in the early 1950s; and he was always as acutely aware as Ivy herself that she never could or would sell like Daphne du Maurier. He never discussed her books with her, before or after publication (doubtless she would have made it impossible, if he had tried). Her manuscripts continued to arrive unannounced at Curtis Brown who forwarded them without comment to Gollancz's office, where Ivy had the reputation of being the only author nobody bothered to read before she went to the printers.

In due course a cheque would be dispatched, the books reached the shops, Ivy's complaints would be parried and dealings would be over for another two years in a relationship which was always, even on strictly business terms, abnormally bleak. Gollancz was or could be a man of extraordinary generosity, warmth, flair, humane and social concern, but he was also arrogant and obdurate, a prince of prevaricators and impossible to worst in a bargain. He and Ivy were perhaps too alike to bring out anything but the worst in one another: he must have realized he had given her grounds to speak disparagingly of him as a Jew, she surely might have recognized the folly of treating him like a tradesman who failed to give satisfaction. Their first meeting in 1948 had not helped matters, and worse was to follow at a second lunch proposed by Gollancz in the early 1960s when Ivy requested a collected edition of her works. She was eighty, and he had published thirteen of her novels to great critical acclaim. Lunch began badly with Ivy declining a drink: 'No, I don't drink. But you have one, if you feel you must.' 'I feel I must,' he said. His polite attempts at making conversation about music and travel were summarily lopped off by Ivy ('No, I know very little about music. I don't care for abroad'), who insisted on getting down to business, whereupon Gollancz asked if she meant that she wanted every single one of her books reprinted. 'Yes,' said Ivy. 'Well, that would ruin you, and ruin me,' said Gollancz. 'I can't do it.' After a pause, Ivy declined his offer of coffee or pudding, said she must go home and went, leaving Gollancz to order two stiff brandies;[54] and (except for a single chance encounter in hospital when they found themselves for once in agreement about institutional food) they never saw or spoke to one another again.

It was a preposterous way to treat an author of Ivy's great age and distinction, but perhaps in a way she left him no alternative. Though her friends tended to blame Gollancz for Ivy's virtual exclusion from London literary life, she herself undoubtedly preferred her fame on terms which included a fair measure of withdrawal and privacy. Gollancz combined the negative merit of non-interference with what was in her eyes the inestimable boon of permanence. 'I am too old to change' was her invariable response to people who urged her to switch to a more appreciative publisher, find a less incompetent maid or move to a pleasanter flat. At the beginning of 1963, Ivy's Polish landlord had hopes of letting her flat to the Dominican Embassy which occupied the other half of the first floor at Braemar Mansions: 'A nice thing if an English gentlewoman is to be turned out by Poles to make room for South Americans,' Elizabeth reported to Robert, though both knew perfectly well that this was no joke for Ivy, whose old terror of disruption and dispersal returned with a force that dismayed her friends. The flat was not simply a place to live in, nor even the home she had shared with Margaret: it contained the whole precious, narrow, intricate, orderly existence the two had built up together inside it, and the prospect of losing it unnerved Ivy, always acutely aware of the precariousness of civilized life.

For two months she could talk and write to her friends of little else. Herman, Madge, and Herman's Dutch friend Riemke Zouthout trudged all over Chelsea and South Kensington in search of more comfortable, convenient and cheaper flats, all of which Ivy rejected out of hand. By the beginning of April, she had forced herself to contemplate moving to a place in Kensington Square, but her trepidation worried everyone who saw it. Cicely, coming to collect the manuscript of *A God and his Gifts* at a more than usually strained luncheon on 5 April, feared some sort of nervous collapse, and so did Vera Compton-Burnett, who well understood the enormity of Ivy's capitulation when the landlord finally agreed at the end of the month to settle for what struck her as a second, exorbitant rent increase. 'I am thankful to stay in my flat, though the rent is vast and will mean resorting to capital which at my age is after all a reasonable thing,' Ivy wrote sombrely to Robert on 5 July. 'Don't follow the example at yours. And stay in your flat. A move is a dreadful thing. And other flats are always worse.' None of Ivy's friends in those days knew how she was placed financially, but the experience had evidently been a great shock. 'I am immensely relieved,' wrote Elizabeth, 'she had a terrible anxiety feeling, and the move might have killed her altogether, and must have as a writer, I think.' Ivy herself felt ever afterwards that she had only narrowly and perhaps temporarily escaped being sucked under by the tide that engulfed so many apparently secure, even affluent old people on fixed incomes in the genteel, residential areas of London in the early 1960s. 'You are the fifth friend of mine to be turned out of her house!' she wrote to her cousin Katie Blackie, that Christmas. 'The threat came on me, but I hope it has passed.'

It left Ivy seeming older, with a sharply renewed sense of the world as a shaky place. Roger Hinks, who had planned to return to London for good in the autumn of 1963, died suddenly that summer: 'It is hard to think of a more wretched misfortune . . .' she wrote to Robert on 5 July. 'I knew him as a very young man, and in the time when he was back in London, got quite dependent on him. And I was so looking forward to having him settle here, and seeing him fulfil himself at last. At 59, he should have had a future before him, and he had not been too fortunate in the past . . .' Helen Rolleston also died at much the same time, and Ivy, who had recovered from her regular winter bout of bronchitis, succumbed to one of her 'old bad throats',[55] brought on she thought by grief and shock. In the past five years she had lost Rose, Ernest, Roger and Helen. Basil Marsden-Smedley fell ill that summer and was surprised and touched to find a case of his favourite burgundy waiting in his hospital room, ordered by Ivy who seldom gave presents and had never shown the faintest interest in his taste in wine.

He died in 1964 (killed, according to Ivy's more cynical friends, by the enforced union between the boroughs of Chelsea and Kensington), followed by the earliest of all her friends, Arthur Waley, two years later. 'I have lost more than one old friend of late, and the world grows emptier,' she wrote to Robert. 'There are many left, and new ones come, but the space is never filled. It is to be expected, but that is no help.'[56] She herself was warned in 1965 by Dr Pasmore that she had a weak heart and must rest, which she did ('Anno Domini really, and tedious!'[57]), amazing Herman by the determination with which she clung to life—'Remember, it's all we've got; remember, it's all we've got,' said Ivy,[58] always strictly practical when it came to mortality. Ten years earlier she had impressed Anne Hill by her matter-of-fact reaction to news of the death of another old acquaintance, who had died of a stroke in her sleep: 'Of a stroke?' said Ivy. 'Good, good. And she had her maid to the last? Good.'[59]

Ivy's nineteenth novel, A God and his Gifts, finished at the height of the crisis in March 1963, had by her own account 'suffered from my months of flat-hunting and threatened upheaval',[60] though its author's distress had by no means damped the spirits of the hero, Hereward Egerton, the god of the title, a novelist of prodigious energy and egotism. The book's period setting is sufficiently elastic to permit an unusually high proportion of characters earning a living, including a working wife ('I thought I would have a change this time,' Ivy said[61]), also a notably casual attitude to sex which somewhat modifies Herman's assertion that Ivy was baffled in the 1960s by the permissive society: 'It was perfectly in vain for me to try to tell Ivy that nobody thought anything of anybody sleeping with anybody, it was just part of daily routine, and that one could not say it was immoral for people to have promiscuous love affairs: she simply couldn't understand it.'[62] Admittedly, Ivy had always insisted that taking a by-blow into a family to be brought up alongside its legitimate brothers and sisters (as the Egertons do in A God and his Gifts) had been standard practice in her own youth.[63] What sounds much more like Herman's account of the Swinging Sixties is the open, uncensorious, wholly businesslike spirit in which this supposedly Victorian family accepts as the eldest son's bride a girl who turns out to be pregnant not by her fiancé but by an unidentified married man. The seducer is revealed in due course as her father-in-law, the godlike Hereward himself, a potent figure unique among Ivy's tyrants in that, far from bottling up his energies as the repressive head of a totalitarian household, he has expended them generously over thirty years by helping himself to every young girl in sight as well as churning out a steady flow of lucrative popular novels.

Hereward is placed in many ways like that other popular author, John Ponsonby in *Daughters and Sons* (1937), who also had a child determined to write something less ephemeral than the trashy bestsellers that bring in enough to support the family and subsidize the ancestral estates. But Hereward's self-centred and coldly contemptuous son Merton is a markedly less sympathetic portrait of an ambitious young writer than France Ponsonby; and the contrast is part of a general shift, for Ivy, drawing closer to old age herself over the past twenty-five years, had grown steadily more cordial towards the older generation in her books, represented here by an irresistibly flighty, amusing, broadminded and soft-hearted couple of grandparents. Sir Michael Egerton and his wife Joanna are both the same age as Ivy herself when *A God and his Gifts* came out. ('"Seventy-nine is not what it is," said Joanna. "Or it would be old age." "Neither is it," said Sir Michael. "I feel as young as I ever did"'[64]). Both are harassed, like their author, by worry over money and property, the catastrophic consequences of drawing on capital, the dread prospect of being obliged by looming debts and pitiless creditors to move, leaving their shabby but beloved old home to the tender mercy of strangers ('I was glad we could keep it. Because what would happen to us without it, I am at a loss to say. It would be the end of our world'[65]). Both end by doting, like every other member of his large and complicated family, on the three-year-old Henry Egerton who is—more than any of his contemporaries, except perhaps Neville Sullivan in *Parents and Children* (and even he had an anxious and tyrannical streak largely foreign to Henry) —Ivy's purest celebration of infancy. Her friends were delighted and even Gollancz, noting that the reviews were more mixed than usual, went so far as to predict record sales for *A God and his Gifts* ('An odd thing about this new novel . . . ,' he wrote to Herbert van Thal on 29 November 1963, a week after publication: 'Quite a little run on it has been started').

If Ivy's central theme in *A God and his Gifts* is one of indiscrimin-ate, explosive, creative vitality, she also attended in a minor key to unfinished business from the past. Hereward has an unmarried sister, Zillah, who, like John Ponsonby's sister Hetta, has willingly submerged her own adult life in his. They represent the final working-out in Ivy's books of the relationship between a brother and sister whose consuming, exclusive love for one another goes back to her own successive absorption in each of her two brothers. The book, which covers a time span of three decades, starts with the lusty young Hereward confessing to Zillah that, since irresistible urges force him to marry, he has selected a wife too humble and dim to pose any threat to his sister ('She may hardly be a friend to you, but she will leave us our friendship. That is a condition I must make, and could not make with every woman. We are not asking nothing, Zillah. We can hardly ask more'[66]). Hereward is equally frank in his proposal to the unfortunate Ada, who meekly endorses his view that her desires must take second place to Zillah's in a marriage designed from the start as a ménage à trois: 'It is safe and open and sound. It carries no doubt and no risk. It will not separate Zillah and me.'[67]

In fact the marriage proves neither safe nor open and, though it does not separate Hereward from Zillah, it reduces her to a self-effacing, spinsterly shadow who barely speaks save in praise or defence of her brother. Her original scheme for collaborating in his work boils down in practice to mounting guard over his door, intercepting his callers and seeing that his meals are sent up on trays, as well as covering up for his love affairs, since both brother and sister openly acknowledge that the satisfaction of Hereward's sexual needs is crucial to their life together:

'Zillah, we are brother and sister. If we were not, what could we be?'

'Nothing that was nearer. It stands first among the relations. There is nothing before it, nothing to follow it. It reaches from the beginning to the end.'[68]

Hetta Ponsonby at a similar junction had pretended to kill herself sooner than accept her brother's marriage. But, whatever Ivy's own feelings may once have been, there is nothing personal about her rueful, humorous, conclusive demonstration in *A God and his Gifts* that 'the brother and sister relation'—at any rate Hereward's idyllic, self-deceiving version of it—is a thoroughly inadequate emotional solution to adult life. Hetta is humiliated and embittered by her attempts to prolong it, Zillah gives in gracefully, each is crushed in the end by her inability to find fulfilment in anyone but her brother. For children and young people the love between brother and sister is often the one wholly satisfactory aspect of family life in Ivy's books. But in middle age it works only for people prepared to settle for the passive, constricted, asexual existence—'the dear little narrow life'—beloved by Elton and Ursula Scrope. Zillah's predicament is not particularly important, or presented in any great detail, but it is Ivy's ironic last word on what had been the major catastrophe of her own early life. It gives *A God and his Gifts* that sense of completion she herself got from Robert's *Stepsons* when (though she had fully intended waiting till the book was in print) she finally read it in manuscript a few years earlier: 'I could not wait any longer. It fulfilled my highest hopes, and they were very high. And I am enjoying the sense of peace that comes from the feeling of gaps filled and curiosity satisfied.'[69]

Robert's book on Jane Austen, also published in 1963, was dedicated to Ivy which made her feel, as she said, highly complacent: 'I agreed with most of it, and got new light on a great deal. I seem rather by myself in thinking the Portsmouth picture a great success'[70] (Portsmouth is the home of the Price family in *Mansfield Park*, always a favourite with Ivy—'I can't understand why people call it *static*. It is so full of movement and life. Even her dull scraps are music to me'[71]). She and Robert exchanged news via go-betweens—Olivia Manning, Kathleen Farrell, and Elizabeth all visited him in Athens—and Ivy (who never gossiped by post) wrote probably more freely to him than to anyone else about the problems and sorrows of mutual friends, and even about her own troubles: 'Yes, Roger's empty place is very empty, and so many of them yawn about me now,' she wrote that Christmas. 'But it is hardly your time to begin to face them yet.'[72]

She still made her annual round of country friends in spring and summer but she was beginning to think twice about accepting invitations in cold or wet weather, to evening gatherings, flats with stairs (climbing was bad for her heart) or houses in outlying parts ('I think if people live in Hampstead, they ought to come to one, don't you?' she said to Barbara Robinson, 'not expect one to go to them').

She missed Julian Mitchell's adaptation of *A Heritage and its History*, directed by Frank Hauser at the Oxford Playhouse in April 1965,[73] and put off seeing it even when it transferred briefly to the West End ('I have not yet seen the play, as I can't do stairs at the time, and they are *everywhere*,' she wrote to Cicely on 25 May. 'And in a way I shrank from seeing it! I felt that a book should be left as it was written. The notices are good . . . Though the *Evening Standard* gave it a fortnight! And some insults!'). Ivy eventually attended a matinée at the Phoenix Theatre, sitting with Julian in the front of the circle, watching through opera glasses and taking tea in a box afterwards with the cast to whom she was polite and congratulatory but diplomatically vague, commenting specifically only on the costumes.

Expeditions were becoming increasingly tiring, for both guest and host, since a formal visit from Ivy in those days was no light matter: taxis had to be called, dogs shut up, the cat put out and the table properly laid, with butter scraped thin on the cucumber sandwiches, crisp toast (Ivy deplored what she called hotel toast as much as bought flowers and shop sponge cake), weak tea and rich cakes (once, at a friend's, when someone complained of a diet that restricted eggs and butter, Ivy said with an encouraging glance at the slice on her plate: 'I don't think you would have any trouble with *this* cake'[74]). Old age made her imperious and sometimes forgetful, but so fond and attentive to her friends that a great many grudged neither time nor trouble to please her. She was growing smaller: after her eightieth birthday, Herman said that there seemed less of Ivy every time he saw her.[75] When vexed or distressed, she would complain under her breath just loud enough to be overheard, like Sabine Ponsonby in *Daughters and Sons*, and people made allowances for her as they had done for Sabine (' "Stephen, of course she is wonderful. People over eighty always are." "It is what they are not. They are more wonderful at any other age . . . Unless you mean they are not blind or deaf, or actually dead, which is what you do mean" '[76]). Ivy had always talked in muttered asides, more and more since Margaret's death, but now her exchanges with imaginary characters slipped over fairly often into conversation with real ones: 'The first time it happened, one stopped politely, and she gave you a sort of blank look, as if nothing had happened. But when you got used to it, you learnt to carry on,' said Kay, who found the habit not so much macabre as companionable. 'Of course

Herman loves her whisperings,' wrote Elizabeth, '—for he is always convinced that he will catch a word or two—but all he has ever heard was when she was going from the dining room to the drawing room after lunch with him, and she whispered, "I hate sauces, I hate sauces, I hate sauces." "And that I am sure I was meant to hear," he said.'

Ivy's Irish housekeeper, Peggy, told Herman she could never get used to hearing her employer talk all day alone. Peggy (who came in 1959 and stayed nearly six years) was herself the most talkative and friendliest of all Ivy's maids: she wore a cap 'as a concession'[77] and was a competent plain cook, what Ivy called a factotum, warm-hearted and willing but untrained, without the habit or discipline that might have enabled her to bear the dismally lonely, ill-paid, uneventful life of a Victorian servant more than fifty years out of date. Ivy, in many ways a considerate employer, could never be induced to offer any advance on what would have been by prewar standards the princely wage of £6 a week, and she sternly discouraged Peggy's sociable custom of waylaying visitors for a chat in the kitchen, offering them drinks without being asked, and making up little gifts for her favourites. But, though Peggy was already talking of leaving at Christmas 1963, she stayed on to see Ivy through the coughs and quinsies of another two winters before she finally returned to Ireland at the beginning of April 1965.

Peggy's successor was a ladylike platinum blonde ('an elderly companion who does everything but is at meals,' Ivy wrote glumly on 6 April to Cecil Gould. 'Thought I should warn you'), chiefly memorable for her reaction to a ribald conversation among Ivy's lunch guests one day about Viva King's latest young man. Willie had died two years earlier and Viva, in her sixties, had opened an antique shop with help from a charming young sailor called Mat, who was systematically rooking his benefactress, filching her china, making off with her etchings and gradually stripping her shelves. The companion had been a buyer in Barkers' eminently respectable department store in Kensington High Street where nothing had prepared her for this sort of depravity. She was incredulous, appealing to each guest in vain before turning in desperation to Ivy: 'Oh, Miss Burnett, won't *you* call the police?' 'Not,' said Ivy politely, 'until I have seen how much Mrs King is enjoying the situation.'[78] The companion lasted two months and was followed by a widowed Mrs Lamin, 'an elderly working woman'[79] who was herself replaced a year later by Mary Maguire. Mary was another Irishwoman, stout, plain, bespectacled, dim, even childlike, and so rough that visitors often complained. But she suited Ivy who relied on her physical strength, understood the need to humour her moods, and found her simplicity such a relief that, when Ivo Pakenham protested about her rudeness, he received a box of sweets with a consolatory note from Ivy explaining that, from the point of view of survival, Mary was far more important to her than any of her friends.

Ivo, who always had the knack of provoking Ivy to frankness, was the person who asked her what quality she valued most in her friends (modestly hoping she might say 'charm', 'affection', 'loyalty such as yours, Ivo') and got the famous reply: 'Availability.'[80] Footloose friends like Madge, who wintered abroad, lived under a cloud only less dark than expatriates like the Robinsons, who did what they could with letters and visits to show Ivy they knew how much she missed them. She grieved now quite unaffectedly over her friends' defection, though her grief had a stoical nip to it:

'I like growing old,' said Herman Schrijver.
'One goes on living and everyone else is dead,' Ivy remarked, spooning up lovingly late strawberries in a sabayon sauce.[81]

Lettice Cooper, introduced by Ivo round about this time, said that her classical education was the thing that made Ivy proudest: 'It was the only thing I ever heard her boast about. She was very Greek, you know. She didn't like trimmings. She liked bare facts and bare lines and brief sentences.'

iii

On 29 November 1965 Ivy caught her foot in a rug on the polished linoleum of her drawing-room floor: 'I seemed to run forward and I couldn't stop myself, and then I fell and I thought I had died. Then I found I hadn't died, but I could not get up.'[82] When the maid came to look for her and summoned Dr Pasmore, Ivy was found to have broken the neck of her right femur. She was admitted for an operation on 2 December to the private wing of University College Hospital where she stayed for the next six weeks. Her room was filled with fruit, flowers and streams of visitors bearing delicacies of all sorts, sweets, honeycombs, home-made cakes and fresh produce in such quantities that much of it had to be redistributed in the wards. Victor Gollancz (who had reluctantly resigned from the firm that year on grounds of ill health and was also in hospital) sent flowers—'Ivy, somebody very rich has bunched you,' said Herman inquisitively[83]—and commiserated about the food, which drew them together as nothing else ever had (though Ivy would not adopt Gollancz's solution of having all meals sent in from a decent hotel—'but then,' as she said, 'I'm not a socialist'[84]).

'I was too badly hurt & helpless to want much for the first few weeks,' Ivy wrote long afterwards in a comforting letter to Sonia Orwell, also recovering from an operation in hospital, 'but later I felt like a schoolboy writing to his mother for supplies, & when I got home I enjoyed the simplest things, a baked potato, a milk pudding, a welsh rarebit, etc, cooked so that they could be put to their proper use.'[85] The nurses treated Ivy with a boldness and disrespect that startled her visitors, giving her a Christmas stocking, calling her 'poppet' and 'sweetie pie' ('I always thought nurses were a tough crowd,' Elizabeth reported to Robert), wheeling her off on Christmas Day to sing carols and be entertained along with the rest by doctors in funny hats, all of which she described sardonically enough to Herman and others. But her account to Elizabeth was amused and accommodating: 'It was very tiring, and I believe that one or two of the patients took a sharp turn for the worse afterwards. But I think the nurses enjoyed it; and, after all, it was for *them*.'[86]

The operation was a success though it was months before Ivy's strength began to come back. In the first few months she was 'dragged daily to a chair' and imprisoned there ('I found it a terrifying experience at first, and always dreaded it'[87]), helpless, immobilized, afraid to stir for fear of jarring her hip. She could not read in hospital, let alone write, and, though she did not complain, the sister told Francis King that she was in great pain.[88] She left hospital on 12 January—'I am at home with nurses, but *at home*! There is still tediousness ahead but the worst is past,' she wrote to the Robinsons next day. She was visited the day after by Cicely who had not seen her since before the accident and found her sadly changed: 'Her face was gaunt, haggard and had a ravaged look. The neat, strong features were puffy; her cheeks sunken, her skin colourless. Even her hair, always so tidily folded away, had an abandoned look. Her dignity, the "iron dignity" critics wrote about, had suffered outrage. I nearly wept at the sight of her.'[89] Two weeks later Ivy was walking feebly with crutches, by March she looked more herself though much older ('The ordeal of all she had been through, and the worry of the expense, and the fear of those jarring pains had left her with a look of weary anxiety'), the following month she had left off night nurses and 'progressed from crutches to sticks, an advance!'[90]

> I went to see Ivy [wrote Elizabeth that spring]. She has bronchitis now, and her breathing is laboured. It was a great shock to me to see her. I felt that I had never seen anyone so old. Her hair is in two little plaits, and she was wearing a rather dashing pink nylon night-gown. Quite a surprise, that. Her eyes look enormous —pale milky blue. She was in marvellous form—exactly the same Ivy, talking a great deal about money. And food. Though one would think not a morsel had passed her lips for months. She took my hand and played with my bracelet—and her fingers, her wrist were just bones. But the same pursed smile and mischievous sideways glance, as if she really must not laugh at her own jokes.[91]

As her health returned, Ivy's friends were increasingly worried by her evident distress over money. The rent increase was now overshadowed by hospital bills, surgeon's fees, the cost of day and night nurses at home. When Ivy had protested at Christmas that she could not afford to stay much longer in hospital, Herman immediately sent a cheque for one hundred pounds, while Lettice Cooper went straight home to telephone John Lehmann on the committee of the Royal Literary Fund which promptly responded, on the recommendation of Francis King and Osbert Lancaster, with an emergency grant of £500. But, when Ivy applied for further relief three months later, the intrepid committee sent its secretary, John Broadbent, to investigate her financial resources: 'He came to see me, you know,' she told Lettice, 'but he found I was too rich.' An application for a Civil List pension was turned down on the same grounds, to her friends' indignation. No one in those days suspected that Ivy's frugality, like Rose's and Arthur Waley's (all three were apt to strike strangers as having trouble in making ends meet), had less to do with actual poverty than with the ingrained, almost superstitious prohibition laid on their class and generation against disbursing capital. For Ivy, the taboo remained unbreakable long after the family trust had been wound up in 1961, and she herself discharged after half a century as her sisters' trustee. People had gone out of their way for years to save Ivy the price of a cab fare and, at a time when even Herman accepted her view of herself as perilously close to destitution ('she had me completely foxed'[92]), nobody could be quite sure she was joking when she said with her pursed smile at tea: 'Soon I may have to ask you all to bring your own buns.'[93]

In January 1967, Ivy slipped backwards in the bathroom and broke her other hip ('She would have broken a third, had she got it,' wrote Viva King tartly[94]), which meant another six weeks in hospital, followed by nurses again at the flat, and a walking frame which she used for the rest of her life. 'Considering my age, my frail bones and lack of muscle, I wondered I had survived, and I suppose the surgeon did too,' she wrote to Cicely a year later, on 25 January 1968. From now on she referred to herself as a cripple, and she seemed to others besides Herman to shrink, sometimes from one month to the next. Several of her friends had suspected after her first fall that she did not mean to go out again and, after the second, she never did. Her world narrowed to the flat with its balcony garden (she was greatly disturbed in the last year of her life when the block of flats opposite her was raised by two storeys, cutting off part of her sky), and nothing anyone could do would persuade her to leave it. Even in spring she contented herself with the bulbs in her window boxes and the constantly replenished pots of snowdrops, violets, primroses, bluebells and cyclamen that she kept drawn up on the floor in front of her chair.

The flat itself, never especially inviting, grew less so. The rooms seemed bare, shabby and dark to Mario Praz, coming to pay tribute in the summer of 1967 (Lady Mander had once proposed lecturing in the 1950s on 'I. Compton-Burnett' in Rome—'We must find a subject that Mario Praz doesn't know more about than any English person,' said Roger Hinks at the British Council, only to find that Signor Praz had already delivered his lecture of the same title).[95] Elizabeth was not the only regular visitor to find herself almost unutterably depressed by a first glimpse each time of what seemed a moral rather than actual dustiness and neglect. The fact was that

Ivy's indifference to material surroundings had been growing steadily more pronounced since Margaret's death. Flowers mattered much to her but flower arrangement meant nothing: she would watch in silence while Sonia or Cicely hunted in vain for a pretty pot, or set about tweaking and fussing over the bunches jammed into the ugly, chimney-pot vases ranged three or four in a row at her feet. She infuriated Herman by allowing Mary to replace Margaret's delicate, striped Coalport cups and saucers—'Cracked and mended and rather rare!'—with cheap, thick crockery from Woolworths. 'To me a room is just a space,' she once said to the music critic, Andrew Porter; and even friends undeterred by the flat's bleakness—'Oh no, it was cosy,' said Lettice Cooper, 'you just sat in front of the fire and talked'—admitted that the only source of comfort and warmth was Ivy's little igloo by the hearth (or later, when laying a coal fire became too much for Mary, where she sat toasting between two electric fires), barricaded by cushions, and chocolate boxes, and a waist-high pile of new novels.

But Ivy herself could still radiate an energy, amusement, humour and sympathy that captivated strangers. 'Her head is lively and finely chiselled; her grey hair is gathered together in the form of a helmet; she has not at all the look of a witch as she appears in many of her photos,' Mario Praz wrote in his diary on 9 June 1967. Herman, who brought him, claimed to have forbidden Ivy beforehand to mention servants or seedlings, 'and for an hour and a half I sat there pouring out cups of tea and listening to the most brilliant lecture on Thackeray'[96] (according to Signor Praz, though they discussed Jean Rhys, Muriel Spark, Joe Ackerley's death and the Sitwells' bad temper, 'Thackeray was not even mentioned'). To the end of her life Ivy read everything anyone ever claimed might be worth reading—'Of all the autumn and spring books I have enjoyed yours the most,' she wrote to Elizabeth on 2 May 1968, when The Wedding Group was published—and, second only to gossip and prices, she liked talking about the contemporary novel. 'She never wrote a word of literary criticism, but it was with unerring precision that she would indicate the defects in the latest work of this or that admired author of the day,' wrote Francis King when she died. 'Yet few people whose literary standards were so exacting have found so much to enjoy in even the most ephemeral of books.'[97]

She admired Francis' own technical skill and confidence but not what she called his 'murkiness',[98] deplored Iris Murdoch's symbolism ('added on top like a layer of thick, hard icing on a cake'[99]), Joyce Cary's facility (Cary once asked her if she didn't find herself thinking of ten or twelve plots at a time: 'I said, "No, I don't," and it would be better for him if he didn't, one must keep an eye on that sort of thing'[100]), and the sentimental side of Evelyn Waugh ('one must not ask people to do more than they can'[101]). 'He has so little talent, so little talent,' she said sadly to Soame of a friend whose novels grew progressively longer, 'but we should be grateful, my dear Soame, because there is so little talent altogether in the world.' Among her literary friends, she loved Rosamond's beauty ('Oh, a water lily,' she told Lettice Cooper), and Olivia's plaintive, funny, faintly waspish style of self-deprecation, which laid her open to much gentle teasing from Ivy ('I always felt she saw Olivia as one of her characters,' said Kay, 'one of her *favourite* characters'), though she was still not entirely happy about Olivia's writing: 'A great many novels nowadays are just travel books disguised, just travel books really. Olivia has just published one about Bulgaria,' she said to Barbara. 'And it is all about Bulgaria, really.' The only travel books for which Ivy regularly made an exception were Robert's; and she thanked him for his novel, *The Deep End*, on 21 May 1968, with perhaps the finest compliment one author can pay another: 'I admired your book very much, not so much because I sometimes felt I had written it myself, as for the deep & subtle treatment of Deadly Nightshade's rise to power & exposure of the theory that honesty is the best policy.'

Ivy depended more than ever in these years of confinement on her friends, especially neighbouring friends like George Furlong, former head of the Irish National Gallery, and Rex Britcher, who shared a tall, thin house in Thurloe Street crammed with furniture, pictures and objets d'art: Ivy laughed a lot about their five crowded drawing rooms, advising them to fit in two more by building on an extra storey, and mischievously aggravating the problem herself by leaving them two each of a set of four grey-painted armchairs in her will. They came frequently to weed, water and restock Ivy's balcony garden. Rex baked her cakes, and so did Lettice Cooper, who took it in turn with Carol Rygate and Elizabeth Sprigge to make tea on Sunday, which was Mary's day off. Ivo came in on Saturdays, Madge on Thursdays, Herman was constantly there, and Soame dropped in every few weeks to catch up on new novels—'There are far too many books about sex, my dear Soame, and far too few about money'—and run through the latest gossip. Country friends came when they could: people like Kathleen Farrell (who had moved, in spite of pleas and remonstrance, to Brighton —'Oh, *don't* go to Brighton,' Ivy said, and, with positive horror, '*Not Hove?*') and Cicely Greig would be asked to come again soon, or pressed to stay behind when everyone else had left for a gossip or to share a companionable silence, 'just sitting in front of her fire chewing chocolates with her'.[102]

Being cheated of this sort of intimacy was what Ivy minded most about exiles like the Robinsons, and the fonder she was, the more unforgiving. Barbara and Walter found themselves punished for living abroad by constant small teases like, for instance, her flat refusal to explain or comment when Arthur Waley died and was found, to the stupefaction of nearly all his old friends, to have left a widow. Arthur had lived for most of his life with Beryl de Zoete (who died in 1962)—'The trouble was they loved, honoured and obeyed each other for thirty years,' said Ivy, 'but whenever one wanted to marry, the other didn't.'[103] But six weeks before he died he had married Alison Grant Robinson, a second lifelong companion whose existence even Ivy had never so much as suspected. Arthur, who had seen Ivy through a lifetime of painful, sometimes catastrophic upheavals as well as two world wars, turned out to have been her match in the art of giving nothing away ('It was no good again today,' he said after one of Ivy's Saturdays,[104] which he attended without fail and often in silence, barely uttering save to say, 'Hello, Ivy, hello, Madge,' and, when he got up to go, 'Goodbye, Ivy, goodbye, Madge'). Alison, his faithful chauffeur on these trips to Braemar Mansions, met Ivy for the first time as his widow when the two talked a great deal about Arthur, whose life had been in some ways as strangely suppressed as Ivy's own. 'I am seeing a certain amount of his widow . . .' she wrote tantalizingly to the mystified Robinsons, 'and find I know our side of him well but not much of the other . . .'

All but the boldest of Ivy's friends had learnt to go carefully when approaching her past, to register inexplicable changes of temperature, sudden comings forth and drawings back indicating the presence of a hidden knot she would not untie or, in Madge's phrase, a stone against which one stubbed one's toe. But at the end of her life Ivy was demonstrative as she had never been in her youth, and she took great pains to help or comfort anyone in trouble. When Carol Rygate fell ill in the summer of 1968, Ivy, who loathed telephoning but knew very well what it meant to be cooped up alone all day in low spirits, rang her every night at six o'clock to talk ('Dearest Carol, I rejoiced much to hear you were on the water, & so on smooth waters at last,' she wrote on 18 December when Carol was convalescing on board ship for Christmas: 'It is a long time of buffeting behind you. I congratulate you on all of it, heat, paucity of fellowship, scope for gluttony and pudding in prospect . . .').

She had done what she could to console Sonia in hospital the winter before, and she wrote copiously several times a week when Madge, too, broke her hip and wrist in a fall in June 1968: 'I felt I had had my third accident, I minded so much. And I mind more & more as I can't get to you & can do nothing . . . I have never been so angry at my own helplessness.'[105] She applied to the Royal Literary Fund (an appeal rejected on Madge's behalf for the same reason as Ivy's) and, when Madge left hospital, arranged for her to be looked after by the nurse, Sister Hallet, who had come to tide Ivy over Mary's summer holiday:

10 July, 1968

Dearest Madge,
      . . . Sister H. will go to you on the day you have fixed. She is kind & reliable & equal to all that has to be done; nervous about her cooking, but manages quite well for warm weather & strawberries for pudding . . . 'Sister' is violently interested in meeting titled people, & no doubt you will oblige her in the matter. She talks & talks & seems always to be everywhere, but is much above the average, & I shall be easy about you in her care . . .
      All my love. I wish I were not such a helpless friend. Fate has not considered us.

Ivy

Julian Mitchell brought Lady Diana Cooper & her son, Lord Norwich to tea last week, & Sister almost expired.

It was a gloomy summer, but of all the misfortunes Ivy dreaded for her friends—'friends are away, & ill, & injured, & domestically harassed & financially oppressed'[106]—loneliness was the worst. Dr Pasmore dropped in often (Ivy told him that summer that, after reading and re-reading Jane Austen for seventy years, she knew the novels so well that she no longer needed to read them[107]). He said that rest and isolation in her flat prolonged Ivy's life by lessening the strain on her heart; and perhaps her seclusion provided a physical equivalent to the moral aloofness that had for most of her life protected perceptions so acute as to be, in her sister's view, almost indecent. Certainly she was loved by more people than ever before in these years of her final retreat from the world when Ivy, who had never seen a hippie or tasted frozen food, never touched a typewriter or entered a tall building, seemed almost infinitely remote from London in the Swinging Sixties. 'She cut herself off, and she lived in the past,' said Kathleen Farrell. 'And then she was thinking.' As her world closed in, as material things fell away, as she herself grew bodily more helpless, Ivy put her faith in gossip and visits, the compensations of the contemplative life—'people will not realise that the pleasure in being well-informed should be intellectual; they make it social.'[108] But above all else she prized the affection of her friends, who were often taken aback in these last years by her energy, constancy and generosity of feeling: 'This zest for life was the counterpart of her dread of death,' wrote Francis King, 'so that, even when she was in the greatest pain and discomfort, one never felt, as often with the extremely old and ailing, that the end would be a mercy.'[109] Selina Middleton had said the same of herself in *The Mighty and their Fall*: 'I would rather be alive than dead. When I die, people will say it is the best thing for me. It is because they know it is the worst. They want to avoid the feeling of pity. As though they were the people most concerned!'[110]

Ivy was made a Dame—'one of nature's Dames' according to the London *Evening Standard*—in the Queen's Birthday Honours the day after Mario Praz's visit in June 1967, receiving the palace envoy alone at home and keeping the insignia ('some little contraption of silk and ribbon, spelt "riband" in the directions . . .'[111]) in a drawer for favoured visitors to take out and play with. She asked Dr Furlong to represent her at the Royal Society of Literature's reception the following year, when she was elected one of their twelve Companions of Literature, along with Dame Rebecca West, Sir Compton Mackenzie and John Betjeman ('quite a nice little honour,' she said to Cicely,[112] though to Madge she was less enthusiastic: 'It is an empty and inconvenient honour, and I am not grateful for it'[113]). These public tributes gave her on the whole much satisfaction and so, for all her misgivings, did seeing versions of her books in the theatre and on television (she missed Julian Mitchell's *A Family and a Fortune* at the Yvonne Arnaud Theatre, Guildford, in July 1966, but watched *A Heritage and its History* with him in 1968 on Mary's television—'It was a very good play, Dame Ivy,' said Mary afterwards, 'but a tiring play'[114]).

> I was surprised and pleased to be a Dame . . . [she wrote on 27 June 1968, to Robert]. I am just beginning to write again—the elaboration is a true one—but the days, which I should find so long, pass by so fast. Being disabled takes time in itself, & I have rather a heavy post . . . The one I miss most, Margaret Jourdain, has now been dead sixteen years; and I still have to tell her things, as you had to, and may still have to tell your brother. I am not fully a Dame, as she does not know about it.

Ivy's last novel had been giving trouble long before illness forced her to lay it aside ('My next novel is in a lamentable state and belongs to the future. I am sorry it is so,' she wrote to Victor Gollancz on 21 August 1964, when delivery should have been nearly due according to her biennial schedule unbroken since the war). Well before her first fall, she told several people that, though she had got the characters, she did not yet know what was going to happen to them and that she had never found a plot so elusive before.[115] She kept her 'little book'—or rather the growing pile of flimsy, tattered school exercise books, thirty in all by the end —stuffed under a cushion with chocolate boxes and newspapers at the end of the sofa (where the pile was discovered the day after she died by Elizabeth Sprigge, a faithful visitor in these years, and later author of the first memoir). All Ivy's manuscripts were endlessly rewritten, crossed out and gone over before being copied in a neat school-girl's hand quite different from the loopy black scrawl in which she wrote letters and composed her first drafts. But the twelve notebooks which contain the fair copy of this last novel[116] are still miserably expressive of labour and effort. They are written in a mixture of both hands, in parts indecipherable and so disturbed that her final revisions are strung out like a chain of islands across a swamp of alterations—five or ten lines left standing on a page criss-crossed with interpolations, corrections, deletions, as many as three or four alternative versions scored through or scrubbed out; and the twelfth booklet, labelled 'Next!', has been dismembered

Pages from the manuscript of *The Last and the First*, showing Ivy's two different handwritings.

A fair copy (printed with minor alterations on p. 132 of the published text) in the neat school-girl's hand she kept for the final version of her manuscripts.

altogether, containing little more than often incoherent notes on scraps or sheaves of loose paper.

Ivy herself was often despairing as her days grew shorter and more cluttered: she would rise at eight, dress slowly, write a little with lunch on a trolley, take tea with friends, perhaps write a little more and retire early to bed. She liked to have her hair done for her ('When I was a little girl, I was very particular about my hair'[117]), and, as she became slower and weaker, would permit Mary to help her dress, telling her little practical things about her mother or the nurse who had looked after her as a child. Ivy's sisters came more often to visit her and, now that the relationship no longer grated on any of them, they slipped back easily to the days when Ivy sat over the others as governess in the schoolroom at Hove ('I am coming to the end of trouble with my naughty sisters,' she wrote to Madge on 1 April 1968, when Vera and Juliet, now running a Rudolf Steiner school at King's Langley, had released capital to finance it by buying an annuity 'against the will of the family lawyer'). She talked more freely of Noel and what he had meant to her. Once she gave Kay without explanation a photograph of Dorothy Kidd as a young woman in a large hat ('We lived together before I lived with

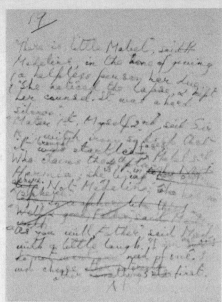

A tentative rough draft written in the mature, loopy hand she used for letters, and showing an early stage in the process of cutting, altering, re-writing and generally working-over to which all her manuscripts were submitted. This is part of a scene omitted from the published text; Mabel was the original name of the child Amy.

Margaret,' she said. 'She married'[118]); and another time, when Dorothy telephoned one Thursday afternoon, Madge heard Ivy change as she answered the telephone, laughing and talking very fast in a voice ('It was a young voice, gay, like a girl's') Madge had never heard her use before.

Many of her friends noticed this general sharpening of memory; and the 'little book', too, returned to the situation in Ivy's own family on which she had based *Dolores* more than sixty years earlier. Ivy had been distressed, round about the time she first began complaining of trouble with her new novel, by Barbara saying that people often took her books to show that human beings were incapable of altruism. 'That was not what I meant at all,' Ivy protested to Barbara, 'with a bleak look'; and in *The Last and the First* (the name eventually chosen for the posthumously published version of Ivy's nameless and unfinished manuscript), she reverts to the theme of unselfishness originally broached in *Dolores*. Her dissatisfaction with that novel had if anything increased with time: she told Barbara how much she envied painters for being able to destroy their early work, and she was scathing whenever admirers—'people who think they are clever'[119]—managed to unearth a copy. Her own published copy is disfigured with a mass of pen-cilled alterations, crossings-out and rearrangements, showing how endlessly Ivy must have tinkered with it in the fallow period when, for fourteen years after the publication of *Dolores*, she wrote nothing at all. Her first and last books both deal among other things with friction between a strong-minded, undervalued, un-wanted eldest stepdaughter and a jealous stepmother ('Whose house is it? Hers or mine?'[120]) closely based in the first instance on Ivy's mother. Dr Compton-Burnett had eased the tension in his own household by removing his eldest daughter bodily (Olive Compton-Burnett had died in 1963, the year Ivy started thinking about *The Last and the First*), setting her up as partner in a girls' school, which is Hermia Heriot's solution to the same problem in *The Last and the First*.

But Dolores Hutton—a characteristically extreme variation on the emotionally agonized, intellectually stultified, morally obdu-rate Victorian heroine idealized by Mrs Humphry Ward and Char-lotte M. Yonge—had insisted on renouncing her own teaching career, her financial independence and hopes of love and marriage, for her family's sake (Ivy, even at this stage, was too honest to represent the recipients of Dolores' repeated sacrifices as anything but ungrateful). Hermia's opportunity for spectacular selflessness comes when, inheriting a small fortune from a rejected elderly suitor, she makes the money over to her father, thereby simul-taneously retrieving the family's financial position and exposing the duplicity of her disgruntled and resentful stepmother. The contrast could hardly be more emphatic. Dolores, conceived by a profound-ly logical mind in terms of a no less profoundly disingenuous morality, remained obstinately blind to the pernicious conse-quences of her saintly self-immolation, while Hermia, embarking on an act of unequivocal altruism, 'behaved as she did as a matter of practical common sense, openly relishing moreover the hold she thus acquired over her stepmother' (the analysis comes from Walter Robinson,[121] always one of Ivy's most perceptive critics). Virtue—the generous virtue of intelligence—prospers for Hermia who puts her trust, as poor Dolores never could, in candour and a shrewd appraisal of the realities of power politics.

But, if *The Last and the First* has an autumnal clarity, there is also an autumnal dryness about this last book which looks back, over more than sixty years and eighteen intervening novels, to the archetypal shapes and outlines laid down in Ivy's childhood. Angus and Roberta Heriot, Hermia's half-brother and -sister by her father's second marriage, are a subdued and chastened pair, hardly more than horrified spectators at a drama in which their own role is negligible ('We have seen some real life, Roberta, a thing I have always wanted to see. But now I don't want to see any more as long as I live'[122]). Madeline, Hermia's cheerful, compliant younger sister, is the last in a long line of optimists, always anxious to smooth over trouble and think only of the happy part ('What is the happy part?' asks one of Ivy's dreadful children, told to run along and not worry about a death in the family in *Darkness and Day*[123]), whose provenance goes back ultimately to Olive's missionary sister, Daisy, the only one of Dr Compton-Burnett's first family on reasonable terms with their stepmother. If there are traces of Ivy herself, they are most evident in young Amy Grimstone, child of a neighbouring household, whose successive mortifications at Hermia's school reflect her creator's experience (Amy's homework essay, quoted verbatim in a cancelled passage of the manuscript, comes in both style and content closer to *Dolores* than anything else in Ivy's subsequent writings[124]); and also perhaps in Amy's grandmother, Jocasta Grimstone, whose laconic speech was recognized by several of Ivy's friends. Hermia's father is an ineffectual figure, kindly but (like Dr Compton-Burnett) too hopeful—or too well-schooled in self-preservation—to register fully the misery and injustice arbitrarily imposed on the whole household by his wife ('You might be a figure in history corrupted by power,' says Hermia to her stepmother. 'It is what you are, only you are not in history'[125]).

Eliza Heriot is unmistakably descended from silly, comic, peevish Mrs Hutton, but the distance Ivy had travelled since *Dolores* may be gauged by the compassion and tragic penetration of this last unfinished, condensed and abstracted portrait of her mother. The last chapter of the printed text of *The Last and the First* was extracted by Cicely, after Ivy's death, from a maze of cancellations (including incestuous complications among the Grimstones, and a whole clutch of alternative marriages for Hermia and others); and among these jumbled and abandoned workings is an episode dealing far more fully than the published Chapter XI with Eliza's public exposure and humiliation: a kind of hunting scene, evidently composed (unlike anything else on this manuscript) straight on to the page, in rich and sombre colours, with Eliza hounded and brought down to the horror of her pursuers before staggering, damaged and in pain, to her feet again. The writing—huge, wild, fierce, lurching diagonally across the page as though the hand that wrote it could scarcely hold a pen—gives a miserable impression of difficulty and weakness. But the scene itself is as crisp in its opening stages, as tautly organized and searching in its exploration of fear, rage, shame, betrayal and their squalid aftermath as anything Ivy ever wrote; and the whole suggests that, if things had not got the better of her in the end, *The Last and the First* might have been a formidable work.

'About a week before she died, she told me it would be "a terrible ms". Her exhaustion was terrible to see,' wrote Cicely,[126] who had begged in vain to be allowed to type the manuscript in the summer of 1969. Ivy complained constantly of being short of time, paying less and less attention to the outside world and seeming scarcely to notice what proved to be a particularly lovely summer. She told Cicely, the last time they stepped out together into a stiff breeze on the balcony, that England was growing windier,[127] as well as emptier. 'It is a dreadful year. Everyone is sick or having operations or gone before. Life is framed in blanks,' she wrote to Katie on 17 February 1969. Ivy, who had been in bed with bronchitis for most of the previous month, was grieving bitterly for Theodora who had died suddenly at Christmas: all that spring she watched over a pot plant that had been Theodora's last present to her, and on 27 February—two months after Theodora's death—she changed her will for the last time.

This was a very long, carefully composed and original document, beginning with twenty-three small bequests: a dozen mirrors were left to friends, mostly other novelists—Olivia Manning, Francis King, Kay Dick, Kathleen Farrell, Lettice Cooper and Julian Mitchell—her diamonds to Carol, her Chinese glass painting (originally a present to Margaret from Soame, it hung over Ivy's desk and was the only picture in the whole flat) to Madge because she loved colour, two urns apiece to Herman and Jim Brandreth (Jim Lees-Milne had a vase, and so did Robin McDouall), small tables to Ivo Pakenham and Cecil Gould, three mirrors to Janet and everything else in the flat to Hester. £15,000 was set aside for Gollancz to produce the collected edition against which Victor had so firmly set his face (he had died at the end of 1967 and been succeeded by his daughter, Livia, who had named half that sum when Ivy asked out of the blue one day at tea how much would be sufficient[128]). The copyrights went to Anthony Compton-Burnett, who was to divide the residue of the estate with Ivy's five friends: Madge, Herman, Robert, Soame and Dorothy's son, Roger Kidd.

Ivy kept her secrets to the end: no one in her lifetime could do more than form often highly inaccurate guesses as to the extent of her resources (eventually sworn at £86,000), her family origins or even her date of birth. She grew desperately frail towards the end, often ill or in pain, and increasingly protected by Mary who did her best in these last months to keep callers at bay. For some time Mary's behaviour had disturbed Ivy's friends. She had long since put a stop to minor pleasures like sitting by a coal fire, or inviting people to lunch, and the thermos-flask teas she left out on her afternoons off were generally considered undrinkable so that tea was available as often as not only to visitors prepared to get it themselves. Access to the flat was in any case not always easy: Mary would invent unlikely excuses, sometimes even try to shut the door in the face of anyone not already deterred by her rudeness, and she frequently refused to fetch Ivy to the telephone on grounds that 'the Dame' was unavailable, resting or 'out'. People disliked her bullying manner, and visitors who knew that Ivy was sometimes pitifully lonely were naturally infuriated by being turned away at the door.

But Mary was probably the only person who realized the full extent of her employer's dependence and weakness; and Ivy, who refused point blank many times to contemplate any change, always said that she and Mary understood each other pretty well. Ivy needed someone who could be relied on to help her dress, move, get about, who would nurse her if necessary without protest or question, someone who would accept both Ivy's helplessness and her reluctance to be coddled or taken in charge. The clause in her will leaving Mary £70 for each year in Ivy's service, provided she was still in it when Ivy died, was a bribe to which Mary responded, enjoying the sense of importance 'the Dame's' celebrity gave her, taking pride in her illustrious visitors (though she remained hazy as to the difference between, say, Lettice and Gladys Cooper), grateful to the Dame as the only employer who had ever given her a radio of her own, let alone promised her money.

In June, just after her eighty-fifth birthday, Ivy, who was in bed with bronchitis again, began hearing hostile foreign voices ('You know I am a writer and have imagination,' she explained afterwards to Hester. 'Perhaps some of the voices were in my imagination, but this did not make them hurt any the less'[129]). Shortage of time worried her dreadfully. Vera and Cicely, meeting over tea at Braemar Mansions in early June, agreed that she could not live very much longer. She re-read *Stepsons* which was at last published that summer:

June 3, 1969

Dear Robert,

I settled back into the old atmosphere with so much ease and pleasure, that I am reluctant to leave it, and other books suffer inattention.

More, I *can't* leave it yet, and other books must suffer.

I hear you have another book on the way, and that must shape the lot of all. But for the moment I am satisfied, and ask no more of Heaven, oblivious of the fact that others may ask much. I hear of you from Olivia and others, and *Stepsons* brings us very near.

Yours affectionately,
Ivy.

Another great pleasure was the diamond brooch which she bought, using up an unexpected windfall from Margaret's American royalties, with a great sense of daring and in defiance of Mr Mowll ('He doesn't understand about a brooch,' said Ivy,[130] clearly thrilled at behaving for once as irresponsibly as her sisters). Hester and Elizabeth Sprigge came to inspect a selection of brooches supplied by a charming young man from a Bond Street shop who produced more and more diamonds as if by magic from his pockets until 'Ivy's eyes shone like the jewels as they were spread on the dining room table'.[131] She chose the prettiest (also, to Hester's consternation, the scratchiest), 'sending us out of the room like school-children while she discussed the price', and afterwards wearing it pinned high up on her dress or her bedjacket, or keeping it by her in a bag with other treasures like her little pearl-studded watch.

On 22 June she wrote a last cryptic letter to Francis King (who was immersed in libel difficulties over his novel, *A Domestic Animal*):

Dear Francis,

You must be fearing I had left the earth; and its binding forces hardly increase. May I ask one question? Has this double world the same significance as it would have here, or anything approaching it? Just *Yes* or *No*, and we will pass on.

The book is the strongest you have done, and quality seems to break in everywhere, or perhaps rather to break out. You have great gifts, and the present misfortunes will not alter its inevitable end. You may come to say you are glad it all happened. It is better to be drunk with loss and to beat the ground, than to let the deeper things gradually escape.

Do come and see me when you can.

Yours always with love,
Ivy.

Vera came for the last time, and they talked about the day that Noel was born. Ivy was becoming too frail to walk easily, her skin irritated her, she had difficulty in eating and sleeping. Julian came on 27 June bringing a friend who had made her a pot of the sort of strawberry jam she liked best with whole berries in it: 'She talked lovingly of Robert Liddell and his novel *Stepsons*. But what really pleased her was the jam. Sometimes she could suddenly shed eighty years and look quite girlish. She did so that afternoon. My last memory is of her licking the jam spoon.'[132] All through July she entertained a procession of old and new friends, seeing someone most days for tea. She had a disconcerting trick of cat-napping, dropping off sometimes in the middle of a sentence. 'I'm not tired, I'm sleepy,' she said sharply to Robin McDouall the last time he saw her on 8 August: 'They are very different things. And I'm surprised that *you* should say tired when you mean sleepy.'[133] On the thirteenth, one of Herman's young friends, Simon Blow, brought a contemporary from Cambridge and Ivy talked without being prompted about Thackeray, saying she was reading *Vanity Fair* and urging them both to another slice of Rex Britcher's plum cake (' "It was made by a member of your own sex," she said encouragingly'[134]).

Soon afterwards she was confined to bed again with bronchitis, and the doctor (Pasmore was away) arranged for a night nurse so as to spare Mary. At their last meeting she had electrified Julian by saying under her breath, as her head went down after a particularly

sweet goodbye, 'Why doesn't he go away and leave me alone?'
Herman sat with her for the last time on 26 August, and her last
words that evening to Mary, who had gone in later to ask if she
needed anything, were 'Leave me alone'.[135] That night she took the
nurse for her brother. She died the next day, Wednesday, 27
August, at about half past nine in the morning. The night nurse had
gone off duty, Ivy had said she would like breakfast and, when
Mary returned with tea, toast and marmalade, had asked for a cup
of hot milk: by the time Mary got back with it, Ivy was dead.

Her mind was clear, her death peaceful, she had kept her maid to
the end. Whatever the question in her last letter to Francis may have
meant, there can, as he said, be no doubt that Ivy herself had been
drunk with loss and beat the ground, and that she had never let the
deeper things escape. She was missed long and sadly by an unusually large circle of friends. Mourners at her funeral, instructed to
return from Putney Vale crematorium to collect their bequests at a
last tea party in Braemar Mansions—many of them meeting for the
first time as they jostled in the hall with their loot—felt they were
taking part in a final strange scene of Ivy's making. She herself had
perhaps foreseen something of the sort when she drew up her will;
and perhaps her own deathbed had not been entirely out of mind
when she made Selina Middleton take to hers in *The Mighty and their
Fall*:

'You don't sound as if you were going to die,' said Hugo.
'No,' said Selina, almost smiling. 'And I can see the nurse
agrees. She feels I am not fit for a higher life; and I would choose
the lower one. And she thinks I should be afraid to die.'
'And you are afraid of nothing,' said her son.
'I don't feel I am going to meet my Maker. And if I were, I
should not fear him. He has not earned the feeling. I almost think
he ought to fear me.'[136]

NOTES

By far the greater part of my information came from talking to people who knew Ivy, so the reader may safely assume that the formula 'x or y said something' means (unless another source is given) that x or y said it to me.

H.S.

Abbreviations used in the notes

The works of I. Compton-Burnett distinguished by initials, as P&M = *Pastors and Masters*, B&S = *Brothers and Sisters*, F&Fate = *A Father and his Fate*, F&Fortune = *A Family and a Fortune*, H&Head = *A House and its Head*, H&History = *A Heritage and its History*, etc. Page numbers refer to Gollancz's uniform edition published in 1972, and are the same for all subsequent reissues.

Burkhart 1	*The Art of I. Compton-Burnett*, ed. Charles Burkhart.
Burkhart 2	*Herman and Nancy and Ivy* by Charles Burkhart.
Burkhart 3	*Twentieth Century Literature*, 'Ivy Compton-Burnett Issue', 1979, guest ed., Charles Burkhart.
Dick	*Ivy and Stevie* by Kay Dick.
Fedden	'Recollections of Ivy Compton-Burnett' by Robin Fedden, *Cornhill*, Winter 1969/70.
Greig	*Ivy Compton-Burnett. A Memoir* by Cicely Greig.
Marsden–Smedley papers	Miscellaneous documents belonging to I.C.-B. and M.J., inherited by Hester Marsden-Smedley and now in the possession of her daughter, Henrietta Williamson.
Mitchell NS	Julian Mitchell in the *New Statesman*, 5 September 1969.
Mowll	Compton-Burnett papers in the possession of Messrs Mowll & Mowll of Dover.
Sprigge	*The Life of Ivy Compton-Burnett* by Elizabeth Sprigge.
V & A papers	Miscellaneous waste papers on the backs of which M.J. compiled her furniture notes, deposited with the Furniture and Woodwork Dept. of the Victoria and Albert Museum.

All letters belong, unless otherwise indicated, to the people to whom they were written.

Foreword   (Pages 9–14)

1   *The Writing on the Wall and Other Literary Essays* by Mary McCarthy, p. 143; and private information from Miss McCarthy.
2   E&B, p. 289.
3   Blurb to first Penguin editions of her novels.
4   B&S, p. 144.
5   D&S, p. 183.
6   Elizabeth Taylor, 28 June 1947.
7   P&C, p. 86.

Chapter One   'Not one of those modern people'   (Pages 15–42)

1   Information from Francis Wyndham (who had it from M.J.).
2   Hester Marsden-Smedley in Burkhart 3.
3   Information from Viva King.
4   Burkhart 2, p. 77.
5   Information from Robert Liddell.
6   David Garnett, letter to H.S., 19 June 1979. The lunch was given by Francis Birrell.
7   Information from R. Mortimer.
8   M.J. was born on 15 August 1876, though Ivy (born in 1884) apparently told Herman and others that there was a gap of ten years between them.
9   P&P, p. 12.
10   P&C, p. 70.
11   *The Weeping and the Laughter*, pp. 126–7.
12   *The Familiar Faces* by David Garnett, p. 221; Lord Hampton (then Humphrey Pakington), another regular on Ivy and Margaret's dining circuit in the early 1920s, said much the same in a letter to H.S., 22 March 1971.
13   D&S, p. 94.
14   D&S, p. 90.
15   Interview with Michael Millgate in 1962, Burkhart 1, p. 35.
16   E. H. Cranton ran this firm, apparently singlehanded, at 6, Fleet Lane, E.C.4, until the Second World War; M.J.'s V&A papers contained fragments of letters to I.C.-B. and statements from Cranton dated 30 September 1933, 31 March 1934, 4 November 1935 and September 1937.
17   Information from Joan Evans.
18   G&G, p. 17.
19   N.S., 20 June 1925.
20   Information from Ralph Edwards who reviewed B&S, M&W and

MWTM anonymously in *Country Life* on 8 June 1929, 6 June 1931 and 26 August 1933 respectively.

21 Hester Marsden-Smedley, Burkhart 3.

22 G&G, p. 21.

23 Burkhart 2, p. 83.

24 MWTM, p. 27.

25 B&S, p. 144.

26 TWTW, p. 149.

27 *Harold Nicolson. A Biography*, vol. 1, by James Lees-Milne (Chatto & Windus, 1980); this account confirmed in conversation with H.S. by Raymond Mortimer, who reviewed P&M in *Vogue*, early April 1925, and H&Head in N.S., 13 July 1935.

28 *A Boy at the Hogarth Press* by Richard Kennedy, p. 69.

29 Correspondence with I.C.-B. (V&A papers); information from Eric Hiscock of *The Bookseller* who worked for the *Evening Standard* when Arnold Bennett's review of B&S was published on 30 May 1929, and discussed it at the time with Cranton.

30 *The Graphic*, 25 May 1929.

31 *Nation and Athenaeum*, 30 March 1929.

32 Letter, V.S.-W. to H.N., 10 April 1929; the diaries of V.S.-W. and I.C.-B. confirm this and subsequent meetings; V.S.-W.'s broadcast review published in *The Listener*, 28 May 1929.

33 Letters to I.C.-B. from David Higham, 12 August 1929, Sylvia Lynd (who had been one of the Book Society's judging panel along with Clemence Dane, J. B. Priestley and George Gordon in May), 7 August, and Donald Brace (V&A papers).

34 P&M, p. 25.

35 Burkhart 1, p. 33.

36 See *Ivy When Young*, pp. 263–4.

37 MWTM, p. 23.

38 See *Ivy When Young*, p. 210.

39 Mitchell N.S.

40 B&S, p. 102.

41 P&M, p. 26.

42 P. C. Kennedy, N.S. 20 June 1925. I am assured by Richard Kennedy that P. C. Kennedy was no relation of his uncle, the architect George Kennedy, who subsequently read B&S in manuscript for Leonard Woolf at the Hogarth Press and was the first to pronounce it a work of genius (see *A Boy at the Hogarth Press*).

43 P&M, p. 47.

44 B&S, p. 39.

45 M&W, p. 203.

46 P&M, p. 32.

47 *New Republic*, 15 January 1930; see also Leo Kennedy, *Common-weal*, 2 April 1930.

48 *Saturday Review*, N.Y., 30 November 1929.

49 Information from Francis Wyndham.

50 Burkhart 1, p. 87.

51 Review of E&B, *Cornhill Magazine*, 1944, reprinted in Burkhart 1, p. 61.

52 D&D, pp. 112–17.

53 MWTM, p. 122.

54 M&W, p. 261.

55 B&S, p. 95.

56 B&S, p. 226.

57 B&S, p. 64.

58 Information from Willie Ranken's niece, Anne Doe; this and subsequent accounts of Ernest Thesiger are largely based on information, papers, press cuttings and the unpublished second half of E.T.'s memoirs provided by his nephew Richard Thesiger.

59 *Eve*, 24 February 1926. (*Eve* was then edited by Ivy's subsequent friend, Madge Garland.)

60 *Pall Mall Gazette*, 28 October 1915.

61 *London Mail*, 20 October 1915.

62 *The Queen*, 19 May 1919.

63 *The Outlook*, 10 May 1919.

64 Information from Francis King.

65 *Daily Sketch*, 22 April 1927.

66 E.T., unpublished memoir.

67 Information from Violet Henriques (daughter of the Hon. Nelly Levy).

68 *Practically True*, p. 159.

69 *Practically True*, p. 31.

70 Information from Yvonne Ffrench.

71 *Practically True*, p. 188.

72 *The Sketch*, 26 May 1926.

73 P&P, p. 69.

74 Burkhart 2, p. 33. This and later accounts of Herman's career based on conversations with him, on Burkhart's admirable memoir, on information supplied by Herman's sister, Elka Schrijver, and on her unpublished ms., 'The Diamonds That Never Were'.

75 £3 a week is the sum given in Burkhart 2 (p. 15), but in fact this was Herman's wage in his first, thoroughly uncongenial job as clerk in a Swiss bank.

76 Information from Jim Brandreth.

77 Burkhart 2, pp. 77 and 79.

78 Sonia Orwell.

79   P&C, p. 126.
80   P&C, p. 79.
81   Burkhart 2, p. 89.
82   Burkhart 2, p. 44.
83   E&B, pp. 14–15.
84   MWTM, p. 33.
85   MWTM, p. 222.
86   Quoted by Arthur Calder-Marshall in *Lewd, Blasphemous and Obscene* (Hutchinson, 1972).
87   C.L., 26 August 1933.
88   *S. Times*, 6 August 1933.
89   N.S., 5 August 1933.
90   Burkhart 3.
91   MWTM, p. 85.
92   Alice Herbert, *Yorkshire Post*, 9 August 1933.
93   See *Ivy When Young*, p. 196.
94   *A Reflection of the Other Person. The Letters of Virginia Woolf, vol. IV 1929–31*, ed. Nigel Nicolson (Hogarth Press, 1978), p. 92.
95   Nathalie Sarraute to H.S., 30 March 1973; see Chap. 9 for a fuller account of this meeting.
96   Information from B. Robinson.
97   Information about Strachey and Cox from Gerald Brenan, letter to H.S., April 1974. (The comment on Cox comes from H. G. Wells.)
98   *Messengers of Day* (Heinemann, 1978), p. 5.
99   *A Writer's Diary* (Hogarth Press, 1954), p. 280.
100   E.W., conversation with H.S.

Chapter Two   *'Playing second fiddle'*   *(Pages 43–64)*

1   F&Fortune, p. 25.
2   P&C, p. 86.
3   MWTM, p. 84.
4   M&W, p. 103.
5   Unpublished memoir.
6   *Eve*, 11 January 1922.
7   *A Moveable Feast* by Ernest Hemingway (Cape, 1964), p. 19.
8   P&P, p. 12.
9   V&A papers.
10   Letter, I.C.-B. to her cousin Katharine (Katie) Blackie, 3 November 1919.
11   Sprigge, p. 94.
12   M&S, p. 79.
13   Robert Liddell in Burkhart 3.

14 Barbara Robinson.

15 Marsden-Smedley papers.

16 D&S, p. 77.

17 M.J., note in diary for 1926; her diary for 1928 records her decreasing weight 'on Dr Heyman's scales' at 27, New Cavendish Street; both her diaries and I.C.-B.'s record regular weighings and trips to fetch pills, etc., from 1929–33. M.J. described this cure and its cost to Ralph Edwards at the time.

18 Hester Marsden-Smedley's account, confirmed by other close friends; but Ivy told James Lees-Milne in 1947 that she always wrote at her little walnut bureau by the window, Caves of Ice, p. 248.

19 P&M, p. 35.

20 This and subsequent accounts of Dorothy Beresford based on an interview with H.S. (1970), also on conversations with her son, Roger Kidd, her sister-in-law, Janet Beresford, and their respective families. For further Beresford history, see Ivy When Young.

21 Dorothy Kidd, unpublished writings supplied by Roger Kidd.

22 G&G, p. 17.

23 Quoted in Sprigge, p. 95.

24 Letter, D.K. to R.K., 27 July 1943.

25 B&S, p. 204.

26 Rosemary Beresford.

27 Burkhart 1, pp. 27–8.

28 Sprigge, p. 95.

29 J. A. Laurence of Laurence, Keen and Gardener.

30 Mowll.

31 Letter, N.C.-B. to I.C.-B., 24 June 1916, see Ivy When Young, p. 242.

32 Letter, Roy Fuller to H.S., 30 July 1974.

33 J. A. Laurence.

34 P&C, pp. 87–8.

35 Their careers reconstructed from conversations with Vera and Juliet Compton-Burnett, and papers, letters, etc., belonging to Mowll & Mowll; see also Ivy When young, passim.

36 D&S, p. 115.

37 Sprigge, pp. 94–5.

38 Information from Sonia Orwell.

39 P&C, p. 70.

40 P&C, p. 185.

41 Burkhart 3, p. 173.

42 H.M.-S., unpublished memoir.

43 Burkhart 3, p. 177.

44 Information from Margaret Hawkins, who worked for the Misses

Noyes before and after the Second World War at Sutton Veney, and remembered 'Miss Burnett's' visits, and often heard them talk about her books.

45 G&G, p. 153.

46 Burkhart 2, p. 93.

47 This and subsequent quotations from Hester Marsden-Smedley come, unless otherwise attributed, from conversations with H.S. between 1970 and her death in 1982.

48 *Regency Furniture 1795–1820*, p. 41.

49 *Ibid.*

50 *Prophesying Peace*, p. 223.

51 Quoted in *Decoration in England from 1660–1760* by Francis Lenygon, p. 12.

52 P&P, p. 68.

53 Sprigge, p. 86.

54 Burkhart 2, p. 81.

55 *Prophesying Peace*, p. 223.

56 *The Work of William Kent*, p. 12.

57 H.M.-S., unpublished memoir.

58 Quoted by M.J. in *Eve*, 7 December 1921.

59 M&S, p. 80.

60 Burkhart 2, p. 75.

61 *The Flowers of the Forest* by David Garnett (Chatto and Windus, 1955), p. 209; so little impression did Ivy make on Birrell at the time that Garnett subsequently confused her and M.J. with the then far more celebrated couple, Miss Moberly and Eleanor Jourdain; and Garnett was obliged to make amends ('Ivy Compton-Burnett was naturally furious with me, and my most abject apologies failed to satisfy her,' D.G. to H.S., 19 June 1979) in his next autobiographical volume, *The Familiar Faces*, p. 221.

62 *Ezra Pound* by Charles Norman (Macmillan N.Y., 1960), p. 246.

63 M&W, p. 264.

64 Fedden (Renée Fedden confirms that the anonymous admirer in her husband's anecdote was Toynbee). Unless both these well-known stories are true, it is the second that must be a myth since Ivy tacitly confirmed the Birrell version in a scathing postcard about Garnett's book to Cicely Greig, dated 5 December 1955.

65 Fedden, p. 429.

66 Burkhart 2, p. 80.

67 This and subsequent attempts to establish M.J.'s financial circumstances are based on her Account Book, which gives detailed figures and sources of income for the years 1902–1924 (Marsden-Smedley papers), and various notes, bills, receipts, bank statements etc.

among her V&A papers; figures for Ivy's income from Mowll & Mowll.

68 MWTM, p. 22.

Chapter Three   'No point in being too Greek'   (Pages 65–105)

1   D&S, p. 68.
2   G&G, p. 62.
3   Letter, R.M. to H.S., 21 September 1980.
4   I.C.-B. to R.L. (Mrs Philipps), 20 March 1938, King's College Library, Cambridge; and conversation with R.L.
5   A typescript of *Buchanan's Hotel*, dated 1933, was loaned to me in 1973 by Ralph Edwards (who had it from the V&A Furniture Department, where it had been found among M.J.'s papers deposited there after her death in 1951), but has apparently since disappeared; Rosamond Lehmann had certainly heard of it, and Hester Marsden-Smedley remembered much talk about it in the mid-1930s when M.J. was applying in vain to London managements.
6   Letters from F. Surgey of Acton Surgey, and several from Hugh Phillips, among the Marsden-Smedley papers; the following account is based also on M.J.'s diaries, trade address book, fragments among her V&A papers; and conversations with Herman Schrijver.
7   *Private History* by Derek Patmore (Cape, 1960).
8   Herman Schrijver; information also from Raisley Moorsom, Mrs Henriques, Viva King; and see 'An Architect's Debt to Country Life' by Oliver Hill, C.L., 12 June 1967.
9   G&G, p. 66.
10   Burkhart 2, p. 96.
11   MWTM, p. 43.
12   P&M, p. 35.
13   Joan Evans, preface to *An Adventure*, p. 15; the following account owes much to conversations with Dame Joan.
14   Conversation with I.C.-B. in February 1957, written down at the time by Rosamond Lehmann.
15   *The Ghosts of Versailles* by Lucille Iremonger, p. 65.
16   To Dr John Rollett, 3 January 1970.
17   Information from Viva King.
18   To Ivo Pakenham.
19   *The Reluctant Pioneer. The Life of Elizabeth Wordsworth* by Georgina Battiscombe (Constable, 1978), pp. 101–2.
20   *Prelude and Fugue. An Autobiography* by Joan Evans, p. 76.
21   *A Childhood*, p. 48.

22 'Reminiscences' by C. M. Jourdain, 1911 (the first part of this typescript is a more intimate, early draft for *A Childhood*, the second is an account of the onset of Milly's illness, her terror, shame, despair and gradual acceptance of her condition). Add. MS, British Library, Darwin and Cornford Papers (these include a correspondence between Milly and her friend, the poet Frances Cornford, giving a detailed picture of the Jourdains at home between 1902 and 1926).

23 Letter, Elizabeth Taylor to Robert Liddell, n.d.

24 D&S, p. 148.

25 Ralph Edwards.

26 Burkhart 2, p. 96.

27 *An Outdoor Breviary*, p. 105, previous reference, p. 84 (the places described are nameless in the published text but identified in M.J.'s handwriting in the margins of the copy she gave Joan Evans).

28 Memoir of Philip by Milly Jourdain, quoted by A. E. Heath in *The Monist*, vol. XXX, April 1920 (a typescript of this essay, 'Philip', corrected in Milly's own hand, is in the library of Trinity College, Cambridge, together with other P.E.B.J. papers deposited by Livia Breglia, Laura Jourdain's daughter by a second marriage). There is another detailed obituary by George Sarton, including a memoir by Philip's wife Laura, in *Isis* (Brussells), vol. V, 1923; and a fascinating account of the relationship with Russell in 'Russell and Philip Jourdain', by I. Grattan-Guinness, greatly expanded in Grattan-Guinness's *Dear Russell—Dear Jourdain*. My account is further indebted to Dr John Rollett for a generous supply of insights, information and Jourdain papers.

29 Russell's journal, November 1902, quoted by Grattan-Guinness, *op. cit.*

30 Frances Cornford to C.M.J., July 1906, B.Lib.

31 C.M.J., *Monist, op. cit.*

32 To Esther Millar, housekeeper to Janette Thesiger.

33 'Philip', *op. cit.*

34 D&S, p. 203.

35 'Some Aspects of Samuel Butler' by M. Jourdain, *Open Court*, vol. XXVII, no. 10, October 1913. (*The Open Court* belonged, with *The Monist* and *The International Journal of Ethics*, to a stable of international, U.S.-based, intellectual journals run by Paul Carus, in all of which P.E.B.J. had an editorial hand.)

36 *Monist, op. cit.*; the original proposal and development of this scheme traced in Cornford papers, B.Lib.

37 P.E.B.J. to Russell, 24 May 1919, *Dear Russell—Dear Jourdain*, p. 150.

38 This was an expanded, updated edition (pub. Marston, 1902) of a work first published in 1865 by Fanny Bury Palliser (Captain Marryat's sister) who had catalogued the lace collection at the S. Kensington (V&A) museum.

39 'Northamptonshire Memories' by W. W. Hadley, *Northamptonshire Past and Present*, vol. II, no. 4; see also 'Alice Dryden' by Joan Wake, *Ibid.*, vol. II, no. 3, 1956; further information from Joan Evans and M.J.'s V&A papers.

40 'Canons Ashby', C.L., 9 April 1981; I am greatly indebted to Mr Cornforth for further advice and information about M.J. and the Drydens.

41 *Dictionary of National Biography*.

42 H.M.-S., unpublished memoir; further quotations and information about the Jourdains at Broadwindsor come from the same source, unless otherwise attributed, or from conversations with H.S.

43 MWTM, p. 213.

44 'The Literary Associations of Dorset' by M. Jourdain, *Memorials of Old Dorset* (Benrose & Sons, 1907).

45 *Outdoor Breviary*, p. 98.

46 *Unfulfilment*, title poem.

47 *Outdoor Breviary*, p. 49.

48 P.E.B.J.'s note scribbled on a letter, 6 March 1911, from Arthur L. Humphreys setting out Hatchard's terms (the *Poems* were eventually published by Truslove and Hanson), V&A papers.

49 M.J.'s salary from Lenygon given in her Account Book; information about Lenygon and his firm from the historian Sarah Coffin, Ralph Edwards, Peter Thornton of the V&A and James Kiddell of Sothebys; M.J.'s authorship of the Lenygon books confirmed by a fragment of a letter to her from the leading American authority on the decorative arts, Fiske Kimball, among her V&A papers (probably written round about the time he published Kent's Houses of Parliament designs in the *RIBA Journal*, August and September 1932): 'I have known and admired your work for a long time —longer than the public, for Francis Lenygon betrayed to me that his two books were written for him, I presume by you. They were the earliest of all recognitions of Burlington and Kent.' See also *English Decoration in the Eighteenth Century* by John Fowler and John Cornforth (Barrie and Jenkins, 1978), pp. 16–17.

50 Fragments of M.J.'s correspondence with Mulliner and Hudson among her V&A papers; their financial transactions listed in her Account Book.

51 'Percy Macquoid and Others' by Ralph Edwards, *Apollo* 4, 1974; see also 'Edward Hudson' by Christopher Hussey, *Country Life*, 26

September 1936, 'Portrait of a Perfectionist. Edward Hudson' by Pamela Maude, *ibid.*, 12 January 1967.

52   Editorial, *Country Life* (opening number), 8 June 1897.

53   Information from Dr Rollett, who had it from a friend of P.E.B.J., Prof. C. D. Broad ('At that time he shared very much the same views of the then war as did Bertrand Russell, and I used to hear from Jourdain a good deal about these matters . . .').

54   Letter, P.E.B.J. to Laura J., 4 July 1915, Trinity College, Cambridge.

55   Frances Cornford to C.M.J., B.Lib. (quotations from F.C.'s and C.M.J.'s letters all come from this correspondence, quotations from P.E.B.J. are from the Jourdain papers, Trinity College, Cambridge).

56   Burkhart 3, p. 175.

57   To Dr Rollett, 26 January 1970; further quotations from V.C.-S. come from the same source.

58   G&G, p. 5.

59   V&A papers; Joan Evans said the *Poems* were financed by Janette.

60   Information from Richard Thesiger, who had it from Janette.

61   *Outdoor Breviary*, p. 103.

62   To Dr Rollett, 26 January 1970.

63   D&S, p. 94.

64   Joan Evans, to whom I am indebted for an account of this affair.

65   A fuller account is in *Dear Russell—Dear Jourdain*, pp. 146–53.

66   *The Work of William Kent*, p. 30.

67   Conditions laid down in correspondence with Waltons of Leadenhall Street (Mrs Levy's solicitors), 26 September 1924–29 September 1931, Marsden-Smedley papers; further correspondence up to and including 1945, V&A papers; Mrs Levy's daughter, Violet Henriques, confirms that the anonymous benefactor was almost certainly her mother, see footnote p. 100.

68   Violet Henriques.

69   Information from Kathleen Farrell, who had it from Elizabeth Sprigge.

70   See *Ivy When Young*, p. 30.

71   Sprigge, p. 95.

72   See *Ivy When Young*, pp. 263–4; M.J. endorsed Butler in *The Open Court*, October 1913.

73   *Traveller's Prelude* by Freya Stark (John Murray, 1950), p. 129.

74   P&M, p. 35.

75   D&S, p. 65.

76   *Spectator*, 19 March 1937.

77   Burkhart 2, p. 79.

78 Information from R. Liddell (letter to H.S., 7 December 1970), who had it from R. Mortimer.

79 *An Adventure*, p. 85.

80 Information from Carol Rygate who was a pupil at St Hugh's at the time; this version of the St Hugh's affair based on Joan Evans' recollections, C.M.J.'s letters, *The Ghosts of Versailles* by Lucille Iremonger and an unpublished, pro-Jourdain memoir by another St Hugh's pupil, 'The Row' by Eveleen Stopford (lent to me by Robert Liddell).

81 Letter, R.L. to H.S., 7 December 1970.

82 Story from Kay Dick, confirmed by Sheila Bush, letter to H.S., 8 April 1983.

83 P&M, p. 26.

Chapter Four '*A woman of blameless character*' (Pages 106–29)

1 TWTW, p. 6.

2 Information from Sonia Orwell.

3 Information from B. Robinson.

4 Detonated by Carol Rygate, whose stories of this affair subsequently gave Ivy much pleasure.

5 Information from Madge Garland.

6 Information from Herman Schrijver; see also Burkhart 2, p. 88.

7 Ivy said this explicitly to Sonia Orwell, and discussed the book's influence on her in more general terms with Francis King and Marion Rawson.

8 *The Real Charlotte*, p. 250.

9 *Week End Review*, 2 September 1933.

10 MWTM, pp. 34 and 37; *The Ghosts of Versailles*, *op. cit.*; information from Joan Evans.

11 See *Ivy When Young*, p. 184.

12 MWTM, p. 85.

13 MWTM, p. 87.

14 MWTM, p. 140.

15 MWTM, p. 142.

16 See *Ivy When Young*, pp. 245–6.

17 MWTM, p. 157.

18 MWTM, p. 158.

19 *The Real Charlotte*, p. 291.

20 MWTM, p. 199.

21 MWTM, p. 173.

22 F&Fortune, p. 235.

23 *Ibid.*, pp. 236–7.

24   In 'Conversation et Sous-Conversation', *Nouvelle Revue Française*,
     January–February 1956 (reprinted in *Tropisms and the Age of Suspi-
     cion*, pp. 117–20).

25   MWTM, p. 265; the comparison with Ivy's illness based on in-
     formation from Vera Compton-Burnett, who nursed her through
     it; and see *Ivy When Young*, pp. 256–7.

26   F&Fortune, p. 271; cf. M&M, p. 290.

27   To James Lees-Milne, *Ancestral Voices*, p. 71.

28   *Lord Byron's Family. Annabella, Ada and Augusta. 1816–24* by Mal-
     colm Elwin (John Murray, 1975), p. 102.

29   MWTM, p. 304.

30   Fedden.

31   MWTM, p. 104.

32   P&P, p. 71.

33   D&S, p. 256.

34   Burkhart 2, p. 30 (the N.S. reviewer was Philip Toynbee on 29
     January 1944).

35   Information from Janet Beresford.

36   MWTM, p. 176.

37   MWTM, p. 143.

38   MWTM, pp. 142–3.

39   See *Ivy When Young*, Chapter 8, for a fuller account of this debt; Ivy
     had certainly read H. Festing Jones' *Samuel Butler. A Memoir* (Mac-
     millan, 1919) when it came out (perhaps also Clara Stillman's
     excellent account of the 'long and painful' correspondence between
     father and son in *Samuel Butler. A Mid-Victorian Modern*, 1932), and
     seems to have borrowed among other things Butler's habit of
     annotating minutes and letters from his father in the same way as
     Felix intersperses his own comments in reports of his father's letters
     and telephone calls.

40   MWTM, p. 20.

41   MWTM, p. 97.

42   MWTM, p. 86.

43   MWTM, pp. 61–2.

44   Interview with Brodie, *Books of Today*, April 1950.

45   MWTM, p. 143.

46   Dick, p. 18.

47   MWTM, p. 174.

48   Burkhart 2, p. 14.

49   *Ibid.*, p. 36.

50   *At Lady Molly's* (Heinemann, 1957), p. 211.

51   This fraud is recorded in 'The Diamonds That Never Were', unpub-
     lished ms. by Elka Schrijver, and my account of Herman's profes-

sional and private life is largely based on conversations with her in
Amsterdam in 1981.

52 *Boswell's Life of Johnson*, ed. G. B. Hill (OUP, 1971), vol. IV, p. 86.
53 Letter, Elka Schrijver to H.S., 24 October 1981.
54 D&S, p. 182.
55 Burkhart 2, p. 49.
56 *Ibid.*, p. 96.
57 *Ibid.*, p. 86.
58 E&B, p. 63.
59 Burkhart 2, p. 93.
60 *Ibid.*, p. 95.
61 Dick, p. 17.
62 *Ibid.*, p. 9.
63 See *Ivy When Young*, p. 272.

Chapter Five   *'Well, and in Swaffham Bulbeck!'*   (Pages 130–51)

1   D&S, p. 123.
2   Information from Barbara Robinson.
3   Letter, D.H. to I.C.-B., July 1935, V&A papers; see also *Literary Gent*, p. 154.
4   Letter, V.G. to I.C.-B., 26 June 1940.
5   *New York Times*, 23 July 1937.
6   Information from Sybille Bedford.
7   R. Ellis-Roberts, *News Chronicle*, 26 May 1937.
8   I.C.-B. to R.L., 27 November 1961.
9   Letter, V.G. to Blanche Knopf, 3 December 1952; information from Livia Gollancz.
10 *Literary Gent*, p. 171.
11 Information from Rupert Hart-Davis.
12 Information from Christopher Sykes.
13 Information from B. Robinson.
14 Burkhart 1, p. 26.
15 C.S. to I.C.-B., 29 March 1937, Marsden-Smedley papers.
16 *Caves of Ice*, p. 115.
17 Information from Cecil Gould.
18 G&G, p. 20.
19 Burkhart 2, p. 100.
20 Quoted in *Rose Macaulay* by Constance Babington-Smith, p. 225.
21 Information from James Brandreth.
22 Greig, p. 26.
23 *Reminiscences of Affection* by Victor Gollancz (Gollancz, 1968), p. 80.
24 Burkhart 2, p. 87.

25   G&G, p. 51.

26   *Ancestral Voices*, p. 61.

27   Greig, pp. 44–5.

28   G&G, p. 63.

29   Liza Banks, to whom I am greatly indebted for information about the Noyeses at Sutton Veney; the following account also owes much to her sister, Anne Northcroft; to Mrs Hawkins and Mrs Gertrude McCracken (both of whom had known and worked intermittently for the Noyeses all their lives); to Mrs John Walker; and to the younger Nicholsons' friends, Humphrey Spender and Clissold Tuely.

30   *Salisbury Plain*, pp. 292–3.

31   Letter, A.N. to H.S., 1 July 1981.

32   Information from the Noyeses' great-niece, Jennifer Adamson; see also *Two Worlds for Memory* by Alfred Noyes (Sheed and Ward, 1953), pp. 9, 42–3, 188.

33   P&C, p. 134.

34   P&C, p. 129.

35   P&C, p. 226.

36   P&C, p. 130.

37   P&C, p. 139.

38   P&C, p. 143.

39   P&C, p. 147.

40   P&C, p. 143.

41   P&C, p. 147.

42   P&C, p. 144.

43   P&C, p. 168.

44   TWTW, p. 310.

45   P&C, p. 129.

46   'Some Notes About Ivy Compton-Burnett, 21 April 1942', unpublished ms. by Lady Anne Hill.

47   Burkhart 1, p. 27.

48   *Ibid.*, p. 192.

49   Typist's bill dated 8 December 1938, V&A papers.

50   Burkhart 2, p. 90, and conversation with Herman Schrijver; but see H.M.-S. in Burkhart 3, pp. 178–9; M.J.'s movements at this time, given in her diary for 1938, were confirmed by Peter Wilson.

51   H.M.-S., unpublished memoir.

52   Letter, Robert Liddell to H.S., 7 December 1970.

53   H.M.-S., unpublished memoir.

54   *Boswell's Life of Johnson*, *op. cit.*, vol. iii, p. 48.

55   Information from Soame Jenyns, to whom this account is largely indebted.

56 *The Weeping and the Laughter*, p. 167.
57 Story from Angus Wilson.
58 TWTW, p. 5.
59 M&M, pp. 12 and 35.
60 D&S, p. 37.
61 Information from Angus Wilson.
62 P&P, p. 155.
63 D&D, p. 19.
64 'Distinguished Evacuee—Miss Ivy Compton-Burnett', unpub-
    lished ms. by Dulcie Pendred; further accounts of Ivy at Bottisham
    supplied by Anna Browne and Ann Graham Bell, both of whom
    were there at the time.
65 P&M, p. 17; the book in question was identified for me as P&M by
    Soame Jenyns.
66 'Distinguished Evacuee', *op. cit.*

Chapter Six   *'When war casts its shadow, I find that I recoil'*   *(Pages 152–82)*

1   Burkhart 2, p. 90.
2   N.S., 13 July 1935.
3   'Notes on Ivy Compton-Burnett' by Robert Liddell, Burkhart 3, p.
    135; subsequent quotations come from the same source unless
    otherwise attributed.
4   Letter, R.L. to H.S., 29 November 1970.
5   Burkhart 2, p. 101 (Herman puts this visit after the war but M.J.'s
    diary and R.L.'s recollection date it 4–10 May 1940).
6   Letter, R.L. to H.S., 7 December 1970.
7   Letter, R.L. to H.S., 13 December 1982.
8   *Ancestral Voices* by James Lees-Milne, p. 71.
9   *Ibid.*, p. 43.
10 Dorothy Kerr, letter to H.S., 30 January 1975; further information
    from Lady Medawar, and the villagers of Sutton Veney.
11 H&Head, p. 274.
12 I.C.-B. to R.L., 5 January 1942.
13 P&C, p. 127.
14 V&A papers.
15 Burkhart 3, p. 179; further information about this period from
    H.M.-S., her daughter Henrietta Williamson, Michael Pinney and
    Marion Rawson.
16 I.C.-B. to R.L., 5 January 1942.
17 N.S., 24 May 1941, reprinted in Burkhart 1, p. 55.
18 Burkhart 2, p. 91.
19 See *Ivy When Young*, pp. 91–2.

20   Information from Francis Wyndham.

21   Letter, I.C.-B. to B. Robinson, 21 November 1964; she had said the same to R.L. in a letter dated 26 July 1950.

22   18 December 1941, V&A papers.

23   V&A papers.

24   E.T., unpublished memoirs.

25   *Ancestral Voices*, pp. 42–3.

26   *Ibid.*, p. 61.

27   Letter from Routledge and Sons Ltd, 9 July 1941, V&A papers.

28   Susan Miles, Sutton Rectory, Sandy, Berks., to I.C.-B., 5 September 1941.

29   *Ancestral Voices*, p. 61.

30   Anne Hill, 'Some Notes About Ivy Compton-Burnett'.

31   *Ancestral Voices*, p. 220.

32   *Julia Strachey* by Herself and Frances Partridge (Gollancz, 1983), p. 190.

33   Letter, John Pope-Hennessy to H.S., 1 June 1981.

34   *Ancestral Voices*, p. 223.

35   Information from James Lees-Milne.

36   *Prophesying Peace* by James Lees-Milne, p. 63.

37   Letter, J.P.-H. to H.S., 1 June 1981.

38   *Ancestral Voices*, p. 65.

39   *Autobiography of Bertrand Russell*, vol. ii, p. 158.

40   F&Fortune, p. 17.

41   Edith Shackleton in *The Lady*, 20 January 1944.

42   M&M, p. 55.

43   M&M, p. 35.

44   Letter, D. G. Muir to I.C.-B., 23 July 1944, Marsden-Smedley papers.

45   D.K. to R.K., 26 January and 9 February 1944.

46   *David Blaize* (Hodder and Stoughton, 1916), p. 149.

47   Letter, n.d., M.J. to Heywood Hill.

48   Information from Livia Gollancz.

49   D. G. Muir to I.C.-B., 23 July 1944, Marsden-Smedley papers.

50   *Collected Poems* by Keith Douglas, ed. John Walker, G. S. Fraser and J. C. Hall (Faber, 1966), p. 150.

51   D.K. to R.K., Royal Lion, Lyme Regis, 18 January 1944.

52   Letter, M.J. to Anne Hill, Cliff Bank, Lyme Regis, 10 February 1944.

53   H.M.-S., unpublished ms.

54   R. Lehmann, 'Tribute to Ivy Compton-Burnett', delivered at the memorial meeting at Crosby Hall on 24 October 1969.

55   'A Conversation between I. Compton-Burnett and M. Jourdain',

Orion, No. 1, 1945; reprinted in Burkhart 1, pp. 21–2.

56 *Ibid.*, p. 27.

57 Reported in a letter from Elizabeth Taylor to Robert Liddell, quoted in his unpublished ms., 'Elizabeth and Ivy'; a slightly different version of this passage appears in the transcript of this interview published in Burkhart 3, pp. 168–9.

58 'An Appraisal. Ivy Compton-Burnett and Elizabeth Bowen', *Horizon*, June 1946; reprinted in Burkhart 1, p. 108.

59 H&Head, p. 172.

60 M&M, p. 22.

61 p. 112.

62 Letter, M.J. to Anne Hill, 10 February 1944.

63 Burkhart 1, p. 22; subsequent quotations come from pp. 23, 25 and 29 respectively.

64 *Regency Furniture, op. cit.*, pp. 41, 47–8, etc.

65 Burkhart 3, p. 139.

66 M.J. to H.H., 22 June 1944.

67 *Ibid.*

68 M.J. to J. Lees-Milne, 5 November 1944.

69 M.J. to H.H., January 1945.

70 M.J. to H.H., 22 June 1944.

71 *Prophesying Peace* by James Lees-Milne, p. 72.

72 M.J. to J.L.-M., 5 November 1944 and 3 March 1945.

73 M.J. to J.L.-M., 3 March 1945.

74 M.J. to H.H., December 1944.

75 Letter, R.L. to H.S., 7 December 1970. Another version appears in Burkhart 3, p. 141.

76 *Ibid.*

77 See *Ivy When Young*, p. 251.

78 Burkhart 3, p. 142.

79 R.L. to H.S., 7 December 1970.

80 Burkhart 3, p. 142.

81 *Ibid.*

82 I.C.-B. to R.L., 17 September 1957 and 2 June 1960.

83 I.C.-B. to R.L., 1 June 1953.

84 On p. 62.

85 I.C.-B. to R.L., 3 June 1969.

86 R.L. to H.S., 7 December 1970.

Chapter Seven   'Truth is so impossible. Something has to be done for it'
                  (Pages 183–214)

1 Letter, I.C.-B. to Cicely Greig, 27 March 1946.

2 I.C.-B. to E.T., 16 July 1947.

3   I.C.-B. to E.T., 28 June 1947.
4   p. 133.
5   I.C.-B. to R.L., 26 July 1950.
6   P&P, pp. 62 and 66.
7   Greig, p. 33.
8   Review of *Darkness and Day*, *Sunday Times*, 5 April 1951.
9   M&M, p. 183.
10 Information from Sonia Orwell.
11 Described in a letter, Rutley Mowll to I.C.-B., 8 January 1946, V&A papers.
12 This and the following quotation from Fedden.
13 Burkhart 1, p. 187 (A. Powell assures me that the boat-race party in question took place in 1952).
14 Letter, Elizabeth Taylor to Robert Liddell, n.d.
15 This and the following quotation from Fedden.
16 Greig, p. 49; the next four quotations are from pp. 17, 36, 20 and 24 respectively.
17 Letter, Graham Greene to H.S., 7 April 1983; the following account is largely based on a three-cornered correspondence between I.C.-B., Victor Gollancz and Spencer Curtis Brown in Gollancz's files.
18 G.G. to I.C.-B., 8 October 1948, Gollancz papers.
19 *Daily Telegraph*, 21 February 1947.
20 I.C.-B. to E.T., 16 July 1947.
21 Information from Elizabeth Taylor.
22 Charles Poore, *New York Times*, 20 June 1948.
23 Greig, p. 43.
24 Cecil Gould, unpublished ms., 1 January 1971.
25 *Important to Me*, p. 193.
26 M&M, p. 67.
27 D&S, p. 69.
28 John Farrelly, *New Republic*, 14 June 1948.
29 Greig, p. 80; the next three quotations from pp. 75, 39 and 44 respectively.
30 Greig, p. 43; possibly there was some confusion about the magazine in question, since *Time*'s verdict ('*Bullivant and the Lambs* . . . is perhaps Author Compton-Burnett's finest novel. Its principal character, Family-Head Horace Lamb, is a typical Compton-Burnett tyrant . . .' 19 July 1948) was by no means among the most perceptive or enthusiastic American review.
31 Information from Vere Watson-Gandy and James Brandreth.
32 Dick, p. 16.
33 Letter, E.T. to H.S., July 1971.
34 Greig, p. 32.

35 Dick, pp. 21–2.

36 Information from Joan Evans.

37 *Caves of Ice* by James Lees-Milne, p. 214.

38 I.C.-B. to V.W.-G., 4 July 1950.

39 Information from Carol Rygate.

40 *Caves of Ice*, p. 254.

41 *Ibid.*, p. 215.

42 Greig, pp. 54–5.

43 *Ibid.*

44 Hester Marsden-Smedley, unpublished ms.

45 D&D, p. 117.

46 D&D, p. 81.

47 *Important to Me*, pp. 188–9.

48 Letter, R.L. to H.S., 7 December 1970.

49 Information from E.T.

50 Summary of medical treatment in M.J.'s diary for 1951.

51 Burkhart 2, p. 76; this scene and its consequences were confirmed privately to me by both Herman Schrijver and Peter Wilson.

52 Information from Margaret Branch.

53 See *Ivy When Young*, p. 263.

54 *Important to Me*, p. 190.

55 See *Ivy When Young*, p. 175.

56 D&D, p. 27.

57 D&D, p. 40.

58 D&D, p. 209.

59 D&D, p. 214.

60 Information from Dr Pasmore.

61 R.E. to H.S., 23 April 1974.

62 Herman Schrijver's version; another, probably apocryphal but much appreciated in design and architectural circles, was: 'Ivy, be sure to lock up the whisky and the biscuits.'

63 F&Fortune, p. 229.

64 I.C.-B. to R.M., 14 April 1951.

65 Information from Joyce Felkin.

66 Information from Olivia Manning, who had it from Basil M.-S.

67 Burkhart 2, p. 76.

68 I.C.-B. to Robin McDouall, 14 April 1951.

69 Information from V. Sackville-West's biographer, Victoria Glendinning.

70 Sprigge, p. 129.

71 Information from James Lees-Milne and Olivia Manning respectively.

72 D&D, p. 215.

73   I.C.-B. to K. Blackie, 14 June 1951.
74   Greig, p. 61.
75   Letter, I.C.-B. to C.G., 4 June 1951.
76   Fedden.
77   Information from Margaret Branch.
78   Letters and information from Dame Janet Vaughan; Lady Mander thought Ivy had also applied to Lady Margaret Hall, Oxford, but the College Secretary was unable to find any evidence among Dame Lucy Sutherland's papers.
79   Information from Ivo Pakenham.

Chapter Eight   'The English Secret'   (Pages 215–55)

1   *Caves of Ice* by James Lees-Milne, p. 192.
2   P&P, p. 8.
3   P&P, p. 44.
4   P&P, p. 164.
5   P&P, p. 188.
6   Information from Sybille Bedford.
7   Fedden.
8   C. Sykes, tribute to Dame Ivy, read at the memorial meeting, Crosby Hall, 24 October 1969.
9   Sprigge, p. 135.
10   Information from B. Robinson.
11   Information from Sybille Bedford.
12   Greig, p. 69.
13   Burkhart 2, p. 100.
14   'A Friendship Without a Thorn', unpublished ms. by Madge Garland.
15   Information from Angus Wilson.
16   Madge Garland.
17   Fedden.
18   I.C.-B. to R.L., 20 October 1954.
19   Burkhart 2, p. 104.
20   I.C.-B. to R.L., 1 August 1951.
21   Letter, I.C.-B. to B. and W. Robinson, 31 January 1965.
22   Burkhart 1, p. 187.
23   Fedden.
24   Anne Hill, diary, 11 February 1956.
25   Fedden.
26   To Robert Liddell.
27   Information from R. Lehmann.
28   Letter, John Pope-Hennessy to H.S., 1 June 1981.

29   *Ancestral Voices*, p. 65; see also Fedden.

30   Betty Miller-Jones.

31   Information from Herman Schrijver.

32   Burkhart 2, pp. 105–7.

33   *Ibid.*, p. 82.

34   J.L.-M. to Madge Garland, 31 August 1969.

35   Fedden.

36   P&C, p. 191.

37   Sprigge, p. 133; the following account based largely on information from O. Manning.

38   E.T. to R.L., n.d.

39   Information from N. Wright.

40   Burkhart 2, p. 96.

41   'A Friendship Without a Thorn', unpublished ms.

42   B&S, p. 88.

43   This and subsequent quotations from Elizabeth Taylor come, unless otherwise acknowledged, from her letters to Robert Liddell, hardly any of which are dated (or dateable, except by internal evidence), and many of which survive only in fragments, the rest having been destroyed at the author's request by R. L., who incorporated much of this extraordinary correspondence in his book, 'Elizabeth and Ivy' (as yet unpublished).

44   *The Bookman*, April 1949.

45   *The Echoing Grove* (it was after this meeting that Ivy came to know Rosamond Lehmann better).

46   Elizabeth Taylor was painfully conscious of some small, barely noticeable burn marks left by a firework on her throat; the heroine of her novel, *The Sleeping Beauty*, had been unrecognizably changed by plastic surgery after a road accident.

47   Information from Angus Wilson.

48   Blanche Knopf to Victor Gollancz, 3 December 1952.

49   M&S, p. 73.

50   M&S, p. 67.

51   Information from Lord Goodman.

52   Information from Sybille Bedford.

53   Information from A. J. Ayer.

54   Dick, p. 25.

55   'A Friendship Without a Thorn', unpublished ms.

56   *Ibid.*, see photograph opposite p. 169.

57   Letter, I.C.-B. to C.G., 22 June 1954.

58   I.C.-B. to B. Robinson, 26 April 1960.

59   Sprigge, p. 151.

60   Letter, Mrs C. C. Baines of Canterbury to C. Greig, 3 June 1972.

61 Sprigge, p. 151.
62 *The Life of Charlotte Brontë*, by E. C. Gaskell (Smith, Elder, 1857), vol. ii, pp. 8–9.
63 G&G, pp. 19 and 51.
64 Dick, p. 14.
65 Letter, I.C.-B. to C. Greig, 5 December 1962; see Greig, p. 88.
66 Dick, p. 18.
67 I.C.-B. to R.L., 29 January 1959.
68 Fedden.
69 This and subsequent quotations from Barbara and Walter Robinson come, unless otherwise attributed, from many conversations with H.S., also from their unpublished ms. notes, 'Conversations Between Ourselves and Ivy'.
70 Greig, p. 21.
71 G&G, pp. 66–7.
72 Information from B. Robinson.
73 Burkhart 2, p. 92.
74 Letter, Valerie Eliot to H.S., 14 June 1983.
75 E.T. to R.L., n.d. (1957).
76 Information from George Furlong and Rex Britcher.
77 This and the subsequent account from 'Some Notes About Ivy Compton-Burnett', unpub. ms. by Anne Hill, 11 March 1958.
78 *Tropisms and the Age of Suspicion*, p. 118.
79 Nathalie Sarraute to H.S., 30 March 1973; this account confirmed by Sonia Orwell.
80 MWTM, p. 92.
81 Burkhart 2, p. 99.
82 I.C.-B. to K. Blackie, 19 December 1959.
83 N.S. to H.S., 30 March 1973.
84 Information from Robin McDouall.
85 *Ibid.*
86 Mowll.
87 Letter, I.C.-B. to B. and W. Robinson, 9 April 1958.
88 Presumably Henrietta Day, whose illness (followed by a change of housekeeper for Ivy) is described in an undated letter which also refers to the murder of a friend and neighbour of E.T.'s by Ruth Ellis in April 1955.
89 I.C.-B. to P.M., 25 July 1954.
90 Greig, pp. 73–5.
91 *The Ghosts of Versailles*, p. 104.
92 Burkhart 3, p. 174.
93 Information from Lucille Iremonger.
94 I.C.-B. to K. Blackie, 14 June 1951.

95   Cancelled passage from 'Herman's Memoir of Ivy', not published in
     Burkhart 2 but kindly shown me by Professor Burkhart.

96   I.C.-B. to Lady MacAlister, 19 April 1968; see also Sprigge, p. 150.

97   See *Ivy When Young*, pp. 127–8.

98   F&Fate, p. 194.

99   F&Fate, p. 75.

100 *Recollections of Virginia Woolf*, ed. Joan Russell Noble (Peter Owen,
     1972), p. 172.

101 R.L. to H.S., 25 February 1983.

102 E.T. to R.L., n.d.

103 I.C.-B. to Robin McDouall, 7 October 1955.

104 I.C.-B. to V. Watson-Gandy, 4 July 1950.

105 Ernest Thesiger, unpublished memoir.

106 Information from Cecil Gould.

107 Burkhart 3, p. 182.

108 E.T. to H.S., n.d. (1971).

109 *Rose Macaulay* by Constance Babington Smith, p. 227.

110 I.C.-B. to R.L., 21 January 1959.

111 H&History, p. 25.

112 I.C.-B. to C.G., 4 November 1958.

113 I.C.-B. to R.L., 17 September 1957.

114 This and the following quotation from H&History, pp. 98 and 134.

115 Letter from I.C.-B., quoted in E.T.'s report to R.L.

Chapter Nine   *'One of nature's Dames'*   *(Pages 256–98)*

1   Dick, p. 24.

2   This and subsequent quotations from Kay Dick come, unless other-
     wise attributed, from conversation with H.S.

3   This and the next two quotations from Ivy come from Dick, pp. 12,
     13 and 9.

4   Mitchell N. S.; this account also based on conversation with J.M.

5   *Important to Me*, p. 193.

6   Information from Madge Garland.

7   Dick, p. 11.

8   Dick, p. 10.

9   Information from Sonia Orwell.

10   I.C.-B. to B. Robinson, 1 October 1959.

11   *Ibid.*, 7 October 1961.

12   *Ibid.*, 21 November 1964.

13   E.T. to R.L., n.d. (1964).

14   Information from Herman Schrijver; my account of this luncheon
     and what followed is based on conversations with both Herman and
     Sonia Orwell.

15   TWTW, p. 66.

16   'A Friendship Without a Thorn', unpublished ms.

17   Information from Madge Garland.

18   M&F, p. 101.

19   M&F, p. 60.

20   M&F, p. 102.

21   *The Mighty and their Fall* 'just coming' on 20 November 1959 (Burkhart, p. 46) and ready for typing by 10 February 1961 (letter, I.C.-B. to C. Greig).

22   M&F, p. 6.

23   M&F, p. 48.

24   M&F, p. 64.

25   Dick, p. 19.

26   Information from Madge Garland.

27   See Burkhart 2, p. 84; Madge Garland confirms that the woman mentioned in this passage was the one with the roses on Brighton Pier.

28   P&C, p. 126.

29   Dick, p. 7.

30   Information from Hester Marsden-Smedley.

31   Kathleen Farrell.

32   'A Friendship Without a Thorn', unpublished ms.

33   I.C.-B. to B. Robinson, 26 April 1960.

34   Christopher Sykes, Sprigge p. 135; Jonathan Cecil and Dorothy Reynolds said the same.

35   Burkhart 2, p. 117. (Balthus' real name was Stanislas Klossowski.)

36   Fedden.

37   'I am well aware . . .' E.T., unpublished memoirs.

38   Information from George Furlong, Rex Britcher and Madge Garland (who were there).

39   '*Thé chez Miss Compton-Burnett*', *Les Nouvelles Littéraires* 10 March 1960 (my translation in this and the following quotations); information from Robin McDouall.

40   E.T. to R.L., n.d.; Madge Garland confirms this account.

41   The following account of Gollancz's dealings with Ivy is largely based on correspondence in Gollancz's files; see also *Gollancz. The Story of a Publishing House* by Sheila Hodges.

42   Greig, p. 41.

43   J. A. Laurence.

44   I.C.-B. to B. Robinson, 1 October 1959.

45   Sprigge, p. 96.

46   Information from Lettice Cooper.

47   Information from Soame Jenyns.

48 I.C.-B. to B. Robinson, 6 January 1960.

49 Burkhart 2, p. 100.

50 I am grateful to Livia Gollancz for a comprehensive survey of Ivy's sales figures, 1937 to date, from which it seems that she sold decidedly more than the 'steady 6,000 copies' quoted on p. 99 of Sheila Hodges' *Gollancz. The Story of a Publishing House*.

51 *Sunday Times*, 8 April 1951.

52 P&C, p. 127.

53 Mowll.

54 Information from Lettice Cooper, to whom V.G. described this meeting.

55 I.C.-B. to K. Blackie, 30 July 1963.

56 I.C.-B. to R.L., 14 December 1964.

57 I.C.-B. to E. Taylor, 1 September 1965.

58 Burkhart 2, p. 96.

59 Anne Hill, 'Notes', 11 February 1956.

60 I.C.-B. to R.L., 5 July 1963; the ms. was ready for typing by 5 April 1963 (p.c., I.C.-B. to C. Greig).

61 Greig, p. 90.

62 Burkhart 2, p. 99.

63 Information from Alison Waley.

64 G&G, p. 53.

65 G&G, p. 10.

66 G&G, p. 38.

67 G&G, p. 39.

68 G&G, p. 49.

69 I.C.-B. to R.L., 20 November 1960.

70 *Ibid.*, 12 March 1963.

71 *Ibid.*, 18 October 1961.

72 *Ibid.*, 10 December 1963.

73 The cast was headed by Dorothy Reynolds as Julia Challoner with James Cairncross as Sir Edward, Christopher Guinee and Alan Howard as Walter and Simon, and a memorable performance from Jonathan Cecil as Simon's youngest child, Ralph; Julian Mitchell's *A Family and a Fortune* was put on the following July at the Yvonne Arnaud Theatre, Guildford, directed by Donald Haworth, designed by Cecil Beaton, with Raymond Huntley as Edgar Gaveston, Catherine Lacey as Blanche, George Benson as Dudley, Avril Elgar as Justine and Joyce Carey as Aunt Mattie.

74 Information from Francis King.

75 E.T. to R.L., n.d.

76 D&S, p. 76.

77 E.T. to R.L., n.d.

78   Information from Sonia Orwell (the other guests included Herman and Dorothy Stroud; and Mrs King did indeed enjoy the situation, see *The Weeping and the Laughter*, p. 236 *et passim*).

79   I.C.-B. to C. Greig, 25 May 1965.

80   Information from Ivo Pakenham.

81   E.T. to R.L., n.d.

82   Greig, p. 102.

83   'Herman's Memoir of Ivy', cancelled passage not published in Burkhart 2.

84   Information from Lettice Cooper.

85   I.C.-B. to S.O., 28 December 1967.

86   E.T. to H.S., 11 May 1971.

87   I.C.-B. to Madge Garland, 29 June 1968.

88   Burkhart 1, p. 196.

89   Greig, pp. 101–2 and 104.

90   I.C.-B. to R. McDouall, 19 April 1966.

91   E.T. to R.L., n.d., but they discussed Truman Capote's *In Cold Blood*, published in February 1966.

92   Burkhart 2, p. 88.

93   Information from Kathleen Farrell.

94   *The Weeping and the Laughter*, p. 237.

95   Reprinted in Burkhart 1; Sr Praz's visit to Braemar Mansions described in his diary for 9 June 1967.

96   Burkhart 2, p. 78; Mario Praz contradicted Herman's report in a letter to Elka Schrijver, 22 December 1981.

97   Burkhart 1, p. 196.

98   I.C.-B. to R.L., 21 May 1968.

99   Interview with I.C.-B., *The Times*, 21 November 1963.

100   E.T. to R.L., n.d.

101   Fedden.

102   Greig, p. 27.

103   Information from Barbara Robinson.

104   Information from Vera Compton-Burnett; and from Madge Garland.

105   I.C.-B. to M.G., 7 June 1968.

106   Letter, I.C.-B. to M.G., 20 June 1968.

107   'Conversation with Miss Compton-Burnett 18 July 1968', unpublished notes by Dr Pasmore.

108   M&W, p. 113.

109   Burkhart 1, p. 196.

110   M&F, p. 60.

111   I.C.-B. to Anne Hill, 17 July 1967.

112   Greig, p. 117.

113 I.C.-B. to M.G., 10 July 1968.

114 Information from J. Mitchell.

115 I.C.-B. to R.L., 14 December 1964; she said much the same to C. Greig and B. Robinson.

116 The ms. of L&F, comprising twelve notebooks (see Sprigge, p. 175), is now in the British Library; the remaining eighteen notebooks, mostly first drafts, all cancelled in Ivy's hand, are in the possession of Henrietta Williamson.

117 Information from Mary Maguire.

118 Dick, p. 29.

119 Information from Lady Mander.

120 L&F, p. 12.

121 Letter, W.R. to H.S., 4 January 1971.

122 L&F, p. 144 (the last five words excised from the published text).

123 D&D, p. 233.

124 See *Ivy When Young*, p. 180.

125 L&F, p. 79.

126 C.G. to H.S., 1 January 1971.

127 Greig, p. 116.

128 Information from Livia Gollancz.

129 Sprigge, p. 171.

130 Information from H. Marsden-Smedley.

131 Sprigge, pp. 172–3.

132 Mitchell, N.S., and conversation with H.S.

133 Information from R. McDouall.

134 Glen Cavaliero, letter to H.S., 11 March 1974.

135 Information from Mary Maguire.

136 M&F, pp. 63–4.

SELECT BIBLIOGRAPHY

ARDEN, JOAN (C. E. M. Jourdain), *A Childhood*, Bowes & Bowes, Cambridge, 1913.

—— *Unfulfilment*, Basil Blackwell, Oxford, 1924.

BALDANZA, FRANK, *Ivy Compton-Burnett*, Twayne, 1964.

BOWEN, ELIZABETH, *Collected Impressions*, Longmans, 1950.

BURKHART, CHARLES, ed., *The Art of I. Compton-Burnett. A Collection of Critical Essays*, Gollancz, 1972.

—— *Herman and Nancy and Ivy. Three Lives in Art*, Gollancz, 1977.

—— *I. Compton-Burnett*, Gollancz, 1965.

—— guest ed., 'Ivy Compton-Burnett Issue', *Twentieth Century Literature*, vol. 25, no. 2, Summer 1979.

DICK, KAY, *Ivy and Stevie. Conversations and Reflections*, Duckworth, 1971; (paperback) Allison & Busby, 1983.

EVANS, JOAN, ed., *An Adventure* by C. A. E. Moberly and E. F. Jourdain, Faber, 1955 (fifth edition).

—— *Prelude and Fugue. An Autobiography*, Museum Press, 1964.

FEDDEN, ROBIN, 'Recollections of Ivy Compton-Burnett', *Cornhill*, no. 1062, Winter 1969/70.

GARNETT, DAVID, *The Familiar Faces*, Chatto & Windus, 1962.

—— *The Flowers of the Forest*, Chatto & Windus, 1955.

GRATTAN-GUINNESS, I., *Dear Russell—Dear Jourdain*, Duckworth, 1977.

—— 'Russell and Philip Jourdain', *Russell: The Journal of the Bertrand Russell Archives* 8: Winter 1972–3.

GREIG, CICELY, *Ivy Compton-Burnett. A Memoir*, Garnstone Press, 1972.

GRILLS, ROSALIE GLYNN, *I. Compton-Burnett, Writers and Their Work*, Longman, 1971.

HIGHAM, DAVID, *Literary Gent*, Cape, 1978.

HODGES, SHEILA, *Gollancz: The Story of a Publishing House 1928–1978*, Gollancz, 1978.

IREMONGER, LUCILLE, *The Ghosts of Versailles*, Faber, 1957.

JOHNSON, PAMELA HANSFORD, *I. Compton-Burnett*, British Council, Longmans, 1951.

—— *Important To Me. Personalia*, Macmillan, 1974.

JOURDAIN, C. E. M. (Melicent), *see* Arden, Joan.

JOURDAIN, E. F. (Eleanor), *see* Evans, Joan.

JOURDAIN, LT. COL. H. F. N., *Ranging Memories*, John Johnson at the O.U.P., 1934.

JOURDAIN, MARGARET (*see also* Lenygon, Francis), *An Outdoor Breviary*, Academy Press, 1909.

—— *Poems*, Truslove and Hanson, 1911.

—— *Regency Furniture 1795–1820*, Country Life, 1934.

—— *The Work of William Kent*, Country Life, 1948.

JOURDAIN, P. E. B., ed., *The Philosophy of Mr B*rtr*nd R*ss*ll*, Allen & Unwin, 1918.

KENNEDY, RICHARD, *A Boy at the Hogarth Press*, Heinemann, 1972.

KING, VIVA, *The Weeping and the Laughter*, Macdonald & Jane, 1976.

LEES-MILNE, JAMES, *Ancestral Voices*, Chatto & Windus, 1975.

—— *Prophesying Peace*, Chatto & Windus, 1977.

—— *Caves of Ice*, Chatto & Windus, 1983.

LENYGON, FRANCIS (M. Jourdain), *Decoration and Furniture of English Mansions During the Seventeenth and Eighteenth Centuries*, T. Werner Laurie, 1909.

—— *Decoration in England from 1660–1760*, Batsford, 1914.

—— *Furniture in England from 1660–1760*, Batsford, 1914.

LIDDELL, ROBERT, *A Treatise on the Novel*, Cape, 1947.

—— *Kind Relations*, Cape, 1939.

—— *The Last Enchantments*, Cape, 1948.

—— *The Novels of Ivy Compton-Burnett*, Gollancz, 1955.

—— *The Novels of Jane Austen*, Allen Lane, 1963.

—— *Stepsons*, Longmans, 1969.

—— *Unreal City*, Cape, 1952.

McCARTHY, MARY, *The Writing on the Wall and Other Literary Essays*, Weidenfeld & Nicolson, 1970.

MOBERLY, C. A. E., *see* Evans, Joan.

NOYES, ELLA, illustrated by Dora Noyes, *Salisbury Plain. Its Stones, Cathedral, City, Valleys and Folk*, Dent, 1913.

POWELL, LADY VIOLET, *A Compton-Burnett Compendium*, Heinemann, 1973.

RUSSELL, BERTRAND, *Autobiography*, vols i–iii, Allen & Unwin, 1967–9.

SACKVILLE-WEST, EDWARD, *Inclinations*, Secker & Warburg, 1949.

SARRAUTE, NATHALIE, *L'Ere du Soupçon*, Gallimard, 1959, trans. by Maria Jolas in *Tropisms and The Age of Suspicion*, Calder & Boyars, 1963.

SMITH, CONSTANCE BABINGTON, *Rose Macaulay*, Collins, 1972.

SOMERVILLE, E. Œ., & ROSS, MARTIN, *The Real Charlotte*, Longmans, 1918.

SPRIGGE, ELIZABETH, *The Life of Ivy Compton-Burnett*, Gollanz, 1973.

SPURLING, HILARY, *Ivy When Young. The Early Life of I. Compton-Burnett 1884–1919*, Gollancz, 1974, Hodder and Stoughton, 1983.

THESIGER, ERNEST, *Practically True*, Heinemann, 1927.

INDEX